陈平语言学文选

THE CHINESE LANGUAGE: FORM, MEANING AND FUNCTION

汉语的形式、意义与功能

◆ 陈 平 著

2017年·北京

图书在版编目(CIP)数据

汉语的形式、意义与功能/陈平著.—北京:商务印书馆,2017
(陈平语言学文选)
ISBN 978-7-100-13980-9

Ⅰ.①汉…　Ⅱ.①陈…　Ⅲ.①汉语—语言学—文集　Ⅳ.①H1-53

中国版本图书馆 CIP 数据核字(2017)第 114513 号

权利保留,侵权必究。

陈平语言学文选
汉语的形式、意义与功能
陈　平　著

商　务　印　书　馆　出　版
(北京王府井大街 36 号　邮政编码 100710)
商　务　印　书　馆　发　行
北　京　冠　中　印　刷　厂　印刷
ISBN 978-7-100-13980-9

2017 年 7 月第 1 版　　　开本 787×1092　1/16
2017 年 7 月北京第 1 次印刷　印张 24¼
定价:79.00 元

目　录

试论汉语中三种句子成分与语义成分的配位原则 …………… 1

汉语双项名词句与话题-陈述结构 …………………………… 14

论现代汉语时间系统的三元结构 ……………………………… 39

释汉语中与名词性成分相关的四组概念 ……………………… 75

语言学的一个核心概念"指称"问题研究 …………………… 96

汉语定指范畴和语法化问题 …………………………………… 121

汉语零形回指的话语分析 ……………………………………… 144

Pragmatic interpretations of structural topics and
　　relativization in Chinese ………………………………… 167

Aspects of referentiality ………………………………………… 196

Referentiality and definiteness in Chinese …………………… 238

Identifiability and definiteness in Chinese …………………… 254

Indefinite determiner introducing definite referent: A special
　　use of "*yi* 'one' + classifier" in Chinese ………………… 335

人名索引 ………………………………………………………… 362

主题索引 ………………………………………………………… 368

后　　记 ………………………………………………………… 379

试论汉语中三种句子成分与语义成分的配位原则

提　要　本文提出两条语义角色优先序列，用以表现汉语句子中主题、主语和宾语与各种语义成分的配位原则。作者试图达到两个目的：一是用高度概括的形式说明相关的语言现象，以收以简驭繁之效；二是揭示在变化多端的配位机制中起根本作用的有关因素。

关键词　主题　主语　宾语　语义格　施事　受事

1. 引言

　　主语、宾语等基本句子成分同施事、受事等语义成分之间的配位问题，是语法研究的中心课题之一。在讨论到这个问题时，吕叔湘先生指出："宾语可以分别为施事、受事、当事、工具等等，主语也可以分别为施事、受事、当事、工具等等。"（吕叔湘 1979：538）他还把句中动词所带的语义成分形象地比作一个委员会里面各有职务的几个委员，把主语这个句子成分比作主席。开会的时候委员们可以轮流当主席，不过当主席的次数有人少，有人多，有人老轮不上。

　　本文顺着吕先生自40年代起形成的有关思路（主要参看吕叔湘 1942—1944, 1946, 1979, 1986 等），参考 Jackendoff（1976, 1987）、Fillmore（1977）、Lakoff（1977）、Hopper & Thompson（1980）、Foley & van Valin（1984）、van Oosten（1986）、Rozwadowska（1988）以及 Dowty（1991）等文献中阐述的有关概念和理论框架，将汉语中主谓宾句及主题句中的主要句子成分同语义成分之间的配位原则归纳为两条语义角色优先序列，希望能以此概括隐藏在大量有关语言现象背后的规律，并且揭示在配位机制中起根本作用的有关因素。我们试图说明的语法现象主要包括：

一、汉语句子中的主题、主语和宾语，最常分别由哪些语义成分充任？它们之间的配位原则是什么？各种配位关系之间的内部联系是什么？

二、有些句子中，句子成分可以互相转化，有些则不行。例如：

（1）a. 纸已经糊了窗户　　b. 窗户已经糊了纸

（2）a. 水浇花儿了　　　　b. 花儿浇水了

（3）a. 张师傅修窗户了　　b.* 窗户修张师傅了

（4）a. 小李浇花儿了　　　b.* 花儿浇小李了

这种转化的条件是什么？它与上面所提到的问题有什么联系？

这类现象早已引起汉语语法学家的注意，人们并对此做了相当细腻的描写。例如，Teng（1974）首先对这类现象进行了全面的研究，范继淹（1984）分析了动词前多项名词性成分的语义类别和排列顺序，李临定（1990）详细讨论了有关语义成分可以与动词构成哪些句法格局。本文所用例句，大部分选自范继俺（1984）和李临定（1990）。语言素材是旧的，但理论表述却是新的。

2. 句子成分的定义

本文所说的三种句子成分，即主题、主语和宾语，均为单纯的结构概念，由有关成分在句子结构中的上下前后位置所决定。

为简单起见，我们将主题定义为位于句首的名词性成分，后接另外一个句子。同为上一个句子的直接成分，如下列例句中的"这本书"和"老李"：

（5）这本书他们看完了　　　（6）老李个儿很高

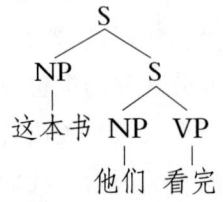
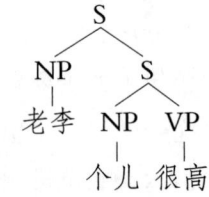

本文把含有这种结构性主题的句子称为主题句。[①]

我们把主语定义为位于句首、后带动词性短语同为句子直接成分的名词性短语，如（5）中的“他们”和（6）中的“个儿”，以及（7）中的“工程队”和（8）中的“孩子们”：

（7）工程队修铁路

（8）孩子们写毛笔字

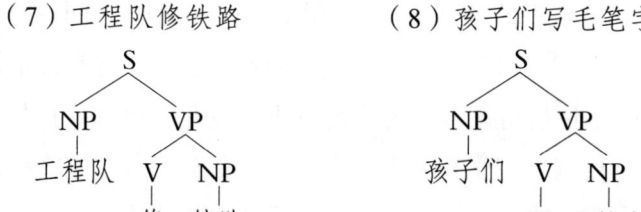

宾语位于动词后面，与该动词同为上一个动词性短语的直接成分，如（7）中的“铁路”和（8）中的“毛笔字”。

这三种结构成分的功能特征和行为特征，不在本文讨论范围之内。

3. 语义成分的定义

语义成分的定义则要复杂得多。虽然施事、受事等术语在文献中使用频繁，但对于它们的内涵、外延以及判断标准，语言学界历来缺乏共同的认识。本文赞同 Hopper & Thompson（1980）、van Oosten（1986）、Rozwadowska（1988）和 Dowty（1991）等著作中的基本思想。我们在这一节里提出的观点，在很大程度上参考了 Dowty（1991）中的某些内容。

首先，我们认为施事、受事等并非初始概念。动词带着种种名词性成分，表现有关事件。这些名词性成分的语义类别，基本上取决于它们在有关事件中所扮演的角色。最基本的语义角色只有两类，我们称之为原型施事和原型受事。如同音位是由更小的区别性特征所组成的那样，原型施事和原型受事分别由两组基本特征组合而成。

① 从线性序列上来看，动词短语前面可以有多个名词性成分。本文所要讨论的主题句，限于“NP+NP+VP（+XP）”这种格式。主题句往往又称作主谓谓语句，参看吕叔湘（1986）。

原型施事特征主要包括：

　　1）自主性　2）感知性　3）使动性　4）位移性　5）自立性

原型受事特征主要包括：

　　1）变化性　2）渐成性　3）受动性　4）静态性　5）附庸性

自主性指的是该成分自主地参与了有关事件，例如，"小王掉了下去，老王跳了下去"，"小王"不具备自主性而"老王"具备自主性。变化性指的是有关事件使得该事物的状态发生了变化，例如"他打破了窗玻璃"中的"窗玻璃"。感知性指的是该成分在有关事件中表现出了感知能力，如"小张喜欢这本书"中的"小张"。渐成性指的是该事物在事件中逐步形成，如"他造了一幢房子"中的"房子"。使动性和受动性、位移性和静态性以及自立性和附庸性是三组对立的概念。使动性指该成分施行某个动作，造成某种事件或状态，而受动性则指该成分承受某个动作或事件的后果。例如，"小李打了小王"，"小李"具有使动性，而"小王"则具有受动性。在"小田去了上海"中，"小田"移动了位置，而"上海"则处于静态。自立性指的是事物先于事件独立存在，而附庸性则指事物的存在是该事件的结果，或是并不存在这个事物。例如，"小刘画了一群山羊"，"小刘"具有自立性，而"一群山羊"则具有附庸性。

　　在具体句子中，同时具备所有的原型施事特征或原型受事特征的名词性成分并不常见，多数情况下，我们所说的施事成分或受事成分只具备上述特征群中的大部分相关特征，而并非全部特征。由此可以推论，所谓施事或受事都有性质强弱的问题。在具体事件中，名词性成分表现出来的原型施事特征数目越多，其施事性就越强；原型受事特征的数目越多，其受事性就越强。另一方面，原型特征的数目越少，其施事性或受事性就越弱，到了一定程度就难分彼此。

　　传统上常用的其他几个语义概念，可以重新解释为上述原型特征的不同组合。根据有关特征的有无、多寡和组合方式，我们把几个语义概念定义如下：

　　感事：＋感知性

工具：＋使动性；＋位移性

地点：＋自立性；＋静态性

对象：＋受动性；＋渐成性；＋自立性

一般所说的系事，指的是跟动词关系比较间接的名词性成分（参看范继淹 1984），在这儿可以理解为缺乏鲜明原型特征的语义成分。

从上面的讨论中不难得出这样的结论：我们平常所说的施事、受事、感事、工具、对象等语义成分在概念上最根本的区别，可以理解为施事性和受事性程度强弱的不同。原型施事和原型受事各自的特征最为明显，因此分别位于同一个连续体上的两极，所有其他的语义成分都可以看作为分布在这个连续体上的一些点，代表有关原型特征的某些典型组合。由于语义性质使然，这些语义点之间的边界往往是模糊的。

具体句子中的名词性成分，它们的语义归类取决于它们当时表现出来的意义与上述哪一种典型组合最为接近。在多数情况下，要确定这一点是不难的。但是，我们也常常碰到一些非此非彼或亦此亦彼的情形，前者如上文中提到的系事成分，后者我们将在下文讨论。

4. 主题、主语和宾语与语义角色的配位原则

4.1 两条语义角色优先序列

三种句子成分与各种语义成分的配位原则可以用以下两条语义角色优先序列的形式表现出来：

一、充任主语和宾语的语义角色优先序列

施事 > 感事 > 工具 > 系事 > 地点 > 对象 > 受事

在充任主语方面，位于">"左边的语义角色优先于右边的角色，在充任宾语方面则正好相反，位于">"右边的角色优先于左边的角色。

二、充任主题的语义角色优先序列

系事 > 地点 > 工具 > 对象 > 感事 > 受事 > 施事

在充任主题方面,位于">"左边的成分优先于右边的成分。

从序列一中可以看出,对于和动词连用的几个名词性成分来讲,优先选择哪一个做主语,哪一个做宾语,主要取决于它们的施事性和受事性的强弱。语义成分的施事性越强,充任主语的倾向性越强;受事性越强,充任宾语的倾向性越强。相对于接近序列两端的语义角色来讲,接近序列中间的语义角色施事性和受事性都较弱,充任主语和宾语的倾向性也相应减弱,从而在句法配位方面表现出一定的灵活性。

从序列二中可以看出,优先选择哪一个名词性成分充任主题,主要取决于它们在语义关系上的疏密。有很多证据表明,各种语义角色中,施事同动词关系最为密切,受事次之(参看吕叔湘 1942—1944;Hopper & Thompson 1980;Foley & van Valin 1984;等等)。与动词关系越是疏离,充任主题的倾向性越强。如前所述,系事与其他语义角色不同之处,在于它没有鲜明的语义原型特征,与动词关系最淡,这使它成为主题成分的最佳选择。

我们以这两条语义角色优先序列来概括汉语中主题、主语和宾语与语义成分的配位原则。用这种方式提出来的理论表述具有高度的可证伪性。我们断言,如果上述概括是准确的,那么,其他条件不变,在配位上遵从这两条优先序列的句子一般是合语法句,并且在功能结构方面(包括主题结构、信息结构和焦点结构等)具有无标记性或中性的特征。而在配位上违反优先序列的句子,要么不合语法,要么在功能方面表现出有标记性的相关特征。

下面,让我们对上述原则进行验证,看它能说明多少已知的语言现象,同时也看它的预测是否同实际情况相吻合。

4.2 主谓宾句

我们先来观察主谓宾句中的配位情况。

施事性或受事性很强的语义成分,一般固定地充任主语或宾语。另外,同时出现的两个名词性成分,如果在施事性或受事性方面强弱程

度相差过大,也就是说在序列一上相距较远,它们在同句子成分的配位上,一般也只能有固定的格局。请看下列句子:

主语:施事＞工具;**宾语**:工具＞施事

  (9)a. 我常听耳机   b.*耳机常听我

  (10)a. 老王喝小杯   b.*小杯喝老王

主语:施事＞地点;**宾语**:地点＞施事

  (11)a. 小张上西单   b.*西单上小张

  (12)a. 他来北京   b.*北京来他

主语:施事＞对象;**宾语**:对象＞施事

  (13)a. 张大爷磨麦子   b.*麦子磨张大爷

  (14)a. 小李修车   b.*车修小李

主语:施事＞受事;**宾语**:受事＞施事

  (15)a. 张大爷磨面   b.*面磨张大爷

  (16)a. 他盖房子   b.*房子盖他

主语:感事＞对象;**宾语**:对象＞感事

  (17)a. 小张喜欢老王   b.*老王喜欢小张

  (18)a. 他怕狗   b.*狗怕他

主语:工具＞对象;**宾语**:对象＞工具

  (19)a. 磨子磨麦子   b.*麦子磨磨子

  (20)a. 毛巾洗脸   b.*脸洗毛巾

主语:工具＞受事;**宾语**:受事＞工具

  (21)a. 卤水点豆腐   b.*豆腐点卤水

  (22)a. 推子推了个光头   b.*光头推了推子

主语:对象＞受事;**宾语**:受事＞对象

  (23)a. 萝卜切丝儿   b.*丝儿切萝卜

  (24)a. 米煮了粥   b.*粥煮了米

上述句子中,在句子成分的和语义成分的配位问题上,凡是符合序列一规定的,全部是自然的合语法句;凡是违反序列一规定的,全部不能说。

根据上述原则，接近序列一中段的语义成分，以及不在序列两端，而彼此相距又较近的语义成分，在充任主语或宾语的倾向性方面差别不大，在配位问题上应该有较大的灵活性。本文开头提到，有些句子中的句子成分可以互相转化。下面再给一些例子：

（25）a. 砖头垫墙了　　b. 墙垫了砖头

（26）a. 杠子顶了门　　b. 门顶了杠子

（27）a. 钉子铆了钢板　b. 钢板铆了钉子

（28）a. 人参泡了酒　　b. 酒泡了人参

我们可以根据上述配位原则，为这种现象提供一种解释。

我们注意到，上面这样的句子都有一个特点，即 a 句中的主语都是工具，而宾语不仅仅是动作的对象，同时也是主语成分通过该动作而抵达的地点。垫的结果，是砖头成了墙的一部分；顶的结果，是杠子靠在了门上；铆的结果，是钉子钻进了钢板；泡的结果，是人参留在了酒里。换句话说，a 句中的宾语兼有对象和地点两种语义角色的特征，可以标作为"地点-对象"。同其他语义成分的组合相比，工具和地点-对象比较靠近序列一的中部，施事性或受事性特征相应较弱。另外，两者在序列上距离不远，在施受性程度方面相差不大。我们认为，正是这些特点，使得它们在配位方面具有较大的灵活性。上面两项条件如有一项不能满足，有关句子成分便不能互相转化。请看下面的例子：[①]

主语：施事；宾语：地点-对象

（29）a. 小赵爬山　　　b.* 山爬小赵

（30）a. 大伙儿逛故宫　b.* 故宫逛大伙儿

---

① 汉语中主宾可以互换的句子，当然不限于我们现在讨论的这一类。下面是几个大家非常熟悉的例子：
（1）a. 这锅饭吃八个人　　b. 八个人吃这锅饭
（2）a. 那张床睡三个人　　b. 三个人睡那张床
（3）a. 桥上走汽车　　　　b. 汽车走桥上
如何处理上面这些句子，笔者目前尚无定见。我的直觉是 a 句的动词和 b 句的动词在同一性方面大大低于诸如"水浇花了，花浇水了"一类的句子。我们说到主宾互换时，前提是 a 句和 b 句是同一个动词。如果所涉及的动词在语义上有较大分别，那么我们也可以说上面的 a 句与 b 句用的是不同的动词。

主语：工具；**宾语**：对象

(31) a. 耳机听音乐　　b.* 音乐听耳机

(32) a. 桨划船　　　　b.* 船划桨

4.3　主题句

我们再来观察有关句子成分和语义成分在主题句中的配位情况。

主题句中哪种语义成分优先充任主题，是由序列二所规定的；而哪种语义成分优先充任句中的主语和宾语，则由序列一所规定，两条优先序列的规定在大多数情况下是一致的。在这样的情形下，句子成分和语义成分在配位上符合序列规定的句子一定是合语法句，而且从功能角度上看是最自然、最中性的语句。不符合序列规定的句子，要么不能说，要么具有附加的特殊功能。请看下面的例句：

主题：系事 > 受事 > 施事 > ；**主语**：施事 > 系事 > 受事；**宾语**：受事 > 系事 > 施事

(33) a. 这事老高有办法

　　 b.* 老高这事有办法

(34) a. 会议经费张主任已经打了报告

　　 b.* 张主任会议经费已经打了报告

主题：工具 > 对象 > 施事；**主语**：施事 > 工具 > 对象；**宾语**：对象 > 工具 > 施事

(35) a. 热水我洗碗了

　　 b.* 我热水洗碗了

(36) a. 这把刀我可剁不动

　　 b.* 我这把刀可剁不动

主题：对象 > 感事；**主语**：感事 > 对象

(37) a. 这种式样小李很喜欢

　　 b.* 小李这种式样很喜欢

（38）a. 那样的人我一点儿也不怕

b.* 我那样的人一点儿也不怕

主题：对象＞受事＞施事；**主语**：施事＞对象＞受事；**宾语**：受事＞对象＞施事

（39）a. 芹菜王师傅包饺子了

b.* 王师傅芹菜包饺子了

（40）a. 那袋米田大爷煮了一锅粥

b.* 田大爷那袋米煮了一锅粥

主题：受事＞施事；**主语**：施事＞受事

（41）a. 交通问题我们解决

b.* 我们交通问题解决

（42）a. 那两幅画儿他还没有画好

b.* 他那两幅画儿还没有画好

上面的 a 句中，主题、主语和宾语三种句子成分同语义成分的配位关系完全符合序列一和序列二的规定。不符合这种最佳选择的句子，大都不能说，如上面的 b 句，少数虽然能说，但却受到很大的功能限制。

范继淹（1984）讨论了"施事＋受事＋VP"这种句式，例如：

（43）a. 我球赛倒看了不少

（44）a. 他火车没赶上

（45）a. 你中药用过吗？

他注意到，"施事＋受事＋VP"式的句子一定有对应的"受事＋施事＋VP"式，而"受事＋施事＋VP"式的句子却不一定有对应的"施事＋受事＋VP"式，例如：

（43）b. 球赛我倒看了不少

（44）b. 火车他没赶上

（45）b. 中药你用过吗？

（46）a. 这张相片他还留着　　b.* 他这张相片还留着

（47）a. 这些东西我不能动　　b.* 我这些东西不能动

（48）a. 自行车老刘修好了吗？　b.* 老刘自行车修好了吗？

另外，他还提到，虽然"施事＋地点＋VP"式的句子一般也能说，但似乎总不如"地点＋施事＋VP"式来得自然。作者敏锐地注意到了上面这种不对称性，但没有进一步加以讨论。

对于这个问题，吕叔湘先生做过深入的观察，得出了精辟的结论。吕先生指出，在"施事＋受事＋VP"式的句子中，受事成分一般前头得有个"连"字，或隐含"连"字的意思，或者表示对比、平行、周遍等特殊意义，例如：

（49）不但笑话我，人家连叔叔都要笑话了。

（50）你怎么外套也不穿就跑出去了。

（51）他呀，天不怕，地不怕，只怕太太一声叫。

（52）这十来个人，从小儿什么话儿不说，什么事儿不做？

而"受事＋施事＋VP"式的句子就没有这个限制（吕叔湘1946：449—452）。换用功能语法的术语来讲，我们可以说"施事＋受事＋VP"是一种特殊句式，其重要功能是标明受事成分一定是该句的焦点信息。同功能结构上无标记的中性句式"受事＋施事＋VP"相比，它违背了序列一和序列二规定的配位方式。我们认为，它正是通过这种手段来传递它的特殊功能信息。这从反面证明，序列一和序列二表现了汉语中三种句子成分与语义成分的常规配位方式。汉语基本句式的一个必要条件，便是符合这种常规配位格局。

最后，我们要指出，在某些主题句中，序列一规定的配位方式同序列二相互冲突。请看下面的例子：

主题：工具＞对象；**主语**：工具＞对象

（53）a. 这把刀排骨可剁不动　　b. 排骨这把刀可剁不动

（54）a. 小卧车冰箱没法拉　　b. 冰箱小卧车没法拉

根据序列一的规定，应该优先选择工具作主语；而根据序列二的规定，应该优先选择工具作主题。在这种情况下，句子成分和语义成分在配位方面一般有较大的自由，如上面a和b两种句式都合语法，在焦点结构方面也似乎难分异同。我们可以把这种现象看成是序列一和序列二的不同规定相互妥协的结果。

5. 结论

本文提出两条语义角色优先序列，用以表现汉语句子中的主题、主语和宾语成分与各种语义成分的配位原则。我们试图达到两个目的：一是用高度概括的形式来说明大量的相关语言现象，以收以简驭繁之效；二是揭示在变化多端的配位机制中起根本作用的有关因素。通过序列一，我们可以看出，在主语和宾语同各种语义成分的配位中起决定作用的，是后者施事性或受事性的强弱。通过序列二，我们可以看出，在主题同各种语义成分的配位中起决定作用的，则是后者与句中动词关系的疏密。

参考文献

范继淹，1984，多项NP句，《范继淹语言学论文集》，北京：语文出版社，1986年，第239—251页。

李临定，1990，《现代汉语动词》，北京：中国社会科学出版社。

吕叔湘，1942—1944，《中国文法要略》，《吕叔湘文集》第一卷，北京：商务印书馆，1990年，第1—463页。

吕叔湘，1946，从主语、宾语的分别谈国语句子的分析，《吕叔湘文集》第二卷，商务印书馆，1990年，第445—480页。

吕叔湘，1979，《汉语语法分析问题》，《吕叔湘文集》第二卷，同上，第481—571页。

吕叔湘，1986，主谓谓语句举例，《吕叔湘文集》第三卷，商务印书馆，1992年，第531—544页。

Dowty, David. 1991. Thematic proto-roles and argument selection. *Language* 67(3):547-619.

Fillmore, Charles. 1977. The case for case reopened. In: Peter Cole and Jerrold Sadock, eds., *Syntax and Semantics*, Vol. 8, *Grammatical Relations*. Academic Press, 59-82.

Foley, William A. and Robert D. van Valin. 1980. *Functional Syntax and Universal Grammar*. Cambridge University Press.

Hopper, Paul and Sandra A. Thompson. 1980. Transitivity in grammar and discourse. *Language* 56:251-299.

Jackendoff, Ray S.1976. Toward an explanatory semantic representation. *Linguistic Inquiry* 7:89-150.
Jackendoff, Ray S.1987. The status of thematic relations in linguistic theory. *Linguistic Inquiry* 18:369-411.
Lakoff, George. 1977. Linguistic gestalts. *Chicago Linguistic Society* 13:236-287.
Rozwadowska, Bozena. 1988. Thematic restrictions on derived nominals, In: Wendy Wilkins, ed., *Syntax and Semantics*. Vol. 21, *Thematic Relations*, Academic Press, 147-166.
Teng, Shou-hsin. 1975. *A Semantic Study of Transitivity Relations in Chinese*. University of California Press.
van Oosten, Jeanne. 1986. The nature of subjects, topics and agents: A cognitive explanation. Distributed by IULC.

（本文原载《中国语文》1994年第3期。）

汉语双项名词句与话题-陈述结构*

提　要　汉语双项名词句可以表现多种类型的信息结构，语法形式与话语语用功能两者之间不存在严整的一一对应关系。最普遍的情形是句首的名词性成分充任话题，句子的其余部分理解为陈述。但是，也有不少时候，位于句首的可以是无定或无指成分，不能理解为一般意义上的话题。汉语双项名词句可以分为许多类别，从信息结构研究的角度来看，最重要的分类之一是根据句首两个名词性成分施事属性的相对强弱将它们分成两大类。一类 NP_1 的施事性弱于 NP_2，另一类则相反。这两类双项名词句在表现话题-陈述结构和其他信息结构上有各自的系统性特点，虽然我们对造成这种现象的原因目前还无法解释。

关键词　双项名词句　主题句　话题-陈述结构　信息结构　有指　无指　周遍成分

1. 话题-陈述结构

　　句子的形式和意义可以从许多不同的角度进行分析，除了句法结构、语义结构、韵律结构等以外，所谓信息结构（information structure）也是句子组织的一个重要方面。发话人话语中涉及的有关事物以及同它们相关的内容，受话人一方是否了解，熟悉程度如何，是否是对方目前的关注焦点，在这些问题上，发话人都得有自己的估量，并以此为根据，决定自己采用的语言形式，以便与上下文顺畅相连，使受话人容易理解，取得最佳的语言交际效果。信息结构所表现的就是具体语境中发话人在这些问题上的判断、预设及意向。语言信息结构方面的内容一般表现在两个主要方面，一是事物的指称形式，二是句子的语法

---

*　本文初稿承蒙方梅教授与陆丙甫教授提出修改意见，谨致谢忱。

组织形式。同一个事物，可以用不同语言形式指称，如各种名词短语、代词，或者零形式，等等；同一个命题，可以用不同的句式表现出来，如主动句和被动句，等等。话题-陈述结构是句子信息结构的一个重要方面，另一个重要方面是所谓的焦点结构。句子可以执行描写、叙述、判断等功能，其描写、叙述、判断的对象称为话题，其他部分则为陈述。句中哪个成分用作话题，哪些部分用作陈述，是发话人选用语言表现形式时的重要考虑因素，并且有时会影响到句子命题的真值条件。①

现代理论语言学发展史上，在话题-陈述结构的研究方面最有影响的语言学家主要有 19 世纪德国语言学家 Georg von der Gabelentz，以及深受德国哲学和语言学界影响的布拉格学派、Charles Hockett、赵元任、Michael A. K. Halliday、Charles Li、Sandra A. Thompson 以及 Jeanette Gundel。Gabelentz（1901）提出心理主语和心理谓语的概念，开启句子信息结构研究的先河。布拉格学派创立功能句子观点理论，使句子信息结构的研究系统化、理论化。Hockett（1958）和赵元任（1968）主张，主谓结构的普遍特征就是话题与陈述，主语通常是话题，谓语是陈述，汉语如此，英语和欧洲其他主要语言一般也是如此。Halliday（1967）深化了对信息结构的系统研究，尤其注重韵律和词序的表达作用。Li & Thompson（1976）将主语突出和话题突出作为两个对立的参项引进语言类型学研究，并且分析了两类语言各自的特点。Gundel 1974 年以"语言理论中的话题与陈述"为题完成了博士学位论文，在随后的 30 年里，主要研究兴趣始终集中在话题与焦点等课题上，发表了许多有影响的著作。值得注意的是，前面六位理论语言学家同时都是汉语语言学家。这恐怕不是巧合，国际语言学界在话题-陈述结构的研究中常见的一些理论概念和观点，在一定程度上是用汉语的眼光看世界的结果。

话题-陈述结构本质上属于话语和语用范畴，同句子的话语功能和

---

① 英国剑桥大学的罗素（Russell）与牛津大学的 Strawson 曾就有关指称问题进行过几次辩论，在哲学、逻辑学与语言学界影响很大（参看 Russell 1905；Strawson 1950, 1964）。Strawson（1964）认为，句子成分在该句话题-陈述结构中的位置会对句子命题的真值条件产生影响。这个观点得到大多数研究者的赞同。

使用语境密切相关。可以把话题和陈述看作连续语流中的一问一答，话题相当于"×××怎么啦？"这类问话中的"×××"，而陈述则提供有关该成分的新的信息。赵元任（1968）指出，汉语正好有一个说明这种观点的现成例子。语气词"啊""呢""吗"等都是一词而兼两任，既可以是疑问词，也可以是提顿词，标明前面的句子成分是句子的话题，见下面的例子（引自 Chao 1968：82）：

（1）问：饭啊？答：还没有呢。　（2）问：饭呢？答：都吃完了。
（1'）饭啊，还没有呢。　　　　（2'）饭呢，都吃完了。
（1"）饭还没得呢。　　　　　　（2"）饭都吃完了。

作为话语和语用概念，话题-陈述结构存在于所有语言之中。但是，这种话语语用概念的表现形式，在不同的语言中却可以有很大差别。虽然话题经常表现为主语，陈述经常表现为谓语，但这与施事做主语、受事做宾语一样，只是一种倾向，两者不对应的情况经常出现。话题可以不是主语，例如：

（3）问：那三位客人呢？
答：我刚才看见那三位客人了，在逛街呢。

主语也不一定是话题，主语为无定或无指名词成分时，不能作为一般的话题看待，例如：[1]

（4）一个大孩子带着弟弟、妹妹出来玩，正好路过那儿。
（5）谁来啦？
（6）谁也没想到会下雨。
（7）人人都抱着个大西瓜。

即使主语是有定成分，SVO 这种句式一般也可以用来表现几种不同的信息结构，这在文献中有广泛而深入的报道。

许多语言都有一些特殊的语法手段，其主要功能就是指示句子的各

---

[1] 汉语句子主语一般由定指成分担任，但是，正如范继淹（1985：328）所说，无定 NP 做主语的句子在汉语中"并不罕见，也不特殊"，Chen（2004）也得出类似的结论。汉语如此，英语也是如此。据 Hopper & Martin（1987：300）统计，现代英语中带不定冠词 a(n) 的名词短语有 27% 左右是在句子中用作主语的。

种信息结构。这些语法手段中，有的是语法助词，如日语中的 *wa*，许多人认为它的主要功能就是表示前面的成分是话题。更常见的语法手段是特殊的句法结构。Gundel（1988）调查了在谱系和地理分布上具有一定代表性的三十种语言，研究它们主要使用哪些特殊语法手段来表现话题-陈述结构。她先将这些语言中主要用来指示话题-陈述结构的特殊句法结构分成两大类，一类是用作话题的语言成分先于用作陈述的句子部分，另一类顺序正好相反。这两类句法结构都称为句法话题结构（syntactic-topic construction），第一类语言位于结构最左边的成分或者第二类语言最右边则称为句法话题（syntactic-topic）。

句法话题位于左边的句法话题结构又可分为两类，一类是左向移位句（left dislocation，简称 LD），其特点是句法话题后接一个完整的句子，句中带有一个语言成分（通常是代词）复指该句法话题，例如：

（8）那套房子，老王后来还是把它买了下来。

（9）王小刚，他不简单啊。

第二类是所谓的话题化结构（topicalization，简称 TOP），句法话题后接的句子在结构上是个不完整的句子，有一个句法成分在位置上是空缺，在语义上复指句法话题。在一些理论语法模式中，该空缺被看成是句法话题的原位，TOP 由 SVO 句派生来。下面是一个 TOP 的例子：

（10）那套房子老王后来卖了。

SVO 是英语中的常态句式（canonical construction），信息结构上的特点之一是可以与多种信息结构相容。与 SVO 句式相比，LD 和 TOP 是非常态句式（non-canonical construction），在语法上受到较大的使用限制，在信息结构上相对而言比较专一。例如，Gundel（1988：223）认为，句法话题结构中的句法话题毫无例外都用作语用话题。

必须看到，句法结构同信息结构的关系相当复杂，不是上面的简单结论所能概括的。Gundel 自己指出，表层句法结构特征与 TOP 一样的句式中，句首成分可以不是语用话题而是与上文中某个疑问词相对应的信息焦点（Gundel & Fretheim，2004）。虽然这两种不同的用法在英语中可以靠韵律特征区别开来，但在其他一些语言中，如芬兰语和挪威语，表现两种不同信息结构的可以是相同的句法和韵律形式，也就是说，这些语法结构在这些语言中是同形异义结构。另外，大家从实际语料中发现，充任句法话题的名词性成分固然以定指和通指性成分为多，但有时也可以是无定甚至无指成分，无法将它们解释为一般意义上的语用话题。

Gundel（1988）发现，她调查的这些语言中还有另外一种句法话题结构，形式上也是句法话题后接一个句子。它的特点是句法话题不是谓语动词的论元（argument），与谓语动词不发生直接的语法关系。句法话题在句中没有复指成分，也不可能挪回到谓语中去。例如：

（11）My work, I'm going crazy.

这种句法话题又称作"悬置话题"（hanging topic）。也有人可能是受Hockett和赵元任等人汉语研究的启发，把这类句法话题结构称为双主语结构（double-subject construction）。Chafe（1976：50）则将这种句式中的句法话题称为"汉语式话题"。下面是文献中经常引用的例子：

（12）那场大火，幸亏消防队来的早。（转引自 Chao 1968：102）

（13）那些树木树身大。（转引自 Chafe 1976：50）

（14）象鼻子长。（转引自 Li & Thompson 1976：480）

LD 和 TOP 是英语和其他主要欧洲语言中的常见结构，而（11）—（14）这类句式则一般限用于非常随便的口语，书面语或正式口语中很少出现。Gundel（1988：224）认为，这类句式代表的正是"最典型的话题-陈述结构"（topic-comment structures par excellence）。这句话的意思是说，在这种句式中句法话题应该一定是语用话题，句子的其余部分为陈述。Li & Thompson（1976）则将这种双项名词句作为话题突出性语言的一个重要特征。汉语是话题突出性语言的主要代表，这类句子既然是区别汉语与英语等主语突出性语言的一个主要特征，自然成为汉语语法学中的重要研究对象。

2. 汉语双项名词句

本文所用的"双项名词句"这个术语，是个比较中性的称呼。句首的名词性成分可以只有一个，也可以不止两个，为了避免将问题过分复杂化，本文的讨论范围限于小句谓语前有两个名词性成分出现的句子，以下面的例句为代表。我们按照 NP_1 的语义角色，大致分成七类。

1. NP_1 为施事。

   （1）有的人，他活着别人就不能活。（转引自吕叔湘 1986：534）

2. NP_1 为受事。

   （2）这套房子他们已经买下了。

   （3）什么话老王都敢说，什么事老张都敢做。

   （4）这几本书你读得很仔细。

   （5）这些话我们还说它干吗！

3. NP_1 为对象。

   （6）这件衣服他并不是十分喜欢。

   （7）那几个人我见到了。

4. NP_1 为工具。

   （8）这把刀我切萝卜。

   （9）这笔钱你交学费。

5. NP_1 为地点（时间或处所）[①]。

   （10）下午我们开个会。

   （11）那个角落我想放一盏灯。

---

① 这儿以及下面的语义角色优先序列中所用的"地点"是个上位概念，至少包含两个下位概念，即后面括号里"时间"和"处所"。用"地点"来涵括"时间"，从理论上讲是有充分理由的。根据许多语言学家（尤其是从心理认知功能角度出发的语言学家）都赞同的所谓"地点理论"（localism），相对其他有关概念而言，空间地点概念在语义和语法上是基本概念，时间概念，甚至动词的使动概念和及物性概念，也大都由地点概念衍生而来。Lyons（1977：第 15 章第 7 节）专门讲了这个问题，立论相当周延。

6. NP₁ 为系事。

(12) 这事老高有意见。

(13) 啤酒你忘了付钱了。

7. NP₁ 与 NP₂ 有隶属关系，或者是整体与部分的关系，另一连带特点是 NP₁ 与谓语没有直接的语义或语法关系。

(14) 小赵胆子大极了。

(15) 十只黄猫九只雄。

可以根据 NP₁ 是否与 NP₂ 后面的谓语成分有语法上的选择关系，将上面的句子分为两大类，1—4 为一类，5—7 为另一类。在少数情况下，NP₁ 在句子中有回指代词，或者可以挪到动词后面。但是，这类与英语中的 LD 和 TOP 相似的句子，在汉语里无论是从句子类型来看，还是从实际话语中出现频率来看，都只占少数。英语中 LD 和 TOP 是非常态句式，同一个常态的 SVO 句相对应，使用非常态句式会产生语用隐涵效果，而上面这些汉语双项名词句在大多数情况下没有一个对应的 SVO 句。

值得注意的是，在绝大多数情况下，句首两个名词的顺序可以互换，例如：

(1')*他有的人活着别人就不能活。

(2') 他们这套房子已经买下了。

(3') 老王什么话都敢说，老张什么事都敢做。

(4') 你这几本书读得很仔细。

(5') 我们这些话还说它干吗！

(6') 他这件衣服并不是十分喜欢。

(7') 我那几个人见到了。

(8') 我这把刀切萝卜。

(9') 你这笔钱交学费。

(10') 我们下午开个会。

(11') 我那个角落想放一盏灯。

(12') 老高这事有意见。

(13') 你啤酒忘了付钱了。

（14'）胆子小赵大极了。

（15'）*九只十只黄猫雄。

以上面例句为代表的双项名词句在汉语里是否属于同一类句法结构，是一个大有争议的问题。以丁声树等（1961）、Chao（1968）以及朱德熙（1982）为代表的结构主义论著将所有这些句子统称为主谓谓语句，根据 NP$_1$ 和 NP$_2$ 的语序，将它们分别称为大小主语，既不考虑它们的语义属性，也不考虑是否可以挪回到动词后面，或者是否有代词复指，对（1）—（15）和（2'）—（14'）不加任何区别。[①] 此外，Gundel（1988）、陈平（1994，1996）以及 Gundel & Fretheim（2004）等论著将（1）—（15）归为一类，统称为句法话题结构，其中又可细分出 LD、TOP 和悬置话题结构，将 NP$_1$ 称为句法话题，相当于结构主义语法论著中所说的大主语。从这个角度出发，有不少问题仍然有待回答，其中包括（2'）—（14'）是否也可归入这一类，在语法和信息结构等方面（2）—（14）与（2'）—（14'）之间是否存在系统差异，等等，这也是本文要探讨的问题。当然，也有许多学者采取不同的分析方法。对于（14）—（15），大家意见比较统一，一般都认为它们是主谓谓语句，但在其他句子的分析上意见分歧极大。许多学者既考虑词序，也考虑语义和其他因素。例如，胡裕树（1979）和吕叔湘（1979：539；1986）都承认（2）—（7）为主谓谓语句，但是对于（2'）—（7'），前者主张将它们看作宾语前置句，后者则主张结合上下文的语法格局做通盘考虑，有的可以看成宾语前置句，有的最好还是看成主谓谓语句。另外，许多传统语法学家，如黎锦熙等，完全从语义出发，将（2）—（7）以及（2'）—（7'）这样的句子都看成是宾语倒装句，按照这种观点，它们自然与（8）—（14）以及（8'）—（14'）分属完全不同的句子类型。所有这些观点在后来的语法著作中都有所反映。当代许多分属不同学派的语法论著，如 Sun & Givón（1985）、Ernest & Wang（1995）、

[①] 有一些主谓谓语句并不是双项名词句，如下面这两个例子（转引自吕叔湘 1986：532，539）：

（1）这椅子坐着很不舒服。 （2）这孩子说话早。

沈家煊（1999）、Zhang（2000）等将（2）—（7）分析为OSV，或同时称之为TOP结构，将（2'）—（7'）分析为SOV，把它们看作宾语倒装句。当然，许多著作里的所谓OSV、SOV、TOP结构、宾语倒装等只是一种方便的说法，但在另外一些著作里，这些用语具有很强的理论涵义。在基本语序为SVO的语言中，将这些句子看作为OSV、SOV、TOP结构或宾语倒装，往往意味着研究者认为存在一个相应的SVO句。这在英语中确实如此，除了悬置话题句以外，所有句法话题结构都有一个对应的、属于基本句式的SVO句，在早期的转换生成语法模式中，前者由后者转换而来。汉语的情况则要复杂得多。上面所举的双项名词句中，只有少数有对应的SVO句，例如：

（2"）他们已经买下了这套房子。

（5"）我们还说这些话干吗！

（6"）他并不是十分喜欢这件衣服。

（7"）我见到那几个人了。

在大多数情况下，谓语前的名词性成分无法挪回到动词后面去。可以用"增字解经"的办法为这些句子设定对应的SVO结构，例如：

（4"）你读（这几本）书读得很仔细。

（8"）我用这把刀切萝卜。

（13"）小赵的胆子大极了。

是不是采取类似的处理方法，一般取决于研究者的理论取向。哪些双项名词句能这么处理、如何避免这种处理方法的任意性、哪些句子由基础部分生成、哪些由转换派生、如何生成或派生，等等，都是国际语言学界在60年代至80年代初热烈争辩的问题。同语法研究中其他许多问题一样，这些问题只有在特定的语法理论框架中才有研究价值。随着主流形式语法理论模式的变化，这些具体问题的理论意义大都逐渐消失。

各种语法理论模式的技术细节及其发展变化固然值得我们研究，但更值得我们认真思索的是有关争论背后的核心问题。现代语言学的发展日新月异，经常有新的理论模式出现，老的不断更新，或者渐渐湮没无闻。透过汗牛充栋的文献资料，我们可以看到，始终存在着一些核心问题，常常在不同的时代、不同的理论背景下以不同的方式成为语言学家的研究课题。我们认为，具体语言中哪些结构属于该语言的基本句式，就是上述争论的一个核心问题。作为语法研究中具有根本意义和全局影响的课题之一，人们对它有持久的兴趣，尽管在表现形式和侧重方面有所不同。本文开头提到的常态句式和非常态句式的区别，在某种意义上可以理解为语言中基本句式和非基本句式的区别，或者是无标记句式和有标记句式的区别（参看 Lambrecht 1994；Birner & Ward 1998；沈家煊 1999；Aikhenvald et al. 2001）。在语言信息结构的研究中，这种区别具有十分重要的意义。

如前所述，英语中的句法话题句是非常态句式，除了极少数的例外情况，它们总是对应于一个常态的 SVO 句。也正是因为英语语言系统中存在这种聚合关系上的对立（paradigmatic contrast），使用者可以用非常态句式表现特殊的信息结构。英语中的所谓分裂句式也是属于同一种情况。那么，汉语中常态句式和非常态句式主要是通过哪些手段表现出来的呢？我们认为，在这个"没有严格意义的形态变化""常常省略虚词"（吕叔湘 1984：466—467）的语言里，各种语义成分在句子中的前后顺序，是区别常态句式和非常态句式的最重要的语法手段。正是基于这种认识，陈平（1994）提出两条语义角色优先序列，试图用以概括各种语义角色和句子中主要语法成分的配位原则。在其他条件相似的情况下，符合该配位原则的是汉语中的常态句式，否则是非常态句式，或者是不合语法的句子。这只是一个初步的尝试，无论在原理上还是细节上都有需要进一步探讨的地方。

许多学者认为，相对于 SVO 而言，OSV 和 SOV 在汉语里是有标记语序，在语义和句法上受到更多的限制（参看沈家煊 1999：第 9 章）。我原则上赞成这个观点，同时想从另外一个角度来看这个问题。如果把 §2 所列（2）—（7）看成 OSV，（2'）—（7'）则为 SOV，（2"）和（5"）—（7"）则为 SVO。值得注意的是，如果采取结构主义语法学家的做法，比照（2）—（7），将所有（2）—（14）中的 S，即 NP_2，都看作主语，同时，将与小句谓语不发生直接联系的句子成分在语义上都看作系事成分，我们可以认为，§2（2）—（14）与（2'）—（14'）的区别在于，前者 NP_2 和 NP_1 的顺序符合陈平（1994）提出的下面这条优先序列，而后者则违反了这条优先序列：

（16）施事＞感事＞工具＞系事＞地点＞对象＞受事

我们可以将 OSV 重新解释为在 NP_2 的选择上符合这条优先序列的句子，而 SOV 则是不符合这条优先序列的句子。我们同时认为，汉语语法组织中在聚合关系上呈对立状态的，可以是 SVO 与 OSV/SOV，即（2"）和（5"）—（7"）与（2/2'）和（5/5'）—（7/7'）的对立，但在很多情况下是 OSV 与 SOV，即（2）—（14）与（2'）—（14'）的对立。理由如上所述，所有（2）—（14）都有对立的（2'）—（14'），而只有少数才有对立的 SVO 结构。这就是说，大多数结构主义语法学家所说的汉语主谓谓语句，即本文所说的双项名词句，在其他条件相同的情况下，可以根据其语义角色排列是否遵照（16）这条优先序列而分成两大类别。相对而言（2）—（14）是汉语里的常态结构，而（2'）—（14'）是非常态结构。方梅（1995）注意到下面这种句子：

（17）你我接管了。

单从词汇意义上看，"你"和"我"理解为"接管"的施事或受事的可能性几乎不分高低，但是，"人们一般把 NP_1 '你'理解为受事，把 NP_2 '我'理解为施事，颠倒过来的可能性几乎没有"。这证明，在 NP_2 的选择问题上，同违反（16）优先序列的"施事＋受事＋VP"相比，"受事＋施事＋VP"是常态句式。

我们在下面会看到，（2）—（14）与（2'）—（14'）在信息结构上分别有自己的系统性特点。

3. 汉语双项名词句的话题-陈述结构

我们现在来分析汉语双项名词句的话题-陈述结构。句子信息结构的分析一般至少从两个方面进行，一是研究有关名词性成分的指称属性，二是研究句子成分在句子的话题-陈述结构、焦点-预设结构中所处的位置及其相互关系，以及它们与上下文中其他成分的联系。前面讲过，我们将§2中（2）—（14）汉语双项名词句称作句法话题结构，与英语 LD、TOP 和悬置式话题结构同属一类。本文同时考察（2'）—（14'）的相关特征，目的是找出两类句子在话题-陈述结构方面的异同。为了方便起见，我们将两类句子中的 NP₁ 统称为句法话题。

3.1　句法话题由定指或通指成分担任

我们先看句法话题由定指或通指成分担任的句子。绝大多数研究者都认为，一个名词性成分要用作语用话题，一个先决条件是它得是个定指或通指成分，这是由话题-陈述结构的话语语用特征所决定的（参看 Strawson 1964；Gundel 1976，1988；Reinhart 1981；Schlobinski & Schütze-Coburn 1992；Lambrecht 1994；Jocobs 2001；Chen 2003，2004；Gundel & Fretheim 2004）。通指成分并不表示确定的个体事物，但就表现一类事物的指称属性而言，它与定指成分有某种相同之处，前者表示言谈双方都能确认的某个事物，后者则表示双方都能确认的某类事物。当然，并不是句子中所有的定指和通指成分都能理解为话题。套用吕叔湘先生讲动词宾语与主语关系时所说的话，句中的定指和通指成分有的做话题的机会多，有的机会少，有的老轮不上。虽然无论是在 SVO 句中，还是在双项名词句中，句法话题与语用话题都不存在一一对应的关系，但在其他条件相似的情况下，句中某些位置上的名词性成分做话题的机会要大于其他位置上的成分。[①] 我们发现，在这方面§2（2）—（14）与（2'）—（14'）表现出不同的特征。先看（2）—（14）。这类句子的句法话题可以做语用话题，句子其他部分为陈述

[①] 这儿讲的其他条件中，最重要的条件之一是有关成分在当前语境中的"激活状态"（activation state），又称突显性（saliency）、话题新/旧信息（discourse new/old）、注意焦点（focus of attention）、心理焦点（psychological focus），等等。相关研究成果在西文文献中有许多报道，汉语文献可参看徐烈炯、刘丹青（1998）和王红旗（2001）。

部分，例如：

(1) 问：这套房子怎么啦？ 答：这套房子他们已经买下了。

NP$_2$ 也可以单独做话题，例如：

(2) 问：他们怎么啦？ 答：这套房子他们已经买下了。

(2)—(14) 看其他句子的信息结构都有同样的特点，例如：

(3) 问：这事怎么啦？ 答：这事老高有意见。

(4) 问：老高怎么啦？ 答：这事老高有意见。

(5) 问：说到小赵嘛， 答：小赵胆子大极了。

(6) 问：说到胆子嘛， 答：小赵胆子大极了。

(2')—(14') 的话题-陈述结构上则受到较多限制。句子中的 NP$_1$ 可单独做语用话题，例如：

(7) 问：他们怎么啦？ 答：他们这套房子已经买下了。

(8) 问：说到胆子嘛， 答：胆子小赵大极了。

但是，这种用法的句子有时显得不太自然，例如，在(9)中，答2和答3比答1更自然一些：

(9) 问：老高呢？

答1：$^?$老高这事有意见。

答2：老高这事有意见。

答3：老高这事有意见，其他事没意见。

与(2)—(14)不同，(2')—(14')中的 NP$_2$ 要么不能用作话题，例如：

(10) 问：小赵呢？ 答：*胆子小赵大极了。

要么带有对比的意思，也就是说，它可以用作对比性的话题，例如：

(11) 问：这套房子呢？

答1：$^?$我这套房子不怎么喜欢。

答2：我这套房子不怎么喜欢，那套250平米的倒想再看一看。

答3：这套房子我不怎么喜欢。

当然，这种句子中的 NP$_2$ 常常不是对比话题而是新信息焦点。这种现象最早是吕叔湘先生指出来的（1946：499—452）。吕先生注意到，句中受事为对比性成分或其他信息焦点成分时，采用"受事＋施事＋VP"词序的（即本文§2（2）—（7））远远不及采用"施事＋受事＋VP"词序的（本文§2（2'）—（7'））多，"而单提一事则相反"。另参看范继淹（1984）、陈平（1994）及方梅（1995）。下面再给两个例子：

(12) 问：抽烟吗？

答1：?/* 我烟不抽。

答2：我烟不抽，酒可以喝两杯。

答3：烟我不抽。

(13) 我不能像你，相干的也问，不相干的也问，问得的也问，问不得的也问。（转引自吕叔湘1946：449）

值得我们注意的是，这种对比意义并不限于文献中所讨论的狭义的"施事＋受事＋VP"句式。比较下面的句子：

(14) a. 象鼻子长。　b. *鼻子象长。　c. 鼻子象最长。

(14b) 不能说，(14c) 能说，两句的区别仅在于 (14c) 的 NP_2 带有对比意义。由此可见，(14) 与 (11) — (13) 在 NP_2 的信息结构属性方面具有一定的共性。同样，"胆子小赵大极了"不能用在 (10) 的语境中，而用在 (8) 的语境中，以"胆子"为语用话题则十分自然。在 (8) 中，"小赵"虽然不是话题而是新的信息焦点，但同样隐含着同其他人对比的意思。与此相对照的是"小赵胆子大极了"，在这句话中，无论是语义角色完全一样的"小赵"还是同在 NP_2 位置上的"胆子"，都没有附带这样的对比意义。从这些现象中我们可以得出三条结论：第一，§2（2）—（14）中的句法话题和 NP_2 都可以做语用话题，§2（2'）—（14'）中的句法话题可以做话题，NP_2 一般不能做话题，除非带有对比意义。第二，§2（2'）—（14'）这种格式的双项名词句有一个共同的特点，NP_2 或明或暗地都带有对比的意思或者是其他类型的新信息焦点。第三，以前讨论的主要是同小句谓语动词有语法选择关系的成分，如 (11) 的"这套房子"和 (12) 的"烟"。我们从上面的例子中可以看到,同谓语在语法上不发生直接联系的系事成分,如(8)的"小赵",(9)的"这事",以及(14)的"象",也表现出完全相同的信息结构特征。这些现象表明,在信息结构方面,(2')—(14')属于同一类句式,与§2(2)—(14)相对立,在 NP_1 为定指或通指成分的情况下,两类句式各有自己的系统性特点。这两类句式的区别性特征在于 NP_1 和 NP_2 在§2(16)这条语义角色优先序列中的相对顺序,(2)—(14)中 NP_1 的施事性比 NP_2 弱,而(2')—(14')中 NP_1 的施事性比 NP_2 强。由此可见,这条语义角色优先序列为概括两类句式之间的区别提供了简洁而有效的判断标准。

3.2 句法话题由无定或无指成分担任

在汉语中,至少有三种情况句法话题可以由无定(indefinite)或者无指(nonreferential)成分担任,在这种情况下,该名词性成分一般不能理解为语用话题,或者不能理解为普通意义上的话题。值得我们注意的是,在这个问题上,§2(2)—(14)同(2')—(14')也有很显著的区别。

首先,NP_1 可以是无定成分,例如:

(15)许多问题我们只能慢慢解决。

(16)两件事咱们得小心,一是饮食卫生,二是交通安全。

(17)我楼里的一个小伙子,胆子大极了。

SVO 句中,无定名词做主语的例子不少,在汉语和英语中都是如此。英语句法话题句中句法话题由无定成分担任的例子在文献中也有过报道,但相对而言比较罕见,而且受到较大的限制(参看 Gundel 1976;Reinhart 1981;Prince 1998;Gundel & Fretheim 2004 等)。上面(15)—(17)这样的汉语双项名词句,同范继淹(1985)讨论的无定 NP 主语句一样,语感上十分自然,只是在实际用法上出现频率更低一些。从信息结构的角度来分析,我们认为可以将这些句子看作一种混合结构。NP_1 形式上是名词性成分,但在信息结构上可以理解为一个全句焦点(sentence focus)的存现句,前面隐含着一个存现句的典型标记

"有"。自 NP_2 开始的其他句子部分为陈述部分，以 NP_1 引进的话题为陈述对象。整个句子同时起着将新事物引进语境并以它为话题对它加以陈述的作用。

其次，在有些双项名词句中，疑问词可以出现在 NP_1 或 NP_2 的位置上。一般来讲，比较常见的是疑问词出现在 NP_2 位置上，§2（2）—（14）和（2'）—（14'）两大类句子都可以有这种用法，例如：

(18) a. 这几个字谁写得最好？　a'. 他哪几个字写得最好？
(19) a. 那部电影谁看过了？　　a'. 你哪部电影没看过？
(20) a. 这事谁有意见？　　　　a'. 老高什么事有意见？
(21) a. 这门课谁得了满分？　　a'. 他们哪门课得了满分？
(22) a. 东京什么最贵？　　　　a'. 物价哪个城市最贵？

疑问词也可以在句法话题的位置上出现，例如：

(23) 问：谁胆子最大？　　答：小赵胆子最大。
(24) 问：哪棵树叶子有毒？答：这棵树叶子有毒。

但这种用法受到很大的限制，一般情况下，只有 NP_1 和 NP_2 有隶属关系的双项名词句才可以有这种用法。当然，隶属关系的理解可宽可严，上面两例的隶属关系较紧，下面则显然偏松：

(25) 问：哪个城市物价最贵？答：东京物价最贵。
(26) 问：谁法文说得最好？　答：小王法文说得最好。

带疑问词的句子成分显然不能理解为语用话题。

第三种情况是，双项名词句的句法话题和 NP_2 可以由无指成分担任，其中最常见的是所谓的周遍成分。陆俭明（1986）讨论了可以用作主语的三类周遍性成分：

(27) 1）含有表示任指的疑问代词的名词性成分
　　 2）含有数词"一"的数量短语
　　 3）含有量词重叠形式的名词性成分

这三类周遍成分都能在双项名词句中充任 NP_1 和 NP_2，例如：

(28) a. 什么话他都敢说，什么事他都敢做，什么时候他都有空，什么地方他都敢去。

a'. 他什么话都敢说，什么事都敢做，什么时候都有空，什么地方都敢去。

（29）a. 一篇像样的文章他都写不出来。

a'. 他一篇像样的文章都写不出来。

（30）a. 家家户户我们都得放在自己的心上。

a'. 我们家家户户都得放在自己的心上。

除此之外，充任 NP₁ 和 NP₂ 的还可以是含有诸如"一切""所有""任何""大多数"等限定词的名词性成分，例如：

（31）a. 一切/所有/任何办法我们都想过了。

a'. 我们一切/所有/任何办法都想过了。

（32）a. 大多数工伤事故我们都让保险公司处理。

a'. 我们大多数工伤事故都让保险公司处理。

从指称属性上来看，所有带有这些周遍性成分和限定词的名词性成分都具有一个共同特点，它们都是无指成分（参看 Milsark 1977；Fodor & Sag 1982；Chierchia & McConnell-Ginet 2000）。与带无定成分的汉语双项名词句和英语句法话题句不同，这种带无指成分的双项名词句在汉语里十分常见，是一种很普通的用法。下面，我们着重研究句法话题和 NP₂ 由周遍性成分充任的句子。

我们注意到，一般说来，周遍性成分在所有的情况下都可以出现在 NP₂ 位置上，但并不是总能出现在 NP₁ 位置上，有时能用，有时不能用。其中的规律是什么呢？请看下面四句一组的例子，注意 NP₁ 和 NP₂ 的语义属性以及它们的词序：

（33）a. 这句话谁都说不好。　　　　　　　（受事＞施事）

b. 什么话他都说不好。

a'. 他什么话都说不好。　　　　　　　（施事＞受事）

b'. ？/*谁这句话都说不好。

（34）a. 这条狗谁都喜欢。　　　　　　　　（对象＞感事）

b. 什么狗他都喜欢。

a'. 他什么狗都喜欢。　　　　　　　　（感事＞对象）

b'. *谁这条狗都喜欢。

(35) a. 这把锁什么钥匙都能开。　　　　　（对象＞工具）
　　 b. 什么锁这把钥匙都能开。
　　 a'. 这把钥匙什么锁都能开。　　　　　（工具＞对象）
　　 b'. *什么钥匙这把锁都能开。

(36) a. 腊八粥什么米都能熬。(小米能熬腊八粥)（受事＞对象）
　　 b. 什么粥这种米都能熬。
　　 a'. 这种米什么粥都能熬。　　　　　　（对象＞受事）
　　 b'. *什么米腊八粥都能熬。

(37) a. 这个地方谁都能睡觉。　　　　　　（地点＞施事）
　　 b. 什么地方他都能睡觉。
　　 a'. 他什么地方都能睡觉。　　　　　　（施事＞地点）
　　 b'. *谁这个地方都能睡觉。

(38) a. 这事什么人都有意见。　　　　　　（系事＞施事）
　　 b. 什么事老高都有意见。
　　 a'. 老高什么事都有意见。　　　　　　（施事＞系事）
　　 b'. *什么人这事都有意见。

(39) a. 这门功课人人都得了满分。　　　　（系事＞施事）
　　 b. 门门功课他都得了满分。
　　 a'. 他门门功课都得了满分。　　　　　（施事＞系事）
　　 b'. ?/*人人这门功课都得了满分。

(40) a. 东京什么都太贵。(东京物价太贵)　（系事＞施事）
　　 b. 哪儿物价都太贵。
　　 a'. 物价哪儿都太贵。　　　　　　　　（施事＞系事）
　　 b'. *什么东京都太贵。

(41) a. 这棵树什么都小。(这棵树叶子小)　（系事＞施事）
　　 b. 哪棵树叶子都小。
　　 a'. 叶子哪棵树都小。　　　　　　　　（施事＞系事）
　　 b'. *什么这棵树都小。

如果我们的语感不错的话，可以根据上面这些句子总结出周遍性成分在双项名词句中的出现规律。如（33）—（41）a和a'句所显示，NP$_2$都可以由周遍性成分充任，不受NP$_1$和NP$_2$语义角色区别的影响。而另一方面，（33）—（41）b和b'句则表明，在其他条件相同的情况下，NP$_1$能否由周遍性成分充任，取决于两个名词性成分在本文第2节（16）这个语义角色优先序列中的顺序，如果NP$_1$的语义角色在NP$_2$的后面，NP$_1$可以由周遍性成分充任；如果它的语义角色在NP$_2$的前面，周遍性成分则不能在NP$_1$的位置上出现。换句话说，如表1所示，两个名词性成分中，只有相对而言施事性较弱的那一个才能以周遍性成分的形式出现在NP$_1$，即句法话题的位置上。

表1　周遍性成分在双项名词句中的出现规律

NP$_1$施事性是否弱于NP$_2$？	NP$_1$	NP$_2$
是（33）—（41）a和b	可用	可用
否（33）—（41）a'和b'	不可用	可用

本文第2节所述（16）这条优先序列原本是用来描写和解释汉语中另外一些语法现象的。上面的分析表明，同一条序列也能用来概括周遍性成分在双项名词句中NP$_1$和NP$_2$位置上的出现规律。这可能不是偶然现象。但是，对于这种现象，我们目前还没有找到一个满意的解释。或许可以认为，如果存在一个逻辑语义上基本对应的SVO句，其中的宾语由一个带周遍性成分的NP充任，那么这个NP可以充任双项名词句的NP$_1$，否则NP$_1$则不能由周遍性名词充任。这种解释可以说明下面这样的情况：

(42) a. 这把钥匙能开任何锁。→ 什么／任何锁这把钥匙都能开。

a'. *这把锁能开任何钥匙。→ *什么钥匙这把锁都能开。

(43) a. 这种米能熬任何粥。→ 什么粥这种米都能熬。

a'. *这种粥能熬任何米。→ *什么米这种粥都能熬。

这似乎是告诉我们，双项名词句中由周遍性成分充任的句法话题，实际上是前置宾语，对于周遍性成分来说，这种前置是强制性的。但是，这种分析适用于上面一些句子，但却无法解释其他的例子。如前所述，汉

语双项名词句大多数都没有相应的 SVO 句,例如:

(44) 什么地方他都能睡觉。

　　 什么事老高都有意见。

　　 门门功课他都得了满分。

　　 哪儿物价都太贵。

　　 哪棵树叶子都小。

这些句子与(33)—(41)中的其他句子在许多方面表现出同样的特征,最好作为同一类句子处理。周遍性成分能否出现在双项名词句 NP_1 这个位置上,起决定作用的是句首两个名词性成分的语义角色和排列顺序。在这方面,符合与违反语义角色优先序列的句子分成相当齐整的两大类,这再次证明,本文上一节和这一节的(2)—(14)/(33)—(41) a 和 b 与(2')—(14')/(33)—(41) a' 和 b' 之间是系统性的区别。句子是否有相应的 SVO 句,有关名词性成分与小句谓语有无语法选择关系,基本上与这两大类句子之间的对立无关。

在这方面,其他无指成分在双项名词句中的表现与周遍性成分相同,例如:

(45) a. 这面盾牌什么样的矛都扎不透它。(对象>工具)

　　　 b. 任何盾牌这个矛都能扎透它。

　　　 a'. 这把长矛任何盾牌都能将它扎透。(工具>对象)

　　　 b'. *什么样的矛这面盾牌都扎不透它。

由无指成分充任 NP_1 或 NP_2 的双项名词句,它的话题-陈述结构不同于其他类型的双项名词句。NP_2 由无指成分充任时,一般都是由句法话题做语用话题,例如:

(46) 问:这段话怎么啦? 答:这段话谁都看不懂。

(47) 问:老高怎么啦? 答:老高什么事都不管。

句法话题由无指成分充任的双项名词句具有比较特殊的话题-陈述结构。首先,这儿的 NP_2 虽然是定指或通指成分,却不能理解为话题,例如:

(48) 问:老高怎么啦?

　　 答 1:*什么话老高都说不出来。

　　　　答2：老高什么话都说不出来。

那么，这种句法话题句还有没有语用话题呢？我们认为，可以参考Gundel（1976）及Gundel & Fretheim（2004）的做法，将这类句子的NP$_1$中表示无指属性的成分与NP的其他意义剥离开来分别处理。形式上，整个名词性成分是无指成分，但在信息结构分析上可以把剥离了无指属性的名词性成分理解为话题，例如：

　　　　（49）大多数工伤事故我们都让保险公司处理。

（49）的语用话题是"工伤事故"，是个通指成分，陈述部分是"我们大多数都让保险公司处理"。因为这个句子有可能具有这种信息结构，所以在话语中能用它来应答下面这样的问题：

　　　　（50）问1：工伤事故呢？
　　　　　　　问2：说到/至于工伤事故嘛，
　　　　　　　答：大多数工伤事故我们都让保险公司处理。

其他由无指成分修饰名词充任句法话题的双项名词句也可以作类似的理解，例如（51）答可以出现在下面的语境里：

　　　　（51）问：说到/至于锁嘛，　　答：什么锁这把钥匙都能开。

也就是说，（51）答可以理解为以通指成分"锁"为语用话题，陈述部分是"这把钥匙什么锁都能开"，也可以用在下面的话语环境中：

　　　　（52）什么锁这把钥匙都能开，铜的、铁的、明的、暗的、新
　　　　　　　式的、老式的，都没问题。

无指成分充任句法话题或NP$_2$的双项名词句也可以有其他种类的信息结构。它可以是一个论元焦点（argument focus）或非谓语焦点句，以无指成分充任的句法话题或NP$_2$为信息焦点，回答上文中一个相应的问题，例如：

　　　　（53）问：小王都试过哪些办法？
　　　　　　　答1：所有办法小王都试过了。
　　　　　　　答2：小王所有办法都试过了。
　　　　（54）问：这把钥匙能开哪些锁？
　　　　　　　答1：什么锁这把钥匙都能开。

　　　　答2：这把钥匙什么锁都能开。
　（55）问：他们哪门课得了满分？
　　　　答1：门门课他们都得了满分。
　　　　答2：他们门门课都得了满分。
　（56）问：谁胆子大？答：人人胆子都大。
它们还可以是句子焦点结构，用在下面这样的语境中：
　（57）问：怎么啦？　答：他们门门功课都得了满分。
限于篇幅，我们将另文详细讨论汉语句子的焦点结构问题。

　　由上面的讨论中可以得出结论，同SVO句中的主语一样，汉语双项名词句中的NP_1虽然一般是定指或通指成分，但无定或无指成分也可以在这个位置上出现，其中以周遍性成分尤为常见。周遍性成分能否在NP_1位置上出现，取决于NP_1和NP_2的语义角色排列顺序。同SVO句一样，汉语双项名词句并没有固定的信息结构。NP_1经常用作语用话题，但也有不少时候它不能用作话题，或者不能用作普通意义上的话题。

4. 结论

　　至少有一部分汉语双项名词句被看作是最典型的话题-陈述句式。但是，我们发现，即使是在汉语这个话题突出性语言中，所谓最典型的话题-陈述句式表现的并不总是典型的话题-陈述信息结构。汉语双项名词句可以表现多种类型的信息结构，语法形式与话语语用功能两者之间不存在严整的一一对应关系。句法话题一般可以用作语用话题，但也有不少时候，担任句法话题的可以是无定或无指成分，不能理解为一般意义上的语用话题。即使是有定和通指成分做句法话题，也并不意味着一定得解释为语用话题。

　　汉语双项名词句可以从不同的角度分为许多类别。从信息结构研究的角度来看，最重要的分类之一是根据句首两个名词性成分施事属性的相对强弱将它们分成两类：一类NP_1的施事性弱于NP_2，另一类则相反。

这两类双项名词句在表现话题-陈述结构和其他信息结构上有各自的系统性特点。在后一类双项名词句中，NP_2 一般得是对比性成分或其他的新信息成分，NP_1 不能由周遍性成分担任，而前一类双项名词句则不受这种限制。对于造成这种现象的原因，我们目前还没有找到一个满意的解释。

参考文献

陈　平，1994，试论汉语中三种句子成分与语义成分的配位原则，《中国语文》第 3 期。
丁声树等，1961，《现代汉语语法讲话》，北京：商务印书馆。
范继淹，1984，多项 NP 句，《中国语文》第 1 期。
范继淹，1985，无定 NP 主语句，《中国语文》第 5 期。
方　梅，1995，汉语对比焦点的句法表现手段，《中国语文》第 4 期。
胡裕树，1979，《现代汉语》（第 2 版），上海：上海教育出版社。
陆俭明，1986，周遍式主语句及其他，《中国语文》第 3 期。
吕叔湘，1946，从主语、宾语的分别谈国语句子的分析，《吕叔湘文集》第二卷，北京：商务印书馆，1990，第 445—480 页。
吕叔湘，1979，《汉语语法分析问题》，《吕叔湘文集》第二卷，同上，第 481—571 页。
吕叔湘，1984，汉语语法要点，《吕叔湘文集》第三卷，商务印书馆，1992，第 466—509 页。
吕叔湘，1986，主谓谓语句举例，《吕叔湘文集》第三卷，同上，第 531—544 页。
沈家煊，1999，《不对称和标记论》，南昌：江西教育出版社。
王红旗，2001，《指称论》，南开大学博士学位论文。
徐烈炯、刘丹青，1998，《话题的结构与功能》，上海：上海教育出版社。
朱德熙，1982，《语法讲义》，北京：商务印书馆。
Aikhenvald, Alexandre Y., R M. W. Dixon, and Masayuki Onishi. eds. 2001. *Non-canonical Marking of Subjects and Objects*. Amsterdam: John Benjamins Publishing Company.
Birner, Betty and Gregory Ward. 1998. *Information Status and Noncanonical Word Order in English*. Amsterdam: John Benjamins Publishing Company.
Chafe, Wallace L. 1976. Givenness, contrastiveness, definiteness, subjects, topics, and point of view. In: Charles N. Li, ed., *Subject and Topic*, New York: Academic Press, 25-55.
Chao, Yuen Ren. 1968. *A Grammar of Spoken Chinese*. University of California Press.

Chen, Ping. 1996. Pragmatic interpretation of structural topics and relativization in Chinese. *Journal of Pragmatics* 26, 389-406.

Chen, Ping. 2003. Indefinite determiner introducing definite referent: A special use of "*yi* 'one' +classifier" in Chinese. *Lingua* 113, 1169-1184.

Chen, Ping. 2004. Identifiability and definiteness in Chinese. *Linguistic* 42(6), 1117-1172.

Chierchia, Gennaro and Sally McConnell-Ginet. 2000. *Meaning and Grammar: An Introduction to Semantics*, 2nd edition. The MIT Press.

Ernst, Thomas and Chengchi Wang. 1995. Object proposing in Mandarin Chinese. *Journal of East Asian Linguistics* 4, 235-260.

Fodor, Janet Dean and Ivan Sag. 1982. Referential and quantificational indefinites. *Linguistic and Philosophy* 9(3), 427-473.

Gabelentz, Georg von der. 1901. *Die Sprachwissenschaft: Ihre Aufgaben, Methoden, Und Bisherigen Ergebnisse*. Ubingen: Gunter Narr Verlag.

Gundel, Jeanette K. 1976. *The Role of Topic and Comment in Linguistic Theory*. Indiana University Linguistics Club.

Gundel, Jeanette K. 1988. Universals of topic-comment structure. In: Michael Hammond et al., eds., *Studies in Syntactic Typology*. Amsterdam: John Benjamins Publishing Company, 209-239.

Gundel, Jeanette K. and Thorstein Fretheim. 2004. Topic and focus. In: Laurence R. Horn and Gregory Ward, eds., *The Handbook of Pragmatics*. Oxford: Blackwell Publishing, 175-196.

Halliday, Michael A. K. 1967. Notes on transitivity and theme in English. Part I & Part II. *Journal of Linguistics* 3, 37-81, 177-274.

Hockett, Charles F. 1958. *A Course in Modern Linguistics*. New York: Macmillan.

Hopper, Paul and Janice Martin. 1987. Structuralism and diachrony: The development of the indefinite article in English. In: Anna G. Ramat et al., eds., *Papers from the Seventh International Conference on Historical Linguistics*. Amsterdam: John Benjamins Publishing Company, 295-304.

Jacob, Joachim. 2001. The dimensions of topic-comment. *Linguistics* 39(4), 641-681.

Lambrecht, Knud. 1994. *Information Structure and Sentence Form: A Theory of Topic, Focus and the Mental Representation of Discourse Referents*. Cambridge University Press.

Li, Charles N. and Sandra A. Thompson. 1976. Subject and topic: A new typology of language. In: Charles N. Li, ed., *Subject and Topic*. New York: Academic Press, 457-489.

Lyons, John. 1977. *Semantics*. Cambridge: Cambridge University Press.

Milsark, Gary L. 1977. Toward an explanation of certain peculiarities in the existential construction in English. *Linguistic Analysis* 3, 1-30.

Prince, Ellen. 1998. On the limits of syntax, with reference to left-dislocation and topicalization. In: Peter W. Culicover and Louise McNally, eds., *The Limits of Syntax. Syntax and Semantics* Vol. 29, San Diego: Academic Press, 281-302.

Reinhart, Tanya. 1981. Pragmatics and linguistics: An analysis of sentence topic. *Philosophica* 27, 53-49.

Russell, Bertrand. 1905. On Denoting. *Mind* 14: Reprinted in Herbert Feigl and Wilfrid Sellars, eds., *Readings in Philosophical Analysis*, New York: Appleton Century Crofts, Inc., 103-115.

Schlobinski, Peter and Stephan Schütze-Coburn. 1992. On the topic of topic and topic continuity. *Linguistics* 30, 89-121.

Strawson, Peter F. 1950. On referring. *Mind* 59, 320-344.

Strawson, Peter F. 1964. Identifying reference and truth value. *Theoria* XXX, 96-118; Reprinted In: Farhang Zabeeh et al., eds., *Readings in Semantics*, University of Illinois Press, 1974, 193-216.

Sun, Chaofen and Talmy Givón. 1985. On the so-called SOV word order in Mandarin Chinese: A quantified text study and its implications. *Language* 61(2), 329-351.

Zhang, Ning. 2000. Object shift in Mandarin Chinese. *Journal of Chinese Linguistics* 28, 201-246.

（本文原载《中国语文》2004年第6期。）

论现代汉语时间系统的三元结构[*]

提　要　本文试图为全面阐释现代汉语中与时间性相关的语法现象建立一个简明的理论框架。作者分析了现代汉语时间系统的三个组成部分：时相结构、时制结构和时态结构，重点放在时相结构方面。作者根据句子的时相结构特点划分出了五种情状类型，同时确定了相应的语法形式特征。作者列出了充任各类情状句谓语的典型动词、动宾结构和动补结构，证明句子的情状归类取决于所有句子成分词汇意义的总和，其中动词是基础，其他成分也起着重要的选择和制约作用。作者并且提出，只有从系统的观点出发，才能够全面阐释现代汉语中与时相、时制和时态特征相关的各种语法现象。

关键词　时相结构　情状类型　状态　活动　结束　复变　单变　时制　时态

1. 前言

　　本文试图建立一个简明的理论框架，以阐释现代汉语时间系统的组织结构，同时指出，要全面而真切地理解与时间性相关的语法现象，最好的途径就是将有关现象置于整个时间系统的框架之中，结合其他系统成分进行分析。这儿所说的时间系统，从本质上来说是一个语法范畴。一方面它由多种相关的语义成分和语义关系结成纵横交错的语义网络。另一方面，这个网络结构伴随着相应的语法形式特征。本文所采用的基本研究方法是先解析相关的语义内容，继而确定与有关语义特征相对应的语法表现形式。

　　现代汉语时间系统的三个主要部分是：（一）句子的时相（phase）结构，体现句子纯命题意义内在的时间特征，主要由谓语动词的词汇意

---

[*] 本文写作过程中，曾就北京话口语格式等问题多次咨询徐丹和王鉴同志。谨致谢忱。

义所决定，其他句子成分的词汇意义也起着重要的选择和制约作用，其中宾语和补语所起的作用尤为显著；（二）句子的时制（tense）结构，指示情状发生的时间，表现为该时间与说话时间或另一参照时间在时轴上的相对位置；（三）句子的时态（aspect）结构，表现情状在某一时刻所处的特定状态。限于篇幅，本文侧重分析句子的时相结构，其他有关内容将在以后陆续讨论。

2. 时间性与时间系统的三个方面

现代语言学调查结果证实，名词与动词的区别存在于古往今来的所有语言之中。这种现象的根本原因要从语言的功能以及人们对于外部世界的认知方式上面去寻求解释。语言的主要功能是用作交际工具。对于周围存在的万事万物，人们首先需要的就是相应的各种名字，可供用作为指代符号。"凡目所见，耳所闻，口所嗜，鼻所嗅，四肢之所触，与夫心之所志，意之所感，举凡别声、被色与无声、无臭，苟可以语言称之者，无非事也，无非物也，无非名也。"论及事物，其主要特点便是它们所执行或者经历的各种行为活动，即所谓"随所在而必见其有行"[①]。因此，人类语言自然又需要有一类符号用以指代形形色色的行为动作。作为两种截然分明的语法类别，名词和动词的出现，便是人类语言顺应这两种最基本功能需求的必然结果。

就最典型的事物而言，它们一般都占据一定的空间，随具体事物类型的不同而表现出大小、多少、高低、厚薄、聚散、离合等特征。行为动作则与此不同。它们最显著的特点表现在时间方面。若将眼光深入到行为动作的内部过程之中，我们往往可以分解辨析其中的各个阶段，例如起始阶段、持续阶段、结束阶段等，同时可以根据有关阶段之间的种种关系确定它们的内部时间结构，并且比较它们的异同。若以时轴上

---

① 参看《马氏文通》"字类"。

的某一点为参照点从外部来观察行为动作，我们往往又可以从中发现已然、方然、未然等时间性特征。与行为动作比较，事物的时间性特征则相对显得单纯。山川河海可以历千载而不改其名，在时间性方面表现出很高的稳定性。从本质上说，语言的语法特征凝聚了语言的交际功能特征。因此，作为所指对象的事物与行为动作在时间性方面的重大区别自然不可避免地要反映到名词和动词这两种基本语法类别各自的语法特征上面。证诸世界上许多有名词变格和动词变位的语言，除了在名词和动词身上都有所表现的一些语法意义，如性（gender）、数（number）等，名词的种种形态变化所表现的语法意义一般与空间位置有关，人们以语法形态为依据，进而把握有关事物在空间分布上呈现出的各种状态，借以理解这些事物在特定情景中所扮演的角色。另一方面，动词变位所表现的语法意义则大多与时间特征有关，利用行为动作在时间流动过程中呈现出的各种状态，人们可以辨识特定的行为动作有别于其他同类行为动作的地方。参见 Langacker（1987）。

句子以动词为核心成分。如果我们将动词在时间性方面展示的丰富内涵理解为动词不同于其他词类的主要区别性特征之一，那么，我们就很容易理解为什么句子的许多语法特征与句子所表命题在时间性方面的种种特点密切相关。诚然，汉语缺乏西方语言中常见的那套外露的屈折形态变化系统，但是，这决不意味着一些基本的语言功能特征在汉语中没有提升到语法平面上凝结为抽象的语法关系。下面，我们围绕与时间性相关的几套重要的语义概念，辨析现代汉语中与它们相对应的语法特征。我们一般以传统所说的单句为分析对象。这些单句一般由单个动词与其他成分结合而成，表现一个简单的命题。

句子的时间性特征，主要取决于时相、时制和时态三个子系统的有关特征以及它们之间的相互联系。下面，我们分别讨论这三个方面的内容。

3. 时相结构

3.0 从句子的词汇意义上来看，有的句子表现静止的状态，也有的句子表现动态的行为。将动态行为进一步细分，有的行为表现一个瞬间动作，有的行为则可以有一定的延续时间；再将可以有一定延续时间的行为进一步细分，有的行为有其内在的终结点，不大可能无休无止地持续下去，而有的行为则没有内在的终结点。以自然时间的流逝为参照点，将所有这些动作行为的发生或展开过程展现在一条时轴上，我们对它们的有关特征会看得更加清楚一些。如果把所有情景的起始点在时轴上定为零点，那么，我们会发现，随着时间的延伸，不同的情景在时轴的有关时点上表现出来的性质并不一致。句子在这方面的表现塑成了它的时相结构。根据句子的时相结构特点而划分出来的类别，称作为情状类型（situation type）。

句子在情状类型方面的归属，主要由句子成分的词汇意义所决定。现代汉语中有一些专用的语法手段，如时态助词"了、着、过"等，经常出现在句子中，表现我们以后将会讨论到的时态特征。在判断句子所属的情状类型时，我们一般先将这些词语从句子中剔除出去，剩下单纯的词汇成分，以后者的语义特点作为分类的出发点。这样做的原因十分简单：我们把"了、着、过"等看作为不同于普通词汇成分的专用时态助词，而这些语法成分本身的特点，有待于我们分析它们与各种情状类型的联系之后才能得出结论。换句话说，既然句子的时相结构是同时态结构等立的部分，那么，"了、着、过"等作为附加在情状类型之上的时态成分，在我们对它们所附着的实体进行分析时，是不宜纳入考虑范围之内的。同时，我们也要指出，同西方语言一样，现代汉语中表现各种时态范畴的语法助词也都是由实词逐渐虚化而来。汉语的特殊之处在于缺乏严格意义上的形态变化，除了"了、着、过"等这些公认的已经几乎完全虚化为语法成分的助词之外，还有不少词语虽然在一定程度上具备了指示时态意义的功能，例如"成、到、好、完"等，但还不能断言它们已经虚化为专门表现时态范畴的语法手段，参见吕叔湘（1982）。这些词语对于原有词汇意义的保留程度，要大大地高于"了、着、过"等单纯语法标记。由于篇幅所限，本文不拟深入讨论这两类词语的异同。我们沿袭惯例，仅将"了、着、过"这类公认的助词作为专用语法手段对待，而将其他诸如"成、到、好、完"等词语一律归入普通词汇部分加以分析。

由此可见，归入各种情状类型的句子，一般要等到带上指示时制特征或时态特征的语法标记之后，才成为我们实际所闻所言的句子。这儿说的语法标记，也包括 Chao（1968）中所提到的"零标记"。换句话说，单纯作为情状类型来考虑的句子都是从实际使用的句子中撇开了时制和时态因素，单独分离出来的语言单位。下面讨论有关情状类型时，读者会发现有些例句离开了时制或时态标记则"不成话"。这是因为这些语言单位本来就不是独立使用的"话"，要成话往往还得加上必要的语法标记才行。

3.1 有关情状类型的研究在西方哲学和语言学研究中具有悠久的传统，最早可以追溯到亚里士多德时代。亚里士多德首先注意到，有些动词的意义必然涉及某种结局，而有些动词的意义则无此连带关系。他同时提出，可以根据这方面的特征为动词分类。近年来，哲学界和语言学界对情状类型的研究兴趣有增无减，陆续发表了一批专著和论文，将这方面的讨论逐步引向深入，其中较重要的有 Vendler（1967）、Verkuyl（1972）、Comrie（1976）、Mourelatos（1978）、Dowty（1979，1982）、Carlson（1981）、Bache（1982）、Smith（1983，1985），等等。从已经发表的研究成果来看，一般把情状类型分为四种，即状态（state）、活动（activity）、结束（accomplishment）和成就（achievement）。值得我们注意的是，尽管作为研究对象的自然语言并非仅仅局限于毫无代表性的那么一两种，尽管各家往这种分类方式中注入的语义差别并非完全一致，所用的名称也远未统一，但是，对于情状类型的四部分类，大家的意见还是相当一致的。这种现象给予我们的启示是，虽然同各类情状相对应的语法形式表现在具体语言中各有不同，类似的情状分类本身确实具有一个超越语言个性特征的逻辑基础。

在现代汉语语法研究领域里，结合时制和时态特征对句子的时相结构做系统分析，这样的研究报告并不多见。但是，同这儿讨论的情状分类相关的现象，却是现代汉语语法研究中的重要课题。在近年来发表的论文中，马庆株（1981）、Smith（1985）和邓守信（1986）尤其引起我们的注意。涉及作为分类对象的语言单位时，各家的做法并不一致。范围最窄的局限于单个动词，最宽的则将眼光延伸至包括时制和时态语法标记在内的整个句子。下面，我们分别以马庆株（1981）和邓守信（1986）为例，讨论他们的分析范围和分类标准。

马庆株（1981）的着眼点主要停留在单个动词上面。他根据动词带时量宾语时表现出来的种种语法和语义特点，检验动词的时相结构。他利用[±持续]、[±完成]、[±状态]三对语义特征，将有关动词分为 V_a、V_{b1}、V_{b21}、V_{b22} 四类。请看下面的表格：

	持续	完成	状态
V_a（死）	−	+	
V_b（等、看、挂）	+		
V_{b1}（等）	+	−	
V_{b2}（看、挂）	+	+	
V_{b21}（看）	+	+	−
V_{b22}（挂）	+	+	+

V_a 类成分，如"死、知道、看见"等，表示瞬间完成、不能持续的动作，后接时量宾语时，该时量短语指动作完成以后经历的时间。请看下面的例句：

（1）已经死了三天了。

（2）手表丢了两天又找着了。

V_b 类成分都能够表示可以持续的动作。其中，V_{b1} 不能表示瞬间完成的行为，因此，后接时量宾语时，该时量短语的所指只能是动作行为持续的时间。请看下面的例子：

（3）等了三天了。

（4）坐了半天了。

而 V_{b21} 和 V_{b22} 既能表示瞬间完成的动作行为，又能表示持续的动作行为，因此，后接时量宾语时，在时量短语的所指问题上会引出歧义。"看了一年了""挂了半天了"可以表示动作持续了那么长的一段时间，也可以表示自动作结束后经过了那么长的一段时间，前一种情况以句（5）为例，后一种情况以句（6）为例：

（5）这本书看了一年了，还没看完。

（6）那场戏我已经看了一年了，还记得很清楚。

另一方面，V_{b21} 和 V_{b22} 的区别在于 V_{b22} 可以表示状态，而 V_{b21} 却不能表示状态。因此，V_{b22} 后接时量宾语时，可以表示动作行为的持续，也可以表示动作行为的完成，还可以表示由该动作行为造成的状态的持续。

马文观察细密，论证谨严。他没有直接提到有关情状分类的名目，但是，文中提出了[±持续]、[±完成]和[±状态]三组区别性特征，并且利用这三组区别性特征对动词进行分类，这种做法与西方语言学家在处理命题的情状分类时所遵循的惯例，在基本原理上是相通的。[①]

邓守信（1986）基本同意 Vendler（1967）区分四类情状的理论观点，并且接过了 Vendler 提出的四类情状的具体名称，将它们直接用于汉语研究。下面是邓守信（1986）分别为各类情状举出的汉语例句：

Ⅰ.活动

（7）张老师在美国教汉语。

Ⅱ.完结（即我们上文所说的"结束"）

（8）他学会法语了。

Ⅲ.达成（即我们上文所说的"成就"）

（9）老王丢了一只手表。

Ⅳ.状态

（10）我们都知道他的名字。

同时，邓守信成功地确定了汉语中这四类情状各自独有的语法特征。他着重分析了副词"一下"和"马上"与各种情状的连用情形，指出由于时相结构的差异而带来的一些语法特点。

---

① 参看 Comrie（1976）、Lyons（1977）中的有关论述。

与马庆株（1981）不同，邓守信（1986）明确指出，文中所谈的情状分类虽然与动词分类有密切的关联，但两者之间并不能画等号。情状分类的对象是整个句子，不是单个动词。从这个角度来看，本文的观点更接近邓守信（1986）。但是，我们从邓文所举的例句和说明中可以看出，他的分类对象是连同时制和时态语法标记在内的整个句子。例如，在讨论达成类情状时，邓文中写道："达成不牵涉到动作而只表明某种情况的出现，如'乾了'的'乾'这个现象在'乾了'之前是不存在的，而且'乾了'也不是某个动作的目标。概括地说，'乾了'只是一个状态的发生，或者说是一个状态的转变。"参见邓守信（1986：31）。在这个问题上，本文采取的是另一种处理方法。

3.2 前面谈过，我们在讨论时相结构的过程中取来作为分析对象的语言单位，既不同于马庆株（1981）中的单个动词，也不同于邓守信（1986）中包括时制和时态标记的整个句子，而是将所有表示时制和时态特征的语法标记排除在外的句子。我们在本文开头便指出，时制指示情状发生的时间，而时态则涉及对于情状内部时相结构的种种观察方法和表现角度。这个定义本身便蕴涵了句子的时相结构同它的时制和时态特征的可分离性。作为各种时制和时态之辨所附丽的主体，句子的时相结构具有自己的独立地位，这应该是不难理解的。[①] 同时，我们也不能无视句子的时相结构同时制和时态之间的密切联系。这种联系主要表现在两个方面。一方面，句子自身的时相结构在很大程度上制约着句子在时制和时态表现方面的选择范围。以时态表现为例，有的情状，如"看电视新闻""唱江苏民歌""把瓶子刷干净"等，因为其时相结构的特点，允许人们从各种角度对它们进行观察。例如，可以把它们作为一个完整的情状加以表述，也可以在情状展开的过程中截取其中的某一点，如起始、中间、结束等，加以表述。而有的情状由于内在时相结构的限制，可供选择的观察角度则远远少于前一类情状，例如"引爆敌人埋下的地雷""跌落在坑里""死去"，等等。换句话说，句子的时相结构决

---

① 至于连同所有时制和时态标记的句子具备什么样的时间性特征，应该如何分类，不在本文讨论范围之内，容以后详加分析。

定了哪些时态种类有出现的可能，哪些时态种类没有出现的可能。另一方面，句子的时相结构在很大程度上制约着时制和时态语法标记在具体使用场合的功能和语义特点。以同样的表面形式出现的指示时制或时态意义的语法手段在不同的语境中表现可以很不一样，其间的差异与有机联系，往往要到作为主体的情状时相结构中去寻求解释。总而言之，理解汉语句子时间系统的关键，是把握句子的时相结构组织同句子的时制和时态三方面的相互联系和相互制约，而要达到这个目的，前提条件是详细分解这三个子系统的结构成分和组织原则。下面，我们重点剖析作为情状分类基础的句子时相结构。

句子成分的词汇意义决定了句子的时相结构，几乎所有的句子成分都有可能在其中起着这样或那样的作用。不过，在决定句子时相结构的过程中，各类成分的力量并不相等。我们按照它们所起作用的大小，将主要的几类句子成分依次排列如下：

  1. 动词
  2. 宾语和补语
  3. 主语
  4. 其他句子成分

其中动词无疑是最重要的因素。动词与其他几类成分的关系简单地说来是这样的：动词的词汇意义，决定了它所在的句子能够表现哪些种类的情状，而与动词连用的其他句子成分则决定了该句实际表现了哪一种特定的情状类型。换句话说，前者提供了可能性，后者在也许不止一种可能性中间进行了具体选择，确定了句子的时相结构。另外，各类动词所提供的可能性范围有大有小。有的动词在适当的条件下可以用于几乎所有的情状类型，而有的动词则限用于某一类或两类情状。下面，在讨论各种情状类型时，我们将同时列出参与表现这类情状的最常见、最典型的动词。但是，这并不意味着所列动词只能用在这类情状之中。实际上，在几种情状类型项下重出的动词比比皆是。关于其他句子成分同动词在确定句子的时相结构中的交互作用，我们将在后面详细讨论。

现在，让我们利用下面的三组区别性特征来分析汉语句子的时相结构，并且据此划分有关情状类别：

1. [± 静态]（static）
2. [± 持续]（durative）
3. [± 完成]（telic）

首先，我们分别对这三组概念略加说明。

静态的对立面是动态。我们把情状沿时轴自零点向前展开的过程看作为该情状在时轴上占据一个时段的过程。如果情状在这个时段中的所有时点上呈现出来的状态都是相同的，那么，我们便称之为静态情状。也就是说，静态情状具有一种均质（homogeneous）的时间结构。静态情状句中最常用的动词有"属于、姓、等于、适合"等属性动词，"相信、知道、爱、恨"等知觉动词，以及"坐、站、睡、躺"等姿态动词。不符合上述条件的情状，我们称之为动态情状。动态情状又可以分出几种情况来谈。有的情状表现的是瞬间性的动作，从它们的时间结构上来看根本无法容纳任何时段，这类情状自然不合静态的要求。这种性质的句子中常用的动词有"认出、发现、死"，等等。有的情状虽然能够延续从而在时轴上占据一个时段，但是，情状在时段的各个时点上呈现出来的性质并不是完全一样的，换句话说，该情状的时间结构是异质的（heterogeneous）。这样的情状也同静态无缘。根据 Comrie（1976）的定义，在一般情况下，静态情状无需外力作用，本身便能将现状维持下去，而动态情状只有在外力的持续作用下才能保持现状。也参见李临定（1985）。

持续是与动态情状相关的特征，静态情状则没有持续与非持续的区别。有的行为动作所占时间很短。从它们的时间结构上来看，这类情状的起始点和终结点在时轴上靠得很近，有时几乎可以说是重合的。它们在时轴上占据的是一个时点，或者是非常短的一个时段。因此，情状本身很难包容一个相对稳定的持续阶段。我们把具备这种特征的情状称作为非持续性情状。这类情状句中常用的动词有"爆炸、跌倒、找到、眨眼"等。另外一类行为动作的起始点和终结点在时轴上则有明显的距离，整个情状因此可以有一个持续过程。这类情状称作为持续性情状，其中常用的动词（及宾语）有"跳舞、唱歌、看电影、读《阿Q正传》"等。显而易见，对于持续性情状来讲，可供观察的角度要多于非持续性情状。

完成与非完成取决于情状有无自然的终结点以及有无向该终结点逐步接近的进展过程。有些情状的语义构成具有内在的自然终结点。情状一旦开始，便一步一步地朝着这个自然终结点演进。抵达终结点便意味着情状的完成。我们举几个例子，"听《贝多芬第九交响曲》、读这两篇文章、看一场电影"等情状都伴随着一个内在的自然终结点，不太可能无休无止地持续下去。换句话说，这类情状在时轴上所占时段的长度已经为情状本身的语义内容所框定，它们的延续时间有一定的常规界限。例如《贝多芬第九交响曲》的演奏时间一般为一小时左右，于是，时轴上自零点后过一个小时，便是情状"听《贝多芬第九交响曲》"的自然终结点。如果这类情状在抵达自然终结点之前中途停止，便不能算作为一个完整的情状。[①] 具备这种性质的情状，我们称之为完成性情状。另一方面，有些情状没有内在的终结点相伴。在时轴上，它们可以在位于起始点之后的任意一个时点上结束，从理论上讲也可以无休无止地延长下去，无论在起始点之后的哪一个时点上结束，这类情状都可以看作为完整的行为动作。具备这种性质的情状，我们称之为非完成性情状。含有诸如"听音乐、读书、跑步"一类动词（及宾语）的句子常常表现非完成性情状。另外，瞬时性行为动作一般也属于非完成性情状。它们虽然有内在的终结点，但却缺乏一个自起始点向终结点逐步接近的中间过程。

3.3 我们根据这三对区别性特征的各种组合方式，将汉语句子表现的情状分成下面五种类型：

	静态	持续	完成
Ⅰ.状态	+		
Ⅱ.活动	−	+	−

---

① 这种性质与许多语法特征有密切关联，例如，它是造成这类情状句中的谓语动词以已然状态出现时一般不能用重叠式的重要原因。参看 Chen(1988)。

（续表）

	静态	持续	完成
Ⅲ. 结束	-	+	+
Ⅳ. 复变	-	-	+
Ⅴ. 单变	-	-	-

现在，我们分别讨论这五类情状的时相结构，同时指出各类情状独具的语法形式特征，最后，分析五类情状彼此间的联系与根本差异。

Ⅰ. 状态（state）

这类情状的最大特点是它的静态性质。我们参考 Smith（1985），将它的时相结构图示如下：

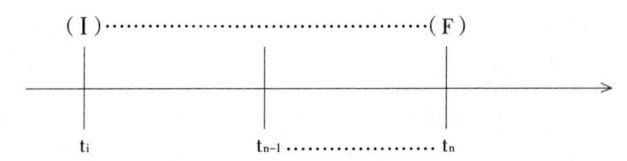

$$(\text{I}) \cdots\cdots\cdots\cdots\cdots\cdots\cdots\cdots(\text{F})$$

$$t_i \qquad\qquad t_{n-1}\cdots\cdots\cdots t_n$$

其中 I 代表情状的起始点，F 代表终结点，箭杆代表时轴，箭头指示时间前进的方向。I 和 F 置于括号之中则表示该类情状缺乏内在的自然起始点或终结点。t_i 和 t_n 等则代表情状在时轴有关时点上的对应状态。根据上面对静态特征所下的定义，我们自然明白 $t_i = t_{n-1} = t_n$。下面是表现状态类情状的一些例句：

（11）他姓刘，属马的，完全符合你们的要求。
（12）铁具有金属的所有特性。
（13）三加三等于六。
（14）这段话包含下面三层意思。
（15）谁都不相信他的话。
（16）你太累了，需要好好地休息几天。
（17）派出的通讯员下去三天还没回来，大家的心里都很焦虑。
（18）我放开她的手，怔怔地站在那里，觉得仿佛是在做梦。
（19）两幅画多年来一直挂在这面墙上。

表现状态类情状的句子，它们的谓语动词通常由下面三类成分担任：

一、表示属性或关系的动词，主要有：

属于　好像　等于　当作　适合　值得　作为　符合
服从　姓　是

二、表示心理或生理状态的动词：
喜欢　高兴　知道　讨厌　相信　重视　焦虑　惊讶
沮丧　需要　明白　舒服　害怕　舍得　愿意　放心
佩服　满意　尊敬　主张　轻视　情愿　失望　懂
嫌　爱　恨

三、表示处所位置的动词，这又可分为两小类，一类表示自身处所位置，另一类表示他身处所位置，有致使的意思。
A. 坐　站　躺　蹲　藏　躲　跪　趴
B. 挂　包　摆　贴　装　腌　铺　捆　盖　穿　戴　垫
叠　顶　堆　存　缝　搁　糊　塞　夹　裹　晾　举
插　搭　钉　架　放

从这三类动词的语义来看，它们的静态性质也有程度强弱的区别。第一类动词的静态性最强，极少与时态助词"着"或时间副词"在"连用，甚至大多数不能与表示状态动作的起始或完成的"了"连用。第二类动词的静态性弱于第一类动词，在一般情况下不能带"着"或"在"，但能够带"了"。另外，这类动词前面能带程度副词，如"很、非常"等。第三类动词能带"着"，但不能单独同时间副词"在"连用。一般也不用在"在+V+着"中。根据一般北京人的语感，"他在跪着""他在趴着"的可接受度又略高于"他在坐着""他在站着"，尽管这四句话都不常说。第一类动词不能出现在"V+（了）+时量短语+了"之中，其他两类可以，时量短语指示状态的持续时间。请看下面的例子：

＊属于了几年了　高兴了半天了　躲了三个星期了
＊姓王姓很久了　知道很久了　　挂了几个月了
＊是了两三年了　坐了一下午了　放了一辈子了

如前所述，就单个动词而言，大多数都可以用来表现两种或更多种类型的情状。以上面所举表示处所位置的动词为例，它们除了可以用在静态性情状之中，几乎全都可以表现动态性情状。因此，下面的语句是有歧义的：

坐在台上　　挂在墙上
站在桌子上　放在地上
躺在床上　　穿在身上
躲在柜子里　晾在外面

它们都可以作静态情状和动态情状两种解释，以"坐在台上"为例，请看下面的句子：

（a）我一眼望进去，只见主席团成员都坐在台上，唯有主席一个人站在那儿做报告。

（b）主席团成员一个个走了上去，坐在台上，主席宣布大会开始。

表现静态情状时，上面语句中的"在＋处所"短语可以移到动词前面来，意思不变：

坐在台上　　→　在台上坐着
站在桌子上　→　在桌子上站着
躺在床上　　→　在床上躺着
躲在柜子里　→　在柜子里躲着
挂在墙上　　→　在墙上挂着
放在地上　　→　在地上放着
穿在身上　　→　在身上穿着
晾在外面　　→　在外面晾着

只能表现动态情状的动词便没有这样的对应关系：

跳在床上　　—/→　在床上跳着
撒在楼下　　—/→　在楼下撒着
摔在桌子上　—/→　在桌子上摔着
砸在头上　　—/→　在头上砸着
甩在墙上　　—/→　在墙上甩着
跌在地上　　—/→　在地上跌着

Ⅱ. 活动（activity）

这类情状具有动态、持续和非完成性的特征，我们将它的时相结构图示如下：

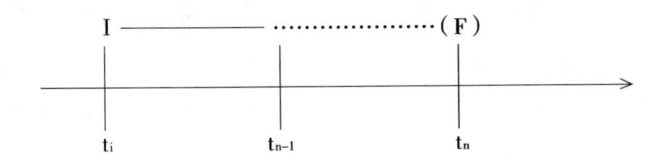

$$I \text{———————}\cdots\cdots\cdots\cdots(F)$$
$$t_i \quad\quad\quad t_{n-1} \quad\quad\quad t_n$$

下面是表现活动类情状的一些例句：

（20）那孩子在门口转悠了半天，就是不敢进去。

（21）我出来时，她正在那儿哭呢。

（22）他抽烟抽了一上午。

（23）他们成天就是游泳、打球、看电视，从来不做正经事。

（24）那群中学生看武侠小说看迷了。

（25）病人听轻音乐对恢复健康有好处。

（26）他每天在操场上跑步。

（27）他教书教了20年了。

（28）老周平时常常写诗。

活动类情状句中，最常用的谓语动词有下面三种类型：

一、动作动词兼表自身或他身所处位置的处所动词，与上面讨论状态类情态时所列举的第三类动词相同。

二、其他表现动态动作的动词，包括表现心理活动的动词，可以分成下面三小类：

A. 跳 走 跑 笑 哭 闹 转 蹦 咳嗽 唠叨

B. 听 看 读 写 教 唱 说 问 念 抽 学 画
　　抄 印 乘 骑 洗 吹 弹 拉 打 吃 吸 喝

C. 想 猜 考虑 琢磨 寻思 回忆 思考 关心 注意 体会

三、带泛指性名词宾语的动宾结构，即一般称作为"离合词"的成分：

读书 唱歌 打仗 开车 铡草 赛球 走路 跑步 跳舞
喝酒 抽烟 捕鱼 吵架 拉琴 说话 写字 鼓掌 告状

用在活动类情状句中的谓语动词可以在"V+着"和"在+V"这

两种句法槽中出现,表现有关动作正处于进行或持续状态。活动类情状没有内在的自然终结点,动作开始后,无论在时轴的 I 以后哪一个时点上终止,都算作为一个完整的动作。这种语义性质同活动类情状句的一个语法特点密切相关。当"V+(了)+时量短语+了"这种格式出现在活动类情状句中时,时量短语指示的是动作自 I 点后在时轴上的持续时间,请看下面的例句:

> 游泳游了一个小时了。
> 抽烟抽了一上午了。
> 教书教了 20 年了。
> 在门口转悠了半天了。

以上句子的时相结构是:t_i = 时量短语的计时起点。

"挂、包、摆、贴"等兼表静态位置和动态动作的动词用在静态情状句和动态情状句中的语法功能是不一样的。用在静态情状句中的时候,动词前面一般不能加时间副词"在",而用于动态情状句中时则可以加"在"。试比较下面两组句子:

> a. 他在往墙上挂奖状呢。
> b. 墙上挂着奖状。
> c. *墙上在挂着奖状。
> a. 她正在贴窗花呢。
> b. 窗子上面贴着纸花。
> c. *窗子上面正贴着纸花。

Ⅲ. 结束(accomplishment)

这类情状具有动态、持续和完成的特征,我们将它的时相结构图示如下:

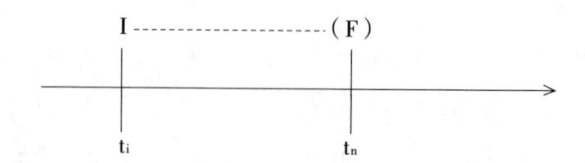

I -------------------- (F)
t_i t_n

下面是表现结束类情状的一些例句：

（29）乐队正在演奏《蓝色多瑙河》。

（30）李建明在操场上看电影《红高粱》呢。

（31）他在写一本谈中国古代建筑的书。

（32）小刚每天绕着操场跑3000米。

（33）到处找不到你，原来你在这儿给儿子剃头呢。

（34）她剪了几朵窗花。

（35）这几本书我读了三四年了。

（36）他上个月做了一只木箱。

表现结束类情状的句子中，最常用的谓语动词有以下两类：

一、动作动词兼处所动词，与讨论活动类情状句时所列的第一类动词相同。

二、其他表现动态动作的动词，与讨论活动类情状句时所列的第二类动词相同。

用在结束类情状句中的谓语动词具有动态和持续的特征，因而，与活动类情状句中的谓语动词一样，可以出现在"V+着"和"在+V"这两种句法槽中。与活动类情状不同的地方是，结束类情状伴随着一个内在的自然终结点。以句（29）和句（30）为例，《蓝色多瑙河》和《红高粱》的时间长度，便是该情状的自然延续时间，乐曲终了，电影结束，意味着情状的自然终结。这种语义特征也带来一个相应的语法现象。当"V+(了)+时量短语+了"这个格式出现在结束类情状句中的时候，时量短语的计时起点可以有两种解释，一是从情状的起始点 I 算起，二是从终结点 F 算起，请看下面的例句：

那支曲子他学了一个月了，

a. 但到现在还没有学会。

b. 早把细节给忘了。（以下例句类此）

他报告听了半天了。

这些问题他问了二三年了。

那本书他读了半年了。

这几幅画他挂了好几个钟头了。

那几条标语他写了好久了。

以上句子的时相结构可以是：t_i = 时量短语的计时起点；
也可以是：t_n = 时量短语的计时起点。

Ⅳ．复变（complex change）

这类情状具有动态、完成和非持续的语义特征。从语义结构上来看，复变类情状由一个动作同指示该动作结果的行为或状态结合而成，因此兼具结束类情状和下面要讨论的单变类情状的某些语义和语法性质。[①] 但同时又有自己的一些独特之处。作为动作，复变类情状可以处于进行状态之中，但是，动作一旦开始，便朝着它的终结点演进，以某个明确的情状变化作为动作的必然结果。作为一个由这种情状变化以及临变前的一段动作紧紧黏合而成的合体性结构，复变类情状中又很难容纳一个相对稳定的持续状态。我们将这类情状的时相结构图示如下：

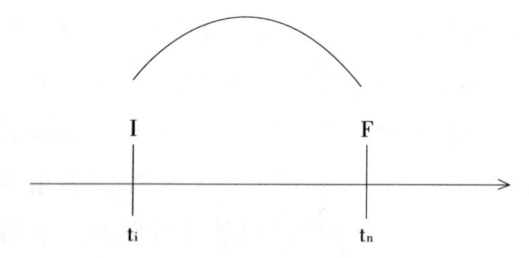

下面是表现复变类情状的一些例句：

（37）农科院正在改良稻种。

（38）这批人正在成为我们所的业务骨干。

（39）两国关系在不断改善。

（40）我想一个人从后门走进去。

（41）太阳正在升起。

（42）他在向我们跑来。

（43）他的病情正在好转。

---

① Comrie（1976：47-48）提到有可能存在这样的合体性情状，但他没有深入地讨论下去。

（44）目前，我们正在理顺价格关系，为经济的进一步发展创造条件。

（45）两国经济实力上的距离正在逐年拉大。

复变类情状句中，常用的谓语动词有以下两类：

一、表示变化的单个动词[①]，例如：

变为 变成 变作 成为 化为 改良 好转 恶化 减少

二、动补结构，主要有下面两类：

A. 动趋结构，例如：

跑来 奔去 走进 提出 爬上 滑下 飞过 送回 收起

拿出 解开 冲出 走上来 溜出去 放进来 赶出去

跑回去 送过来 抬下去 搬过去

B. 动形结构，例如：

长大 拉长 缩短 展宽 放松 理顺 变好

用在动形结构中的动词，一般都表示变化，典型成分有"变、长、加、拉、缩、扩"等，参见范晓（1985）、郑怀德（1987）等。用在这种场合中的形容词，一般是所谓的渐变成分（grade term），从语义性质来看，这种成分与其反义词构成对立的两极，但两极之间是一个逐渐过渡的连续体（continuum），不存在截然分明的界线。

表现复变类情状的词语有与其独特的时相结构相对应的语法特点。这些成分一般不能与"着"连用，但前面可以出现时间副词"在"。换句话说，复变类情状的时相结构，限定了人们在观察角度方面的可选范围。可以把这类情状表现为一个正在进行之中的过程，但不能表现为相对稳定的持续状态。请看下面的例子：

（37）'* 农科院正在改良着稻种。

（38）'* 这批人成为着我们所的业务骨干。

（40）'* 我想一个人从后门冲着进去。

（41）'* 太阳升起着。

---

① 参看傅承德（1988）。

(43)'* 他的病情好转着。

(44)'* 我们正在理顺着价格关系。

表现复变情状的动词可以用在"V+(了)+时量短语+了"之中，时量短语指的是复变动作结束后结果状态的持续时间。请看下面的例句：

稻种改良了三年多了。

病情恶化了一个星期了。

他溜出去一上午了。

信送来很久了。

这条马路展宽了好几年了。

围墙加高一年多了。

表现渐变的情状在汉语中自成一类，具备独有的语法特征，就已经发表的论著来看，这在其他语言中还没有人谈过。我们在前面说到，Vendler(1967)等所做的四部分类具有一定的逻辑基础。如果把时相结构看作为这个逻辑基础的重要组成部分，那么，汉语的例子启示我们，在语法范畴的意义涉及相同的逻辑或认知领域时，各种语言的组织原则可以非常接近，但是，作为表现（coding）相同领域的语言形式，不同语言中的语法范畴对于该领域的覆盖方式却可以有所不同。只有将汉语的语法范畴置于这样的坐标之中，才能真正发现它与其他语言的相同与相异之处。

Ⅴ. 单变（simple change）

这类情状具有动态、非持续、非完成的语义特征。它与其他四类情状的最大区别之处，在于这类情状的发生和结束都是一瞬间的事，在时轴上，它的起始点和终结点几乎是重叠在一起的。

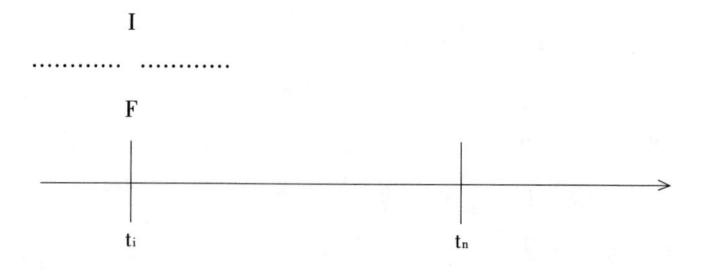

```
            I
    ············ ············
            F
    ────────┼──────────────────┼────────▶
           t_i                 t_n
```

下面是表现单变类情状的一些例句：

（46）村东头人家养的那条大黄狗前天死了。

（47）邻居厨房里的煤气罐突然爆炸了。

（48）他上午在操场上把钱包弄丢了，下午去找了半天，最后总算找到了。

（49）他站到麦克风前，大声宣布……

（50）宋科长一下子坐在椅子上，半晌说不出一句话来。

（51）俘虏跪倒在地，嘴里不停地讨饶。

单变类情状句中，最常用的谓语动词有以下三类：

一、表示瞬时变化的动词：

死　塌　垮　炸　断　熄　倒　摔

认出　发现　找到　遗失　想起　记得　忘记

二、表示瞬时动作的动词：

坐　站　躺　蹲　藏　躲　跪　趴

三、动补结构，主要有下面两类：

A. 动动结构，例如：

打破　推倒　掀翻　学会　吃完　看见

常用来做补语的动词有：

倒　翻　完　见　成　破　死　掉　病　疯　懂

B. 动形结构，例如：

磨好　烧焦　砸烂　敲扁　切碎　写错

用来表现单变类情状的谓语动词，不能在"V+着"或"在+V"这样的句法槽中出现，因为情状本身的时相结构决定了它不可能被表现为一个处于进行或持续过程之中的动作。前面讲过用于状态类情状句的第一类和第二类动词，一般也不能与"在"和"着"连用。那是因为动词本身就指示一种状态，没有必要再带表现类似意义的语法成分。"V+（了）+时量短语+了"这样的格式出现在单变类情状句中的时候，时量短语计量的是作为变化结果而存现的有关状态的持续时间。

用于 I 和 V 类情状句中的谓语动词，它们的语法特征可以概括如下：

	I			II	III	IV	V
	（1）	（2）	（3）				
很 +V	-	+	-	-	-	-	-
V+ 着	-	(-)	+	+	+	-	-
在 +V	-	(-)	-	+	+	+	-
V+（了）+ 时量短语 + 了（动作持续）	-	-	-	+	+	-	-
V+（了）+ 时量短语 + 了（状态持续）	-	+	+	-	+	+	+

  上面，我们分别讨论了五类情状的语义特征，展示了它们的时相结构，同时确定了与各类情状句相对应的语法特征。相关讨论，可参见范继淹（1982）、傅承德（1988）、马希文（1984）、孟琮等（1987）、潘文娱（1980）、于根元（1981）、Li & Thompson（1981）、Li, Thompson & Thompson（1984）等。现在，让我们回到本节开头提出的问题：这五种情状类型之间的联系和根本差异表现在什么地方？

  对比上面五类情状的时相结构示意图，我们认为，情状起始点与终结点在时轴上的间距大小，是这五种情状类型彼此有别而又彼此相连的根本因素。I 类情状自有其独特之处。它表现的是状态而不是动作，情状的起始点和终结点相对而言显得比较模糊。如前所述，就常常用来表现这类情状的三小类典型动词而言，它们的静态性也有一个由强渐弱的过渡过程。静态性最强的第一小类，其中的大多数成分甚至不能带"了"以指示状态的开始。因此，我们不妨认为，对于静态性最强的情状类型来说，因为它们表现的是一个相对恒定久远的状态，其起始点和终结点之间的距离在人们的感觉中仿佛是无限的。至于其他四种情状，对比一下它们的时相结构示意图，其间的区别一目了然。自 II 类情景经 III 类、IV 类，直到 V 类情景，它们的起始点和终结点之间的距离在时轴上由长至短逐类缩小，最后完全重叠在一起。它们在时相结构上展现出来的这种区别和联系，是对上述各组相应语法特征的最好说明和解释。从这个时相结构特点出发，我们可以探讨和发掘与汉语时间系统相关的种种语法现象。有关研究结果，我们将另文发表。

3.4 上面，在讨论和分析各种情状类型时，我们分别罗列了出现在各类情状句中的典型动词，并且以这些动词为主要依据，阐释了各种情状类型句的主要语义和语法特征。但是，我们希望不致因此而造成一种误解，认为这些情状句的有关特征，包括它们的时相结构特征，实际上就是句中谓语动词的特征。所以，有必要再次强调指出，句子在情状类型方面的归属，并不单纯取决于谓语动词本身，而是由动词和其他句子成分共同决定的。动词的重要作用在于，它的语义性质为句子的情状归属提供了数量不一的可能性，而其他句子成分所起的作用，则是在有关可能性中进行选择，具体确定了句子的情状类别。下面，我们侧重分析其他句子成分在句子的时相结构定型过程中所起的作用。

我们注意到，同样的动词，往往出现在不止一类情状的项下。例如，用在状态类情状句中表示自身处所位置的动词同时又作为表示瞬间动作的动词出现在单变类情状句之中。另外，处所动词在状态类情状句、活动类情状句和结束类情状句中重出。事实上，表示动态动作的动词大都有可能表现活动类情状、结束类情状、复变类情状或单变类情状，其间起关键作用的控制因素是与动词连用的其他句子成分。动词与其他句子成分在确定句子的情状类型归属的过程中各自所起的作用以及相互联系，是有相当严整的规律可循的。下面，我们剖析三种比较典型的情况。

首先，我们讨论"读、说、写、打"等动态行为动词。这些动词因所带宾语的不同，可以分别表现活动类情状和结束类情状。请对比下面左右两列词语：

    读书   读那两本书
    说话   说几句应酬话
    写字   写几个字
    打球   打一场球
    跑步   跑 5000 米
    念佛   念几句咒语
    喝酒   喝两瓶茅台

弹钢琴	弹一首肖邦的练习曲
拉小提琴	拉《梁祝》
看电视	看电影《红高粱》
背英文	背第五课课文
听大海的涛声	听德彪西的《大海》
听音乐	听一场音乐会
写大楷	写一页大楷
画水彩	画几个苹果
抽烟斗	抽一支烟
吃零食	吃晚饭
洗冷水	洗脚

左列一般表现活动类情状，用在"V+（了）+时量短语+了"框架中没有歧义，时量短语一律指示动作的持续时间。右列一般表现结束类情状。用在同样框架中会产生歧义，时量短语可以指示动作持续时间，也可以指示动作完成后的状态持续时间。

上面两列词语中，所用的动词完全一样，差别在于它们所带的名词宾语。这两组名语之间的显著区别是，右列表现的都是具备固定的物质形体或者明确的时间界限的物体或事件，而左列的名词则正好相反，它们表现的物体或事件缺乏固定的物质形体或明确的时间界限。造成这种差别的主要原因有两条。其一，在左列出现的名词很多都是不可数名词或抽象名词，没有专用量词，无法根据其内在的自然形态按件论个地计量，如"酒、电视、英文、大海的涛声、音乐、大楷、水彩、零食、冷水"等。如果没有外加的量词作为计量单位与这些名词连用，这些名词本身所指事物是没有明确的空间或时间标界可言的。其二，在左列出现的名词虽然本身是可数名词，但是用在该动宾结构中的时候是无指性（nonreferential）或通指性（generic）成分[1]，如上面所举的"书、字、球、钢琴、小提琴、烟斗"等。作为无指性或通指性成分，这些名词在

---

[1] 有关这些语义概念的定义和形式特点，参看陈平（1987）。

这些动宾结构里并不指示具体的单个实物。这样一来，因为作为动作所及对象的名词成分缺乏固定明确的空间或时间界线，所以，整个动作情状当然也不可能有一个内在的自然终结点。恰成鲜明对照的是，出现在右列中的名词都是有指性（referential）成分，有的是带量词的不可数名词或抽象名词，有的本身就是可数名词或专有名词，共同特点是具备明确的空间或时间界线，因此，带这类名词做宾语的动作一般有其内在的自然终结点，在时轴上占据一个有界的（bounded）的时段。在这里，名词宾语的空间性和时间性特征与整个动宾短语的时相结构存在着清晰的对应关系。

上面，我们分析了同样的动词如何因为所带宾语的不同而用来表现活动类情状或结束类情状。接着，我们来讨论动词所带补语的性质对整个句子情状归类所产生的影响。

我们前面讨论复变类情状和单变类情状的时候指出，两类情状都包含一个共同的语义内核，即从一种状态变为另一种状态。所不同的是，复变类情状涉及的是一个过程性变化，而单变类情状则涉及一个瞬时性变化。这个区别体现在用来表示这两种情状的典型动词上面。用于复变类情状的典型动词，如"变化、成为、变成"等等，前面可以加时间副词"在"，表示有关情状正处于一个变化过程之中。而用于单变类情状的典型动词，如"摔、炸、断、塌、死"等，表现的都是瞬时性的变化，当然无法在前面加上时间副词"在"。但是，我们同时也注意到，另有不少动词，既可用在复变类情状句中，又可用在单变类情状句中，对于这些动词来说，在句子的情状归类中起决定作用的一般是动词后面所跟的补语成分。请对比下面两列词语：

跑来　　　　跑完 跑完3000米
走去　　　　走到门口
滑下去　　　滑落
奔上来　　　奔到广州
爬进去　　　爬累
剔出来　　　剔起来 他们坐地上剔起烂土豆来了

拉大	拉断
理顺	理错 他把卡片的顺序理错了
缩小	缩掉
放松	放倒

上面两列动补结构中，左列一般用来表现复变性情状，不能加"着"，但可以与"在"连用。右列一般表现单变性情状，不能与"着"或"在"连用。所用动词完全相同，其间的语法差别是由补语造成的。

右列动补结构中的补语成分品类比较复杂，有的是动词，如"落、倒、断、掉"，有的是形容词，如"累、完、错"，有的是介词短语，如"到门口、到广州"，有的是表示时态意义的成分，如"剔起来"中的"起来"。左列动补结构中的补语成分则一般由两类成分充当。一类是趋向补语，如"来、去、下去、上来、进去、出来"，一类是形容词，如"大、顺、小、松"等。深入考察左右两列补语成分的语义性质，我们发现，补语成分与时间性相关的特征是造成两组动补结构之间语法差异的根本因素。左列的补语成分，其语义组织中都蕴涵着一种渐变性质。所谓趋向补语，顾名思义，表现的就是一个由此向彼的渐变趋势，与动词结合后，由动词指示渐变的动因，在从一种状态变化到另一种状态之间允许有一个逐渐发展的过程。仅就词类来看，形容词既出现在左列动补结构中，又出现在右列动补结构中。但是，左列中的形容词都具备一个共同的语义特点，它们所表现的性状特征在程度强弱之间允许有一定的变化幅度，其间自然寄寓着沿时轴由弱渐强逐步过渡这样一种可能性。而这样的语义特征是右列中的形容词所缺乏的。这种语义差别有一个相应的形式特征，可供我们取来作为区分这两类形容词的测试标准。凡是容纳"渐变"特征的形容词都可以用在"（正）在+Adj+起来/下去"这个句法结构之中，反之则不行。请比较下面的例句：

（52）他的胆子在一天天地大起来。

（53）合格的人才正在一天天地少下去。

（54）*工作正在一天天地完下去。

(55)* 他在慢慢地错起来。

我们由此得出的结论是，对于同一类动词来说，如果所带补语的语义性质包容一个由此及彼、由弱渐强的过程，那么，在有关情状的时相结构中，作为起始点的动作和作为终结点的最后结果之间也相应地允许有一个渐变的过程存在。我们因此而得到一个复变类情状。另一方面，如果补语成分在语义性质上更多地表现为一个有无截然对立的状态，很难同渐变的概念相容，那么，在相应的动补结构所表现的情状中，起始点和终结点之间自然也不大可能存在一个过渡阶段。我们因此而得到一个单变类情状。

我们注意到，即使是在上文中归入复变类情状项下的有关词语，用在"在+V"格式之中时，句子的可接受度也并非完全相同。有的常用一些，有的在口语里基本上不说，只是用在书面语里。考虑到这类情状的时相结构特点，这种现象完全是在意料之中的。既然是渐变，必然涉及一个程度问题。动词和补语两部分在语义上的渐变性越强，与"在"连用时可接受程度也就越高，随着两部分在语义上的渐变性逐步减弱，句子的可接受度也随之下降，有时会造成一些介乎于合法与不合法之间的句子，人们对它们是否能说意见并不一致。对于同一个动词来说，形容语做补语时，动补短语前面能否用"在"，与该形容词能否用在"（正）在+Adj+起来/下去"之中，两者的可接受度高低成正比关系。这恰好证明了补语的时间性特征对于动补短语时相结构的重要制约作用。

最后，我们来分析主语在句子的情状归属中所起的作用。

在讨论用于单变类情状的典型动词时，我们指出，它们一般都表现瞬时性的变化，起始点和终结点在时轴上几乎重合。但是，有一种现象是值得我们注意的：并非所有表现瞬时行为动作的词语都只能用在单变类情状句之中。诸如"拍手、眨眼、点头"等词语，虽然也表示瞬时性的动作，但却常常用在活动类情状句之中。活动类情状句中所用的典型动作动词表现出来的语法特征，这些词语一般也都具备，例如，我们可以说"拍着手、眨着眼、点着头""正在拍手、正在眨眼、正在点头""拍手拍了三分钟了（动作持续）",等等。在这些方面,基本上无异于"跳、走、跑、笑、听、看、读、写"等动作动词。就单次动作来说,"拍手、眨眼、点头"等动作确实是瞬时行为,但在日常生活中,这些动作不太可能只做一次,一般都是以多次态（iterative）的形式出现的。于是,由多次瞬时动作构成的动作流便在语义结构和语法表现形式上获得了与一般动作相等的地位。

一般情况下,"死、摔、爆炸"等表现瞬时变化的动词较少,如"拍手、眨眼、点头"那样用来表示多次态行为。但是,如果句子中的其他成分提供了适当的语义环境,这类动词所在的语句也会表现出只有其他类型的情状句才具备的语法特征。试比较下面三组句子。

(56) a. 埋在土里的定时炸弹"轰"的一声炸了。

b. 大火终于烧到仓库,那满库房的军火劈里啪啦炸了足足20分钟。

(57) a. 小明手里的大炮仗突然响了。

b. 昨晚是年三十,炮仗响了整整一宿。

(58) a. 他家养的那只鸡死了。

b. 农场里养的鸡正在大批地死去。

上面三组句子中,b句中的主语为瞬时行为的多次态用法提供了条件,因此,以"炸、响、死"这些表示瞬时变化的典型成分为谓语动词的句子,无论在时相结构还是语法形式上,都表现出其他情状类型句才具备的特征。

上面,我们详细考察了时间系统组织的第一个方面——句子的时相结构,并且根据时相结构特征和相应的语法特征划分出五种情状类型。我们讨论了各类情状的语义性质,同时列举了用于各类情状句中的典型动词。最后,我们剖析了其他句子成分在确定句子的情状归属中所起的重要制约作用。为了使读者对于汉语时间系统的三元结构有一个概括性的了解,我们在下面非常扼要地介绍一下其他两个方面的情况。限于篇幅,有关细节将另文讨论。

4. 时制结构

时间系统的第二个方面是情状的时制结构。所谓时制，指的是情状的发生时间、说话时间和时轴上的另外一个时间（又称为参照时间）三者在时轴上的相互关系。我们用 E 代表情状时间，用 S 代表说话时间，用 R 代表参照时间。它们在时轴上的前后关系可以呈现出多种多样的格局。我们下面举几个例子略加说明：

（59）他学过几年日文。

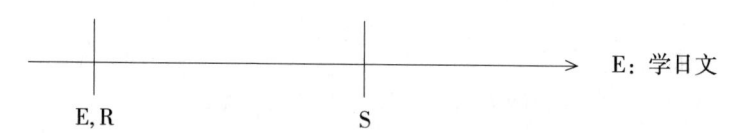

```
            |              |              →  E：学日文
           E,R             S
```

（60）老王上个月来信说要调到深圳去工作。

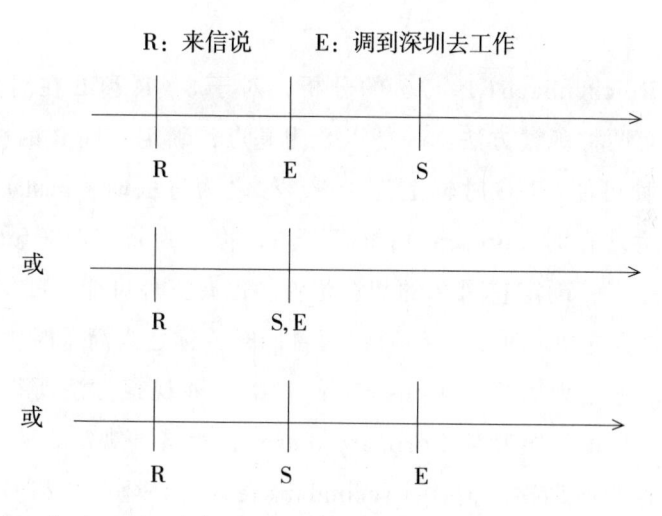

```
         R：来信说    E：调到深圳去工作
            |         |         |         →
            R         E         S

   或       |         |         |         →
            R        S,E

   或       |         |         |         →
            R         S         E
```

（61）大家赶到车站时，车已经开出了。

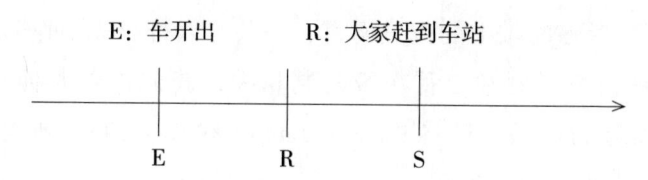

```
         E：车开出      R：大家赶到车站
            |         |         |         →
            E         R         S
```

（62）他现在正在那儿喝酒呢。

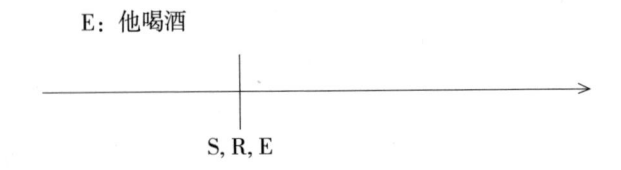

　　　　E: 他喝酒
　　　　　　｜
　———————————————————→
　　　　　S, R, E

（63）你打算什么时候交稿？

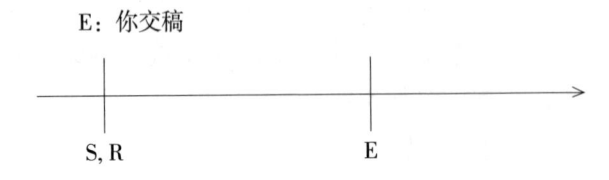

　　　　E: 你交稿
　　　　｜　　　　　｜
　———————————————————→
　　　S, R　　　　　E

（64）等到你下个月把书借到手，我的文章早就写好了。

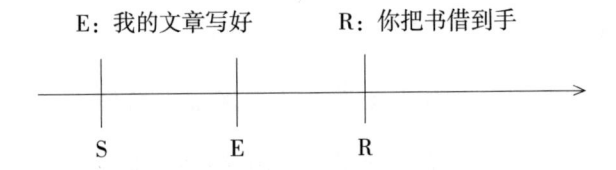

　　　E: 我的文章写好　　R: 你把书借到手
　　｜　　　｜　　　｜
　———————————————————→
　　S　　　E　　　R

　　根据 Reichenbach（1947）的分析，对于 S、R 和 E 在时轴上的相对位置，有两种观察方法。一是以 S 为基点，确定它同 R 的相对位置。一共有三种可能：R 在时轴上先于 S，称之为过去时（past）；两者同时，称之为现在时（present）；R 后于 S，称之为将来时（future）。二是以 E 为基点，确定它同 R 的相对位置。也有三种可能，E 在时轴上先于 R，称之为先事时（anterior）；两者同时，称之为简单时（simple）；E 后于 R，称之为后事时（posterior）。第一种观察方法所得结果，一般被看作为所谓初级时制（primary tense），第二种观察方法所得结果，一般被看作为所谓次级时制（secondary tense）。至于 S 和 E 在时轴上的相对位置，一般认为对语法形式没有直接的影响。这样一来，虽然就 S、R 和 E 三者在时轴上的位置而言，一共可以排出 13 种格局，但是，将上述三种初级时制和三种次级时制相乘，我们得到九种基本形式，以此统摄所有的格局。现将 Reichenbach（1947：297）所得结果排列如下：

时制结构	名称
E—R—S	先事过去时（Anterior past）
E，R—S	简单过去时（Simple past）
R—E—S R—S，E R—S—E	后事过去时（Posterior past）
E—S，R	先事现在时（Anterior present）
S，R，E	简单现在时（Simple present）
S，R—E	后事现在时（Posterior present）
S—E—R S，E—R E—S—R	先事将来时（Anterior future）
S—R，E	简单将来时（Simple future）
S—R—E	后事将来时（Posterior future）

以上只是一种逻辑分类。我们铺陈的目的，并不是就此断言现代汉语中有相应的九种语法时制，而只是为深入探索汉语的时制系统提供一个起参照作用的坐标。一种流行已久的观点认为，汉语语法中只有时态的分别，没有时制的分别。对于类似的观点要从两个方面来进行分析。一方面，如果以有无专用的语法助词为标准，那么，直到目前为止，从大量的分析"了、着、过"等助词的研究结果来看，它们的语法意义的确同时态密切相关，把这些语法成分看作为表现有关时态的专用语法手段，也是一种合适的处理方法。另一方面，我们也不能忽略过去、现在、将来、先事、后事等时制特征在汉语语法中的重要地位。尽管从表面上看，似乎还没有发现表现时制区别的专用语法助词[①]，但是，如果就此得出结论，认为如此重要的时间性特征在汉语语法中缺乏相应的语法表现形式，那就显得过于轻率了。实际上，这种观点也不符合已经发掘出来的汉语事实。不少研究报告证明，许多同句子的时间性相关

---

① 也有人把"我前天来的"中的"的"看成是过去时的标记。

的语法形式特征最后都只能归结为句子的时制特征使然。例如，王还（1963）、刘月华（1984）等在讨论动词重叠式用法时，刘月华（1988）在讨论"过₁"和"过₂"的区别时，都发现某种语法格式或某个语法助词是否能用，常常取决于有关句子表现的是先事情状还是后事情状。下面，我们也来举两个例子，分别说明句子的时制特征对于"V+了"和"V+了+V"这两种语法格式的影响。首先，请比较下面的一组句子（E：洗澡）：

　　（65）a. 他洗了澡了。　　　　E—S，R（先事现在时）
　　　　　b. 他想洗澡。　　　　　S，R—E（后事现在时）
　　　　　c.*他想洗了澡。　　　　S，R—E（后事现在时）
　　　　　d. 他洗了澡就吃饭去了。E—S—R（先事过去时）
　　　　　e. 他想洗了澡就吃饭去。S—E—R（先事将来时）

由此可见，只要是先事情状，无论是现在时、过去时，还是将来时，都可以用"V+了"这种格式。再比较下面一组句子（E：看看孩子）：

　　（66）a. 他看了看孩子。　　　　E—S，R（先事现在时）
　　　　　b. 他想看看孩子。　　　　S，R—E（后事现在时）
　　　　　c.*他想看了看孩子。　　　S，R—E（后事现在时）
　　　　　d. 他看了看孩子就走了。　E—R—S（先事过去时）
　　　　　e.*他想看了看孩子就走。　S—E—R（先事将来时）
　　　　　f. 他想看看孩子就走。　　S—E—R（先事将来时）

"V+了+V"也用于先事情状，但只限于现在时和过去时，不能用于将来时，有（66）e 为证。由这两组例子得出的结论是，"V+了+V"的使用场合上比"V+了"受到更多的限制，而只有从句子的时制特点入手，才能阐明这种限制的本质。

　　从上面的简短讨论中，我们可以看到，汉语句子在时制结构方面的差异，确实伴随着相应的语法形式特征。只是同英语等西方语言相比，汉语时制的语法特征在表现方法上显得比较隐蔽，只有通过深入细致的挖掘和分析才能够逐步为人们所知晓。同时，我们也要指出，汉语中与时制有关的语言现象以前也并非无人提起，只是在许多情况下往往将它们全部同时态现象笼而统之地混为一谈。的确，时制同时态关系密切，但它们毕竟是彼此有别的两类现象，除了在毗邻的地界上有一些难解的重叠与纠葛以外，在大多数情形下还是能将两者区别开来分别处理的。

5. 时态结构

时间系统的第三个方面是情状的时态结构，如前所述，时态表现的是观察有关情状的种种方式，指示情态所处的特定状态。对于相同的情状，可以有形形色色的观察角度。因此，在讨论时态类型时，首先要判明分类的标准和层次，在这样的前提下确定具体时态在整个时态系统中的地位。下面，我们以一个结束类情状为例，说明有关时态的特点。首先，请看下面的示意图：

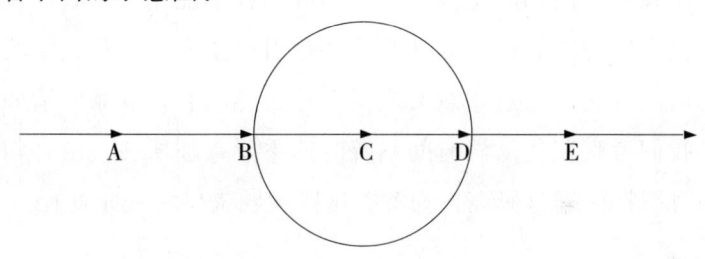

时轴上的字母代表情状的各个发展阶段，其中 B 和 D 分别为该情状的起始点和终结点。

发话人从该情状的表现角度着眼，可以对其内部时相结构不加分析而把它表现为一个整体性的情状，也可以把它表现为一个正处于持续状态或进行过程之中的情状。我们称前者为完全态（perfective），后者为不完全态（imperfective）。

发话人也可以从情状的各个发展阶段着眼，表现情态本身所呈现的存在方式，其中又可分为两种主要的类别。

一是以 B 为界，B 以前的状态称作为未然态，B 以后称作为已然态。

二是以 D 为界，一组表现情状在到达 D 以前所处的各个阶段，常用的时态助词有"了""起来""下去""着"等；另一组则表现情状到达 D 以后所呈现的各种状态,常用的助词有"过""来着""了"等。

限于篇幅,我们不可能在此详加讨论。前面说过,由于时相结构的限制,各种情状所能允许的表现方法并不完全相同,有的能同各种时态相容,有的则只能同少数时态连用。其间的相互关系,我们将另文讨论。

另外,我们也要指出,有关语法手段在指示特定时态意义的同时,也往往会有一些延伸性的用法,所表现的语法意义可以同它的主要意义有比较密切的关系,也可以同后者有相当大的距离。这种现象并非仅见于汉语。英语中的"to be + V-ing"通常都被看作进行态的表现形式,但它有时也并不表示正在进行中的动作。例如 I am leaving tomorrow(我明天动身),现在进行时态的语法形式,表现的却是未然动作,详细讨论参见 Leech(1970)、Quirk(1985)等。"了、着、过"等在现代汉语中使用频率最高的时态标记,在哪些场合下能用,哪些场合下不能用?什么是它们的核心语法意义?什么是引申意义?在什么情况下表现什么样的语法意义以及这些意义之间有什么样的有机联系?诸如此类的问题,是我们考察现代汉语时间系统时的主要兴趣所在。结合句子的时相特征和时制特征进行研究,为解答这些问题提供了一条途径。

6. 结论

我们分析了现代汉语时间系统的三个组成部分,时相结构、时制结构和时态结构,重点放在时相结构方面。我们根据句子的时相结构特点分出五种情状类型,同时确定了相应的语法形式特征。我们列出了充任各类情状句谓语的典型动词、动宾结构和动补结构,证明句子的情状归类取决于所有句子成分词汇意义的总和,其中动词是基础,其他句子成分也起着重要的选择和制约作用。

现代汉语时间系统的全貌,目前还远未为人们所认识,"了、着、过"等助词错综复杂的用法、变化多端的意义,常常引出许多悬案,带来无穷困惑。我们认为，解答这些问题的前提是——辨析分解汉语时间系统的组成部分，确定各个部分中的基本成分和结构关系。然后，从考察对象与时间系统内其他成分的种种关联中把握其内在的规律。换句话说，只有从系统的观点出发，才能全面阐释现代汉语中与时相、时制和时态特征相关的各种语法现象。

参考文献

陈　平，1987，释汉语中与名词性成分相关的四组概念，《中国语文》第 2 期。
范继淹，1982，论介词短语"在 + 处所"，《语言研究》第 1 期。
范　晓，1985，略论 V—R，《语法研究和探索》(3)，北京：北京大学出版社。
傅承德，1988，试论"在"和"着"的语境分布和时态表达作用，第五次现代汉语语法讨论会论文。
李临定，1985，动词的动态功能和静态功能，《汉语学习》第 1 期。
刘月华，1984，动词重叠的表达功能及可重叠动词的范围，《语法研究和探索》(2)，北京：北京大学出版社。
刘月华，1988，动态助词"过$_2$过$_1$了$_1$"用法比较，《语文研究》第 1 期。
吕叔湘，1982，《中国文法要略》，北京：商务印书馆。
马建忠，1898—1899，《马氏文通》，北京：商务印书馆，1983。
马庆株，1981，时量宾语和动词的类，《中国语文》第 2 期。
马希文，1987，北京方言里的"着"，《方言》第 1 期。
孟　琮等，1987，《动词用法词典》，上海：上海辞书出版社。
潘文娱，1980，谈谈"正""在"和"正在"，《语言教学与研究》第 1 期。
邓守信，1986，汉语动词的时间结构，《第一届国际汉语教学讨论会论文选》，北京：北京语言学院出版社。
王　还，1963，动词重叠，《中国语文》第 1 期。
于根元，1981，关于动词后附"着"的使用，《语法研究和探索》(1)，北京：北京大学出版社。
郑怀德，1987，带结式动词和不带结式动词，《句型和动词》，北京：语文出版社。
Bache, Carl. 1982. Aspect and aktionsart: Towards a semantic distinction. *Journal of Linguistics*. 18:57-72.
Carlson, Lauri. 1981. Aspect and quantification. In: Tedeschi and Zaenen, eds., 31-64.
Chao, Yuen Ren. 1968. *A Grammar of Spoken Chinese*. Berkeley and Los Angeles: University of California Press.
Chen, Ping. 1988. Language variation and autonomous linguistics. Plenary session paper at the First Hong Kong Conference on Language and Society.

Comrie, Bernard. 1976. *Aspect*. Cambridge: University Press.

Dowty, David. 1979. *Word Meaning and Montague Grammar*. Dordrecht : D. Reidel.

Dowty, David. 1982. Tenses, time adverbs, and compositional semantic theory. *Linguistics and Philosophy*. 5. 1:23-55.

Hopper, Paul. ed. 1982. *Tense and Aspect: Between Semantics and Pragmatics*. Amsterdam: J. Benjamins.

Langacker, Ronald. 1987. Nouns and verbs. *Language*. 63. 1:53-94.

Leech, Geoffrey. 1970. *Towards a Semantic Description of English*. Bloomington: Indiana University Press.

Li, Charles N. and Sandra A. Thompson. 1981. *Mandarin Chinese: A Functional Reference Grammar*. Berkeley and Los Angeles: University of California Press.

Li, Charles N., Sandra A. Thompson, and R. McMillan Thompson. 1982. The discourse motivation for the perfect aspect: The Mandarin particle *le*. In: Hopper, ed., 19-44.

Lyons, John. 1977. *Semantics*. Cambridge: University Press.

Mourelatos, Alexander. 1978. Events, processes, and states. *Language and Philosophy*. 2:415-34.

Quirk, Randolph et al. 1985. *A Comprehensive Grammar of the English Language*. London: Longman.

Reichenbach, Hans. 1947. *Elements of Symbolic Logic*. New York: The MacMillan Company.

Smith, Carlota. 1983. A theory of aspectual choice. *Language*. 59.3:479-501.

Smith, Carlota. 1985. Notes on aspect in Chinese. *Proceedings of Texas Linguistic Forum* 26.

Tedeschi, Philip J. and Annie E. Zaenen. eds. 1981. *Tense and Aspect*. New York: Academic Press.

Vendler, Zeno. 1967. *Linguistics and Philosophy*. Ithaca: Cornell University Press.

Verkuyl, Henk. 1972. *On the Compositional Nature of the Aspects*. Dordrecht: D. Reidel.

（本文原载《中国语文》1988 年第 6 期。）

释汉语中与名词性成分相关的四组概念

提　要　本文系统分析了有指与无指、定指与不定指、实指与虚指，以及通指与单指这四对概念的含义及其相互关系，研究了这些概念在汉语中的表现方法，同时揭示了相关的各类名词性成分的语法特点。

关键词　有指　无指　定指　不定指　实指　虚指　通指　单指

在语法研究中，人们讨论较多的是名词性成分与动词性成分之间的种种结构关系和语义关系。本文要探讨的则是同实际话语中出现的名词性成分自身相关的下列四组语义概念：

　　有指（referential）　　与　　无指（nonreferential）
　　定指（definite）　　　与　　不定指（indefinite）
　　实指（specific）　　　与　　虚指（nonspecific）
　　通指（generic）　　　与　　单指（individual）

本文所说的名词性成分，包括人称代词和用作名词的"的"字结构。

在涉及上面四组概念的有关著作中，定指与不定指等术语有时用来指语义概念，有时用来指表现形式，在本文中这四组概念则一律用来指语义概念。

首先，我们逐节讨论这些概念的准确含义，然后，我们要研究这些概念在现代汉语中的表现形式，同时探讨具有这些语义特征的名词性成分表现带来的语法特点。

一

这里要讨论的四组概念，都是描写名词性成分的所指对象

（referent）同实际语境中存在的事物之间的关系，与发话人当时当地的所持意图和所做假设等因素密切相关。只有紧紧扣住具体语境，才能准确地把握这些概念的含义。下面，让我们来分别讨论这四组概念。

1.1 有指与无指

如果名词性成分的表现对象是话语中的某个实体（entity），我们称该名词性成分为有指成分，否则，我们称之为无指成分，请看下面的例句：

（1）去年八月，他在新雅餐厅当临时工时，结识了一位顾客。

除去句首的时间词不算，我们有四个名词性成分"他""新雅餐厅""临时工"和"一位顾客"。其中三个都是实有所指。"他"和"新雅餐厅"分别代表语境中发话人和受话人都知道的两个身份明确的实体。"一位顾客"在这儿也代表语境中的一个实体，虽然我们一时无法把这个实体同语境中某个具体的人联系起来，但是我们相信这个人在语境中是存在的。"临时工"这个名词性成分则与其他三个成分不同，它在这儿表示一种身份，不是一个实体，我们不能把这个名词同语境中某个具体的人等同起来。换句话说，发话人在提到"临时工"这个名词时，着眼点是该名词的抽象属性，而不是语境中具有这种属性的某个具体人物。"临时工"在这儿是无指成分。再举几个例子。下面句子中，底下加点的是有指成分，加线的是无指成分：

（2）路旁种了许多苹果树和梨树。
（3）我们下车买了许多苹果和梨。
（4）他从来不同别人打架。
（5）这一架你可打输了。
（6）王老头种的西瓜，个个都有篮球大。
（7）地摊上卖的西瓜，个个都有你手里的篮球那么大。

判断一个名词性成分是有指还是无指，有一个简捷的方法：有指成分可以用种种方式加以回指（anaphoric reference），而无指成分则无法回指。请看下面的句子：

(8) 他们下星期要考研究生。

这是一个歧义句。"考研究生"既可理解为"对研究生进行考查",也可理解为"报考研究生"。做第一种理解时,名词性成分"研究生"在语境中实有所指,可以后接回指成分,例如:

(9) 他们下星期要考研究生。这批研究生进校两个多月了,这是第一次对他们进行考查。

"这批研究生"和"他们"回指第一分句中的有指成分"研究生"。做第二种理解时,该名词性成分表示一种资格,并不代表语境中的任何实体。这样的无指成分自然无法加以回指。详细讨论参见 Chen(1986a)。

1.2 定指与不定指

发话人使用某个名词性成分时,如果预料受话人能够将所指对象与语境中某个特定的事物等同起来,能够把它与同一语境中可能存在的其他同类实体区分开来,我们称该名词性成分为定指成分。这里又有两种情况。一是语境中没有其他同类实体,所指对象在特定语境中是独一无二的。二是虽有其他同类实体,但受话人可以凭借种种语言信息和非语言信息将所指对象与其他实体区分开来,关于这一点,我们下面还会谈到。相反,发话人在使用某个名词性成分时,如果预料受话人无法将所指对象与语境中其他同类成分区分开来,我们称之为不定指成分。这里也可分两种情况:一是发话人是首次把所指对象引进话语,把它作为一个陌生的实体介绍给受话人;二是发话人仅仅是用该名词性成分虚指该成分所代表的事物,至于这个事物是否存在于特定语境之中,发话人本人也不清楚。关于这一点,我们将在下一节中详细讨论。例如:

(10) 那天,一辆草绿色的解放牌卡车悄无声息地滑至淮海别墅顾而已家门……车停稳后,只见跳下一群身着去掉了领章、帽徽的空军服装的人。他们一进屋,就把守好每扇门窗,拉好窗帘。

让我们来研究一下上面这段话中底下带直线的八个名词性成分。"一辆草绿色的解放牌卡车"和"一群身着去掉了领章、帽徽的空军服装的人"两个名词性成分的所指对象在上文中从来没有露过面,在这段话中是第一次出现。读者无法根据任何语言信息或非语言信息把它们跟其他的草绿色的解放牌卡车和身着去掉了领章、帽徽的空军服装的人区分开来,作者是把它们作为两个对读者来说是陌生的事物引进话语的。因此,它们都是不定指成分。其他六个名词性成分的情况则有所不同。在上文中,作者提供了上述事件发生的时间与地点——1966年的上海。在这个特定的语境中,"淮海别墅顾而已家门"的所指对象是独一无二的,读者要把它辨认出来应该不成问题。至于"车"和"屋"两个名词,虽然实际语境中可能出现不止一辆车和一幢屋子,但读者运用他的语言能力,可以明白无误地判断出句中这两个名词的所指对象,就是指前面提到的那辆解放牌卡车和淮海别墅顾而已家。同样,读者判断出"他们"指的是那群身着去掉了领章、帽徽的空军服装的人,"门窗"指的是顾而已家里的门窗,"窗帘"指的是顾家窗子上挂的那些窗帘。这六个名词性成分都是定指成分。

根据上面所给的定义可以知道,只有有指成分才有定指与不定指的区别。对于无指成分,这种区别是没有任何意义的。

需要强调的是,定指与不定指这对概念涉及的核心问题,是发话人对于受话人是否有能力将名词性成分的实际所指事物从语境中同类事物中间辨别出来所做的判断。这同发话人本人是否具有这种辨析能力并无直接关系。发话人本人也许早就将所指人物"验明正身",也许自己也不知道该名词性成分指的是语境中哪一个特定的人物。例如:

(11)1981年3月30日,美国总统里根在华盛顿劳联-产联建筑工会的集会上讲演后,从希尔顿饭店走出来,……就在这一刹那,<u>记者群中一个身穿棕褐色雨衣的金发青年</u>,蓦地拔出左轮手枪,对着里根"呼!呼!"连射两枪。……开枪者是25岁的约翰·欣克利。

(12)1966年8月,一股摧残文物、捣毁名胜古迹的狂风,扫荡着川西平原。<u>高悬在新津县纯阳观中的一口著名黄钟</u>,首当其冲了。

在(11)中,写稿人在第一次提到"记者群中一个身穿棕褐色雨衣的金发青年"时，不会不知道所指的人就是下文中要讲到的25岁的约翰·欣克利。同样，（12）的作者在写到"高悬在新津县纯阳观中的一口著名黄钟"时，完全明白他讲的是一个确定的事物，因为他在下文中交代得很清楚，当时当地，那座道观中只有那一口黄钟。尽管作者对两个名词所指事物的身份早已辨明，但在第一次向读者提到它们时，还是把两个名词作为不定成分处理，将两个新的人物引进话语。其所以这样做，完全是从读者的角度出发，考虑到他们是第一次碰到这两个事物，当然对它们的身份不甚了了。再如：

（13）<u>一位从广州中山大学来的同志</u>登上城楼，只见天安门广场南端、人民英雄纪念碑的前面，端端正正树立着孙中山先生的巨幅画像，不禁心中一热，哭了。<u>一位姓杨的先生</u>，是几个月前从台湾回到大陆定居的。他说：今能亲登天安门，毕生荣幸。（《光明日报》1986.10.3《唯有今日好——国庆天安门城楼记盛》）

国庆期间从广州中山大学来北京的人很可能不止一位，几个月前从台湾回归大陆的姓杨的人也许也不止一位。写上面这段话的记者也许知道这两个人的名字、住址等，也许知道的仅仅是上面写出来的这些。无论如何，记者判定读者是无法把他们与同类人区分开来的，因此把他们作为不定指成分介绍给了大家。

接着要问的问题是，发话人是根据什么来判断受话人具备或者是不具备将实际所指对象从语境中辨析出来的能力的？换个角度来提问题，要具备什么样的条件，名词性成分的所指对象才能由发话人以定指形式表现出来？一般说来，只有在下面三种情况下，名词性成分才能以定指形式出现。

第一种情况是，所指对象在上文中已经出现过，现在对它进行回指。例如：

（14）9月6日，<u>一个农民打扮的人</u>在翠微路商场附近摆了个摊子，声称专治脚鸡眼，一青工决定让他看看。"病可治，挖一个鸡眼四元钱。"为了治病，青工欣然同意。

（15）他已经游到岸的另一侧，发现<u>一根漂在水面的碗口粗的</u>

毛竹，便爬上去。真棒，毛竹竟一点也不往下沉。

（14）中的"他"回指首句的"一个农民打扮的人"，末句的"青工"回指前面说的那位让他治病的青工。（15）末句中的"毛竹"则回指上面他发现的那根毛竹。在这种情况下，语言环境（linguistic context）提供的信息帮助受话人确定这些名词性成分在语境中所指的特定对象。

上面讨论中谈到的语言环境，只是一种狭义的语言环境，就广义来说，语言环境不限于同一篇文章、同一次交谈，而是可以延伸到在这以前进行的全部语言交际活动。这种广义的语境所提供的信息，同样可以帮助受话人确定某个名词性成分在当时当地所指的特定对象。例如，如果受话人以前知道某人的姓名，那么，在以后的语言活动中，这个姓名便成了定指成分，因为受话人听到姓名便能将所指对象同语境中存在的某个特定人物联系起来。可是如果受话人以前没有听说过这个姓名，那么，在首次提到时，光有名有姓可能还不足以使所指对象以定指身份出现。例如：

（16）某机关宿舍中，<u>一位名叫蒋红春的女中学生</u>，在屋里打完驱赶蚊虫的"DDT"……

（17）"这个来钱容易，出去一天能弄个百八十块的……"<u>一个28岁，叫刘金顺的农民</u>说。

虽然有名有姓，作者还是将这两人以不定指名词性成分的形式介绍给了读者。

第二种情况是，名词性成分的所指对象就存在于交际双方身处的实际环境中，可以靠眼神或手势做当前指示（deictic reference）加以辨识。请看下列例句：

（18）（漫画：病人床头放着一瓶利眠宁，医生手里举着一篇文章）医生：你看这篇文章比吃那个利眠宁有效。

（19）瞧，那老大爷已经套了两次虎了，可再次都被"中途犯规"罚下了场。

在这种情况下，非语言环境（nonlinguistic context）提供的信息帮助了受话人确定名词所指的特定对象。

第三种情况是，所指对象与其他人物之间存在着不可分离的从属或连带关系，我们在认识周围世界万事万物的同时，也必然会注意到事物之间的这种关系，把有关这类的知识纳入我们的常识范畴。这样，一旦某个事物的身份在话语中被确定之后，与它有着这种从属或连带关系的其他事物也可借此与语境中同类的其他事物区别开来，获得定指性身份。这种现象在语言交际中是十分常见的。例如：

(20) 晚上八点半，他们两人走出丽都饭店自动启闭的玻璃大门。停车坪上有十几辆"的士"，他俩立即扑向最靠近的一辆。这辆"丰田"改装的"的士"黑着灯，空着座。温良谨拉开车门，卢小婷一闪身便钻了进去。黑影里的司机回头一瞥，迅即转过头去。

主语位置上的"停车坪"和"黑影里的司机"都是定指成分。读者虽然没有在上文中碰到过它们，但是同样能够辨析出这两个名词在这儿所指的特定对象。"停车坪"指的是附属于丽都饭店的停车坪，"黑影里的司机"指的是那辆"丰田"改装的"的士"的司机。作者预料读者能够做出这样的判断。大饭店一般都建有停车坪，而出租汽车一定都有一位司机，对于生活在现代文化背景下的读者群来说，这些知识都属于常识范畴。借助这种从属或连带关系，甚至上文中从来没有提到过的人物也能以人称代词的形式出现，例如：

(21) 副书记张侃精明得很，他晓得这位女书记要说什么。她是个老处女，虽结过婚，但刚办完结婚登记手续，他就告别了她，把一腔热血洒在朝鲜的三千里江山上，成为名震全国的战斗英雄。

"他"所指的对象，不是别人，就是这位女书记的丈夫。虽然上文中从来没有出现，作者在他第一次露面时就把他以定指形式介绍给了读者。这是因为作者知道读者都具有这样的常识：得是一男一女才能办理结婚登记手续。

1.3 实指与虚指

发话人使用某个名词性成分时，如果所指对象是某个在语境中实际存在的人物，我们称该名词性成分为实指成分。反之，如果所指对象只是一个虚泛的概念，其实体在语境中也许存在，也许并不存在，我们称该名词性成分为虚指成分。前面讲过，定指与不定指的基础，是发话人对于受话人能否把所指对象与语境中同类事物区分开来所做的判断，同发话人本人是否能够确认所指对象并无直接关系。这里讨论的实指与虚指这一对概念的基础，却是发话人本人所持的意图，同受话人没有直接关系。例如：

（22）A：请你从我桌子上取支笔来好吗？

　　　B：您要什么笔？

　　　A：我的那支灰杆儿钢笔。

（23）A：请您从我桌子上取支笔来好吗？

　　　B：您要什么笔？

　　　A：随便什么笔都行。

"笔"在（22）和（23）首句中的形式相同，但语义不一样，根源在于发话人当时心里所持意图不同。发话人说（22）时，"笔"实有所指，他心中想到的是某个在语境中实际存在的具体事物。而在说（23）时，"笔"的所指对象则是任何一个属于"笔"类的个体，至于最后落实到哪个个体身上，发话人并无定见。因此，我们把（22）首句中的"笔"看作实指成分，而把（23）首句中的"笔"看作虚指成分。同样，下面也是一个歧义句，"北京姑娘"可以做实指或虚指两种理解：

（24）老杨想娶一位北京姑娘。

这个句子可以理解为老杨已经有了意中人，此人是一位北京姑娘。也可以理解为老杨正在找对象，条件是女方得是北京人。再分别举几个实指和虚指的例子。在下面的句子中，底下加点的是实指成分，加线的是虚指成分：

（25）他不知道自己一个亲生儿子已被造反派以"三反"为罪名活活打死……他更不知道，海外还有一位知名人物心急如焚，万般焦虑，各方打听自己的消息。这位知名人物就是号称"世界船王"的包玉刚先生。

（26）你冷静想想，如果突然换一个同志接替你的工作，他即使是善于经营广大华行，也不可能很快取得敌人信任。

（27）由西安来京出差的邵某欲买一台录像机，可奔波多日没买到合适的。

只有不定指成分才有实指和虚指的区别，顾名思义，定指成分都是实指。参见 Lyons（1977）。

1.4 通指与单指

名词性成分的所指对象如果是整个一类事物（class），我们称该名词性成分为通指成分。相反，所指对象如果是一类中的个体（individual），我们则称之为单指成分。上面所举的例子中，大都是单指用法的名词性成分。下面例句中，带点的名词性成分是通指成分。

（28）麻雀虽小，但它颈上的骨头数目几乎比长颈鹿多一倍。

（29）苍蝇、海星、蜗牛都是聋子。

通指成分在语义上有两个特点值得我们注意。一方面，它并不指称语境中任何以个体形式出现的人或物。从这个角度看，它与无指成分有相同之处。另一方面，通指成分代表语境中一个确定的类。从这个角度看，它与定指成分有相同之处。

二

现在，我们来研究现代汉语中具有上述语义特点的各类名词性成分的表现形式和语法特点。

我们先从名词性成分的词汇形式上着眼，把汉语中的各种表现形式归并为以下七组：

A 组　人称代词

B 组　专有名词

C 组　"这／那"+（量词）+名词

D 组　光杆普通名词（bare noun）

　　　　E 组　　数词+（量词）+名词
　　　　F 组　　"一"+（量词）+名词
　　　　G 组　　量词+名词
D 组的光杆普通名词指不带数词、量词、指代词等附加成分的名词，包括用作名词的"的"字结构。E 组中的数词包括指定数的"一""二"和指约数的"几"等数词。F 组中的"一"是个虚化了的数词，同 E 组中的正规数词相比，它的指数功能弱化到可以忽略不计的程度。它在句子中总是轻读，不能带句子重音或逻辑重音，往往可以省略而对句子意义没有任何影响。试看下面的句子：

　　　　（30）我和老高关系不错，有时他下楼来聊聊，我就递上一支烟，他便躲到我家房间里抽起来。
　　　　（31）还有一个小伙子挺招人，手里提着一个赛过 14 吋电视机那么大的录音机。

在上面带直线的名词性成分中的"一"，不能重读，可以省去而不影响意义，请看下面的句子：

　　　　（32）……我就递上支烟，……
　　　　（33）还有个小伙子挺招人，手里提着个赛过 14 吋电视机那么大的录音机。

（32）和（33）中带线的名词性成分这时就属于 G 组了。比较下面的句子：

　　　　（34）单有一只飞燕，还算不了春天。
　　　　（35）我不需任何特殊待遇，如果大家有一碗饭就够了，我也不要求给我两碗饭。

"一"在这儿是普通数词，可以重读，不能省略，所在的名词性成分属于 E 组。

　　下面，我们逐节讨论各类名词性成分的表现形式和语法特点。

2.1　有指与无指

　　本节中，我们侧重讨论无指成分，有指成分则作为定指与不定指成分在下节中详细讨论。

在一些熟语性用法中，人称代词可以用作无指成分。例如：

（36）今年先种他几亩试验田，取得经验后再大面积推广。

（37）我不管他三七二十一，去了再说。

这种用法限于一些固定格式，本文暂不讨论。一般说来，无指成分的词汇形式限于 D 组至 G 组的格式，而有指成分则可用 A 组至 G 组的各类格式表现。请看表 1。

表 1 有指成分与无指成分的表现格式

	有指成分	无指成分
A 组	+	
B 组	+	
C 组	+	
D 组	+	+
E 组	+	+
F 组	+	+
G 组	+	+

这四组格式的无指成分分别在下列场合中出现：

（一）复合词的构词成分。例如，下列复合词中底下加线的都是无指成分：

鸡蛋糕　桃子树　羊毛　饭桶　冬至　霜降　肇事
恼人　方言调查　商品展销　汽车配件　啤酒大王

一般说来，用于这种场合的是 D 组格式，即光杆名词。

（二）分类性表语成分。例如：

（38）雍士杰曾是一名菜农，今年 50 多岁。

（39）抗日战争胜利后，他又赴美国，在美国华盛顿州立大学任特约教授。

一般说来，用于这种场合的是 D 组、F 组和 G 组三种格式。

（三）比较结构中用在"像""如""有"等词语后面的成分，例如：

（40）王大在运河里捞到一只螃蟹，乖乖，足有小脸盆大。

（41）公社机关铁门外那两盏葫芦瓢一般大的电灯，依旧亮在那儿。

（42）他目瞪口呆，像一根木头棒子楔在原地，一动不动。

D组、E组、F组和G组四种格式都可以用在这种场合。

（四）否定结构中在否定成分管界内的成分，例如：

（43）我这些天来没买书，口袋里没钱。

（44）没想到他的所谓办公室连张桌子都没有。

D组、E组、F组和G组四种格式都可以用在这种场合。

（五）构成所谓"短语动词"的动名组合中的名词性成分，例如：

读书　吵架　打仗　谢幕　打牌
洗澡　捕鱼　酗酒　告状　抽烟

一般来讲，只有D组格式用于这种场合。这类动名组合语义单一，名词性成分不代表语境中任何一个具体的事物，而只是作为补充动词语义的外延性成分进入组合。

除非出于对比或者强调的目的，无指成分一般不能以主语身份出现。下面句子中底下带点的都是有指成分：

（45）A：书读完了吗？　　B：读完了。

（46）曹禺是《雷雨》的作者。→《雷雨》的作者是曹禺。

试比较下面的句子：

（47）曹禺是剧作家。→ *剧作家是曹禺。

2.2　定指与不定指

汉语名词性成分的定指与不定指的区别在语言形式上由三个方面表现出来：一是该成分本身的词汇表现格式，即以A组至G组的哪一种格式出现；二是该成分所带定语的性质；三是该成分在句子中所担任的句法功能。这三方面的因素相互联系，相互制约，构成了极具汉语特色的错综复杂的局面。

我们先讨论名词性成分本身的表现格式。

吕叔湘先生（1985）指出，"他"在由古汉语中"其他"的意义发展成为第三人称代词的演变过程中，经历过一个专指（即本文所说的"实指"）而无定的阶段。请看下面的例句：

（48）长房曾与人共行，见一书生……无鞍骑马，下而叩头。长房曰："还他马，赦汝罪。"人问其故，长房曰："此狸也，盗社公马耳。"（《后汉书 82 下·费长房》）

（49）终不能如曹孟德、司马仲达父子，欺他孤儿寡妇，狐媚以取天下也。（《晋书 105·石勒》）

这儿的"他"均专指一人，但确切所指对象是谁，并不能从语境中判断出来。这种用法一般已不见于现代汉语。

在前面所列的七组格式中，自 C 组而上居于上端的三组格式一般只用来表现定指成分，自 F 组而下居于下端的两组格式一般只用来表现不定指成分，位于中端的 D 组和 E 组则表现出相当大的灵活性。请看表 2：

表 2　定指成分与不定指成分的表现格式

	定指成分	不定指成分
A 组	+	
B 组	+	
C 组	+	
D 组	(+)	(+)
E 组	(+)	(+)
F 组		+
G 组		+

上面说过，除名词性成分本身的格式体现定指与不定指的区别，该成分所带定语的性质和该成分的句法功能也是有决定作用的因素。但是，需要在这里指出的是，在表 2 中越是接近两端的格式，所表现的定指性或不定指性的程度越强，而受其他两个因素的影响也就越小。相反，越是接近中间，本身所表现的定指性或不定指性的程度越弱，受其他两个因素的影响也就越大。比较下面两个句子：

（50）客人从前门来了。

（51）前门来了客人。

"客人"在（50）中做主语，是定指成分。在（51）中做存现句的宾语，是不定指成分。同属 D 组格式的名词，句法功能不同，定指与不定指方面的理解也就不同，这是汉语中大家熟知的事实。但是，这种由句法功能左右定指或不定指区别的现象只出现在表 2 中接近中间的那几组词汇格式身上，接近两端的格式并不受其影响。试比较下面的句子：

（52）屋门"吱呀"一声被推开了，从外面走进一位陌生女子。

（53）屋门"吱呀"一声被推开了，一位陌生女子从外面走了进来。

（54）王经理、李处长，还有财务科的大刘、小孟伫立在车站的出口处。

（55）车站的出口处伫立着王经理、李处长，还有财务科的大刘、小孟。

同样是做主语，属于 F 组的名词性成分"一位陌生女子"在（53）中仍作不定指理解；同样是做存现句的宾语，属于 B 组的"王经理、李处长，还有财务科的大刘、小孟"在（55）中仍作定指理解。句法功能的变化对这些名词性成分作定指或不定指理解不产生任何影响。

在掌握了其他两个因素的作用范围的前提下，让我们先来研究名词性成分所带定语对于该成分的定指性或不定指性的影响。

领属性定语具有强烈的定指性质，带有这类定语的名词性成分一般作定指理解，请看下面的例句：

（56）走进办公室，他的办公桌上端端正正地放着一封匿名信。

（57）一位德国作家还根据门森的日记为他撰写了一本书。

一般性的定语成分，限定性越强、越具体，该名词性成分的定指性也就越强。除了特殊情况以外，表 2 中接近顶端的格式难得带限定性的定语成分，就是因为格式本身已经表现出强烈的定指意义。对于自 C 组而下的格式来讲，限定性定语起着增强定指性质的作用。请看下面的句子：

（58）小敏兴冲冲地奔到桌前，拉开抽屉，抽出那本《江苏画刊》，翻开，几页掉了下来。

属于 E 组格式的名词"几页"在最后一个小句中做主语，根据一般人的语感，句子读起来不太自然。但是，同样的名词，加上限制性定语成分以后，全句的自然度便大大地提高了。试比较：

(59)……印着秋色图画的几页掉了下来。

(60)……印着张顺义《太湖风情》组画的几页掉了下来。

有时，限制性定语本身提供的信息具有相当强的区别功能，名词性成分所带的数量词或者指别词等附加成分可以省略而不影响对该成分的理解。例如：

(61) 1985 年 6 月，她大学毕业，同年嫁给了一位在新加坡航空公司驻洛杉矶办事处工作，名叫马利克的办事员。

(62)……同年嫁给了在新加坡航空公司驻洛杉矶办事处工作，名叫马利克的办事员。

(63) 他慢慢地踱到一土坟前，缓缓地从怀中掏出一本《中国作家》杂志，翻过了几页，把登载着小说《黑纽扣》的那几页撕了下来。

(64)……把登载着小说《黑纽扣》的几页撕了下来。

(61)和(63)中，各词性成分所带的限制性定语足以确立所指对象的定指性，体现 C 组特征的"那"和 F 组特征的"一位"在这儿成了羡余成分。

最后，我们来探讨名词性成分的句法功能与定指和不定指区别之间的关系。

名词性成分的句法功能同它的定指性或不定指性两者之间关系十分密切。这种密切的关系主要表现在三个方面：第一，有的句子成分强烈倾向于由定指格式的名词性成分充当，而另有一些句子成分则强烈倾向于由不定指格式的名词性成分充当；第二，对于本身不明确地指示定指性或者不定指性的格式来讲，名词性成分位于某些句法位置上时，有作定指理解的强烈倾向，而位于另一些句法位置上时，则有作不定指理解的强烈倾向；第三，有的句法位置只接受不定指格式，完全排斥本身具有强烈定指意义的格式，而另有一些句法位置则只接受定指格式，完全排斥本身具有强烈不定指意义的格式。下面逐一讨论。

根据我们的观察，下面一些句子成分有由定指格式的名词性成分充当的强烈倾向：

主语
"把"字的宾语　　　　　数量宾语前的受事宾语
双宾语结构中的近宾语　领属性定语①

例如：

（65）他派周摄影把玉莲送到县招待所，安排食宿。

（66）并且当场夸下海口，保证在两个月之内要叫姓程的垮台撤职，给程某一个沉重的打击。

（67）你往北走哇，正顺路，我捎你们娘俩一截儿。

（68）源新从床下费力地拖出一只用蒲包扎得牢牢的木箱，眼睛看着玉珍，踢了那只木箱两脚。

（69）偶然，他在爸爸的提包里发现一只哨子。

下面所列的句子成分则有由不定指格式的名词性成分充当的强烈倾向：

存现句中的宾语　　　　处所介词短语前的宾语
双宾语结构中的远宾语　复合趋向补语后的宾语

例如：

（70）奇怪，摆书摊的屋里走出一个晾衣服的中年妇女……前面靠墙根坐了个哄娃娃的上年纪妇女。

（71）林野递给我一条用热水刚刚洗干净的毛巾，无言地望着我。

（72）请你立刻来一趟，我要报告你个好消息。

（73）我放一张纸在这里，请你画个老鼠在上头。

---

① 同列举的其他句子成分相比，领属性定语的定指倾向性要稍微弱一些。
不定指格式充当领属定语的例子也时有所见，例如：
（1）他在一个旅客的提包里发现了……
（2）一个人的一生应该这样度过。
（3）一个地方的气候跟它的纬度有关。
（4）一个案子的真相不是一下子就能弄清楚的。
不过，在许多类似情况下，有关名词性成分实际应该看作通指性用法，如上面（2）、（3）和（4）中带线的成分。有关通指性名词成分与定指性名词成分在概念上的相通之处，参见本文§1.4。上述现象和四句例句都是吕叔湘先生向作者指出的。

(74) 保卫处长叫护士端进来一盆热水。

这儿所谓的强烈倾向，指的是在自然话语中，从出现的频率上来观察，上面这两大类句法成分在大多数情况下分别由定指格式和不定指格式的名词性成分充任。相关讨论可参见范继淹（1985）、李临定（1986）、吕叔湘（1982）及 Li & Thompson（1981）。

表 2 中介乎定指格式与不定指格式之间的 D 组和 E 组格式的名词性成分，如果充任上述定指倾向性句法成分时，则有作定指理解的强烈倾向；如果充任不定指倾向性句法成分时，则有作不定指理解的强烈倾向。先举几个用作定指倾向性句法成分的例子：

(75) 门一打开，进来一男两女三个青年，都很精神，其中一个女孩子很像英格丽·褒曼。大鸣直起了腰。三个客人嗅嗅鼻子，似乎不习惯这屋子的烟味和臭袜子味。

(76) 甲嘎次仁拣起一颗豆子，用大拇指把豆子弹了出去，豆子准确地飞进了巴桑的嘴，大概一直飞进了食道。

(77) "请喝茶。"老王递给客人一杯热腾腾的香片茶。①

(78) 将军的部下都晓得将军的厉害，对于触犯军纪者都是毫不留情的，拔出手枪，就赏给违法者一粒"花生米"。

(79) 他还给妻子准备了一件礼物：一只精美的陶瓷花瓶。地震后，人们从废墟中扒出了田所良那只已经压扁了的皮箱。箱中有花瓶的全部碎片。

上面的句子中，带点的 D 组和 E 组格式的名词性成分都作定指成分理解。值得我们注意的是，D 组和 E 组的表现也并不是完全一样的。即使是在这些定指倾向性句法位置上，较接近不定指一端的 E 组格式有时也还作不定指理解，例如：

(80) 忽然，两道冰冰的目光直射向我，几个干枯的手指触到了我的鼻尖。我吃了一惊！面前站了一个瘦削的老头。

而较接近定指性一端的 D 组格式则很少会出现这种情况。

---

① 我们暂把这个句子中的"递给"和（78）中的"赏给"作为一个词看待。

在下面的例句中，D 组和 E 组格式的名词性成分充任不定指倾向性句法成分。

(81) 在车站只等了一会儿前面就来车了。

(82) 你穿了一件鹅黄色的毛衣，手里拾了一大把红叶。临别时，还给了我两片。

(83) 好不容易等到上午十时，才见里面慢慢悠悠地踱出两个办事员来。

(84) 他在口袋里掏了半天，摸出来几张皱巴巴的票子，递了过去。

上面的句子中，带线的 D 组和 E 组格式的名词性成分都作不定指成分理解。

在这些句子中，名词性成分的句法功能决定了所指对象的定指性或不定指性，这是汉语区别于印欧语言的一个特征。其他语言中的相关现象，参见 Chen(1986b)、Du Bois(1980)、Givón(1984) 及 Hopper & Thompson(1981)。

在讨论表 2 中七组词汇时，我们提到，这七组格式本身所体现的定指性或不定指性在程度上有强弱之分。我们现在讨论的这些句法成分，它们所表现的定指倾向或不定指倾向在程度上也有强弱之分。有的只接纳体现出强烈的定指性或不定指性的格式，而把其他格式干脆排斥在外，有的则比较宽容一些，除了中立的 D 组和 E 组格式以外，也容纳语义对立但程度稍弱的格式。这些句子成分与表 2 所列的格式之间存在着相当有趣的配应关系。一般说来，主语只能由自 F 组而上的格式担任，双宾语结构中的近宾语和数量宾语前的受事宾语只能由自 E 组而上的格式担任，双宾语结构中的远宾语只能由自 C 组而下的格式担任[①]，处所介词短语前的宾语和复合趋向补语后的宾语只能由自 E 组而下的成分担任，不在范围内的格式一般不能使用。例如：

(85) a. 一个老汉伸手拦住汽车，接着又来敲车窗。
　　　b. *个老汉伸手拦住汽车……

---

① 这里所说的远宾语，不包括"称""叫""称呼"等动词后的成分，例如：
(5) 别人都叫他大赵。　　(6) 称他李主任吧。
也有人把这种名词性成分看作补语。

(86)a. 我在桥头等了他半天，就是不见影子。

　　　b. 我在桥头等了老李半天，……

　　　c. 我在桥头等了那个人半天，……

　　　d. *我在桥头等了一个人半天，……

　　　e. *我在桥头等了个人半天，……

(87)a. *写这个名字在上头

　　　b. *写名字在上头

　　　c. 写几个名字在上头

　　　d. 写一个名字在上头

　　　e. 写个名字在上头（参见吕叔湘（1980：573））

具体语境不同、各人的语感不同，对各种句法成分在表2所给格式的"切割点"这个问题上大家的意见未必能取得一致。但是，我们断言，对于同一种句法成分来说，不管把切割点判定在哪一个格式上，如果这是个定指倾向性句法成分，高于该切割点的格式一定可用；如果是不定指倾向性句法成分，低于该切割点的格式一定可用。

2.3　实指与虚指

就词汇形式来说，实指成分可用自A组至G组任何一种格式表现。前面说过，定指成分全是实指，没有虚实之别，因此，虚指成分的词汇表现形式限于自D组而下的格式。详见表3。

表3　实指成分与虚指成分的表现格式

	实指成分	虚指成分
A组	+	
B组	+	
C组	+	
D组	+	+
E组	+	+
F组	+	+
G组	+	+

虚指成分一般用在表示未然、条件、疑问、否定等意义的句子中。请看下面的例句：

（88）箱子太沉，我得去楼上找几个人帮着抬上去。

（89）只要能给他弄到一辆汽车，他一定肯来。

（90）你能不能去拿把扳子来？

这些场合中的名词性成分常常又可以作实指成分理解。以（88）中的"几个人"为例，发话人也许知道楼上有几个人，现在就去找他们帮忙，也许他只是想找人帮忙，楼上有人没人他并不清楚。如果是前一种情况，该名词短语作实指理解，如果是后一种情况，作虚指理解，但是，如果把（88）由表示未然状态的句子改成表示已然状态的句子，则"几个人"只能作实指理解，请看下面的句子：

（91）箱子太沉，我去楼上找了几个人帮着抬了去。

2.4 通指与单指

单指成分可用由 A 组至 G 组各格式表现。除了靠名词重叠或名词前加"所有""一切"等限定词等方法以外，通指成分可用由 C 组至 G 组的格式表现。见表 4。

表 4　通指成分与单指成分的表现格式

	通指成分	单指成分
A 组		＋
B 组		＋
C 组	＋	＋
D 组	＋	＋
E 组	＋	＋
F 组	＋	＋
G 组	＋	＋

用 C 组格式表现通指成分时，都有"种""类"等表示类别的量词相随，如：

（92）算了算了，那种瓜以后再也不买了。

这种用法同定指格式的单指成分如"那只瓜"有许多相通之处。上面所举的定指成分的那些语法特点也完全适用于这里表现通指的 C 组格式。

其他几组格式中，最常用的是 D 组和 F 组，例句 §1.4。

三　结语

我们在本文中首先分析了有指与无指、定指与不定指、实指与虚指以及通指与单指这四对概念的含义及其相互关系。接着，我们研究了这些概念在现代汉语中的表现方法，同时揭示了相关的各类名词性成分表现出来的语法特点。本文所做的工作将有助于我们进一步从功能的角度进行汉语的句法研究和话语分析。

参考文献

范继淹，1985，无定 NP 主语句，《中国语文》第 5 期。
李临定，1986，《现代汉语句型》，北京：商务印书馆。
吕叔湘主编，1980，《现代汉语八百词》，北京：商务印书馆。
吕叔湘，1982，《中国文法要略》，北京：商务印书馆。
吕叔湘著，江蓝生补，1985，《近代汉语指代词》，上海：学林出版社。
Chen, Ping. 1986a. Referent Introducing and Tracking in Chinese Narratives. Ph.D. Dissertation, UCLA.
Chen, Ping. 1986b. Discourse and particle movement in English. *Studies in Language*. 10.1:79-95.
Du Bois, J. 1980. Beyond definiteness: The trace of identity in discourse. In: Wallace Chafe, ed., *Pear Stories: Cognitive, Cultural, and Linguistic Aspects of Narrative Production*. Ablex Publishing Corporation, 203-274.
Givón, Talmy. 1984. *Syntax*. Vol. I. John Benjamins Publishing Company.
Hopper, Paul and Sandra A. Thompson. 1980. Transitivity in grammar and discourse. *Language*. 56.2:251-299.
Li, Charles N. and Sandra A. Thompson. 1981. *Mandarin Chinese: A Functional Reference Grammar*. University of California Press.
Lyons, John. 1977. *Semantics*. Cambridge University Press.

（本文原载《中国语文》1987 年第 2 期。）

语言学的一个核心概念"指称"问题研究

提　要　指称是语言学研究中的一个核心概念，贯穿语言本体研究的许多方面，词汇、语义、句法、语用、话语分析等领域，都要涉及指称问题。指称问题有四个主要的研究角度，分别是逻辑和哲学角度、语义学角度、语用学角度和话语分析的角度。本文分别从这四个角度出发，探讨汉语指称研究的理论背景、重要概念、研究方法及主要研究成果。
关键词　指称　语言哲学　语义指称　语用指称　话语分析　主题性

我们今天讨论语言学研究中的一个核心概念"指称"问题，英文是"referentiality"，以及与它同源的几个词如"refer、reference、referent、referential"，等等。我们昨天的讨论范围是以索绪尔结构主义理论为开端的现代语言学，今天将目光延伸到自古希腊时期直到现在的整个时段。

为什么说指称问题是语言学研究中的一个核心概念？首先，这个概念的研究在西方学术传统中源远流长，从古希腊时代起直到21世纪的现在，一直是哲学、逻辑学、文学和语言学等专门研究领域里大家密切关注并深入探讨的对象；语言学研究中有许多十分常用的理论、原则、概念和方法，要对它们有深刻理解并且能熟练运用，一个前提条件是掌握它们的来龙去脉，从历史的角度看问题，往往能使我们站得更高，看得更远。我们今天以指称问题为例，说明为什么要这么做。其次，指称现象贯穿语言本体的许多方面，词汇、语义、句法、语用、话语分析等领域，都要涉及指称问题。指称问题尤其是语义学和语用学研究的主要内容，语义学课程常用的一本教科书 *Knowledge of Meaning—An Introduction to Semantic Theory*（Richard Larson & Gabriel Segal,

The MIT Press, 1995），600多页，几乎一半的篇幅是讲与指称相关的问题。指称现象在功能语法和话语分析中的重要性自不待言，就是在形式句法学研究中也占据着独特的地位。自1960年代开始，乔姆斯基（Chomsky）的生成语法理论模式就将两个名词性成分的同指和异指作为许多语法结构特征的主要判断标准，例如：

（1）小王经常表扬他。

（2）小王认为他能够拿到这份工作。

句（1）中的"他"如果与小王同指，必定会强制触发反身代词转换，现在这个位置上是"他"而不是"自己"，可证"小王"和"他"两个名词性成分一定是异指。与句（1）不同，句（2）中两个名词性成分可以是同指，也可以是异指，因此可证两个名词性成分在句（1）和句（2）中所处的结构位置不同。Chomsky 的生成语法理论经过了好几个主要发展阶段，从所谓的标准理论、扩充标准理论、管约理论、原则与参数框架直到现在的最简方案，名词性成分的同指和异指始终是重要的理论分析手段。

指称问题在语言学研究中十分重要，这是由许多原因造成的，其中包含深厚的历史因素。指称研究可以一直追溯到西方学术的源头。以前讽刺别人唯洋是举，会说此人"言必称希腊"。这种说法其实是有一定原因的，我们现在熟知的西方学术的源头是古希腊，许多重要的思想、概念、命题，包括观察问题的角度、提出问题和解决问题的方法等，都可以上推到古希腊时代，其中也包括我们今天讲的指称问题。

古希腊最重要的三位哲学家是苏格拉底、柏拉图和亚里士多德。我相信我们都读过这么一句话："人不能两次跨入同一条河流。"这句话出自柏拉图的著作《对话录》Cratylus 篇，该著作记录了苏格拉底同 Hermogenes 和 Cratylus 两人的对话，讨论内容很多涉及语言问题。Cratylus 是另一位哲学家 Heraclitus 的学生，也可以说是柏拉图的老师，在名与物的关系上主张神授论。在柏拉图的书中，苏格拉底转述了 Heraclitus 的观点"人不能两次跨入同一条河流"。我们现在一般都把这句话主要作为一个哲学命题看待，从哲学的角度谈"常"与"变"

的关系，什么是恒常的，什么是变动的，以及两者的联系和转化，等等。但是，仔细研读这本书的原文，就会认识到这个命题还有另外一层意义，从根本上来说涉及一个语言学中的指称问题，涉及 identity。所谓 identity，也就是我们每天用的 ID（identity）card "身份证"中的那个 identity。我们对着镜子看看我们自己是谁，这个就是 identity。涉及指称问题时，我将它译作"同一性"，同一性是同指或异指的判断依据。"人不能两次跨入同一条河流"这个哲学命题如果是对的，那我们就会面对一个同一性问题，同时也是指称问题。你昨天跨入一条河，它叫苏州河，你今天又跨入这条河，你说昨天和今天跨入的一定不会是同一条河，因为人不能两次跨入同一条河流。那么，这就带来一个很实际的指称问题：你昨天称它为苏州河，你今天就不能称它为苏州河，因为它们不可能是同一条河流。但是，不是苏州河，你今天称它什么呢？明天、后天呢？Cratylus 本人的观点甚至更为激进，他认为一次跨入同一条河流都是不可能的，你左脚先跨进去，右脚接着跨进去的不可能是同一条河流，根据同一性规定，自然也不能共用一个名称。所以，说到底，这是个很难回答的指称问题。我们也许可以觉得这些哲学家真会钻牛角尖，但人类两千多年的智力进步许多都起源于这批人的苦思冥想。晚年的 Cratylus 不说一句话了，他觉得语言没办法表达自己想表达的意思。那他日常生活怎么办？就是用手指。英文中的 refer 源自拉丁语 re-（"回"）与 ferre（"带"），"带回"的意思，我觉得汉语用"指称"这个词更为贴切和传神，就是 Cratylus 晚年做的事情。

苏格拉底、柏拉图以后，指称现象一直是古希腊哲学家和后人所关注问题的一个重要方面。为了便于大家理解，我下面将时代顺序倒过来讲。

我们知道当代语言学有两个最主要的学派，一个是形式学派，以美国麻省理工学院（MIT）乔姆斯基创立的生成语法理论为代表，另一个是功能/认知学派，主要从语言的功能、话语和认知的角度研究语言，也包括现在许多人感兴趣的构式语法。这两大学派各自提出许多新颖的思想、理论，取得许多独创的研究成果，体现了语言学领域 20 世纪下半叶直到现在所取得的巨大进步。但是，从学术思想发展史的角度来看，它们也都各自从前人那儿继承了丰厚的理论资源。现代语言学作为一门独立学科在世界范围里迅速发展主要是 20 世纪下半叶的事情，欧美国家大学成立独立的语言学系，几乎都在 60 年代以后。在这之前，语言学家大都散布在哲学系、人类学系、心理学系、教育系、英语系、外语系等部门。实际上，三四十年代以前，专业语言学家人数也不多，伦敦大学直到 1944 年才设立英国第一个普通语言学讲座教授的席位。但是，这并不是说我们现在研究的语言现象以前大都没人关心。当代语言学家现在研究的许多语义学、语用学问题，包括我们今天讨论的指称问题，以前主要是逻辑学家、哲学家感兴趣的问题。

以德国哲学家、逻辑学家和数学家弗雷格（Gottlob Frege, 1848—1925）和英国哲学家、逻辑学家和数学家罗素（Bertrand Russell, 1872—1970）为主要代表人物的分析哲学，对语言研究尤其是语义研究，起了非常有力的推动作用。我们下面会谈到，现代语言学家说到指称问题，往往都是从弗雷格和罗素开始。弗雷格更被看成是推动 20 世纪初期哲学向语言转向（linguistic turn）的关键人物，所谓语言转向，指的是主张哲学分析的研究重点应该是哲学和语言的关系。但是，弗雷格和罗素对于自然语言本身并没有太大的研究兴趣，他们研究语言的出发点和目的地都是逻辑和哲学问题。这两人加上早期的维特根斯坦（Ludwig Wittgenstein, 1889—1951）等人在这方面的主要贡献，是用逻辑分析的方法，将日常语言的表述形式化为逻辑语言，揭示单从自然语言词语字面上未必能看得出来的深层意义。基本接受罗素等人学术思想和研究方法的哲学家大都在罗素本人所在的英国剑桥大学工作，在 30 年代尤其活跃，一般被称为剑桥分析学派。20 世纪下半叶的 MIT 形式学派从学术谱系上来看接近剑桥分析学派，在学术思想上传承借鉴之处很多，尤其是在形式语义学研究方面。

另外有一批志趣相投的哲学家，主要有 Gilbert Rile（1900—1976）、John L. Austin（1911—1960）、Peter F. Strawson（1919—2006）、Paul Grice（1913—1988），以及后期的维特根斯坦等人，这些人除了维特根斯坦，40 年代到 60 年代末都在英国牛津大学工作，人称牛津日常语言学派（Oxford school of ordinary language）。这一学派人物大都认为，要研究人们的思维，唯一途径是通过语言研究，尤其是日常自然语言研究。同剑桥学派注重公理化、形式化的研究相比，牛津学派更关注非形式化的日常语言现象，包括一些在他们看来很重要的日常用语。20世纪下半叶功能/话语/认知学派的许多基本理念和思路，都是直接从牛津学派那里传承而来。牛津学派的一位重要学者，堪称现代语用学奠基人之一的 Paul Grice，1967年更是从牛津转入美国加州大学伯克利分校工作。我们都知道，加州大学伯克利分校60年代后期一直到现在都是功能/话语/认知学派的大本营，牛津学派对他们的巨大影响是显而易见的。

剑桥学派和牛津学派是不是无所依傍、平地起高楼那样出现的呢？当然不是。可以很清楚地看到，他们在许多方面与古希腊哲学家以及后来两千多年间有关学者、学派和学术思想一脉相承，并在此基础上推陈出新。就指称研究而论，柏拉图以后有两个学派特别值得我们注意。

一个学派以亚里士多德为代表人物，亚里士多德是一位人类思想史上的巨人，我们现在学科体系中分属自然科学、社会科学、人文艺术的许多领域里，都能看到他做出的奠基性的工作。亚里士多德创建了形式逻辑理论，侧重研究语言和思维的形式特点，主词谓词、命题、判断、演绎推理的三段论，传统思维定律如矛盾律、排中律和同一律，等等，我们现在几乎每天都要用到的概念和定律，或是由他本人创立，或是前人提出而经由他做出深入阐述。同时要指出的是，西方几乎很少有一个学派找不到直接对立面，无论造诣多么深厚的学者，都会听到对他质疑辩难的声音，一条条地批驳那些看似无懈可击的观点，这在亚里士多德也不例外。

古希腊时期离雅典30多公里的城市 Megara，有一个史称 Megarian School 的哲学学派，是由 Euclides 创立。对语言学家来说，最值得关注的是他的学生 Eubulides，是 Eubulides 提出的一些悖论（paradox）。什么是悖论？前提和推理有效，但结论自相矛盾、论断无法立足。最有名的就是所谓说谎者悖论。柏拉图、亚里士多德等人主张的排中律、矛盾律等，是传统逻辑思维的基本定律。排中律规定，一个命题 p，不是真 p，就是假 ~p，没有介乎 p 和 ~p 之间的第三种可能；矛盾律则规定，

p 和 ~p 不可能同时成立。例如，"我是张三"这句话表现的命题，要么是真的，我就是张三；要么是假的，我不是张三，两者必居其一，也不可能我既是张三，又不是张三。但是，Eubulides 提出的悖论揭示，世界上有一些命题并不是如这些思维定律所规定的那样非此即彼、黑白分明。例如，"我在说谎"，你说这个命题是真是假。你说这个命题是真的，我是在说谎，那你的判断同时意味着我讲这句话的时候没有说谎，说的是真话；你说这个命题是假的，我在说真话，那同样意味着我讲这句话的时候实际上是在说谎，说的不是真话。由此可见，柏拉图、亚里士多德等人的定律在这儿不起作用。我们现在知道，造成这种现象的原因是有关成分在思维层面和语言层面上所指对象可以有所不同，涉及指称问题。Eubulides 其他几个悖论同语言学的关系更为密切，有一个是 Electra 悖论。Electra 是希腊神话中一个女子的名字，是一个国王的女儿。她的父王被她的母亲谋杀了，她哥哥 Orestes 先是逃了出去，后来装扮成一个蒙面的乞丐回来报仇。他路过 Electra 的住处，敲开门讨水喝，Electra 没有认出此人是谁，将他引进厨房。Eubulides 问道，在这个时候，"Electra 知道她的哥哥 Orestes 在厨房里"这句话表现的命题是真还是假？蒙面乞丐和 Electra 的哥哥 Orestes 是同一个人，如果根据指称对象相同的两个语言成分可以互相替换而不影响命题真假值的原理，这个命题应该是真的，但几乎所有的读者都会将这个命题判断为假的。造成这个悖论的原因很大程度上是指称同一性问题，两千多年后的弗雷格提出的有关理论，为回答这类问题提供了一条思路。Eubulides 还提出所谓的"沙堆悖论"（the sorites paradox），说的是有一个沙堆，一个显然有效的逻辑思维前提是"从一个沙堆中拿走一粒沙，它还是一个沙堆"。因此，你拿走一粒沙，这还是一个沙堆，接着一粒一粒地拿走，如果严格根据所给前提推理，哪怕拿净，这还应该是一个沙堆。另外，从实际观察和判断角度来看，要拿走多少粒沙才能说这不是一个沙堆，谁也说不清楚。因此，一定会存在这样一种状态，"这是一个沙堆"这个命题我们不好说是真还是假。造成这个悖论的原因是谓词属性边界模糊，在这种情况下，柏拉图、亚里士多德等人提出的传统逻辑思维定律又失效了。另外，Eubulides 还提出一个"头角悖论"（the horns paradox），主要涉及预设（presupposition）问题。Eubulides 提出的这些悖论，都是用来驳斥亚里士多德形式逻辑理论中的主要公理。面对 Eubulides 的质疑，亚里士多德无法为自己辩解。

语言学史专家 Peter Seuren 认为，Eubulides 悖论对于后来自然语言语义学研究的发展起了极为重要的作用，"可以不带夸张地说，20 世纪以及今后自然语言语义学的中心问题，是由 Eubulides 在公元前 4 世纪提出来的"（Seuren 1998：428）。20 世纪剑桥学派的罗素等人继承了亚里士多德的形式逻辑研究传统，并在此基础上将有关语言、思维和外部世界关系的研究在深度和广度方面大大地往前推进。牛津学派则对形式化系统兴趣不大，同时不断对剑桥学派的理论、原则、方法和有关论点提出质疑（参见陈平 2012：4）。Seuren 在上文中同时指出，古希腊亚里士多德学派和 Megarian 学派之间的历史，又在 20 世纪剑桥学派和牛津学派之间重演，连无关要旨的细节都是那么相似。

指称现象涉及的范围广，研究的历史长，观察的角度多，所有这些因素造成了指称研究复杂多端，需要我们认真观察，仔细分辨。对自然语言中的指称问题，有四个主要的研究角度：第一是逻辑和哲学的角度，第二是语义学的角度，第三是语用学的角度，第四是话语分析的角度。因观察角度的不同，研究者的出发点、动机、重点关注的对象、分析论证的方法以至术语的内涵和外延往往并不一样。如果你告诉我你在研究指称问题，我常常要问一句，是从哪个角度研究指称问题？同时也要看到，这四种研究路径相互之间又有非常密切的联系，在许多问题上相互借鉴，相互促进。今天我就分别从这四个角度出发，向大家介绍指称研究中的背景知识、重要概念、研究方法及主要研究成果。

1. 逻辑和哲学角度

现代语言学家广泛深入地研究自然语言的意义问题，主要是 20 世纪 60 年代以后的事情。在此之前，自然语言同语义、语用相关的现象，包括指称问题，主要是逻辑学家和哲学家的研究对象。哲学有一个专门的分支，叫语言哲学（philosophy of language），专门从哲学的角度研究同语言有关的各种现象，从 20 世纪初开始到现在，一直是哲学学科最受重视的领域之一。语言哲学家主要关注的是语言、思维和外部世界的关系，研究兴趣侧重围绕"意义"这个主题，自 19 世纪末到 20 世纪上半叶，主要研究对象就是指称问题。前面提到的德国学者弗雷格，以及剑桥学派和牛津学派的代表人物，是语言哲学研究领域里的主力。此外，还有一些美国学者，如 William Van Orman Quine（1908—2000）、Zero Vendler（1921—2004）等，也是这个领域里的很有影响的人物。

弗雷格对语言哲学研究的主要贡献是 Frege（1892）提出的 Sinn 和 Bedeutung 的概念。这两个对立概念在英语文献中有好几种译法，如 "sense/referent, sense/meaning, meaning/denotation, sense/nominatum" 等，同一个词 "meaning"，有人用来对译 "Bedeutung"，也有人如罗素则用来对译 "Sinn"，如果不对照德语原文很容易产生误解。另外，文献中与 Sinn 相同或相似的概念，还有 intension（内涵）、connotation 等，与 "Bedeutung" 相同或相似的概念，还有 extension（外延）、designatum 等。我将这两个词分别译为"意义"和"所指对象"。弗雷格提出这两个概念，主要是针对有学者认为专名没有意义的观点，也有助于消解类似上面所讲的 Electra 悖论问题所带来的困惑，尽管根据历史记载，弗雷格当时还不知道 Electra 悖论。弗雷格主张，起指称作用的语言符号可以有两层意思：一是该符号形式本身表现的内容，可以看成是所指对象的表现方式，以这种形式显示它的有关属性，此为意义；二是外界存在的被指事物本身，此为所指对象。符号的意义决定它的所指对象，词语是否具有意义以及是否存在所指对象，有待满足的条件是不一样的，可以只有意义而不存在所指对象，如"现任法国国王"。两个词语可以有不同的意义，但所指相同，文献中常见的例子是"启明星就是长庚星"（The Morning Star is the Evening Star），因为两个专名虽然所指对象相同，就是金星，但意义不同，所以这句话不能看作为同义反复。弗雷格的著作中，这两个概念主要用于专名，但也可以将这种区别延伸到概念词（Begriffswort）和句子，如句子的意义是命题，所指对象是真假值。有不少同这两个概念相关的重要问题，弗雷格没有给出明确的说明。另外，弗雷格的关注对象主要是理想化的语言而不是自然语言，如何将他的整套理论用于分析自然语言，还有许多问题有待回答。弗雷格之后，意义和所指对象这两个概念的性质、使用范围及相关问题成了20世纪语言哲学研究的中心课题，弗雷格也因此被一些人称为"语言哲学之父"。

罗素是位极为优秀的学者和真正意义上的知识分子，1950年获得诺贝尔文学奖，其实"诺贝尔文学奖"中的"文学"（literature）用的是广义，指文字作品，并不专限狭义的文学作品，这又是一个翻译可能会导致误解的例子。罗素获奖，不是因为他发表的优秀诗歌小说，而是表彰他在多种重要的著作中大力倡导人文理想和思想自由。在"指称"概念和种种语言形式的关系问题上，罗素比弗雷格严格得多。弗雷格认为，不但专有名词和指代词（如"那个人"）可以是有指（referential）成分，限定摹状词，即带定冠词的名词短语也可以是有指成分。而罗素则认为，只有当所指对象是独一无二的事物（singular reference）的时候，才谈得上有指。因此，有指成分只能是逻辑专名、指代词以及如"我"这样的标示词（indexical）。他将其他的语言成分，包括限定摹状词、带不定冠词的无定名词短语、带量词的名词短语、光杆名词等等都归为一类，称之为"指谓成分"（denoting expressions），他认为指谓成分不是有指成分。

罗素对语言哲学的最大贡献是他提出的限定摹状词理论（Theory of Descriptions）。他（Russell 1905，1919）提出，限定摹状词指示外部世界有关事物的方法与专名完全不同，专名直接指称所指对象，不必依靠其他词语，而限定摹状词只能间接指示外部事物，先一般性地描摹事物的性状，凡是符合描摹性状的事物，就是该名词性成分的所指事物。罗素认为，脱离句子孤立地看专名和摹状词这两种语言成分，也许不容易说明这种区别，但它们在句子主语位置上出现的时候，这种区别就看得比较清楚了。专名做主语的句子，该句的语法主语和语法谓语同时就是逻辑主语和逻辑谓语，构成单纯的主谓句。但是，如果主语位置上出现的是一个限定摹状词，如句（3）：

（3）现任法国国王是秃头。（The present King of France is bald.）

那么，表面上这是一个句子，但实际上表现了三个命题，我们可以用下面的逻辑表达式来说明，三个命题分别由 & 连接：

∃x[现任法国国王（x）& ∀y [现任法国国王（y）→ y=x] & 秃头（x）]

从表面语言形式上来看，限定摹状词在句（3）中做主语，而通过逻辑表达式，可以看到该摹状词以受量词约束的谓词形式出现。罗素由此认为，限定摹状词以及其他的指谓成分，都是所谓的量化（quantificational）成分，属于无指成分。罗素对句（3）中摹状词的逻辑分析，被看成是哲学领域里语言分析的典范之作，被誉为开创了分析哲学的新范式。在专有名词、指代词、标示词，以及带定冠词、不定冠词或量词的名词性短语及光杆名词等各种名词性成分的指称属性和分类方法等问题上，罗素的理论统治语言哲学界达五十年之久，其影响力至今不衰。语言哲学界乃至语言学界，尤其是从事形式语义学研究的学者，有不少人仍然基本接受罗素的理论思想和分析方法，一般称为新罗素学派（neo-Russellians）。在有指（referential）和无指（nonreferential）等概念的使用范围上，他们几乎完全遵循罗素的原则。

对罗素理论提出异议并得到广泛重视的首先是牛津学派的领军人物 Peter Strawson。罗素认为指称是词语形式的属性，而 Strawson（1950）则强调指称的语用性质，认为指称是人们使用词语所做出的行为，应归入词语的应用范畴，而不是看作为词语的自身属性，如 "法国国王"，1750 年指的是路易十五，到了 1770 年指的却是路易十六。因为我们常常用摹状词指称独一无二的事物，所以带定冠词的名词短语也可以看作为有指成分。说话人甚至可以用其他形式的语言成分，如带不定冠词的名词短语，来表示当时在他的思想里是独一无二的事物，因此也可以看成是有指成分。同时，语言形式完全一样的词语，可以作有指成分用，也可以作无指成分用，如下面两句中的"the whale"（鲸鱼），在句（4）中为无指成分，句（5）中为有指成分：

（4）The whale is a mammal.（鲸鱼是哺乳动物。）

（5）The whale struck the ship.（鲸鱼撞到了船。）

美国哲学家 Keith Donnellen 1966 年写的一篇文章在指称研究领域里也有很大影响。Donnellen（1966）提出，罗素和 Strawson 都没有注意到摹状词的两种不同用法，一是有指（referential）用法，一是属性（attributive）用法，完全相同的词语在指称问题上可以有这样两种迥然不同的用法，他的一个有名的例句是句（6）：

（6）Smith's murderer is insane.（杀害 Smith 的人精神不正常。）

"Smith's murderer"（杀害 Smith 的人）作有指用法理解时，指的是某个特定的人，这个人杀害了 Smith，这句话说的是这个人精神不正常。这个短语还可以有另一种理解，即 Donnellen 称之为"属性用法"的理解，说话人并不知道是谁杀了 Smith，只是说能把 Smith 杀了的人，无论他是谁，一定是个精神不正常的人。Donnellen 提出的指称用法和属性用法这两个概念，在文献中被广泛引用。

上面讲的是逻辑学家和哲学家对指称问题所做的主要研究。他们提出的概念、术语、研究思路和研究结论，对语言学家影响极大。语言学家研究指称问题，很难完全脱离语言哲学家设定的基本理论框架。语言学指称研究领域各家各派的著作中，时时可以看到上面这些逻辑学家和哲学家的影子。因此，我们要研究指称问题，一般都得从上面所给出的这些文献开始，否则很可能连基本概念、常用术语都说不清楚。其实，这不仅仅限于指称问题，语义学、语用学很多研究领域都是这种情况。我以前谈到，语言学家 20 世纪下半叶之前对语义和语用学的了解可以说是乏善可陈，语言意义研究不是他们的传统强项和主要兴趣所在。语言学家开始重视语义和语用问题时，先是主要是向逻辑学家和哲学家学习，我知道有好几位同行将维特根斯坦后期的著作奉为至宝，后来又越来越多地将目光投向心理学和认识科学。这样做非常好，语言的意义问题极为复杂,语言学家必须借鉴相关学科的理论、概念和研究方法,以促进这方面的研究工作。

同样是研究语言的指称现象,逻辑学家/哲学家和语言学家还是有许多不同之处。就指称对象来说,语言哲学家所说的有指成分,必须指的是现实世界中存在的某个事物。语言学家则没有这样严格的要求,涉及的事物无论是存在于外部客观世界,还是语言构建的篇章话语或是发话人自己的思维空间,只要符合一定的条件,都可以看成是有指成分。从研究目的上来看,语言哲学家更多的是通过研究语言探索人们的思维活动规律以及知识的起源、获得和运用等问题,重点是语言、思维和外部世界的关系。语言学家最感兴趣的是语言本体,侧重研究语言形式同语言意义两者之间的对应关系,研究语言的运用以及历史发展等。从研究方法上来看,逻辑学家和哲学家大都围绕抽象概念做文章,而语言学主要是一门实证科学,论证必须建立在通过自省、观察或试验得到的大量语料之上,往往还得研究多种语言之间在有关问题上的异同,各种语言理论假说都得通过语料的检验。

2. 语义学角度

从语义学角度研究指称现象主要涉及两个方面,一是词语的形式,二是该形式表现的同指称有关的意义。

语言成分通过本身的形式表示种种意义,有些意义可以说能脱离使用者和上下文而独立存在。从语义学角度观察,所谓有指成分就是说话人可以利用这个语言形式,通过它的内在语义指称外部世界、话语环境或自己思想中的某个特定对象,否则为无指成分。同有定/无定(definite/indefinite)这对概念不同,有指/无指(referential/non-referential)是从发话人立场出发(speaker-oriented)的概念,详细论证参见 Chen(2009,2015)。就语义有指成分来说,一般情况下,说话人只要使用这个词语,受话人不言而喻地认为该词语指称某个特定的事物。我随便用一个专有名词"张大成"来做例子：我、祝老师和蒋老师三个人坐在一起说话，我突然说，张大成怎样怎样，我知道祝老师认识张大成，而蒋老师如果不知道张大成是什么人，或许便会觉得不太自在。因为他知道我用"张大成"这个专有名词，一定是特有所指的，如果他对此人毫无所知，会觉得难以参与我们的讨论。如果换一个名词短语，比如说，"我今天来复旦路上碰到的一个人"，大家就不会有那种感觉。这证明，有些语言成分，如专有名词，本身形式表示的内在语义决定了它们是有指成分。在这儿我要说明两点，第一，上面这个似乎是没有任何问题的判断，实际上是有很大争议的。许多语言学家认为，这类论断是错误的，脱离了使用语言的人和上下文，语言形式本身无意可言。这种观点是从语言哲学家那里转来的，说到底是个哲学问题。如同大多数哲学命题一样，不太可能截然分出是非对错。当然双方都各有许多论据和论证，因为时间问题，我今天无法细说，大家知道有不同观点就行了。第二点同第一点密切相关，就是专有名词为什么会有指称用法，它的指称功能是怎么来的，除了指称功能以外还有什么意义，等等。这些主要是语言哲学界内部的问题，从弗雷格、罗素直到现在，讨论非常热烈，不过同语言学家感兴趣的问题没有什么直接关系，在大多数语言学家看来，专有名词只有指称意义或指称功能。

　　从语义学的角度看指称问题，一些词语的语义能分解成两个部分，一部分表现词汇意义，另一部分表现指称意义。我们以英语中带定冠词"the"的名词短语"the city"为例，"city"是城市的意思，只有词汇意义而没有其他，如果没有其他成分同现，我们不知道这个词语是有指还是无指；"the"就很有趣了，这个词没有具体的词汇意思，只有语法意义或者更准确地说只有指称意义，它表示同它连用的这个名词指称一个特定的事物，在这儿就是指称一个特定的城市。指代词也有类似用法，比如说"那把椅子"，光说"椅子"一般不知道是有指无指，但"那"的意义决定了这个名词短语指的是语境中一把特定的椅子。"那"与"the"相比，"那"除了表示有指以外，还多了一点意义，就是同说话人距离相对较远，另外，在与"那些"对立的场合下还有单数的意思。而"the"只有单纯的指称义，不表示同远近、单复相关的任何其他属性（参见 Chen 2004）。

相反，有些词语的内在语义决定了它们是无指成分，如分量词（partitive quantifier）或带分量词的名词短语。分量词的语义作用是指整体中的一部分，如"大多数学生"指的是所有学生整体中的一个部分，这部分超过总数的二分之一。分量词表示的是从整体切出来的一部分，从语义上来看不可能指称构成这个部分的特定成员，也就是说不可能指称特定对象，所以说带分量词的成分是语义无指成分。还有一些名词短语从语义上来看既不包含内在的有指属性，也不包含内在的无指属性，发话人使用这些词语时，受话人既可以作有指理解，也可以作无指理解。

从语义学的角度研究指称现象，可以根据语言成分同指称相关的内在语义属性把它们分成三大类：一类是有指成分，主要有三种表现形式——专有名词、代词及指示词；一类是无指成分，是带分量词的名词短语；还有一类有指无指两可。表 1 列出了这三类语言成分的主要语法形式。

表 1　汉语名词性短语的语义有指与无指

名词性短语的语法类别		语义有指	语义无指
有定名词短语	专有名词	+	−
	人称代词	+	−
	指代词"这/那"（+NP）	+	−
无定名词短语	"一"+（量词）+ NP	+	+
	量词 + NP	+	+
不定名词短语	数词/"几"……+ 量词 + NP	+	+
	光杆名词	+	+
分量词（+NP）	"每"	−	+
	"所有"	−	+
	"一切"	−	+
	"大多数"	−	+
	"多数"	−	+
	"少数"	−	+

表 1 的分类参考了 Fodor & Sag（1982）对英语有关词语的讨论和分类，这种语义学角度的指称成分分类方式，在世界语言中是大同小异的。表

中有定、无定和不定这些概念的定义和表现形式，汉语文献有我 1987 年《中国语文》上的那篇论文。因为今天我们的题目是"有指/无指"，不是"有定/无定"，所以我就不多说了，对这些概念感兴趣的也可以参考 Chen（2003，2004，2015）。

归入无定和不定名词短语的词语，从语义学的角度来说，既可以是有指，也可以是无指。这是由词语本身的语义属性所决定的。英语带不定冠词的名词性成分也具有相似的指称属性，有些例句可以直译成汉语，说明同样的有指/无指现象。例如，"Jenny wants to marry a linguist"（Jenny 想嫁给一位语言学家），"一位语言学家"的语义属性决定了这个无定名词短语在这句句子中可以有有指和无指两种理解。一是有指，Jenny 已有一位意中人，是语言学家，她想嫁给他；二是无指，Jenny 还没有意中人，她只想嫁给语言学家，是张三还是李四都没有关系。如果将"一位语言学家"换成"Chomsky"，这个句子就没有歧义，Jenny 想嫁给 Chomsky。换成"那个捧了一束花的人"，也没有歧义。为什么？语言成分的语义性质决定了它们只能作有指/无指成分理解。

3. 语用学角度

从语用学角度研究指称现象，关键着眼点是词语的实际用法，主要涉及的三个方面，一是词语的形式，二是该形式表现的同指称有关的意义，三是发话人的意图以及具体语境。语言成分在语义学意义上的有指无指，为使用者如何使用这些成分提供了各种可能性，而在具体语境中实际上是如何使用的，是语用学研究的课题。

根据 Chen（2009）提出的观点，语用学意义上的有指语言成分，必须要满足三个条件：

（一）语言成分所指的特定对象必须存在于语境之中，所谓语境，可以是周围的客观世界，可以是篇章话语构造的情景，也可以是说话人脑海里的景象；

（二）该指称对象对说话人来讲是一个特指事物，说话人知道具体指的是什么，至于对话人知道与否与我们讨论的有指无指无关，这也是有指无指区别于有定无定的一个重要方面；

（三）说话人具有使用该语言成分指称一个特定对象的意图。

语用学意义上的有指成分必须符合上面三个条件。只满足一个或两个条件而没有满足所有三个条件，都是语用学意义上的无指成分。要详细说明两者的区别，最好从语用无指成分的五大类别讲起。

1) 类指或者说通指（generic）用法

类指用法指的是名词所表示的是物种的某个类别，不是特定的个体事物。前面的句（4）是一个例子。我同时要说明的是，类指是一个较复杂的概念，专门研究类指的著作非常多。类指用法也可以说有有指的属性。它虽然不指称任何特定个体，但指称一个特定的类，从非严格意义上来说也是有指，具有一定程度的双重属性。将类指用法的词语看作为无指成分，很大程度上是因循语言哲学研究的惯例，从单纯语言学的角度来看，比如从有关词语的表现形式以及回指用法等语法特点上来看，类指用法和有指用法有时并无很大区别。

2) 属性（qualitative）用法

这类无指用法一般指的是用作定语、表语等成分的一些名词性成分，如"冰箱修理厂"中的"冰箱"、"老王去年提拔为船长"中的"船长"等，表示的是有关属性，不是特定的个体事物。如"船长"指的是身份、官衔、职务，不是具体哪条船的船长，因此这些名词是无指用法。

3) 惯用语（idiomatic）用法

如"上大学""吃馆子"等说法中的名词性成分。

4) 非特指（non-specific）用法

这类无指用法又包含好几个小类，其中主要有上面讲的"Jenny 想嫁给一位语言学家"那种用法，是所谓模糊语境（opaque context）造成的有指无指两种可能解释中的一种；还有如"班上每位同学都学一门外语"中的"一门外语"，大家可能学的是同一门外语，也可能小张学的是英语，小李学的是法语，小王学的是德语，在后一种情况下，"一门外语"显然不是用来指称哪门特定的外语（narrow-scope nonspecific）；另外还有英国语言学家 John Lyons（1977：189）指出的一种情况，"一位朋友刚刚给我送了一张漂亮的情人节贺卡"中的"一位朋友"无疑符合上面所列出的有指成分的第一个条件，因为这个人存在于语境之中，但发话人说的可能是一位特定的朋友，也可能不知道他是谁，后一种情况下，这个非特指用法的名词性成分是无指成分。

5）非指向性（non-ostensive）用法

这种用法的例子如"我是从一位医生那儿听来的""有个小偷来过"等句子中的名词性成分，说话人可能想到的是一位特定的人物，但在这儿他只是提过而已，无意将注意力"指向"该人。

对照有指用法的三项标准，上面的前三类用法一项都不符合，第四类用法有些符合第一条标准，但不符合第二和第三条标准；第五类有些可能符合第一和第二条标准，但不符合第三条标准。我们由此得出的推论是，语言成分的语用有指无指可以说是一个程度问题，一条标准都不符合的用法，无指性最强，符合一条标准的用法，其无指性又要强于符合两条标准的用法。

语言学家研究语义和语用问题，最后的工作大都要落实到语言形式上来，观察种种语义和语用特点在语言形式上，包括词汇、词法和语法形式上是如何体现出来的。用 Chen（2009）提出的方法剖析语用学意义上的有指无指用法，可以更清楚地描写和解释语言意义和语言形式两者之间的关系。

在能否可以有回指成分以及可以有什么样的回指成分这个问题上，语用有指和无指程度的强弱展现出明显的区别。语用无指性很强的用法，如属性用法和惯用语用法，不能用回指成分对该名词性成分进行回指，因为语境中不存在一个可以回指的特定事物。相反，对于语用无指性很弱的用法来说，如某些非特指和非指向性用法的无指成分，后面可以用代词、指示词、名词等形式对它进行回指，许多情况下同语用有指成分没有什么区别。

到目前为止，还没有发现哪种语言从语言表现形式上全面地区分语用有指用法与无指用法的区别，也就是说，两种用法的语言表现形式往往是相同的，这在上面英语和汉语的例子中也体现了出来。但是，语言学家也发现，西班牙语、俄语、土耳其语等语言里，有些语用有指和语用无指用法有相应的语言形式区别。需要强调指出的是，这种语言形式区别，只限于语用无指性最强的用法，无指性相对较弱的用法即使是在这些语言中也同有指性用法没有什么区别。

语用有指用法和语用无指用法的区别，在汉语语言形式方面没有全面的体现，但是，汉语中这样一个倾向性的规律，语用无指性很强的用法大多数以光杆名词的形式出现，"老王去年提拔为船长"不会说成"老王去年提拔为一位船长"；其他属性用法也是这样，汉语表语成分一般是光杆名词，比如"他是老师，我是工人"，受到西化的影响，现在常常说成"他是一位老师，我是一位工人"，我听起来往往觉得有些别扭，我们读传统白话文作品如《红楼梦》等很少碰到这样的说法。

4. 话语分析的角度

从话语分析的角度研究指称现象，主要涉及三个方面：一是词语的形式；二是该形式表现的同指称有关的意义；三是发话人在话语环境中使用有关词语的目的。上面讨论语用无指用法的时候，五类中最后一类非指向性用法已经涉及发话人使用有关词语的目的。从话语分析的角度研究指称问题，指称词语的使用目的是最重要的考虑方面之一。

我先举两个英语例子：

(7) I walked out of the café, and bumped into *a boy on bike.*

(8) I walked out of the café, and bumped into *this boy on bike.*

这两句句子的意思差不多，都是"我走出咖啡厅，撞到一个骑自行车的男孩"。句（7）的宾语是个带不定冠词的名词短语"a boy on bike"，句（8）的宾语换成另外一种表现形式"this boy on bike"，句（8）的用法较新，应该不会超过五十年，至少在书面英语中首次出现的时间不会早于 20 世纪 60 年代。宾语所指对象"骑自行车的男孩"在语境中第一次出现，是个无定成分。这两个句子的区别单句情况下看不出来，要联系上下文才行。在大多数用句（7）宾语形式的情况下，说话人可能接着说这个男孩如何如何，也有可能再也不提这个孩子，说其他事情去了；而用句（8）宾语形式时，绝大多数情况下说话人后面会接着谈论这个男孩。这两个例子说明，一个首次出现的事物，在说话人话语组织中重要性如何，可能会反映在它的语言表现形式上面。从话语分析的角度研究指称问题，主要就是考察指称成分在话语中的重要性与其表现形式的关系。

说话人在实际话语活动中使用指称成分要达到的目的是什么？主要可以分为两种，一种是用它提到的所指事物，在话语组织中所起功能仅仅是提供背景信息，如时间、地点、方式等，或者所用的只是语用学意义上的无指成分，用来补足有关语义信息或语法位置；另一种目的是先将表述对象引进话语组织，接着以之为主要话题对它做详细的描写和说明。这两种目的说明，指称成分所代表的所指对象，在话语组织中的重要性可以有很大的不同。确定有关事物在话语组织中的重要性有什么客观判断标准呢？话语分析领域里最常见的做法就是统计它在后续话语里的出现次数，出现次数越多，重要性越强。这种做法用的是拙劲，虽然看上去比较简单，但一是操作性很强，二是从道理上来讲也还是非常合理的。

从话语分析的角度观察指称问题，我的研究重点是指称词语的形式、语法位置同所指对象在话语组织中的重要性三者之间的关系，所涉及的许多是汉语语法研究中讨论多年的问题。话语分析文献中也常用"主题性"（thematicity）这个概念代表话语组织中出现事物的重要性。我在今天介绍的研究中将其分为四级，分别是弱（后续话语中出现次数为 0—3）、中（4—9）、强（10—19）和超强（20+）。为了便于理解，我今天将"弱"这一级简化了，还可以把它细分为后续话语中出现次数为 0 以及 1—3，详情可参见 Chen（2009）。我研究的指称形式是两种，一种是"一＋量词＋NP"，另一种是光杆名词，语法位置是主语、宾语、"有"字句宾语、方位结构以及其他句法成分。我的统计语料全部来自《中国寓言故事》（远方出版社 1999 年版），文体偏向通俗易懂的口语风格。统计数据分别在下面六个表中列出。

首先看表2，展示的是首次由两类名词性成分引进话语的有关事物的主题性特征。

表2 "一+量词+NP" vs. 光杆名词

主题性	"一"+量词+NP	光杆名词	总数
弱	74（22%）（45%）	263（78%）（91%）	337（100%）（74%）
中	24（52%）（14%）	22（48%）（8%）	46（100%）（10%）
强	23（92%）（14%）	2（8%）（1%）	25（100%）（6%）
超强	45（100%）（27%）	0（0%）（0%）	45（100%）（10%）
总计	166（37%）（100%）	287（63%）（100%）	453（100%）（100%）

（$\chi^2 = 146$，df=2，$p < 0.001$）

表2显示，从事物主题性强弱的角度看，主题性弱的事物78%首次以光杆名词的形式出现，22%首次以"一+量词+NP"的形式出现。呈鲜明对比的是，主题性超强的事物一共有45个，首次出现全部用"一+量词+NP"的形式，主题性强的23个事物中，只有一个以光杆名词的形式引进语境。从词语形式的角度看，首次以光杆名词形式出现的事物，91%要么一次都没有重提，要么重提不超过三次。首次以光杆名词出现而主题性强的事物只有两个，占总数1%，可以算是例外；而以"一+量词+NP"的形式首次出现的事物，从主题性强弱分布上来看则比较均匀。文献中有观点认为，以"一+量词+NP"的形式引进语境的一般是主题性强的事物，从表2的数据来看，这种观点不能完全成立，因为45%引进的是主题性弱的成分。表2得出的总的结论是，首次以光杆名词形式出现的事物，一般来说是主题性弱的成分；两种语言形式相比，以"一+量词+NP"的形式引进的事物主题性较强，这两种语言形式在主题性上的区别具有统计学上的意义。

接着看表3，展示的是首次以两种语言形式在主语位置上引进的事物，在主题性上有什么特点。

表3 主语位置上的"一＋量词＋NP"vs. 光杆名词

主题性	"一"＋量词＋NP	光杆名词	总数
弱	8（18%） （27%）	37（82%） （82%）	45（100%） （61%）
中	64（46%） （21%）	7（54%） （16%）	13（100%） （18%）
强	6（86%） （21%）	1（14%） （2%）	7（100%） （9%）
超强 （20+）	9（100%） （31%）	0（0%） （0%）	9（100%） （12%）
总计	29（39%） （100%）	45（61%） （100%）	74（100%） （100%）

我们先从语言形式上观察，一共有45个光杆名词在主语位置上出现，有37个主题性弱，占82%；在主语位置上出现的光杆名词主题性超强的一个没有，主题性强的1个，主题性中的7个。我们是否能说主语位置上引进的事物主题性一般较强呢？如果词语形式是光杆名词，这种观点显然完全不能成立。再看"一＋量词＋NP"，一共有29个。这29个例子中，有8个主题性弱，6个中，6个强，9个超强，这说明首次在主语位置上出现的无定NP，在话题性强弱问题上没有明显的倾向性。此外，有些汉语语法论著说"一＋量词＋NP"一般不能做主语，表3的数据不支持这种观点。

表4对比主语和非主语位置上的"一＋量词＋NP"的主题性强弱。

表4 主语和非主语位置上的"一＋量词＋NP"

主题性	主语	非主语	总数
弱	8（11%） （27%）	66（89%） （50%）	74（100%） （46%）
中	6（27%） （21%）	16（73%） （12%）	22（100%） （13%）
强＋超强	15（23%） （52%）	51（77%） （38%）	66（100%） （41%）
总计	29（18%） （100%）	133（82%） （100%）	162（100%） （100%）

（$\chi^2 = 4.892$，df=2，p = 0.087）

表 4 展示无定 NP 在主语和非主语位置上引进事物的主题性强弱的对比。我们讨论表 3 时指出，出现在主语位置上的"一+量词+NP"，在主题性强弱方面没有明显的倾向性。表 4 显示，非主语位置上出现的"一+量词+NP"共有 133 个例子，66 个主题性很弱，占 50%，51 个主题性强或超强，占 38%。两种语法位置上出现的"一+量词+NP"在主题性上有一定差异，但这种差异严格说来没有统计学上的意义，这个结果也颠覆了我以前对这个问题的一些认识。

表 5 说明首次在宾语位置上以两种语言形式引进的事物在主题性方面的强弱。

表 5 宾语位置上的"一+量词+NP"vs.光杆名词

主题性	"一"+量词+NP	光杆名词	总数
弱	41（22%） （61%）	143（78%） （91%）	184（100%） （82%）
中	11（48%） （17%）	12（52%） （8%）	23（100%） （10%）
强	8（80%） （12%）	2（20%） （1%）	10（100%） （5%）
超强	7（100%） （10%）	0（0%） （0%）	7（100%） （3%）
总计	67（31%） （100%）	157（69%） （100%）	224（100%） （100%）

首次在宾语位置上出现的光杆名词一共有 157 例，91% 即 143 例主题性弱，12 例中，2 例强；"一+量词+NP"一共出现 67 例，61% 即 41 例主题性弱，主题性强或超强的有 15 例，占 22%。从主题性的角度来看，主题性弱的事物的 78% 以光杆名词的形式引进，22% 以"一+量词+NP"的形式引进。强和超强的事物共有 17 例，15 例以"一+量词+NP"的形式引进，占 88%，2 例以光杆名词的形式引进，占 12%。两种语言形式引进的事物在主题性上的差异是明显的。

下面两句是"有"字句的例子：

（9）有一个商人在外面做生意，赚了不少钱。

（10）有人专门拜访他，向他请教。

表6展示在"有"字句宾语位置上首次出现的两种语言形式主题性的强弱。

表6 "有"字句中的"一+量词+NP" vs. 光杆名词

主题性	"一"+量词+NP	光杆名词	总数
弱	14（50%） （25%）	14（50%） （100%）	28（100%） （41%）
中	5（100%） （9%）	0	5（100%） （7%）
强	8（100%） （15%）	0	8（100%） （12%）
超强	28（100%） （51%）	0	28（100%） （40%）
总计	55（80%） （100%）	14（20%） （100%）	69（100%） （100%）

表6显示，即使是在"有"字句中，由光杆名词首次引进的事物无一例外主题性都弱，这也符合大家的语感，"有人来了"，很可能后面就不会再提这个人了。以"一+量词+NP"的形式引进的事物共55例，有14例即25%主题性弱，5例中（9%），8例强（15%），28例超强，占51%。从这些数据来看，恐怕不能说"有"字句中"一+量词+NP"引进的一定是重要的事物，因为也有25%的例子引进的是主题性弱的成分。但另一方面，表6显示，主题性超强的事物在"有"字句中都是以"一+量词+NP"形式出现的，尽管这句话不能倒过来说。

表7对比"一+量词+NP"在"有"字句和其他句法位置上出现时主题性的强弱。

表 7　"有"字句和其他句法位置上出现的"一 + 量词 + NP"

主题性	"有"字句	其他句法位置	总数
弱	14（19%） （25%）	60（81%） （54%）	74（100%） （46%）
中	5（23%） （9%）	19（77%） （17%）	22（100%） （13%）
强 + 超强	36（55%） （66%）	32（45%） （29%）	66（100%） （41%）
总计	55（18%） （100%）	111（82%） （100%）	162（100%） （100%）

（$\chi^2 = 20.43$, df=2, $p < 0.001$）

表 7 显示，同样的"一 + 量词 + NP"形式，用"有"字句引进的事物，主题性要高于在其他句法位置上引进的成分。

最后，让我们来看首次在方位结构中 NP 的位置上引进话语的有关成分（如"主人将客人引到院子里散步"中的"院子"）的主题性强弱，结果请看表 8。

表 8　方位结构中的"一 + 量词 + NP" vs. 光杆名词

主题性	"一" + 量词 + NP	光杆名词	总数
弱	11（15%）	63（85%）	74（100%）
总计	11（15%） （100%）	63（85%） （100%）	74（100%） （100%）

结果非常清楚，首次在方位结构中引进话语的事物，绝大多数（85%）用光杆名词的形式，少数（15%）用"一 + 量词 + NP"的形式。无论用哪种形式，主题性都非常弱。

参考文献

陈　平，1987，释汉语中与名词性成分相关的四组概念，《中国语文》第 2 期。
陈　平，2012，话语分析与语义研究，《当代修辞学》第 4 期。
Chen, Ping. 2003. Indefinite determiner introducing definite referent: A special use of "*yi* 'one' + classifier" in Chinese. *Lingua* 113, 1169-1184.
Chen, Ping. 2004. Identifiability and definiteness in Chinese. *Linguistics* 42(6), 1129-1184.

Chen, Ping. 2009. Aspects of referentiality. *Journal of Pragmatics* 41, 1657-1674.

Chen, Ping. 2015. Referentiality and definiteness in Chinese. In: William S.Y.Wang and Chaofen Sun, eds., *The Oxford Handbook of Chinese Linguistics*. Oxford University Press, 404-413.

Donnellan, Keith S. 1966. Reference and definite descriptions. *Philosophical Review* 75, 281-394.

Frege, Gottlob. 1892. Über Sinn und Bedeutung. *Zeitschrift für Philosophie und philosophische Kritik*. Vol. 100, 25-50; (English translation) "On sense and reference", In: Zabeeh et al., eds., 1974, 117-140.

Fodor, Janet Dean and Ivan Sag. 1982. Referential and quantificational indefinites. *Linguistics and Philosophy* 5, 355-398.

Lyons, John. 1977. *Semantics*. Vols. I-II. Cambridge University Press.

Russell, Bertrand. 1905. On denoting. *Mind* 14; Reprinted in Zabeeh et al., eds., 1974, 141-158.

Russell, Bertrand. 1919. *Introduction to Mathematical Philosophy*. London: G. Allen & Unwin.

Seuren, Peter. 1998. *Western Linguistics—An Historical Introduction*. Blackwell Publishers.

Strawson, Peter F. 1950. On referring. *Mind* 59, 320-344; Reprinted in Zabeeh et al., eds., 1974, 159-192.

Zabeeh, Farhang, E. D. Klemke and Arthur Jacobson. eds. 1974. *Readings in Semantics*. Urbana: University of Illinois Press.

（本文为作者 2014 年 12 月在上海复旦大学所做 "光华人文杰出学者讲座" 第二讲的整理稿，原载《当代修辞学》2015 年第 3 期。）

汉语定指范畴和语法化问题

提　要　自然语义在语言中可以有各种各样的形式表现，是否构成特定的语法范畴则要看该语言是否具有强制性的专属语法表现手段。对于有定与无定来说，最典型的专属语法表现手段是英语中的冠词，判断其他语言是否具有定指范畴，一个惯用指标是该语言是否具有冠词那样的语法成分。定冠词一般由指示词演变而来，两者之间的最大区别，是后者具有前者没有的直指属性。不定冠词一般起源于数词"一"，后者演变成为前者的过程，就是数词的计量功能不断虚化以至于消失的过程。汉语指示词"这/那"是最接近定冠词的表示有定的语法表现手段，但同后者相比还保留了一定程度的直指属性，语法化程度还不够高。汉语"一"的语法化程度较高，在许多用法中几乎完全失去原生计量功能。汉语在定指问题上不同于英语和其他欧洲语言的一个显著特点，是名词性成分在可辨识性表现方面缺乏语法上的强制性。汉语有异于英语的另一个重要方面，是光杆名词和数量名词在可辨识性方面的不定性用法，其解读往往取决于名词性成分在句中的语法位置。作为一个语法范畴，定指/不定指在现代汉语中尚未得到充分发展。

关键词　语法范畴　有定　无定　指示词　直指　数词"一"　光杆名词　定指倾向性位置　无定倾向性位置

语言学文献中，"语法范畴"这个术语使用频率高，指涉面广，最普通的用法是指下面两类语言成分：

1. 具有相同语法属性的语言成分/单位的集合

2. 具有基本相同的语义基础及专属语法表现手段的语法属性的集合

第一种用法历史久远，传统语法著作中所见"语法范畴"这个术语，早先应用范围较窄，主要指词类，如名动形等，后来也指句子成分，如主谓宾等。现代语言学文献中，这个术语更多的时候是用来指第二类语言成分，常见的语法范畴包括数、性、格、时、体、肯定/否定、传信/传疑（evidentiality）等。我们今天讲的定指范畴指的是第二种意义上的语法范畴。

第二种意义上的语法范畴有什么特点呢？根据上面的定义，它具有基本相同的语义基础。比如说数，作为语法范畴，数的语义基础是自然数量，包括可数、不可数、单个、多个、一个、两个、三个等；性作为语法范畴，它的语义基础是自然性别，包括雄性、雌性和中性；格作为语法范畴，它的语义基础是名词性成分与其他语言成分之间的关系，如施事、受事、归属等。时、体、肯定/否定、传信/传疑等类此。共同语义基础是语法范畴的一个方面，另一个更重要的方面是专属语法表现手段，包括内部屈折、语缀、语法虚词、语序以及种种语法行为特征等。同一个语法范畴，各种语言所用的专属语法手段可以有很大的不同，这是早已广泛确认的事实。语言之间是否有共同的自然语义基础，则是一个历来争议不休的问题。许多语言学家都认为，世界语言有共同的自然语义基础，那正是不少语言普遍现象的起源之处。信奉 Sapir-Whorf 假说的语言学家则对此持有异议，认为不能先验地认为人类语言有共同的自然语义基础，随着对以前所知甚少的许多土著语言的深入研究，支持这种论点的证据似乎越来越多。这个话题不属我们今天讨论的内容，我们存而不论，为了方便起见，姑且以语言之间有基本相同的自然语义基础为假设作为我们讨论的前提。

专属语法表现手段是语言形式，语言形式表现的意义与自然语义基础有密切联系，但两者之间往往有很大的区别。虽然我们暂且认定种种自然语义属性在语言中普遍存在，但是，对特定的自然语义属性而言，并非所有语言都有相应的语法范畴，都具备专属语法表现手段。数量是普遍存在的自然语义属性，但不是所有语言都有"数"这个语法范畴。英语有"数"这个语法范畴，但我们可以说这个语法范畴在汉语中却不存在，在绝大多数情况下，汉语名词没有指示单复数的语法成分或其他语法表现。即使在具有"数"这个语法范畴的语言中，该语法范畴对于自然语义现象的切割归类方式也可以很不相同。英语有单复数的区别，books 是复数名词，复数语法标记 -s 表示大于一，从 books 这个词上无法看出是指两本、三本还是更多本书。然而有些语言则有分别表示单数、双数、三数或更多的独特语法手段。还要指出的是，语法范畴的归类，可以同自然语义归类相悖甚至相反。性的自然语义基础非常明显，可以清楚地分成雄性、雌性和中性三种。作为语法范畴的性，却可以与自然性别并不一致。德语中的"男人"der Mann 语法上是阳性，与阳性定冠词 der 连用，"女人"die Frau 是阴性，与阴性定冠词 die 连用，语法性和自然性相同。但是，"姑娘"das Mädchen 语法上却是中性，与中性定冠词 das 连用；将太阳和月亮拟人化时，我们一般会将太阳看成雄性，因为它光芒四射，有阳刚之美，而月亮则比较柔和，应该看成雌性，然而这两个事物在德语中的语法性别正好与我们的预期相反，太阳 die Sonne 是阴性名词，而月亮 der Mond 却是阳性名词，其中似乎并没有什么规律可循，外国人学德语碰到这些情况只能死记。个体量词是汉语中最典型的语法范畴之一。"条、头、枝、张、滴"等个体量词同自然语义有密切联系，通常表现物体最具代表性的形状或功能特征，但也有许多用法并无自然理据可言。我们说"一头猪""一条狗"和"一个人"，可是一般不说"一条猪""一头狗"或"一头人"，尽管猪狗形状差不了多少，狗和人也都有头。与其他语法范畴一样，汉语个体量词在语法上有一定的强制性，与数词连用的名词性成分一般都得带量词。

我们研究任何一个语法范畴，一是看它的共同语义基础是什么，二是看它的专属语法表现手段是什么，这两个主要问题就是研究语法范畴的基本出发点。至于研究顺序，可以从专属语法形式出发，研究它们的语法意义，也可以从自然语义出发，观察是否在我们研究的语言中有专属语法表现手段。无论研究顺序是什么，语法范畴的专属语法手段表现的语法意义同自然语义基础之间的关系，都是我们研究语法范畴时的重点关注内容。

研究作为语法范畴的定指／不定指，主要工作是确定它的自然语义基础、专属语法表现手段以及它们之间的关系。定指范畴的自然语义基础属于语言信息结构表现的内容，那语言信息结构表现的主要内容是什么呢？说话人决定说什么和怎么说的时候，除了要考虑自己说话的目的之外，一定得对受话人对于自己要讲的内容了解多少、是否是当前关注的对象、他们对有关内容有什么预期等做出自己的判断。用语言学的术语来说，就是对有关信息在对方脑海里的认知状态做出自己的判断，以便组织和调整自己的说话内容与方式。信息结构研究涉及的常用概念包括新信息、旧信息、已知、未知、激活状态、未激活状态、主题、焦点，等等。文献中对这些概念的定义形形色色，很少有两位研究者的用法会完全一致，内涵和外延彼此参差或相互交叉的情形相当常见，我们在阅读或使用这些术语时得十分仔细。信息结构是决定语句表现内容和形式的过程中十分重要的因素，以所谓新信息和旧信息为例，我们说的每一句话，从信息结构的角度来看，一般都得包含两部分的内容，一部分是旧信息，就是发话人认为受话人已经知道的内容，另一部分是新信息，是对方不知道的内容。发话人一般都是以旧信息带出新信息，就是以旧信息为出发点，在这个基础上再引进新的信息内容。定指/不定指也是信息结构的一部分，其涉及的关键因素是，就某个具体事物而言，发话人认为受话人对该事物知道多少，是否能够把它从其他同类事物中辨识出来，我们下面对此做详细讲解。

我们首先讨论术语问题。"定指/不定指"，或"有定/无定"，英文是 definite / indefinite。我们开头说到，语法范畴有两个主要方面，形式和意义。需要特别指出的是，definite / indefinite 这对术语在英语文献中，有时指形式，就是该范畴专用的语法手段；有时指意义，就是该语法手段所表现的语法意义。我们会发现，这对术语有时在同一页甚至是同一句中既用来指形式，又用来指意义。请看下面的例子：

(1) From a grammatical point of view, we may recognize three main kinds of singular <u>definite</u> referring expressions in English: (a) <u>definite</u> noun phrases, (b) proper names and (c) personal pronouns. (Lyons 1979: 179)

句(1)中，definite 出现了两次，第一次用在 singular definite referring expressions 这个短语中，指的是意义，但紧接着用在 definite noun phrases 这个短语中，指的是形式。不仔细分辨，很容易带来理解上的困难。

同数、性、格等语法范畴一样，世界语言有的有定指范畴，有的没有定指范畴，主要判断标准是语言中有没有表现有定无定的专属语法手段。如何判定有没有专属语法表现手段呢？一个行之有效的方法是首先研究具有典型定指范畴的那些语言，观察那些语言中的专属语法手段有哪些形式特点，它们表现什么样的语法意义，如何对自然语义进行切割、划界和归类。然后以此为基础，剖析我们要研究的语言，考察其中有没有表现类似语法意义的专属语法手段，它们的语法意义是什么，同相关的自然语义现象是什么关系。

英语有定指语法范畴，专属语法表现手段包括定冠词、不定冠词、弱化 some、零形式（又称"bare NP"，光杆名词），等等。其中定冠词 the 和不定冠词 a(n) 是最典型的语法表现手段。Chesterman(1991：4)下面这段话简明扼要地道出了冠词在定指范畴研究中的重要性：

> It is via the articles that definiteness is quintessentially realized, and it is in analyses of the articles that the descriptive problems are most clearly manifested. Moreover, it is largely on the basis of the evidence of articles in article-language that definiteness has been proposed at all as a category in other languages.（定指最典型的表现方法是冠词，通过分析冠词，能最清晰地描述有关问题。此外，其他语言是否具有定指范畴，大都取决于能否证明这些语言具有冠词语言中的冠词那样的成分。）

要判断一种语言有没有像英语冠词那样的语法成分，并不是一件容易的事情。如前所述，与定指范畴相关联的自然语义特征可以说存在于所有语言之中，各种语言中也往往会有表现相关语义特征的语法手段，关键问题是如何判定具体语言中的有关表现手段是否具有英语冠词的典型特征，从而回答该语言是否有表现有定/无定的专属语法成分，最终回答该语言是否具有定指语法范畴。要回答这些问题，我们首先要做的是研究英语冠词具有哪些语法特点，冠词同其他相关的语法表现手段有哪些异同，它们的语法意义是什么，与相关的自然语义基础有哪些联系等一系列的问题。

下面，我们先分析英语中冠词的语法意义，然后研究汉语中是否具有类似的语法表现手段，考察与定指范畴相关的语法意义在汉语中的形式表现特点。

我们首先研究定冠词 the。在 the 赋予名词性成分什么样的语法意义这个问题上，我们在相关文献中能读到好几种不同的观点。哲学家如 Russell（1905）、Strawson（1950）等人认为 the 主要是表示"独一无二"（uniqueness），Jespersen（1949）等语法学家提出主要是表示"熟悉"（familiarity），就是发话人认为受话人应该熟悉该名词性成分所指称的事物，Hawkins（1978）主张定冠词的主要作用是引进某个事物，让受话人在双方共有的知识范围中找出该事物，同时将所有符合名词性成分描写属性的指称对象整体包括在内。我本人则赞同 Lambrecht（1994）等人的观点，认为"可辨识性"（identifiability）是 the 和其他定指语法表现手段的主要语法意义。

什么叫可辨识？它是一种认知属性。发话人认为受话人可以将某个事物从同类的事物中辨识出来，它就具有"可辨识"这个认知属性，否则就是不可辨识。举两个例子：

（2）a. 老王花许多钱买了<u>这部手机</u>。

　　b. 老王花许多钱买了<u>一部手机</u>。

什么情况下我们会说 2（a），什么情况下我们会说 2（b）？世界上有无数手机，我如果判定你们应该知道我说的是哪部手机，因为我现在将它举在手里，我就用 2（a）；我如果判定你们不知道我说的是哪部手机，我就用 2（b）。前一种情况下，手机具有可辨识性，所以我采用了定指语法手段，就是指示词"这"；后一种情况下，我判定你们不知道我说的是哪部手机，手机不具有可辨识性，我就采用了无定语法手段"一"。

"可辨识性"这个概念具有两个特点：第一，它本质上是一个语用学的概念，离开实际语境，离开上下文，谈不上是否具备可辨识性。第二，它是个基于受众（addressee-oriented）的概念，是从受话人角度出发的一个认知概念，也就是说，是否具有可辨识性，是发话人对于受话人是否具有将它从同类事物辨认出来这个认知能力所做的一个判断，与发话人自己能否将它辨认出来没有直接关系。采用2（a）定指形式时，言语双方都知道说的是哪部手机。但是，用2（b）无定形式时，也许我自己并不知道老王买的是什么手机，但也有可能我知道得很清楚，这部手机现在就在我口袋里。但我判定，对受话人来说，你没有辨识我说的是哪部手机的认知能力，所以我就采用无定语法手段。在这方面，有定无定同有指无指有根本的不同。有指和无指是从发话人的角度出发（speaker-oriented）的概念，发话人如果用名词性成分指称自己认知领域里某个具体事物，它就是有指成分，否则是无指成分。

我们接着要探究的是"可辨识性"这个概念的认知属性。发话人根据什么来判定某个事物对于受话人来说具有可辨识性，或是不具有可辨识性。也就是说，可辨识性这个概念的认知基础是什么？

事物主要可以通过下面四种方式获得可辨识性。

第一种方式最简单，就是所谓的物理同现。比如我说"这部手机"，英语可以说 this phone 或 the phone，大家都知道我说的是哪部手机，因为咱们大家现在都位于同一物理空间，都在同一间教室，我认定大家都能看见我手里举着的这部手机，这个事物由此获得可辨识性。今天的演讲有全程录音，如果以后有人听今天演讲的录音，那他不会知道我说的到底是哪部手机，物理同现的条件没有满足，可辨识性的认知基础也就不复存在。

第二种是语篇同现。我们先看句（3）和句（4），两句句子的意思是一样的：

(3) There is a dog and a cat in my backyard. The dog loves to chase the cat.

(4) 我家后院有一条狗和一只猫。那条狗老是喜欢追那只猫。

两句句子中，dog 和 cat 以及"狗"和"猫"在第一分句中首次出现，在第二分句中用定指形式回指。在座的并没有去过我家，所以我知道大家没有见过我养的狗和猫，因此第一次提到的时候将它们作为不可辨识的事物对待。第二次提到的时候它们都以可辨识事物的身份出现，与定指形式 the 和"那"连用。听到第二分句时大家还是没有见到我家的狗和猫，但是都知道我说的不是随便哪条狗哪只猫，而是我在第一句话中提到的那条狗和那只猫，这种情况下，可辨识性的认知基础建筑在语篇同现之上。

第三种是共有背景知识。孩子回家了，一进门，开口第一句话就是句（5）或句（6）：

（5）Where is the dog?

（6）狗呢？

显而易见，这种情况下物理同现和语篇同现的条件都未能满足，但发话人还是将狗作为可辨识性事物看待。这种情况下可辨识性的认知基础是什么呢？是共有背景知识。发话人和受话人都知道家里有一条狗，虽然不在视线之中，说话之前谁也没有提过这条狗，但发话人完全可以认定受话人知道说的是哪条狗。由共有背景知识带来的可辨识性，是最常见也是最复杂的一种情况。我们再看句（7）和句（8）：

（7）David bought an old car yesterday. The horn didn't work.

（8）戴维昨天买了辆旧车，喇叭不响。

"喇叭"也是第一次出现，既不是物理同现，也不是语篇同现，但发话人还是把它作为可辨识事物处理，用定指形式指称。原因是前面提到一辆旧车，我们都知道汽车都有喇叭。说喇叭不响，受话人应该知道这儿说的是一个特定的喇叭，就是戴维昨天买的那辆旧车的喇叭，可辨识性的认知基础建筑在我们的共有背景知识之上，就是汽车都有喇叭。再看句（9）和句（10）：

（9）David bought a used car yesterday, but the seller later claimed that he did not get the money from David.

（10）戴维昨天买了辆旧车，但卖主后来声称他没从戴维那儿拿到钱。

除了"喇叭"以外，"卖主"和"钱"虽然是第一次出现，但都作为可辨识事物对待，用的是定冠词。受话人明白，发话人这时指的不是随便哪个卖主，而是那部旧车的卖主，钱是卖旧车的钱。为什么发话人认定受话人一定知道说的是什么呢？因为在我们的知识系统中，在我们的共有背景知识中，买卖至少涉及四个主要事物：买主、卖主、交易物和钱。只要提到买卖，这四个事物便在受话人脑子里得到激活（activated），从而获得可辨识性。语义上紧密相连的概念在人们的认知中集群聚合、集群激活的思想在心理学、语言学、人工智能研究领域中由来已久，大家提出很多理论概念来概括这类现象，如 frame、script、scenario、schema、file、domain 等，其定义和所指大同小异。

Nature（《自然》）2016 年 4 月 28 日刊登了美国加州大学伯克利分校研究人员在相关领域里的最新研究成果（Huth et al. 2016）。他们利用核磁共振（MRI）技术，探究种种语义概念在大脑里的储存部位、联结状态与激活方式。他们让七位受试人听两个小时的故事，用核磁共振仪实时观察大脑中 60000—80000 个绿豆大小的部位，记录它们对总共 985 个词语概念的反应。主要发现包括：(a) 不同词语概念激活大脑的不同部位，也就是说，词语代表的概念定点于大脑的不同部位；(b) 我们学心理语言学时都学过，人脑里有两个区位专职处理同语言有关的信息，Broca 区和 Wernicke 区，这两个区位一般都在人的大脑左侧。Huth 等人的研究发现，词语概念的分布遍及整个大脑，包括左右两侧；(c) 意义密切相关的词语概念定位于大脑中相连的部位，如家庭、妻子、母亲、怀孕等词语概念在大脑的所在部位紧密相连，而且同样的概念在七位受试人大脑里的所在部位基本相同；(d) 同一个词语因为其多义性可以位于大脑的不同部位。*Nature* 发表的这项研究报告，颠覆了某些传统观念，也为以前提出的 frame、script、scenario、schema、file、domain 等理论概念提供了客观的实验证据。

Huth 等（2016）研究项目中的七位受试人，都在西方社会成长和接受教育，就一般日常生活经验来说，可以认为他们具有大致相同的共有背景知识。共有背景知识实际上可广可窄，可深可浅，发话人往往必须根据具体受话对象做必要的调整，否则就会造成交流上的障碍。我相信我们都有这样的经验，读其他专业领域里的论文，有时每个字、每个词都认识，但就是不知道整个篇章段落说的是什么意思。主要原因之一是基本概念不明，因此往往无法理解词语之间的逻辑关系，明明是文章中第一次出现的事物，作者却把它们作为可辨识事物对待。缺乏必要的背景知识，缺乏对有关概念之间关系的基本了解，我们就很难读懂文章的内容。不难想象，如果对汽车缺乏最基本的知识，根本不知道汽车会有喇叭，要看懂句（7）和句（8）是有一定困难的。把"旧车"换成"房子"，这两句句子谁也看不明白。如何处理共有背景知识，也是研制人工智能系统工作中最具挑战性的领域之一。

　　第四种是所谓自含式定指。虽然第一次出现，没有物理共现，没有语篇同现，也不属于严格意义上的共有背景知识，但是名词性成分自身带有一个较长的限制性定语，因为这个定语包含大量对受话人来说是已知的信息，凭借这些已知信息，受话人能够将该定语中心词所指事物从同类事物中辨识出来，如例（11）和（12）：

　　（11）Do you know the man that she went to dinner with last night?
　　（12）你认识昨晚同她一起吃晚饭的那个男人吗？

"那个男人"第一次出现，但通过自含定语成分"昨晚同她一起吃晚饭的"获得唯一性，也就是可辨识性，因此可以定指成分的形式出现。相比其他三种情况，自含式定指的出现频率不是很高。

　　未能满足上面所说任何一项条件的事物，发话人一般将之作为不可辨识事物对待，在语言形式上表现为无定成分，英语中最典型的方法是加不定冠词 a(n)。英语中有定无定是截然分明的两类语法表现形式，对于所有名词性成分来说，有定无定是一种强制性的分别，不是表现为有定形式，就是表现为无定形式，两者必居其一。这样的强制性归类也是语法范畴的重要定义标准之一，如前面讲到的英语的数范畴、德语的性范畴和汉语的量词范畴都是对名词性成分做强制归类。但是，从意义上来看，可辨识性和不可辨识性之间有一个程度问题。我们知道，无论是英语还是汉语，无定名词做主语都会受到一定限制，一句话能不能说，有时得由整个句子的及物性特征决定。例如，"一个小孩很聪明"，这句话一般不这么说，但是"一个小孩慌慌张张地冲了进来"，这句话就完全可以说。这个问题还有另外一个观察角度：无定名词主语句是否可以说，同主语的可辨识性强弱也有关系。从例（13）可以看得很清楚，其他句子成分保持不变，主语所表示的事物可辨识性越强，该句可接受度就越高（例句引自 Prince 1981：246）：

（13）a. A friend of mine bought a Toyota.

b. A friend of Steve's bought a Toyota.

c. A friend of my neighbor bought a Toyota.

d. A friend of a guy I know bought a Toyota.

e. ?A friend of a guy's bought a Toyota.

句 13（a）能说。虽然主语以无定形式出现，但从语义上来看，这个名词性成分的可辨识性程度相对较高。为什么呢？因为它的定语"我的"可辨识性很强，句 13（b）—（d）也可以说，但可接受度随着主语可辨识性减弱而逐渐降低，到了例 13（e），定语成分和中心词的可辨识性都很弱，大多数人认为这句话不能说。

讨论了有定无定这个语法范畴的语义基础，我们接着研究该语法范畴的形式表现特征。我们先观察英语中的情况。

英语有定成分主要有三种表现形式：专有名词、人称代词以及定指名词（definite NPs）。定指名词的专属语法成分主要是定冠词 the、指示词 this/that/these/those、物主代词以及全称量词。我们今天主要讨论定冠词和指示词。

世界语言中的定冠词绝大多数都是由指示词演变而来，或者说是经过语法化的过程演变而来。顾名思义，指示词的主要特点是"指示"，直指性（deixis）是它最重要的特征。而所谓直指性，就是其所指对象必须参照具体语境中的时间、地点、角度等条件才能确定，例如"我、你、他"，"这儿、那儿"，现在时、过去时、将来时，等等。"这部手机"，在座的都知道是哪部手机，我现在说"那部手机"，大家顺着我手指的方向也能知道我指的是哪部特定的手机。但是，听演讲录音的人脱离了现场的语境，就无法将这两个直指成分同两部具体的手机连接起来。英语定冠词与指示词最大的区别，是前者的语法意义是单纯地表示可辨识性，不具备指示词表示远近的直指属性。Greenberg（1978：61—

62)、Diessel（1999：128—129）等人指出，指示词语法化为定冠词的过程，就是其直指属性逐渐弱化以至于消失的过程，可以图示如下：

语法化前　　　　语法化中　　　　　语法化后
物理同现　　＞　语篇同现　　＞　共有背景知识/自含式定指

如前所述，可辨识性成分的认知基础主要可以分为四大类，分别是物理同现、语篇同现、共有背景知识以及自含式定指。英语定冠词与指示词在直指属性问题上的区别，突出地反映在它们可以与哪些可辨识性成分连用这个方面。

定冠词是定指范畴最典型的专属语法表现手段，所有四类可辨识性成分都能通过定冠词来表现它们的定指语法意义，例句前面已经给出。指示词主要表现物理同现，也可以表现语篇同现，例（14）是语篇同现的例子：

(14) George went out again without permission. I don't like that.

从某种意义上来讲，语篇同现往往可以看成是物理同现的心理延伸，只是具有程度不等的抽象性。因此，指示词用来指经由语篇同现的可辨识成分时，仍然可以保留一定程度的直指属性，由物理距离的远近转化为心理距离的远近，常常有对比意义。如句（14），说话人不喜欢George的做法，有意拉开距离，这种情况下一般都是用that。相反的情形请看句（15）：

(15) Thank you for your detailed post. This is much appreciated.

同样是回指同一语篇出现的事物，但说话人有意拉近与它的距离，用this就更得体。由例（14）和（15）可见，this/that用于语篇同现的可辨识事物时，仍然可以表现出较强的直指属性。从使用频率来看，语篇同现用得更多的还是定冠词。例（16）是有关文献中常常提到的两个例子：

(16) a. Beware of the dog.（当心狗。）
　　　b. Beware of that dog.（当心那条狗。）

两句中的"dog"都以定指形式出现，也就是说发话人判定受话人知道他说的是哪一条狗。但是，这两句话有一个重要区别：如果那条狗位于受话人视线之内，两句都可以说；但是，如果狗不在受话人视线之内而属于双方的共有背景知识，只能说16（a），不能说16（b）。这说明指示词一般来说不能用于源自共有背景知识的可辨识性事物，至少在比较正式的文体中不能用，另见例（17）、（18）和（19）：

(17) Be quiet. *Don't wake up that baby (who is sleeping in the next room).

(18) *That sun was covered by dark clouds.

(19) They bought a used car. *These/those tires are all worn out.

正式文体中，指示词也不能用于自含式可辨识成分，见句（20）：

(20) *Do you know that man that she went to dinner with last night?

句（17）、（18）与（19）中名词性成分的可辨识性源自共有背景知识，句（20）是自含式定指。指示词不能用于这些场合的原因是，它们的直指属性与这两类可辨识性成分的认知基础互不相容。

不可辨识事物在英语中最重要的专属语法表现形式是不定冠词a(n)。大多数语言中的不定冠词都起源于数词"一"。数词"一"演变为不定冠词的语法化过程，就是它的计量意义不断虚化的过程，Givón（1981）、Heine（1997）等人将这个过程分成五个阶段，现转述如下。

第一阶段，它是个数词，主要功能是计量，见例（21）：

(21) I need an hour.

这句是说我需要一个小时，不是两个、三个小时，句中的 an 可以用数词 one 取代。

第二阶段，它的主要用法是表示某个事物的存现，典型场合是所谓的存现句，如例（22）：

(22) A guy came up the front stairway.

这种情况下 a 的计量用法开始弱化了，翻译类似（22）这样的句子有时甚至不必将计量的意思表现出来，译成"有人从前面的楼梯走了上来"

就行了。

第三阶段，该词用于无定有指成分，指称一个对于发话人来说是特定的事物，但是发话人认为受话人不知道是哪个特定事物，也就是说对受话人来说是不可辨识事物，如例（23）：

（23）He bought a house last year.

说这句话的时候，我判定你们不知道他买的是哪座房子，但我自己知道，这就是无定有指用法。

第四阶段，用于无定无指事物，如例（24）：

（24）He wants to buy a house in this area; any house will do.

他想在这个区买座房子，什么房子都行。

如果说前面四个阶段，该词还或多或少地保留了计量的意思，到了第五阶段，它就完全虚化为一个单纯的语法标记了，名词性成分可以不指任何个体而只是表示类别或是有关属性，如例（25）：

（25）He is a good chef.

例（25）的表语名词前加不定冠词，完全是由于英语有定／无定语法范畴的强制性要求，同计量没有什么关系，翻译成汉语不必译出。欧化汉语也有类似句（25）这样的用法，如"我是一个厨子，他是一个工人"，这儿的"一"跟数字"一"没有什么关系，把它去掉，丝毫不影响句子的意思。

语法化过程除了语义虚化，往往还伴随语音弱化和词法自主性弱化，这在英语定冠词和不定冠词身上表现得十分清楚。定冠词 the 除特殊情况以外从不重读，而指示词 this/that/these/those 则常常重读；指示词可以用作形容词，后接名词，也可以单独用作代词，而定冠词不能单用。不定冠词也是同样情况，a 是 an 的弱化形式，而 an 又是 one 的弱化形式，弱化程度最高的 a 最常用。one 可以单用，a(an) 同 the 一样，完全失去了词法自主性，不能单用。所有这些特征都表明，英语定冠词 the 和不定冠词 a(n) 都是语法化程度非常高的专属语法成分。

世界上许多语言没有英语冠词这样语法化程度非常高的专属语法成分，在这些语言中，可辨识／不可辨识事物有无专门的语法表现手段，这些形式手段有哪些特点，有没有正处于语法化过程之中的指示词和数词，如果有，它们处于什么样的演变阶段——这些问题都是过去几十年间语言学界重点研究的问题。我们现在探讨这些问题在汉语中的情况。

陈平（1987）将汉语同指称问题相关的语法表现手段从词语形式出发归纳为七类：

  A. 人称代词
  B. 专有名词
  C. "这/那"+（量词）+（NP）

  D. 光杆名词
  E. 数词 + 量词 + NP

  F. "一"+（量词）+ NP
  G. 量词 + NP

七类形式分为三组，在有定无定方面各有特点。第一组是 A、B 和 C，这组特点是三组语法形式都表示可辨识事物，我们称之为定指（definite）形式；第三组是 F 和 G，都表示不可辨识事物，我们称之为无定（indefinite）形式。这两组成分指代的事物，在可辨识和不可辨识这个属性的解读方面一般说来是固定的。第二组是 D 和 E，与其他两组不同，在所指事物可辨识与不可辨识这个问题上，D 和 E 这两种语言形式本身没有固定的解读，我们称之为不定（indeterminate）形式。就语言形式来说，英语、法语及日耳曼和拉丁语族的其他语言也有 D 和 E 这两种形式，与这些欧洲语言相比，汉语在 D 和 E 的语法功能和可辨识/不可辨识的解读方面表现出自己的特点。下面我们分别研究这三组形式的有关特点。

  与其他语言中的人称代词和专有名词相比较，第一组中的 A 和 B 在有定无定方面没有什么特别值得注意的地方。一般情况下，发话人选用这两种语言形式时，都是指称某个他认为受话人非常熟悉的事物。汉语没有英语定冠词那样的语法成分，与定冠词最接近的语言形式就是第一组中的 C，即指示词"这/那"。我们研究汉语"这/那"在有定无定方面的特点，主要侧重两个相互之间有密切联系的问题：首先是判断"这/那"是否在向定冠词方向演变，它们的语法化程度如何，然后是比较这两个指示词语法化程度的高低，其中涉及的关键因数是这两个指示词的直指属性。

我们上面谈到，事物可辨识性的来源归为四大类，分别是物理同现、篇章话语同现、共有背景知识和自含式结构。现在，我们考察"这/那"与四类可辨识事物的连用情况。

源自物理同现的可辨识事物，汉语可以用"这/那"，前面已经举了几个例子。"这/那"也可以用于语篇同现，如例（26）：

（26）一个小孩子……路中的时候呢，碰到了一个女孩子，这个时候，<u>这个小孩子</u>又看了<u>那个女孩子</u>，看了一眼。

"这个小孩子"指第一次出现的小孩子，"那个女孩子"指他碰到的那个女孩子，"这"和"那"的用法有对比的意思，"这"指心理距离较近的成分，"那"指较远的成分，同例（14）和（15）中 this/that 的用法有相似之处。再看例（27）：

（27）在通向城里的一条大路旁，长着一棵大树。<u>这棵树</u>的树干上有一个很大的洞。一天，一个打鱼的人进城卖鱼……<u>这位渔夫</u>急忙跑到<u>那棵有大树洞的树</u>下躲雨，……一天，<u>那位往树洞里放鱼的渔夫</u>又经过这里。

例（27）中，用"这"回指刚刚引进话语的某个事物，如"这棵树""这位渔夫"。后面隔了一段距离再次回指时，用"那"不用"这"，反映出有关事物在语篇中距离的远近。例（26）和（27）说明，"这"和"那"在用于语篇共现时仍然可以保留较强的直指属性。但是，汉语指示词也可以用在没有什么远近对比意义的语篇同现场合，如例（28）：

（28）有一个猎人养着一只狗。<u>这只狗</u>很懂事。

用"那"取代句（28）中的"这"，整个句子也很自然，选用"这"还是"那"语义上没有什么区别，由此可见，这种场合中的"这/那"原生的直指属性已经相当弱化了。

经由共有背景知识而获得可辨识性的事物，可以用"这/那"指称，但仅限于高度口语化的非正式文体，如例（29）：

（29）他买了辆旧车，那轮胎都磨平了。

自含式可辨识成分，可以用"这/那"，如例（30），但通常也只是在非正式文体中出现：

（30）上个月来看你的那个人，我今天又见到他了。

例（28）、（29）和（30）中名词性成分表现的有关事物，其可辨识性的认知基础同直指属性没有什么关系，"这/那"可以作为定指形式与这些名词连用，虽然目前一般还是仅限于高度口语化的非正式文体，尤其是例（29）和（30）这样的用法，但我们都知道，语言演变基本上都是从口语开始的，书面语相对而言则比较保守。"这/那"在上面这些场合中不读原字字调而读轻声，这进一步说明这两个指示词，或者用更严谨的语言来说这两个词分化出来的同形语素，在某种程度上正处于语法化的过程之中，但离完全失去直指属性的 the 那样的定冠词还有很长的距离。

我们要问的另一个问题是，"这/那"这两个词哪个语法化程度更高，或者说哪个词的直指属性弱化程度更高？在这个问题上，语言学界意见不一。我的看法是"那"的语法化程度比"这"高，证据是什么呢？例（30）中这类自含式成分，其可辨识性源自同它连用的限定性定语成分，与直指属性没有什么关系，所用定指成分的语义内容相对来说比较单纯，就是指示某个发话人认为受话人应该可以辨识的事物，可以说是最接近定冠词 the 的一个用法。根据我们的统计，例（30）这种场合中，"那"的使用频率是"这"的十倍以上，详细讨论参见 Chen（2004：1155）。

我们接着分析第三组 F 和 G 这两个无定形式。F 形式中的量词可以省略，如例（31）：

（31）她去年交了一（个）男朋友，比她小两岁。

"一"后面个体量词省略，在今天的北京口语中是十分常见的现象。这种省略现象似乎出现时间并不很久,也就是最近几十年的事情,较早口语化程度很高的文学作品如老舍的《茶馆》中,这种现象一例未见。《茶馆》里"人还不如一只鸽子呢"及"一个乡下丫头,要二百银子"这样的话,现在北京人说起来,往往会省略"只"和"个",在青年人中间尤其如此。

G 形式"量词 + 名词"的例子见下:

(32)她去年交了<u>个男朋友</u>,比她小两岁。

例(32)的名词性成分"个男朋友",一般都作为"一个男朋友"的省略形式看待。

F 和 G 形式中"一"是数词,其本质功能是计量。我们现在要问的是,这个词在汉语中是否有计量意义虚化的用法?从下面的例句中可以看出,Givón 和 Heine 等人指出的数词"一"计量意义虚化的五个阶段性用法,汉语中全都可以看到,下面例(33)—(36)中的"一"分别是存现用法、有指无定、无指无定及类指:

(33)<u>一只小企鹅</u>摇摇摆摆走了上来。

(34)我昨天请<u>了个电工</u>查了一下线路。

(35)快去找<u>一辆车</u>,什么车都行。

(36)他说话就像<u>(一)个痞子</u>。

"一"从计量到表示有指无定、无指无定直到类指,就是初始计量功能不断虚化的过程,到最后如句(36)的用法,可以说已经同数字"一"没有一点关系了,主语可以换成复数,句子照样可以说,如:

(37)他们父子俩说话就像<u>(一)个痞子</u>。

从数词"一"计数功能虚化的角度来看,该词的语法化程度同英语不定冠词 a(n)已经可以说是不相上下,英语不定冠词的主要用法同样可以在汉语"一"身上看到。但是,无论是正处于语法化进程之中的定指形式"这/那",还是已经高度语法化的无定形式"一",同英语定冠词与不定冠词相比,两者之间有一个非常重要的区别:英语有定无定的区别具有语法上的强制性,也就是说,只要是名词短语,一定得与表现有定无定的语法成分(包括零形成分)连用,不是表示可辨识事物，就是表示不可辨识事物，执行这项功能最常用的语法成分，就是定冠词和不定冠词。在汉语中，可辨识与不可辨识在语法表现形式方面缺乏强制性，虽然"这/那"和"一"分别表现可辨识与不可辨识的事物，但并非所有的名词性成分都一定得明白标示它们的有定无定属性。有没有语法表现方面的强制性，是判断一个语言中有没有某个语法范畴的一个非常重要的标准，在这方面，汉语同英语的区别非常明显。

汉语在有定无定问题上有异于英语的另外一个重要方面，是上述七类中第二组的两种形式 D 和 E，即光杆名词和数量名词，在语法功能和语义解读上表现出来的特点。如前所述，我们将 D 和 E 称为不定形式，有别于第一组的有定形式和第三组的无定形式。英语也有光杆名词和数量名词，但都归为无定形式，表现不可辨识事物。而汉语以 D 和 E 形式出现的名词性成分，可以是可辨识事物，也可以是不可辨识事物，在实际语句中如何解读，很大程度上取决于该名词性成分在句子中的语法位置。

我们根据同有定无定相关的特征，将相关汉语句子成分分为两大类，一类是定指倾向性位置，另一类是无定倾向性位置：

　　a）定指倾向性位置

　　　　主语

　　　　"把"字句宾语

　　　　动词前宾语

　　　　双宾语结构中的近宾语

　　b）无定倾向性位置

　　　　"有"字句"有"后位置

　　　　存现句动词后位置

　　　　双宾语结构中的远宾语

多种话语分析统计结果显示，第一组（A、B、C）有定形式入句时，一般出现在定指倾向性位置上，而第三组（F、G）无定形式入句时，一般出现在无定倾向性位置上。相反的用法则受到很大限制，有的是不合语法，如例（38）及（39）：

(38)*我明天送<u>一瓶好酒</u>你。

(39)*? 后面跑来了<u>王小二</u>。

有的虽然可以说，但使用频率较低。无论使用频率是高是低，以第一组有定形式出现的名词性成分都作可辨识事物理解，以第三组无定形式出现的名词性成分都作不可辨识事物理解，不受它们句中语法位置的影响。

第二组不定形式 D 和 E 有着与第一组和第三组完全不同的特点。首先，就句中出现位置而言，同其他两组相比，它们所受限制较少，尤其是 D 光杆名词，可以出现在绝大多数句法位置上；其次，以不定形式 D 和 E 出现的名词性成分在可辨识和不可辨识方面的解读，通常取决于它们在句子中的语法位置，在定指倾向性位置上出现，往往作可辨识事物理解，在无定倾向性位置上出现，往往作不可辨识事物理解。"客人来了"和"来客人了"的区别，早已成了汉语语法的基本常识。

在有定无定的解读方面，不定形式 D 和 E 有另外两个特点值得我们注意。首先，作有定理解的光杆名词和数量名词涵盖了前面讨论的所有四大类可辨识事物——物理同现、语篇同现、共有背景知识及自含成分，分别见例（40）、（41）、（42）及（43）：

(40) 小心，别把<u>孩子/两个孩子</u>吵醒了。

(41) 他养了一只猫和几条狗，<u>猫</u>又肥又大，<u>几条狗</u>却瘦得皮包骨。

(42) 我买了辆旧车，<u>轮胎/四只轮胎</u>都磨平了。

(43) 你认识刚才来的<u>学生/三个学生</u>吗？

其次，光杆名词和数量名词作有定还是无定理解，同它们在句中所处位置相关，必须指出的是，这只是在大多数情况下表现出来的一种倾向，有统计数据支持（参见 Chen 2009），但是，倾向毕竟不是说一不二的严整规律，请看例（44）和（45）：

(44) 丈夫找来了<u>几位泥瓦工</u>，<u>几位泥瓦工</u>用了一天时间把房顶修好了。

(45) <u>两个强盗</u>从这里走过，看到周围没有人，只有欧寄这么一个小孩子，就起了坏心……<u>两个强盗</u>把欧寄的双手反绑在……

词语形式完全相同的数量名词，在例（44）宾语位置上出现时作不可辨识事物理解，在主语位置上作可辨识事物理解，回指上句引进的成分。但在例（45）中，词语形式和句中位置完全相同，"两个强盗"第一次出现作不可辨识事物理解，但第二次出现就必须作可辨识事物理解。

甚至某些情况下我们说不清楚以光杆名词或数量名词出现的名词性成分到底是应该作可辨识还是不可辨识事物理解，请看例（46）和（47）。

(46) 昨晚炼油厂大火，<u>铁门</u>都烧化了。

(47) 小李的病很严重，<u>医院的三位心脏病专家</u>说得立刻动手术。

句（46）的"铁门"可以有不止一种理解：一是你我都知道炼油厂有铁门，或是有几扇铁门，这种情况下"铁门"指可辨识事物，它（们）烧化了；也有另外一种可能，你不知道炼油厂有几扇铁门，或是根本不知道炼油厂有没有铁门，我这句话的意思是说，大火温度高到连铁门都烧化了，这种情况下"铁门"指不可辨识事物。例（47）的情况与句（46）类似，有可能这个医院只有三位心脏病专家，他们都说得立刻动手术，这时该数量名词指的是可辨识事物；也有可能该医院有很多位心脏病专家，有三位说得立刻动手术，这种情况下，同样形式、同样位置上的名词性成分作不可辨识事物理解。自然语言的许多用法往往不是那么齐整，类似这样可作两可解读的情况随处可见。我们要正视和尊重语言事实，就得承认我们研究得出的语言规律往往同时带有很大的局限性。许多语法理论模式看上去的确很美，但要在涉及实证语言材料的细节上都经得起推敲还是有大量的工作待做。

下面是讨论的总结：

（a）定冠词一般由指示词演变而来。同英语定冠词 the 相比，汉语指示词"这/那"的语法化程度还不够高，直指意义还没有充分弱化。相比之下，"那"的语法化程度要高过"这"；

（b）不定冠词一般由数词"一"演变而来，汉语"一"语法化程度较高，在许多用法中几乎完全失去初始计量功能；

（c）汉语和英语的一个重要差异，是名词性成分在可辨识性表现方面缺乏语法上的强制性；

（d）汉语和英语的另一个重要差异，是汉语中光杆名词和数量名词在可辨识性方面的不定性用法，其解读往往取决于名词性成分在句中的语法位置；

（e）作为一个语法范畴，定指/不定指在现代汉语中尚未得到充分发展。

参考文献

陈　平，1987，释汉语中与名词性成分相关的四组概念，《中国语文》第2期。

Chen, Ping. 2004. Identifiability and definiteness in Chinese. *Linguistics* 42(6), 1129-1184.

Chen, Ping. 2009. Aspects of referentiality. *Journal of Pragmatics* 41, 1657-1674.

Chesterman, Andrew. 1991. *On Definiteness*. Cambridge University Press.

Diessel, Holger. 1999. *Demonstratives: Form, Function and Grammaticalization*. Amsterdam: John Benjamins.

Givón, Talmy. 1981. On the development of the numeral "one" as an indefinite marker. *Folia Linguistica Historica* 2(1), 35-53.

Greenberg, Joseph. 1978. How does a language acquire gender markers? In: Greenberg, Joseph H., ed., *Universals of Human Language: Vol. III: Word Structure*, Stanford University Press, 47-82.

Hawkins, John. 1978. *Definiteness and Indefiniteness: A Study in Reference and Grammaticality Prediction*. London: Croom Helm.

Heine, Bernd. 1997. *Cognitive Foundations of Grammar*. Oxford University Press.

Huth, Alexander G. et al. 2016. Natural speech reveals the semantic maps that tile human cerebral cortex. *Nature* 532, 453-458.

Jespersen, Otto. 1949. *A Modern English Grammar on Historical Principles*. London: Allen and Unwin.

Lambrecht, Knud. 1994. *Information Structure and Sentence Form: A Theory of Topic, Focus, and the Mental Representation of Discourse Referents*. Cambridge University Press.

Lyons, John. 1977. *Semantics*. Vols. I-II. Cambridge University Press.

Prince, Ellen F. 1981. Toward a taxonomy of given-new information. In: Cole, Peter, ed., *Radical Pragmatics*. New York: Academic Press, 223-255.

Russell, Bertrand. 1905. On denoting. *Mind* 14; Reprinted in Zabeeh et al., eds., 1974, 141-158.

Strawson, Peter F. 1950. On referring. *Mind* 59, 320-344; Reprinted in Zabeeh et al., eds., 1974, 159-192.

Zabeeh, Farhang, E. D. Klemke and Arthur Jacobson. eds. 1974. *Readings in Semantics*. University of Illinois Press.

（本文原载《当代修辞学》2016年第4期。）

汉语零形回指的话语分析

提　要　汉语话语结构特征对于零形回指的使用起着重要的制约作用。所指对象在话语中具有强烈的连续性，是回指时以零形式出现的必要条件。连续性有微观和宏观之分。微观连续性取决于先行词和回指对象在各自句子中的地位，宏观连续性取决于先行词和回指对象各自所在的句子在话语组织中的关系。本文为衡量所指对象微观连续性和宏观连续性的强弱设定了具体的评判标准。
关键词　零形回指　话语结构　先行词　宏观连续性　微观连续性

1. 引言

　　话语中提到某个事物之后，再要论及该事物时，一般使用各种回指（anaphoric）形式，同上文取得照应。汉语中的回指形式共分三大类：零形回指（zero anaphora）[①]、代词性回指（pronominal anaphora）以及名词性回指（nominal anaphora）。请看下面的例句：

　　　　（1）唐明德$_i$惊慌地往外跑，ϕ$_i$撞到一个大汉$_j$的身上。他$_i$看清了那人$_j$的眉眼，ϕ$_i$认出那人$_j$是谁。

第二小句和第四小句句首的主语 ϕ，以及第三小句的主语"他"回指第一小句中的"唐明德"。第三小句和第四小句中的名词短语"那人"回指在第二小句中出现的"一个大汉"。为了便于下面展开讨论，我们首先明确区分四个不同的概念。它们是回指形式（anaphora）、回指对象（anaphor）、先行词（antecedent）以及所指对象（referent）。上面的例

---

　　① 很多著作中把同类现象称作为"省略"。限于篇幅，本文不讨论"零形回指"和"省略"这两个术语的异同。

句中，无实在语音表现的 φ、"他"以及"那人"，各自代表一种回指形式，我们分别称之为零形回指、代词性回指和名词性回指。这些回指形式在本句中指代的事物叫作回指对象。在上文中出现，与回指对象指称相同的事物叫作回指对象的先行词。[1] 比如，在例（1）中，第一小句的"唐明德"是后面的零形回指对象和代词回指对象的先行词。第二小句的"一个大汉"是后面的名词回指对象的先行词。这里所说的回指对象和先行词都是与其表现形式所在的句子联系在一起的，而所指对象这个概念则总指体现它们之间同一性关系（coreference）的那个事物。

本文结合话语组织，探讨汉语中零形回指的用法。至于代词性回指和名词性回指（合称非零形回指，下文用 P/N 代表），作者另有专文论及（参看 Chen 1987），本文从略。所依据的语料，几乎全部选自以书面语形式出现的叙述材料。有关汉语话语中句子的划界问题，作者另行讨论。本文中一般以标点符号为标记，把用逗号、句号、问号等断开的语段算作小句，在同一节话语中，用英文字母顺序标记各个小句的先后。

顺便指出，本文所做的是话语分析工作。[2] 语言学研究得到的结果，极少能表现为说一不二的"法则"。同句法分析相比，话语分析得来的结论，更是常常表现为一种倾向、一种规律性（regularity），而不是概括性很强、仅有少许例外的所谓规则（rule）。这是话语本身的性质使然，是不以我们的主观意志为转移的。

2. 零形回指的适用范围

与非零形回指不同，零形回指没有实在的词语表现形式可供我们辨

---

[1] 认真地分析起来，有严格意义上的同指，也有松散意义上的同指。请看下面的例句：
那只白瓷花瓶$_i$（a）没有摆稳，φ$_i$（b）掉在地上摔得粉碎，这下子谁也不想要 φ$_i$（c）了。
（b）中的零形回指对象同（a）中的先行词是严格意义上的同指，而（c）中的零形回指对象同先行词则是松散意义上的同指。这种区别涉及语言哲学上的一些问题，本文不拟深究。文中所引例子，一般都属于严格意义的同指。

[2] 有关话语分析方法的讨论，详见陈平（1987）。

认，因此，如何确定这种回指形式在具体场合中存在与否，如何判断回指对象的有关性质，成了我们必须首先解决的问题。简单地说，在这个问题上我们主要依靠全句的语义和语法格局。如果从意思上讲句子中有一个与上文中出现的某个事物指称相同的所指对象，但从语法格局上看该所指对象没有实在的词语表现形式，我们便认定此处用了零形指代。所谓词语形式上没有而意思上有的成分，在本文中一般限于下面两种情况：

（一）谓语动词的支配成分

（二）主谓谓语句、名词谓语句、形容词谓语句等非动词谓语句中的主语

先说第一种情况，动词与名词性成分之间可以发生种种语义和语法上的联系。从语义上来看，名词性成分可以直接参与动词所表示的动作、过程、状态、关系，表示相关的施事、受事、感受者等各种角色，也可以附着于动词，表示与后者相关的方式、时间、地点等背景信息。就具体动词而言，它同各种语义成分的关系有疏有密。为了动词意义上的完备，有些语义成分一般是不可缺少的，而有些则可有可无。以动词"跑"和"买"为例。"跑"一般要求带一个表示施事的名词性成分，而"买"则一般要求带分别表示施事和受事的两个名词性成分。这类语义成分如果在动词用作谓语时出缺，便会影响句子意义的完整。至于这两个动词在具体场合中是否随带表示时间、地点的语义成分，则一般关系不大。语言学文献中，通常把关系较密切、语义上不可或缺的名词性成分称为动词的参与成分（participant role），而把关系较疏远、语义上可有可无的称为附带成分（circumstantial role）。从语法关系上来看，动词直接支配一定数目的名词性成分。这些成分一般是参与成分，进入句子格局时做主语、直接宾语、间接宾语，等等。被直接支配的名词性成分的数目，决定了具体动词的价（valence）。在句子中，动词的语法支配成分和所带的各种语义成分如何配应，由动词本身的价、整个句子的格局以及使用情景确定（可参见吕叔湘 1982）。在动词谓语句中，本文中所说的零形指代只适用于作为句子中谓语动词的支配成分的所指对

象。请看下面的例子：

（2）拂晓，云雾濛濛的大树林子里，朱亚光_i不辨东南西北，ф_i跌跌撞撞地往前挣扎着。

(2b) 中，主语用零形回指，先行词是 (2a) 的主语。从意思上来看，(2b) 中动作发生的时间和地点，也都是从 (2a) 承接过来的。但是因为表现时间和地点的名词性成分在这里并非句中动词的支配成分，所以并不算作零形回指。

再说第二种情况，回指对象在语义上充任非动词谓语句的主语。请看下面的例句：

（3）厉秀芳_i自从城里回来后，ф_i整天心神不安。
（4）他还有个弟弟_i，ф_i当兵的。
（5）她_i丑，ф_i老，ф_i厉害。
（6）小田已经找到了合适的对象_i，ф_i在燕山公社。

在首句之后的小句中，非动词谓语的主语都由零形回指充任，先行词是上句的主语或者动词宾语。事实上，汉语中动词谓语句和非动词谓语句常常并列使用，两种类型的零形回指也常常相随出现。请看下面的例句：

（7）摊前过去个人_i，ф_i高身量，ф_i大眼睛，ф_i小胡黑子，ф_i提着两个点心匣子。
（8）那狗_i黄毛，ф_i黑眼圈，ф_i长身材，ф_i细高腿，ф_i特别地凶猛，ф_i要咬住人，ф_i不见点血腥味儿，ф_i决不撒嘴。

在句（7）和句（8）中，首句之后所有小句的主语都以零形回指的形式出现，有的带动词谓语，有的带非动词谓语。

3. 零形回指的使用条件：制约因素的多样性

零形回指的使用条件是什么？我们出于直觉、基于常理的回答是这样的：因为零形回指本身并没有任何实在的表现形式，所以，所指对象所在的语言环境和非语言环境必须能够提供足够的信息，保证受话人不至于对回指对象的身份感到费解或者产生误会，否则，发话人便违反了语言交际一要明确、二要经济的基本原则。但是，如果我们想要提高对于这个问题的认识，使它超越直觉和常理的水平，就必须比较准确地判定导致受话人对回指对象的身份做出正确判断的所有因素，条分缕析地研究这些因素各自的性质和评价标准，研究它们之间的相互关系。

我们生成和理解话语的生理-心理活动，包含着一系列极其复杂的判断和推理过程。在这些过程中，往往要调动储存在我们头脑里各个方面的语言信息和非语言信息。确认零形回指对象的先行词，涉及受话人对于相关词语和句子的各种词汇、语义、句法、语用知识，是多种因素交互作用的结果。如果想让计算机具备处理自然语言的功能，前提就是得将有关判断和推理过程的各个方面全部研究透彻。众所周知，在计算机自然语言处理中，回指形式的生成和理解是最难对付的几个问题之一。然而，如果我们不满足于把处理范围局限于单句，而是想跨入连贯话语的领域，我们又不得不正视摆在我们面前的这个难题。尤其是汉语话语中的零形指代，出现频率大大高过西文，语境中又缺乏丰富的形态标志，更需要我们从各个方面去努力探索。

要把缠绕一团的有关因素一一分解剖析，理出头绪，不是一件容易办到的事情。我们在研究具体的例子时，主要采取对比等手法，根据特定的语境判断在众多因素中起主要作用的因素。请看下面的句子：

（9）刘四爷$_i$就这么一个女儿$_j$，ϕ_j眼看是没有出嫁的希望了。（9b）中的零形回指对象是（9a）中刘四爷的独养女儿而不是刘四爷。做出这个判断的主要依据显然是句中动词"出嫁"与"刘四爷"在词汇意义上的不相容性。换个中性动词，脱离了上下文，第一小句中的两个名词都有做先行词的可能。对比（10）：

（10）刘四爷$_i$就这么一个女儿$_j$，$\phi_{i/j}$眼看是没有回来的希望了。

本文侧重研究的不是单个词语的词汇意义，而是所指对象所处的话语结构特征在确定所指对象、排除误解可能的过程中所起的作用。下面我们会看到，所谓话语结构特征，实质上凝结了话语作为交际工具的功能特征。只有结合连贯的话语，才能把握其主要性质，光是把眼光局限在单词单句的范围里是很难说明有关现象的。请看下面的例子：

（11）颜秀芳_i 从丈夫_j 手里接过儿子_k，ϕ_i 冷冷地说……

（12）她_i 上姑妈_j 家去找小芹_k，ϕ_i 打听老头子的消息。

（13）她_i 从手袋_j 里的名片夹_k 中取出一张名片_l，ϕ_i 递给了对方 ϕ_l。

如果只是从词汇意义的角度来看，以上三句句子中，（a）中出现的带直线的三个名词性成分都可以做（b）中带直线的零形回指对象的先行词。但是，显然没有人会如此任意地理解这三句句子。我们可以把句（10）拿来同这三句句子做一个对比。在这四句句子中，第一小句中的带直线的名词性成分与第二小句中的谓语在词汇意义上同样具有相容性，但是，（10b）中的零形回指对象可以有两种选择，而（11b）、（12b）、（13b）则只有一种选择。这就告诉我们，词汇意义之外的其他信息在这儿起了决定作用。

在词汇意义相容、其他条件大致相等的情况下，什么样的话语结构特征能使所指对象在回指时以零形式出现而不至于引起误解，这是我们试图在下面解答的问题。

4. 话语结构特征对于零形回指的制约作用

话语结构特征对于零形回指的制约作用主要体现在所指对象的连续性（continuity）上面。所谓连续性，指的是回指对象与其先行词彼此之间在话语中的联系。连续性的强弱则取决于所指对象在话语组织中所处的地位。这种地位主要表现在下面两个方面：

（一）话语中先行词与回指对象在各自句子中的地位

（二）话语中先行词所在的句子与回指对象所在的句子之间的关系

第一个方面决定了所指对象的微观连续性（micro continuity），第二个方面决定了所指对象的宏观连续性（macro continuity）。宏观连续性在话语层次上位于微观连续性之上，宏观连续性弱，微观连续性一定也弱；宏观连续性强，微观连续性则可强可弱。只有在宏观连续性和微观连续性两者俱强的情况下，才能断言所指对象具备很强的连续性。所指对象的连续性越强，回指时使用零形式的可能性就越大。下面我们分别讨论连续性的两个方面。

4.1 微观连续性

所指对象的微观连续性本身受两方面的因素制约，一是先行词的启后性，二是回指对象的承前性。启后性和承前性越强，所指对象的微观连续性也就越强。这种现象同话语内容的展开方式密切相关。话语组织的基本单位是句子。句子与句子首尾相连，前后呼应，构成话语的篇章段落。从信息构成的角度来看，一般可以把句子分成两大部分，一部分表现作为发话人和受话人双方都知道的已给信息（given information），以这一部分同上文相连。另一部分以第一部分为出发点，对它有所评述，一般包含受话人以前不知道的新信息（new information），以此将意欲传递的内容渐次展现。在语言学文献中，通常把第一部分称作为话题（topic），第二部分称作为评述（comment）。大多数句子中既有话题部分，也有评述部分。但是，也有一些句子只有评述部分，没有话题部分。请看下面的例句（T 代表话题，C 代表评述）：

（14）A：(T) 我 (C) 看见大兄弟了。
　　　B：(T) 他 (C) 在哪儿？
　　　A：(T) 他 (C) 在村西头的晒麦场上。
（15）A：(T) 姑父 (C) 哪儿去了？
　　　B：(T) φ (C) 里头躺着呢。
（16）(C) 来车了！

话语展开过程中起推进作用的评述部分，它们最常见的出发点一是上句的主题，二是上句评述部分中的某个新的信息成分。所谓新的信息成分，在这里有两层含义，或者是该成分以前没有提到过，这次以不定指的身份首次被引进话语，或者是该成分虽然是定指成分，但是在这个命题中出现却是受话人未曾想到的。以上句的主题或者评述部分中新的信息成分的身份出现的所指对象最容易成为下句的主题，因而启后性最为强烈。话语中的句子如果以上句的主题为本句的主题，我们称之为平行推进；如果以上句评述部分中某个新的信息成分为主题，我们称之为层继推进。请看下面的例句：

(17) 他$_i$擦车，ϕ_i打气，ϕ_i晒雨布，ϕ_i抹油。

(18) 机手$_i$停车以后，ϕ_i打开车门，ϕ_i跳下去，ϕ_i急步地奔到正翻腾着山洪的道沟岸边。

(19) 那个人$_i$也意识到跑不脱，ϕ_i只好扔掉麻袋，ϕ_i原地站住，ϕ_i同时战战兢兢地扭过脸来。

(17)(18)(19) 的展开方式图示如下：

$$T_1 + (C_1 \rightarrow C_2 \rightarrow C_3 \rightarrow C_4)$$

再看下面的例句：

(20) 他$_i$必定也看见了那些老弱的车夫$_j$，ϕ_j穿着薄薄的破衣$_k$，ϕ_k根本抵御不住冬日的风寒。

(21) 前面停了一辆没熄火的拖拉机$_i$，ϕ_i装满了西瓜$_j$，ϕ_j在阳光下透出翠绿的颜色。

(22) 上面有个干部模样的人$_i$，ϕ_i托着一个袖珍半导体收音机$_j$，ϕ_j正响着。

(20)(21)(22) 的展开方式图示如下：

$$\begin{array}{ccc} T_1 & + & C_1 \\ & & | \\ & T_2 & + & C_2 \\ & & & | \\ & & T_3 & + & C_3 \end{array}$$

在 (17)(18)(19) 中，(b)(c)(d) 三个小句子都承接 (a) 的主题，围绕同一个所指对象做平行铺述。(20)(21)(22) 则不同，(b) 和 (c) 分别以 (a) 和 (b) 的评述部分中的某个所指对象作为自己的主题，逐层相继，层层深入。这六句句子分别代表最常见的两类话语展开方式。①

　　联想到实际话语的组织过程，这种现象是不难解释的。一方面顺着上面已经确立的主题继续说下去，对于发话人与受话人双方来讲，无疑是一种自然省力的方式。另一方面，刚刚介绍给受话人的新的信息成分很容易成为对方注意的焦点，受话人一般预期接着会得到有关该成分的进一步叙述或者描写。因此发话人在选择评述部分的主题时，舍旧而就新，也是一种十分顺应对方心理的做法。从语法表现手段上来看，启后性最强的这两类所指对象，前一类通常以主语的身份出现，以有定形式居多，后一类一般以存现动词后的名词性成分或者普通及物动词后的宾语成分出现，以无定形式居多。请看下面的例句：

　　（23）楚世杰$_i$坐起来，ϕ$_i$发了阵子愣，ϕ$_i$才摆脱睡意。

　　（24）他$_i$想到这里，ϕ$_i$紧走几步，ϕ$_i$到了十字路口，ϕ$_i$一屁股坐下。

　　（25）村口上有一个扶着水平仪三脚架的工人$_j$，ϕ$_j$在观察着，远处还有个打小红旗的工人$_j$，ϕ$_j$跟他遥相呼应。

　　（26）来了一群作家$_j$，ϕ$_j$发动社员写诗歌。接着又来了一批画家$_j$，ϕ$_j$教给社员作画。

　　（27）欧有旺$_i$续了个离婚的"活人妻"$_j$，ϕ$_j$带过来一大车东西。

　　（28）他$_i$手里牵着一头灰毛驴$_j$，ϕ$_j$又瘦又小，ϕ$_j$湿淋淋的。

（23）和（24）中，后续句的主题是充任上句主语的名词性成分。（25）和（26）中，后续句的主题换成了上句存现动词后的名词性成分。与此相似的是（27）和（28），（a）的评述部分中以动词宾语身份引进的新的信息成分，成了后续句的主题。回指对象的先行词如果像这些句子中带线的名词性成分一样，在话语中具备一定的信息特征和语法特征，我们便据此断言它表现了强烈的启后性。

---

　　① 这儿讲的两种话语展开方式最早是 Henri Weil 于 1844 年概括出来的，常为后人所沿用，可参看 Sgall et al.（1986：58）。Daneš（1970）还在这两种方式的基础上做了一些引申，排出五种话语展开方式。

但是，话语信息结构同句法结构有时也有不一致的地方。因为具备强烈的启后性而常常成为后续句主题的所指对象，除了出现在上面讨论的三种句法位置上之外，还经常附属于占据这三种位置的其他名词性成分，以后者的定语成分的形式出现，尤为常见的是用作主语的定语成分。请看下面的例子：

(29)[祥子$_i$]的右肘很疼，ф$_i$半夜也没睡着。

显而易见，(b)的主语不是上句的"祥子的右肘"，而是其中的定语成分"祥子"。下面再给一些同类型的句子：

(30)[祥子$_i$]的心中很乱，ф$_i$末了听到太太说怕流血，ф$_i$似乎找到了一件可以安慰她的事。

(31)[祥子$_i$]的脸通红，ф$_i$手哆嗦着。

(32)[大家$_i$]的眼跟着祥子，ф$_i$腿也想动，ф$_i$都搭讪着走出来。

(33)[文博士和唐先生$_i$]的名片递上去，ф$_i$还没有等到传见，车又开了。

(34)门儿先推开一道缝，伸进一张[女人$_i$]的圆脸，ф$_i$看看屋里没旁人，ф$_i$才把整个身子移了进来。

这种格局的句子不少可将主语中的定语标志"的"除去，把句子改造成标准的主谓谓语句。请看下面的例子：

(29)'祥子$_i$右肘很疼，ф$_i$半夜也没睡着。

(30)'祥子$_i$心中很乱，ф$_i$末了听到太太说怕流血，ф$_i$似乎找到了一件可以安慰她的事。

(31)'祥子$_i$脸通红，ф$_i$手哆嗦着。

这样一来，首句便含有平常所说的一大一小两个主语。上面的三句句子中，大主语做了后续句的主题。我们也常常碰到小主语做后续句主题的例子。请看下面的句子：

(35)乔连科$_i$爸爸$_j$是剃头的，ф$_j$勒着裤腰带过日子，ф$_j$攒几个钱供养乔连科上学念书。

(36)他$_i$右臂$_j$受过重伤，ф$_j$至今都有点儿往内弯曲。

(37)这种树$_i$树叶子$_j$很小，ф$_j$呈卵圆形，ф$_j$冬天也不凋落。

如果词汇意义相容，而上下文又没有提供其他可资辨析的信息，这种格式的句子有造成歧义的可能。请看下面的句子：

（38）小王$_i$父亲$_j$生病，ϕ$_i$/$_j$请假回家了。

孤立地看，大主语"小王"和小主语"父亲"都有做（b）中零形回指对象的先行词的可能。

不具备以上所说特征的名词性成分，其启后性相对较弱，同启后性较强的成分相比，使用零形回指的可能性相对较小。但是，这并不意味着这类成分一定不能用零形回指。启后性强弱程度不等的名词性成分如果同时出现在后续句中，发话人在选择回指形式时，逻辑上有下面四种可能（P/N=代词或名词）：

（一）[NP$_i$ 强 ......NP$_j$ 弱]...[ϕ$_i$ ......ϕ$_j$]

（二）[NP$_i$ 强 ......NP$_j$ 弱]...[P/N$_i$......P/N$_j$]

（三）[NP$_i$ 强 ......NP$_j$ 弱]...[ϕ$_i$ ......P/N$_j$]

（四）[NP$_i$ 强 ......NP$_j$ 弱]...[P/N$_i$ ......ϕ$_j$]

从实际话语的出现频率上来看，（一）（二）（三）这三种格局最为常用，而最后一种格局则比较罕见。这种现象说明，一般只有在启后性相对较强的所指成分采用零形回指的前提下，启后性相对较弱的成分才有可能用零形回指。请看下面的例句：

（39）阎光$_i$一直把赵百万$_j$当成"死老虎"，ϕ$_i$既没喂过ϕ$_j$，ϕ$_i$也没打过ϕ$_j$。

（40）屠老二的儿子小五$_i$一边走一边摘刚红了圈的枣子$_j$吃，ϕ$_i$还往衣兜里装ϕ$_j$。

（41）支书$_i$笑眯眯地朝他$_j$打个手势，ϕ$_i$切断他$_j$的话。

（42）屠老二$_i$见赵百万$_j$那样急了眼，ϕ$_i$就挡住他$_j$，ϕ$_i$小声说……

（43）他$_i$睁大眼睛监视着欧有旺$_j$的一举一动，ϕ$_i$不给欧有旺$_j$空子钻。

（39）—（43）全都选自浩然的中篇小说《赵百万的人生片断》中

的十页。以第二种格式出现的句子不在本文讨论范围之内。在这十页中，如例句所示，两个回指对象与其先行词在前后句中同时出现的句子共有17例。其中如同（39）和（40）那样用第一种格局的共有6例，如（41）（42）（43）那样用第三种格局的共有11例。采用第四种格局的则一例都没有发现。换句话说，如果后续句中只有一个零形回指，其先行词一般应该是上文中启后性较强的名词性成分。我们由此可以解释，在前面的（11）（12）（13）中，尽管首句中各有三个名词性成分与后续句谓语在词汇意义上完全相容，我们并没有因此而对后续句零形回指对象的身份感到费解。

除了先行词的启后性以外，所指对象的微观连续性还取决于回指对象的承前性。所谓承前性，是站在回指对象的角度上，观察它与前面先行词之间联系程度的疏密。在其他条件大致相同的情况下，承前性越强，微观连续性就越强。从语法表现手段上来分析，位于主语位置上的名词性成分一般承前性最强，位于动词宾语位置上的次之，位于其他位置上的又次之。联想到各种句法成分的话语功能，这种现象是不难理解的。主语通常是全句的主题所在，评述部分要依靠它才能与上文相连。因此，句子中包含的各种名词性成分中，一般只有同上文联系最为密切的才会被选拔到主语的位置上去。必要时，得同时对句子的格局做些适当的调整，如采用被动式，等等。根据 Chen（1984）所做的统计，在57例零形回指中，如果将所在句子中的有关参与成分按照句子的原型（prototype）式样组织起来的话[①]，零形回指对象在句子中做主语的有43例，占75.4%，做直接宾语的有11例，占19.3%，其他有3例，占5.3%。廖秋忠（1984）也得到相似的统计数字。

综上所述，所指对象在话语中的微观连续性取决于先行词的启后性与回指对象的承前性，这些性质都同话语的组织方式密切相关。从语法形式上来看，启后性强的所指对象大都表现为句子的主语，以及作为新

---

① 例如，带施事、受事和受惠三个参与成分的动词谓语句，在汉语中的原型是：
施事　V　受惠　受事
我　　送　小李　两本书

的信息介绍给受话人的存现动词后成分或动词宾语,而承前性强的所指对象一般表现为句子的主语。所指对象的启后性和承前性越是强烈,使用零形回指的可能性也就越大。

4.2 宏观连续性

上面谈到微观连续性强的所指对象回指时以零形式出现的可能性很大。这句话只有在所指对象于更高层次上的宏观连续性也很强的前提下才能成立。如果宏观连续性很弱,一般不能使用零形回指,相关研究可参看 Givón(1983)、Li & Thompson(1979)、van Dijk(1985)等。

本文中所说的所指对象的宏观连续性取决于先行词所在的句子与回指对象所在的句子两者在话语结构中的联系。这种联系表现在两个方面,一是句子与句子之间的线性顺序,二是句子与句子之间的层次关系。

我们先来说线性顺序。先行词和回指对象各自所在的句子前后邻接时,宏观连续性相对较强;中间插入其他句子时,宏观连续性相对较弱。请看下面的例句:

(44)天赐$_i$被赶脚的搀上去,驴$_j$一动,他$_i$趴下了身。

(45)虎妞$_i$服下去神符,陈二奶奶$_j$与"童儿"$_k$吃过了东西,虎妞$_i$还是翻滚的闹。

(46)大太太$_i$撩袍拖带的浑身找钱,φ$_i$预备着代付客人$_j$的车资;客人$_j$让了两句,大太太$_i$仿佛要拼命似的喊……

插入的成分越长,结构越复杂,对所指对象的连续性所造成的削弱作用就越大。由于人脑短期记忆容量的限制,与靠近先行词的回指成分相比,同先行词相隔较远的回指成分一般需要更为明白的表现形式,以弥补由于阻隔而造成的信息衰减。在(44)(45)(46)中,假如用零形回指取代所有现用的回指形式,就会给读者带来理解上的困难,甚至会导致误解。

接下来说层次关系。句子与句子之间的层次关系可以分成两种,一种是句法结构中的层次关系，另一种是语义结构中的层次关系。我们常常观察到这种情况：先行词与回指对象各自所在的句子，从线性顺序上看，中间隔着其他句子，但是，从层次关系上来看，插入句同前后有关句子不属于同一个层次。在这种情况下，虽然插入成分对所指对象的宏观连续性也有影响，但是与位于同一层次的插入成分相比，它所造成的削弱作用要轻微一些，回指对象往往仍然可以以零形式出现。请看下面的例子：

（47）王亦东$_i$推了自行车进了门，ϕ_i瞧见李贵在刷油漆，他的老伴儿$_j$陪在一旁给打扇子，ϕ_i真是从心里羡慕。

（48）田云$_i$知道，小刚$_j$这一去，ϕ_j三年五载是回不来的，ϕ_i不禁心中一阵发酸。

（49）涂大妈$_i$见二女儿$_j$说完这句话，ϕ_j转身走了，ϕ_i只好冲着背后骂一声……

在上面三个例子中，先行词所在的首句与回指对象所在的末句从线性顺序的角度来看隔着其他句子，但是只要分析这些句子的句法结构就可以发现，起间隔作用的句子是最前面的小句中某个动词的支配成分，与先行词和回指对象各自所在的小句不属同一个层次。

句法关系只能解释句子与句子在较低的话语组织平面上的联系，单纯利用这种关系很难说明一个较长的话语段落所包含的所有句子之间的联系。比这种关系更具普遍意义的是句子与句子在话语的语义结构中的关系。对于汉语这样缺乏丰富的形态标志的语言来讲，语言单位在语义结构中的相互关系是左右许多语法现象的重要因素。只有分析先行词和回指对象所在的句子在话语语义结构中的联系，才能比较全面和准确地把握所指对象的宏观连续性，从而完整地说明话语结构对零形回指的制约作用。

我们先来看下面的八个句段：

（50）他刚把车拉到窗下，虎妞从里头出来了。

（51）曹宅饭食不苦，而且决不给下人臭东西吃。

（52）假若祥子想不起孔圣人是什么模样，那就必应当像曹先生，不管孔圣人愿意不愿意。

（53）小刘参加了春节马拉松赛跑，今天累得起不了床。

（54）老者吃完自己的份儿，把杯中的酒喝干，等着小马儿吃净了包子。

（55）他的跑法可不好看：高个子，他塌不下腰去，腰和背似乎是块整的木板。（老舍《骆驼祥子》）

（56）一个队员倒挂金钩将球打入网内，吐一口痰罚五毛钱。

（57）他外出总带着保镖，花棚里到处都是萝卜味儿。

（50）至（55）的意思，我们都能看明白。（50）至（52）三段中，带点的词语明示了句群里各个小句之间的语义关系。（53）至（55）三段中虽然找不到类似的词语，我们凭借有关知识，还是可以推断出各个小句之间的语义联系。但是，（56）和（57）则使我们感到莫名其妙，尽管我们理解各个小句的意思。造成这种现象的原因有两条：（一）我们读到相邻的两句句子，一般不会把它们视为语义上毫不相关的两个单位，而总是要根据句子的意思、当时的环境等，尽力判断它们之间的联系；（二）有关这种性质的句间关系，我们头脑里储存着一定数量的固定模式，这是我们语言知识中很重要的一个组成部分，同我们获得的有关大千世界的各种非语言知识有着千丝万缕的联系。看到一连串在线性顺序上前后相连的句子，我们总是试图将句间关系同固定模式中的某一个配应起来。自然语言中也总是有一些词语，专门用于指示这种关系，如（50）至（52）三句中带点的成分。即使句中没有这类专职词语，我们也总会根据上下文提供的有关信息，结合我们各方面的知识揣摩分析，将句间关系套入某个模式之中。有些句子之所以看上去费解或者不通，原因之一是我们无法将任何一个体现句间关系的固定模式安在这些句子上面。

上面所讲的固定模式，我们把它们称作语式（schema）。话语语义结构的最小组织单位是命题，一般表现为句子。所谓语式，正是体现了句子与句子在语义结构中的最基本的组织方式。下面我们扼要讨论语式的几个特点。

（一）可以把语式看作为高次谓词（higher-order predicate），带各种小句做论元（argument）；如同低次谓词，如动词，有"价"的限制，各种语式对所带小句的数量、性质、相互关系（等立或主从）、前后顺序等常常也有一定要求。

（二）除了小句以外，语式还可以带其他语式做论元。这个特点决定了话语的语义结构同句法结构一样，具有递归（recursive）的性质。也就是说，整段话语，实质上是由各种语式由低到高、逐层相合构筑而成的语义结合体，同一种语式可以在不同层次上反复出现。透过句子在话语表面的线性序列，我们可以看到其内部隐藏着一个语义层次结构。在这个结构组织中位于较高层次的语式与语式的联结之处，在言谈中一般表现为时间较长的停顿，在篇章中则表现为各个章节段落的起讫。

（三）上面说过，这些抽象性质的语式在数量上是有限的。不过，在具体数量和关系等问题上，大家没有比较一致的意见（参看Chen 1986；Grimes 1975；Longacre 1983；Mann & Thompson 1983, 1985）。下面给出的一些最常见的语式，只是取来作为例子，没有穷举的意思。

    顺连——所带论元无数量限制，但按时间先后排列的前后顺序不能颠倒。

    罗列——所带论元无数量限制，前后顺序可以颠倒。

    对比—— 一般带两个论元，有前后顺序的限制。

    交替——所带论元无数量限制，前后顺序可以颠倒。

上面四种语式所带论元之间是等立关系。请看下面的例子：

（58）他停下来，把一篓篓水果通通搬到车上，然后走了。

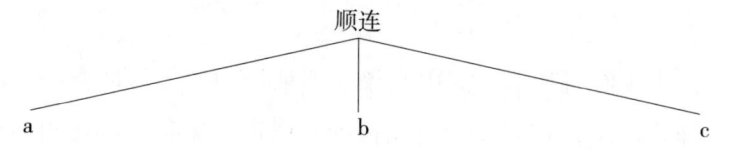

```
              顺连
         /     |     \
        a      b      c
```

（59）他一口气冲到对方门前，并不立即起脚射门，而是将球拨给了后面接上来的左锋。

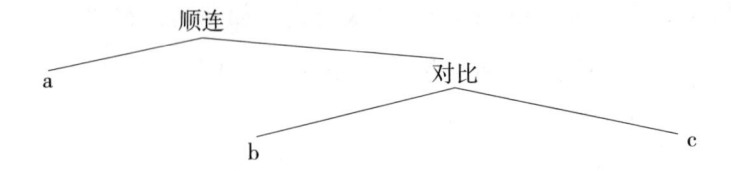

```
        顺连
       /    \
      a      对比
            /    \
           b      c
```

背景——带一主一从两个论元,从部在前,主部在后。
因果——带一主一从两个论元,从部在前,主部在后
让步——带一主一从两个论元,从部在前,主部在后。
条件——带一主一从两个论元,从部在前,主部在后。
说明——带一主一从两个论元,主部在前,从部在后。

上面五种语式所带论元之间是主从关系。话语中有明确标示语式内容的专职词语时,主部和从部的前后顺序相对要自由一些。请看下面的例子:

(60) 因拉惯了车,祥子很有些辨别方向的能力。

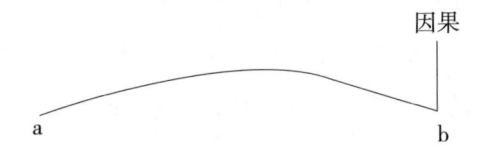

```
           因果
          /    \
         a      b
```

(61) 汗还没有完全落下去,他急忙地穿上衣服,跑了出来。他怕大家看他的赤身。

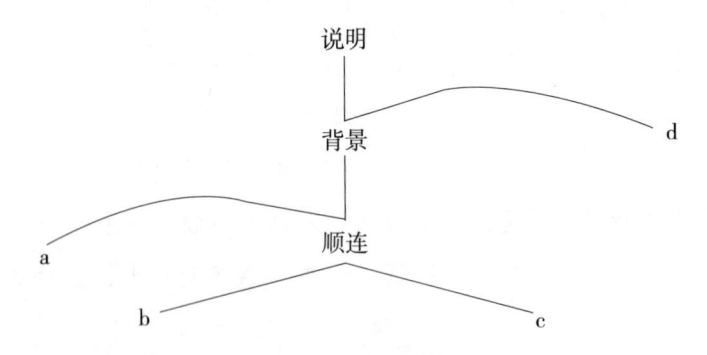

```
              说明
             /    \
          背景      d
         /    \
        a      顺连
              /    \
             b      c
```

现在,让我们回到本文的中心议题即话语中的零形回指上来。借助语式这个理论概念,我们在分析先行词和回指对象各自所在的句子在话语中的关系时便有了一个参照系统,由此可以比较准确地判定所指对象

的宏观连续性，从而说明零形回指使用中的制约因素。①

如上所述，言谈篇章中所有的小句都是通过高高低低各个层次上的语式彼此发生联系而组织成为一个语义结构体的。连接先行词所在小句和回指对象所在小句的语式在这个语义结构体中所处层次越低，所指对象的宏观连续性越强。随着所处层次的升高，宏观连续性随之减弱。请看下面的例子：

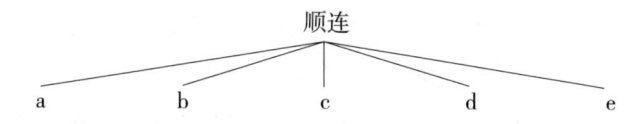

（62）他_i冲到干沟子跟前，ф_i闸住车子，ф_i翻身跳下，ф_i急转身，ф_i伸出两只带有茧子的大手……

```
         顺连
    ┌──┬──┼──┬──┐
    a  b  c  d  e
```

---

① 汉语话语中有一种反指（cataphoric reference）现象，也可以借助语式这个概念加以说明。本文所举例子中，零形回指的先行词都要到上文中去寻找。但是，在下面的句子里，零形回指对象的身份要从下文中探求：
（1）ф_i把虎妞的话从头到尾想了一遍，他_i觉得像掉在这个陷阱里。
（2）ф_i灭了灯，ф_i把头完全盖在被子里，他_i想就这么睡去。
（3）ф_i因为来自乡间，他_i敢挨近牲口们。
（4）ф_i在买上自己的车以前，祥子_i拉过人和厂的车。
（5）ф_i能在天亮的时候赶到，ф_i把骆驼出了手，他_i可以一进城就买上一辆车。
这种反指现象在汉语话语中十分常见。但是，同零形回指相比，零形反指受到更大的限制。零形反指对象所在的句子在话语结构上一定得从属同指成分所在的句子。我们以（1）（3）（5）为例，分析它们的语义结构：

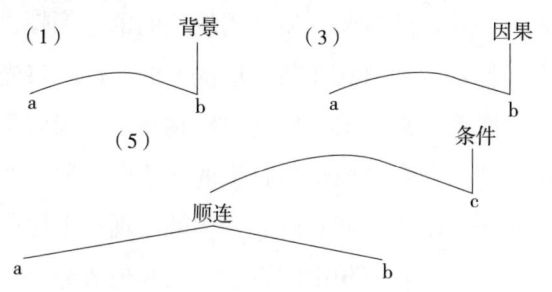

```
(1)      背景           (3)      因果
    ┌─────┐                ┌─────┐
    a     b                a     b
         (5)                        条件
                                     │
                                     c
         顺连
    ┌─────────┐
    a         b
```

如果反指对象所在的句子与同指成分所在的句子在语式结构中是等立关系，或者是主从关系，反指对象则不能以零形式出现。试比较（6）（7）（8）三句句子：
（6）他_i不想打架，虽然ф_i不怕打架。（老舍《骆驼祥子》）
（7）虽然ф_i不怕打架，他_i不想打架。
（8）*ф_i不想打架，虽然他_i不怕打架。
这三句句子属于同一种语式，但在（6）和（8）中，主部在前，从部在后，在（7）中，从部在前，主部在后。从部主题可以用零形回指，如（6），也可以用零形反指，如（7），但主部主题则不可以用零形反指，如（8）。

（63）他ᵢ虽然认识这个人的面貌态度，ϕᵢ可是不敢上去招呼。

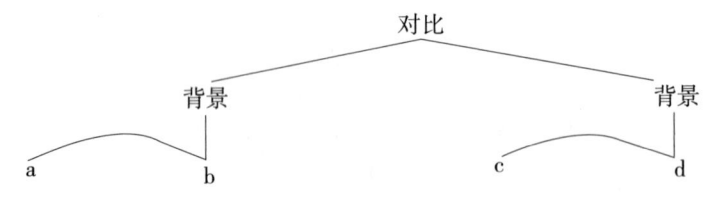

```
        让步
    ┌────┴────┐
    a         b
```

（64）祥子ᵢ找到了包月，ϕᵢ就去住宅门；ϕᵢ掉了事而又去拉散座，ϕᵢ便住在人和厂。

```
              对比
      ┌────────┴────────┐
     背景              背景
    ┌─┴─┐            ┌─┴─┐
    a   b            c   d
```

在（62）和（63）中，先行词和回指对象所在的小句位于同一层次上，直接受同一个语式的管辖。而在（64）中，回指对象所在的小句（c）同先行词所在的小句在语义结构的最底层分别隶属两个语式，只是升到第二个层次才由对比语式将它们联结起来。我们检查了约 40 万字的材料，对相关的例子进行了类似的语义结构分析，结果表明，零形回指对象所在的句子同先行词所在的句子在话语语义结构中相隔一般不超过三个层次。在一定长度的话语篇章中，即使所有小句的主题都由同一个所指对象充任，回指时也不太可能通篇都以零形式出现。话语的展开和深入，必然意味着将所有句子联为一体的语式层次渐次提高。为了便于受话人把握话语的语义组织，发话人到了一定的时候，便利用较长的语音停顿、标点符号、章节段落等语言手段标示各种语式在某一层次上的起讫。将先行词与回指对象各自所在的小句联系起来的语式所处层次越高，所指对象的宏观连续性就越弱。这说明为什么在章节段落里打头的句子中，回指对象很少使用零形式，即使它是句子的主语，而它的先行词就出现在上面段落的最后一句之中。虽然从线性顺序上看两句中间没有插入其他成分，但是从语义结构上看，两者在层次上相隔较远，所指对象的宏观连续性较低。

另一方面，我们也注意到这样的现象：先行词和回指对象所在的句子中间插进了其他句子，但回指对象还是以零形式出现。我们分析了这些句子的话语语义结构，发现它们一般都有以下两个特征：（一）插入句在语式里要么从属于先行词所在的句子，要么从属于回指对象所在的句子，它不能以等立的身份与这些句子同时成为某个语式的论元；（二）插入句本身的结构不能太复杂。请看下面的例子：

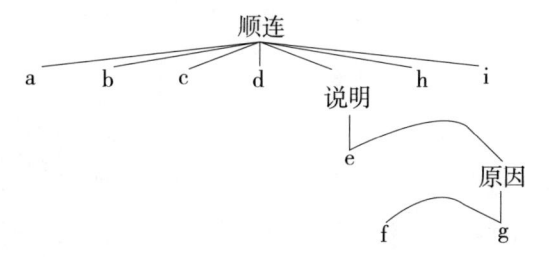

（65）张大嫂$_i$做菜，φ$_i$端茶，φ$_i$让客人，φ$_i$添汤，φ$_i$换筷子——老李$_j$吃高了兴，φ$_j$把筷子掉在地上两回——φ$_i$自己挑肥的吃，φ$_i$夸自己的手艺。（老舍《离婚》）

作为各个小句的主题，所指对象"张大嫂"一直贯通到小句（e），然后为（f）和（g）所打断，到（h）再续接起来。插入成分仿佛打了个岔，为（e）做了补充性的说明，（h）则又回到原来的主题上来。（f）和（g）前后两个破折号显然用于指示插入成分的性质，表明在语义结构中它同前面和后面的句子不是属于同一语式的等立成分。再看下面的句子：

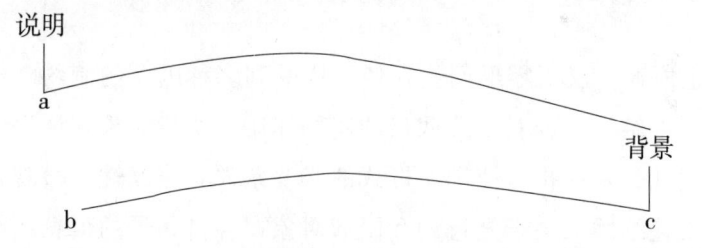

（66）娃娃$_i$老爱跟着她$_j$，φ$_j$走到哪，φ$_i$跟到哪。

回指对象所在的（c）同先行词所在的（a）中间隔着（b）。讲到（b）时，（a）的主题，即回指对象的先行词"娃娃"，并没有被忘记，而只是暂时被作为（b）中主题的另一个所指对象"她"压在下面，到了（c）才弹回（pop back）到表面。虽然语言结构具有递归的性质，但是，我们在语言的实际运用中处理这类递归结构的能力却受到记忆容量等因素的限制。插入成分在话语结构中的从属性质，减少了被压进（push down）的主题弹回时可能给受话人带来的理解上的困难。最后，让我们来分析下面这句句子（选自吕叔湘1986）：

（67）他ⱼ十分信服老队长ⱼ，ϕⱼ吩咐他ᵢ做什么，总是ϕᵢ话才出口，ϕᵢ拔腿就走。

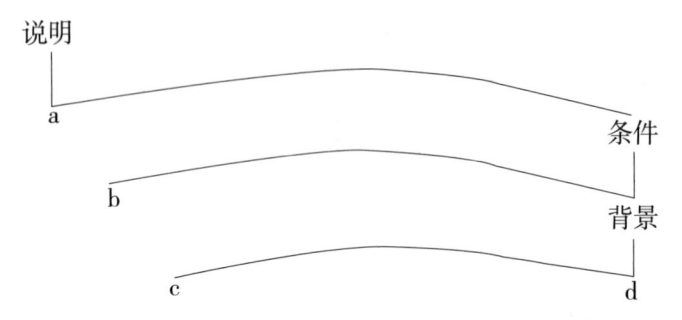

```
       说明
        ┌─────────────────────────┐
        a                         │ 条件
                                  │
            ┌─────────────────────┐
            b                     │ 背景
                                  │
                c                 d
```

（a）的主题为"他"，到了（b）和（c）为"老队长"所取代，到了（d）又成了句子的主题。从话语语义结构上来看，先行词所在小句和回指对象所在的小句中间隔着的成分都是从属成分，结构也比较简单，对所指对象的宏观连续性没有产生可观的削弱作用。如果所指对象被压进的层次较多，插入成分相当冗长复杂，回指时便不适宜以零形式出现。

5. 结论

综上所述，汉语零形回指在使用中受到多种因素的制约。本文侧重分析了话语结构特征对零形回指的制约作用。所指对象在话语中具有很强的连续性，是回指时使用零形式的必要条件。连续性有微观和宏观之分。微观连续性取决于先行词和回指对象在各自句子的信息组织中的地位，体现在先行词的启后性和回指对象的承前性上。先行词在两种情况下启后性最强，一是做主语，二是作为新的信息成分出现在存现动词后面或者做普通动词的宾语。回指对象做主语时承前性最强，做宾语时次之。先行词的启后性和回指对象的承前性越强，所指对象的微观连续性就越强。宏观连续性取决于先行词和回指对象各自所在的句子在话语组织中的关系。直接管辖这两个句子的语式在话语结构中所处层次越低，两句之间插入成分越少、越简单，所指对象的宏观连续性就越强。为了衡量所指对象连续性的强弱而设定的这些评判标准，都以话语的结构组织作为自己的基本出发点。在这些相关的语言特征身上，凝结着话语的交际功能特征。

在有关著作中，常常用"主题链"（topic chain）或者类似的概念来说明零形回指的用法。这类概念的有用之处是比较形象地体现了我们的直觉，使用起来相当方便。但是，也有两个缺点：（一）由于缺乏精细深入的分析，这类概念的内涵相当模糊，在有关主题链的本质、相关因素、适用范围等问题上，我们找不到明确的答案；（二）由于缺乏客观的评判标准，这类概念在运用时带有一定程度的任意性，有时会使人陷入循环论证。如果我们要为计算机理解和生成汉语话语篇章设计一个可行的模式，能够比较顺利地处理零形回指，那么，首先要解决的问题就是分解零形回指的各个制约因素，明确各个因素的性质和相互关系。本文的研究，就是这个工作的一个组成部分（Chen 1985），相关文献，可参看 Berwick（1983）、Mckeowan（1985）和 Sidner（1983）。

参考文献

陈　平，1987，话语分析说略，《语言教学与研究》第 3 期。
廖秋忠，1984，现代汉语中动词的支配成分的省略，《中国语文》第 4 期。
吕叔湘，1982，《中国文法要略》，北京：商务印书馆。
吕叔湘，1986，汉语句法的灵活性，《中国语文》第 1 期。
Berwick, Robert C. 1983. Computational aspects of discourse. In: Brady and Berwick, eds., 27-105.
Brady, Michael and Robert C. Berwick. eds. 1983. *Computational Models of Discourse*. Cambridge: The MIT Press.
Chen, Ping. 1984. A discourse analysis of third person zero anaphora in Chinese. Bloomington: IULC.
Chen, Ping. 1985. Implementation of a mini discourse model in PROLOG. UCLA ms.
Chen, Ping. 1986. Referent introducing and tracking in Chinese narratives. UCLA Dissertation.
Chen, Ping. 1987. A discourse analysis of pronominal and nominal anaphora in Chinese. Presented at the 14th International Congress of Linguists (Section: Text and Discourse), Berlin.
Daneš, František. 1970. Zur linguistischen Analyse der Textstruktur. *Folia Linguistic*

IV, 72-78.

Daneš, František. 1974. Functional sentence perspective and the organization of the text. In: František Daneš. ed. 1974. *Papers on Functional Sentence Perspective*. The Hague: Mouton, 106-128.

Givón, Talmy. 1983. Topic continuity in discourse: An introduction. In: Talmy Givón, ed., 1983. *Topic Continuity in Discourse: A Quantitative Cross-Language Study*. Amsterdam/Philadelphia: John Benjamins Publishing Company, 1-41.

Grimes, Joseph E. 1975. *The Thread of Discourse*. The Hague: Mouton.

Hopper, Paul and Sandra A. Thompson. 1980. Transitivity in grammar and discourse. *Language* 56:251-299.

Li, Charles N. and Sandra A. Thompson. 1979. Third-person pronouns in zero-anaphora in Chinese discourse. In: Talmy Givón, ed., 1979. *Syntax and Semantics*, Vol. 12. *Discourse and Syntax*. New York: Academic Press, 311-335.

Longacre, Robert E. 1983. *The Grammar of Discourse*. New York: Plenum Press.

Mann, William and Sandra A. Thompson. 1983. Relational propositions in discourse. USC/Information Sciences Institute, Technical Report RR-83-115.

Mann, William and Sandra A. Thompson. 1985. Assertions from discourse structure. USC/ISI, Technical Report RS-85-155.

McKeown, Kathleen R. 1985. *Text Generation*. Cambridge: Cambridge University Press.

Sgall, Petr, et al. 1986. *The Meaning of the Sentence in Its Semantic and Pragmatic Aspects*. Dordrecht: D. Reidel Publishing Company.

Sidner, Candace L. 1983. Focusing in the comprehension of definite anaphora. In: Brady and Berwick, eds., 267-330.

van Dijk, Teun A. 1985. Semantic discourse analysis. In: Teun A. van Dijk, ed., *Handbook of Discourse Analysis*. Vol. 2. *Dimensions of Discourse*. London: Academic Press.

（本文原载《中国语文》1987年第5期。）

Pragmatic interpretations of structural topics and relativization in Chinese[*]

Abstract The correlation between the topic construction and the relative construction has long been observed in the literature. This paper demonstrates that, in Chinese, this correlation is best accounted for not in terms of the syntactic characterization, but in terms of the pragmatic interpretation of the syntactic topic involved. Specifically, independent of the syntactic characterization of the topic construction in question, three pragmatic interpretations of syntactic topic are identified in Chinese, namely, instance topic, frame topic, and range topic, each characterized by its special thematic structuring of the topic construction involved. It is established that whether and how the topic construction can be converted into a relative constructionin Chinese depends crucially upon the differentiation between the three types of pragmatic interpretation of syntactic topic. The findings reported here suggest that what is defined as a syntactic topic does not constitute a homogeneous grammatical function in Chinese. They may also suggest further investigations of how the pragmatic differentiations of syntactic topic relate to other

---

[*] Following is a list of the abbreviations used in this paper following the convention in Li and Thompson (1981):

BA: *ba* (proposed object marker)
CL: classifier
CRS: currently relevant state
CSC: complex stative construction
EXP: experiential aspect
PFV: perfective aspect
Q: question

grammatical processes in Chinese, and whether and how such differentiations are established in other languages.

Keywords   topic construction; relative construction; syntactic topic; pragmatic topic; instance topic; frame topic; range topic; thematic structuring

1. Introduction

In this paper, I will try to show that, contrary to claims proposed in the literature, the correlation between the topic construction and the relative construction in Chinese is best accounted for not in terms of the syntactic characterization, but in terms of the pragmatic interpretation of the syntactic topic involved. This finding suggests that what is defined as a syntactic topic does not constitute a homogeneous grammatical function in Chinese as far as its relevance to relativization is concerned. Independent of the syntactic characterization of the topic construction in question, three pragmatic interpretations of syntactic topic are identified in this paper, namely, instance topic, frame topic, and range topic, each characterized by its special thematic structuring of the topic construction involved. I will demonstrate that the pragmatic differentiations established here play a crucial role in accounting for whether and how the Chinese topic construction can be converted into a relative construction.

Section 2 and section 3 will be respectively devoted to a brief discussion of topic constructions in Chinese, with three types of syntactic topic that are differentiated on syntactic basis, and a brief discussion of relative constructions in Chinese. In section 4, I demonstrate how the approach based on the concept of syntactic topic as a homogeneous grammatical function fails to offer a satisfactory account of the correlation between the topic construction and the relative construction in Chinese. In section 5, I discuss the pragmatic interpretation of syntactic topic, and show how three pragmatic interpretations of syntactic topic are identified. In section 6, I present a neat account of the correlation between the topic construction and the relative construction in Chinese that depends crucially upon the pragmatic differentiation of syntactic topic drawn in section 5. In section 7, I summarize the findings in this paper.

2. Topic construction and three types of S-topics

The syntactic topic (henceforth called S-topic) is a structural constituent of a topic construction (TC), which in English and Chinese is defined as assuming the general form of NP S', as exemplified by the following sentences:

(1) *This proposal*, the review committee does not like ____ at all

(2) *John* I haven't seen him for a long time

(3) *xiangjiao* wo hen ai chi ____
    banana I very love eat
    "Bananas, I like very much."

(4) *nei jian shi*, ni zuihao ba ta wangdiao
    that CL thing you better BA it forget
    "That issue, you had better forget it."

The initial NP in a TC, as exemplified by the italicized expressions in (1)-(4), is referred to as the S-topic. According to Gundel (1985 : 86), an S-topic is formally defined as follows:

(5) A constituent, C, is the syntactic topic of some sentence S, iff C is immediately dominated by S and C is adjoined

to the left or right of some sentence S' which is also immediately dominated by S.

In the literature, three types of S-topic are distinguished on the basis of that constituent's syntactic relationship with the rest of the sentence. First, it is well-known that (1) and (2) belong to two distinct types of TC in English, the former representing what is called TC of Topicalization (TOP), and the latter, TC of Left Dislocation (LD). The TC of TOP features a gap in the remaining part of the sentence into which the S-topic can be moved without affecting the propositional content of the sentence. On the other hand, instead of having a slot for the S-topic in the remaining part of sentence, the TC of LD has a pronoun that is coreferential with the S-topic (cf. Chomsky, 1977, 1981, inter alia). In view of the above distinction, the S-topics in (1) and (2) are respectively called the S-topic of the TOP type and that of the LD type.

TCs of both types are commonly attested in Chinese, as illustrated by (3), which is a TC of the TOP type, and (4), a TC of the LD type. Following are more examples:

(6) nei ji   feng xin   ta kuai   xie wan   le
    that several CL letter he almost write finish CRS
    "Those several letters, he has almost completed."

(7) zhexie shi   wo conglai meiyou   tingshuo guo
    these things I   ever   not-have hear:say EXP
    "These things, I have never heard of."

(8) nei ge ren   wo yiqian jian guo   ta ma?
    that CL person I before see EXP he Q
    "That person, have I met him before?"

(9) ni   shuo de neixie ren   tamen dou lai   le
    you say   DE those people they   all come CRS

"The people you mentioned, they are all here."

The S-topics in (6) and (7) belong to the TOP type, and those in (8) and (9), to the LD type.

In addition to the above two types of S-topics, there is a third type of S-topic that is particularly common in Chinese, which is illustrated by the following sentences:

(10) zhe ben shu wo du de hen lei
 this CL book I read CSC very tired
 "Concerning this book, I have a hard time reading it."

(11) nei chang huo xingkui xiaofangdui lai de kuai
 that CL fire fortunately fire-brigade come CSC fast
 "As for that fire, fortunately the fire brigade arrived promptly."

(12) xiang bizi chang
 elephant nose long
 "The elephant has a long nose."

(10)-(12) differ remarkably from (6)-(9) in that, unlike these former examples, there is neither a syntactic slot for the S-topic, nor a coreferential pronoun in the remaining part of the sentence. The S-topic either bears a participant semantic relationship, as in (10), or a circumstantial semantic relationship, as in (11), to the predicate verb in the remaining part of the TC, or has no direct relationship to the latter, as in (12) where longness is predicated of the nose, not of the elephant. S-topics like these, if they have corresponding expressions at all in English, are often encoded in terms of prepositional phrases, as can be seen from the English translations. Representing what Gundel (1988: 224) calls topic-comment construction par excellence, (10)-(12) are also generally known as "Chinese-style" TCs in the literature, in contrast to typical "English-style" TCs that are represented by the TOP and LD types (cf. Chafe, 1976 : 50-51; Xu and Langendoen, 1985, inter alia). NPs as represented by the initial expressions in (10)-(12) will henceforth be referred to as the Chinese-style S-topic.

Thus, three types of S-topic, namely TOP, LD, and Chinese-style, have been identified, which are differentiated on the basis of the syntactic relationship that holds between the S-topic and the remaining part of the TC.

3. Relative construction in Chinese

Before exploring the correlation between the TC and the relative construction (RC), let us have a brief discussion of the features of the Chinese RC first.

An RC, as defined in Lehmann (1992: 333), is one consisting of a (possibly empty) nominal, called the head, and a subordinate clause, called the relative clause, which semantically modifies the nominal. A distinction is drawn between two types of RCs, one with a head NP, and the other without a head NP. The latter type is also known as headless relative clause or free relative clause in the literature (cf. Bresnan and Grimshaw, 1978; Lehlnann, 1986, 1992). In Chinese linguistics, it is customarily referred to as nominalization (cf. Li and Thompson, 1981). In the following discussion, the term relativization will be confined to the RCs with a head, and those without a head will be referred to as nominalizations.

Relativization in Chinese is marked by the particle *DE*, which connects a truncated clause to the following head NP, as illustrated by the following instances:

(13a) lüxingtuan   tizao   chufa   le
      tour-group   ahead-of-schedule leave   CRS

"The tour group left ahead of schedule."

(13b) [tizao chufa DE] lüxingtuan

"The tour group that left ahead of schedule."

(14a) Xiao Wang qing   lai   le   keren

Xiao Wang invite   come   PFV   guest

"Xiao Wang has invited some guests."

(14b) [Xiao Wang qing lai DE] keren

"The guests that Xiao Wang has invited."

(15a) neixie shi   nimen bu   zhidao

those thing   you   not   know

"Those things you do not know."

(15b) [nimen bu zhidao DE] neixie shi

"Those things that you do not know."

(16a) zhexie ren   women gu   tamen lai   dang   guwen

these person   we   hire they   come serve-as advisor

"These people, we hire them as advisors."

(16b) [women gu tamen lai dang guwen DE] zhexie ren

"Who we hire as advisors."

(17a) zhe   ke   shu   yezi   da

this   CL   tree   leaf   large

"This tree has large leaves."

(17b) [yezi da DE] zhe ke shu

"The tree that has large leaves."

As is evident from the above examples, RCs in Chinese can be derived from non-TCs, as in (13)-(14), and TCs, which can be a TOP TC, as in (15), or an LD TC, as in (16), or a Chinese-style TC, as in (17).

Nominalization in Chinese, as elaborated in Li and Thompson (1981), is formed by placing the particle DE after a truncated clause, which, in contrast to the case with relativization, is not followed by a head noun. As is the case with relativization, a nominalized construction in Chinese can be derived either from a non-TC, such as (13c)-(14c), or from a TC, such as (15c)-(17c):

(13c) shuodao　　　lüxingtuan,　　[tizao　　　　　chufa DE]
　　　speaking-of　tour-group　　ahead-of-schedule　leave
　　　fan'er　　　　　zuihou　dao
　　　on-the-contrary　last　　arrive
　　　"Speaking of tour groups, the one that left ahead of schedule, on the contrary, arrived last."

(14c) [Xiao Wang　qing　lai DE]　houlai　dou　zou　le
　　　Xiao Wang　　invite come　later　all　leave CRS
　　　"Whomever Xiao Wang invited left later."

(15c) [nimen bu　zhidao DE]　hai　　duozhe le
　　　you　not　know　　　still　a-lot　CRS
　　　"There is still a lot that you do not know."

(16c) [women gu　tamen lai　dang　　guwen DE] qishi　　dou
　　　we　　hire they　come serve-as advisor　　actually all
　　　shi　xie　　　waihang
　　　be　several　layman
　　　"Those whom we hire as advisors are actually all laymen."

(17c) [yezi da DE] haokan
　　　leaf　large　beautiful
　　　"What has large leaves is beautiful."

　　A nominalized construction like the above is, by definition, one whose semantic head is lexically empty. Its reference depends upon which participant is left unspecified in the truncation of the relative clause. If there is one participant that is missing, then the referent of the nominalization is the same as that of the missing participant, as illustrated by (13c)-(17c). If more than one is missing, then the nominalization can refer to either of the missing participants, as illustrated by (18c):

(18) ta feichang xihuan zhe ge guojia
he very like this CL country
"He likes this country very much."

(18a) [ta feichang xihuan DE]
"What he likes very much."

(18b) [feichang xihuan zhe ge guojia DE]
"Whoever likes this country very much."

(18c) [feichang xihuan DE]
"Whatever is liked very much." or
"Whoever likes ... very much."

When a TC is converted into a nominalization, it is always the S-topic that is left unspecified. In other words, the referent of the nominalization that is derived from a TC in Chinese is the same as the S-topic of the corresponding TC, as shown in (15)-(17).

It must be noted that, in Chinese, whatever sentence can be nominalized can be relativized, but the reverse is not true. There are many sentences which can be relativized, but cannot be nominalized, in spite of the fact that the reference of the nominalized construction would be predictable from the context, as is illustrated by (19):

(19a) nei ci bisai Lao Li de le guanjun
that CL match Lao Li get PFV champion
"In that match, Lao Li won the championship."

(19b) [Lao Li de le guanjun DE] nei ci bisai, wo
Lao Li get PFV champion that CL match I
meiyou canjia
not-have participate
"That match in which Lao Li won the championship, I

did not participate."

(19c) shuodao bisai, *[Lao Li de le guanjun DE], wo
speaking-of match Lao Li get PFV champion I
meiyou canjia
not-have participate

"Speaking of the match in which Lao Li won the championship, I did not participate."

4. Previous accounts of correlation between TCs and RCs

4.1 Syntactic approach

The correlation between the two syntactic constructions of TC and RC has long been observed in the literature (cf. Chomsky 1977, 1981; Jiang 1991; Justus 1976; Kitakawa 1982; Kuno 1973; J. McCawley 1976, 1988; N. McCawley 1976; Schachter 1976, etc.). For example, it is claimed in Kuno (1973: 254) that a relative clause is derived from a TC in Japanese, and what is relativized is not an ordinary NP, but the theme [S-topic] (NP-*wa*) of the source construction. Although there is no morphological topic marker in Chinese like the Japanese *wa*, similar claims are also made for Chinese. It has been maintained that if an NP can be an S-topic, it can also be relativized on in Chinese (Tsao, 1990: 430). Jiang (1991 : 140) further argues that only an S-topic can be relativized on, and non-S-topics cannot. Such views have been generally accepted in Chinese linguistics, and, to the best of my knowledge, have not been challenged before.

What must be pointed out here is that the correlation between TCs on the one hand, and relativization and nominalization on the other hand, cannot be characterized solely with reference to the syntactic types of S-topic. While S-topics of the TOP and LD types can be relativized and nominalized, as illustrated above, the situation is more complicated with Chinese-style S-topics. Some of the TCs with a Chinese-style S-topic can be relativized and nominalized, and some can not, as exemplified by the following.

(20a) shuiguo wo zui ai chi xiangjiao
fruit I most like eat banana
"As for fruit, I like bananas best."

(20b) *[wo zui ai chi xiangjiao DE] shuiguo

(20c) shuodao shuiguo, *[wo zui ai chi xiangjiao DE]
speaking-of fruit

(21a) wujia Dongjing bi Beijing gui
price Tokyo than Beijing expensive
"As for prices, Tokyo is more expensive than Beijing."

(21b) *[Dongjing bi Beijing gui DE] wujia

(21c) shuodao wujia, *[Dongjing bi Beijing gui DE]

Some can be relativized, but not nominalized, as has already been illustrated by (19).

The initial NPs in the a-sentences in (19), (20) and (21) are all classified as Chinese-style S-topics, yet the three a-sentences behave differently with respect to whether they can be relativized or nominalized. Any explication of the relationship between TCs and relativization or nominalization in Chinese that operates exclusively in terms of the syntactic types of S-topic would find it difficult to account for the differences displayed by the Chinese-style S-topics in this respect.

It must be emphasized that what is at issue here has significance that goes beyond the resolution of the issue of whether the correlation between the TC and the RC can be captured exclusively in syntactic terms and with sole reference to the S-topic. A proper account of the phenomena involved will lead to a better understanding of the status of S-topic in Chinese grammar.

Since the stimulating paper by Li and Thompson (1976), topic as a grammatical notion has attracted much attention from linguists, particularly those working with special reference to languages such as Chinese that are now generally known as topic-prominent. On the other hand, relativization, as a syntactic process, has come under meticulous scrutiny since the 1960s, as it is considered to be a syntactic mechanism that offers special insight into the organization of grammar. The correlation of relativization and specific syntactic functions like subject and object was established in Keenan and Comrie (1977) in the form of the so-called Accessibility Hierarchy, which specifies how specific grammatical functions are amenable to particular strategies in a particular language in an orderly way. The findings in Keenan and Comrie are considered to be of great theoretical significance in that they are taken to provide evidence for the existence of specific grammatical functions. Although no mention was made in Keenan and Comrie of whether and how a base-generated S-topic in topic-prominent languages like Chinese should be accommodated in terms of its place in the Accessibility Hierarchy, it is generally maintained that it should be treated on a par with subject, at least in so far as relativization is concerned (cf. Chen 1986, 1994; Jiang 1991; Tsao 1990, inter alia).

If it can be demonstrated, as I have done above, that no proper account of the correlation between the TC and the RC in Chinese is possible that operates exclusively in terms of the syntactic types of S-topic, then we are justified in asserting that, at least as far as the correlation between the TC and the RC is concerned, what is defined as an S-topic does not constitute a homogeneous grammatical function in Chinese.

4.2. Pragmatic approach

J. McCawley (1976) and N. McCawley (1976) are among the first to approach the phenomena from the perspective of the pragmatic interpretation of the S-topic. In his insightful discussion of this issue in Japanese, J. McCawley (1976: 305) points out that, aside from syntactic constraints upon the types of NPs that can be relativized, (restrictive) relative clauses in Japanese can be formed by relativization on an NP that corresponds to an instance topic, but not on an NP that corresponds to a range topic, as illustrated by (22) and (23):

(22a) Nihon wa   syuto ga   sumi-yo-i (instance topic)
       Japan   capital   live-good-present
       "As for Japan, its capital is a good place to live."

(22b) [syuto ga sumiyoi]   kuni
                            country
       "A country whose capital is a good place to live."

(23a) Nihon wa Tookyoo ga sumi-yo-i (range topic)
       "As for Japan, Tokyo is a good place to live."

(23b) *[Tookyoo ga sumiyoi] kuni
       "A country whose Tokyo is a good place to live."

Whether, and to what extent, the correlation is attested in other languages has so far been little investigated.

5. Pragmatic interpretation of S-topic

It is concluded above that whether a Chinese TC can be relativized or nominalized cannot be accounted for in terms of the distinctions between the three types of S-topics, namely TOP, LD, and Chinese-type, that are distinguished on the basis of the syntactic features of the construction. Before I demonstrate how a neat account of the correlation is couched in terms of the pragmatic differentiation of the S-topic, let us first discuss the pragmatic interpretation of S-topic in Chinese, and how three pragmatic interpretations of S-topic, namely, instance topic, frame topic, and range topic, are identified independent of the syntactic characterization of the TC in question.

5.1. Definition of pragmatic topic: Aboutness

The S-topic, as we will see below, is closely related to the notion of pragmatic topic (henceforth called P-topic). The P-topic is generally defined in terms of pragmatic aboutness in the literature. According to Gundel's formulation (1985: 86):

>(24) An entity, E, is the pragmatic topic of a sentence, S, iff S is intended to increase the addressee's knowledge about, request information about or otherwise get the addressee to act with respect to E.

For a similar point of view, cf. Dik (1978), Kuno (1972), Reinhart (1981) and others.

Just how the P-topic is represented at the sentence level has been an issue under close examination during the past decades (cf. Chafe 1976,

1994; Davison 1984; Dooley 1982; Gundel 1977, 1985, 1988; Halliday 1967; Kuno 1972; Li and Thompson 1976, 1981; Prince 1981, 1985, 1992; Reinhart 1981; Tsao 1990; van Dijk 1977, 1981; van Oosten 1986, etc.). It is observed that with a sentence like (25) it is possible to have different sentential constituents serving as the P-topic:

(25) Felix invited Rosa to dance with him.

for example, can be used to assert about Felix that he invited Rosa to dance with him, or about Rosa that Felix invited her to dance with him, as in the contexts of (26)A and (27)A respectively:

(26) A: How about Felix?

(27) A: How about Rosa?

The same observation applies to Chinese. (28) can be used felicitously in the contexts of (29)A and (30)A, which require different sentential constituents being interpreted as P-topic:

(28)   Lao Zhao ba   kerenmen dou dai   chuqu le
       Lao Zhao BA   guests   all take out   CRS
       "Lao Zhao took all the guests out."

(29) A: Lao Zhao zenme le?
        Lao Zhao how   CRS
        "What happened to Lao Zhao?"

(30) A: Kerenmen zenme le?
        "What happened to the guests?"

In the face of such evidence, few people presently insist on sentence-initial position as the necessary and sufficient condition for the pragmatic topichood of an NP (cf. Halliday 1967, 1985; Huddleston 1988). On the other hand, it is generally assumed, and sometimes asserted, that the S-topic in all types of TC is always to be interpreted as the pragmatic topic (cf. Gundel 1988: 211). Speaking of TCs like (31) and (32),

(31) Felix, it's been ages since I've seen him.

(32) Your second proposal, the board found unfeasible.

Reinhart (1981:63) also observes that, under normal intonational and stress patterns, they can be used appropriately in a given context only if the fronted NP is understood as the P-topic, i.e. if the sentence is used to assert something about the referent of its S-topic (cf. Davison 1984; Gundel 1985: 86; 1988: 211, for the same observation).

5.2. Three types of pragmatic interpretations of S-topic in Chinese

While it is debatable whether the correlation between the S-topic and the P-topic is as high in Chinese TCs as in English, there is little reason to doubt that, all other conditions being equal, the S-topic, of all sentential constituents in a Chinese TC, is the most likely candidate for the role of P-topic as defined above. What concerns us here, however, is to identify finer distinctions with regard to the pragmatic interpretation of the S-topics in Chinese TCs that will play an indispensable role in the account of the correlation between the TC and the RC, and at the same time, to show how such distinctions are correlated with characteristic features of the thematic structure of the constructions in question.

Formulated in general terms as it is, the definition of P-topic in (24) is applicable to the S-topic in Chinese. Thus, given the following three instances of TC in Chinese with the underlined S-topic interpreted as the P-topic,

(33) *Lao Li* women yijing qing lai le
Lao Li we already invite come CRS
"Lao Li, we have already invited here."

(34) *shang ci jiaoyou* haizimen dou lei ji le
   last CL outing children all tired extremely CRS
   "On the last outing, the children were all exhausted."

(35) *wujia* Niuyue zui gui
   price New-York most expensive
   "Speaking of prices, New York is the most expensive."

It may be maintained, based on (24), that (33)-(35) are uttered with the intention to increase our knowledge about Lao Li, the last outing, and prices respectively.

Granted the general applicability of (24) to (33)-(35), it should be pointed out that the definition, as it is, fails to capture some important distinctions between the three sentences in the way the S-topic is interpreted in relation to the rest of the construction.

First, let us consider (33) and (34). While it can be claimed in general terms that the two sentences are about Lao Li and the last outing respectively, strictly speaking, it is only in (33) where the S-topic represents the sole expression about which an assertion is made. With regard to (34), on the other hand, being exhausted is asserted of the children, not the outing. The S-topic in (34) actually serves to provide the frame within which the assertion about the children is made.

(35) represents another sub-type in so far as the pragmatic interpretation of the S-topic is concerned. On the one hand, (35) is like (34) in that the S-topic expression, unrelated to the predicate verb in the remaining part of the TC in terms of case frame, provides a frame within which an assertion is made of another expression. On the other hand, it differs from (34) in that it features a special focus structure in the TC involved, which serves to identify a member of the set of all possible values that is specified by the S-topic expression. For instance, (35) specifies that, speaking of prices in all places, it is New York that

is most expensive. I will elaborate on this point later.

We have thus established that, while the S-topic in Chinese TCs is interpreted as the P-topic in general terms, finer distinctions can be made with regard to the pragmatic interpretation of the S-topic. What is more important, as I will demonstrate later, it is precisely these finer pragmatic differentiations that will play a crucial role in the account of the correlation between the TC and the RC in Chinese. Following the practice in the literature (cf. Chafe 1976; Dooley 1982; J. McCawley 1976; N. McCawley 1976; Jiang 1991, etc.), the three types of P-topic as illustrated in (33)-(35) are called instance topic, frame topic, and range topic, respectively. Following are more precise definitions of these subtypes of P-topic.

(36) An *instance topic* represents an instance of the object about which a predication is made and assessed. It is typically a definite entity in the cognitive inventory of referential entities in the context.

(37) A *frame topic* is one that provides the spatial, temporal and individual frame within which the proposition expressed by the remaining part of the TC, typically a predication made of another expression in the sentence, normally that of the subject, holds true.

(38) A *range topic* is one that delimits the range of a variable of which the predication is made.

Take for illustration the sentence (35), the S-topic *wujia*, as a range topic, in the words of J. McCawley (1976: 304), "restricts the range of the variable x in 'x was high' to price levels in various places, and say that of the things in that range, it is the member corresponding to New York for which 'x was high' is true."

While the instance topic and frame topic have been clearly

differentiated in the literature, the difference between frame topic and range topic is not as well recognized. As a matter of fact, the two are found to be collapsed in some literature, as is the case in J. McCawley (1976) and Jiang (1991:12). The two types of P-topic, as noted above, share the characteristics of delimiting the validity of the predication that is made by the remaining part of the sentence, but differ with regard to the thematic structuring of the TC as a whole. On the other hand, it must be pointed out that, when carrying the normal intonation and stress contour, a TC with a frame topic is characterized by the flexibility of the scope of new information, whereas a range topic TC must be interpreted as having a fixed scope of new information. This is demonstrated by the fact that the former can be used as a felicitous answer to questions that demand various portions of the TC as new information, while the latter, in contrast, does not display such flexibility. Compare the following sentences:

(39) zhe ci kaoshi Xiao Li cuo le san dao ti
this CL test Xiao Li do-wrongly PFV three CL question
"In this test, Xiao Li got three questions wrong."

(40) shuiguo Xiao Li mai le xiangjiao
fruit Xiao Li buy PFV banana
"As for fruit, Xiao Li bought bananas."

(39), which is a frame topic TC, can be felicitously used in the contexts of (41)A-(43)A:

(41) A: zhe ci kaoshi Xiao Li cuo le duoshao?
this CL test Xiao Li do-wrongly PFV how:many
"How many questions did Xiao Li get wrong in this test?"

(42) A: zhe ci kaoshi Xiao Li zenme le?
this CL test Xiao Li how CRS
"How did Xiao Li go with this test?"

(43) A: zhe   ci   kaoshi   zenme   le?
     this   CL   test   how   CRS
     "How about this test?"

In contrast, (40), which is a range topic TC, can only be used as a felicitous answer to (44)A, but not to (45)A-(46)A:

(44) A: shuiguo   ta   mai   le   shenme?
     fruit   he   buy   PFV   what
     "As for fruit, what did he buy?"

(45) A: #shuiguo   ta   zenme   le?
     fruit   he   how   CRS
     "As for fruit, what did he do?"

(46) A: #shuiguo   zenme   le?
     fruit   how   CRS
     "What happened to the fruit?"

That a range topic TC is characterized by a narrow focus scope is also evident from the placement of *shi* (or its interrogative form *shi bu shi*) in the Chinese TCs. As a focus marker in Chinese (cf. Li and Thompson 1981; Teng 1979), *shi* is used in front of a sentential constituent to mark the following as the focus of new information. Consider the following examples:

(47)   ta   zu   le   liang   tao   gongyu
     he   rent   PFV   two   set   apartment
     "He rented two apartments."

(47a) ta zu de *shi* liang tao gongyu
     "It is two apartments that he rented."

(47b) ta *shi* zu le liang tao gongyu
     "He RENTED two apartments."

(47c) *shi* ta zu le liang tao gongyu
     "It is him who rented two apartments."

Shi can occur quite freely, within syntactic constraints observed in Li and Thompson (1981) and Teng (1979), in a frame topic TC, as shown in (48a-d). In a range topic TC, however, it is confined to the place in front of the NP that provides the value for the variable, as shown in (49a-d):

(48) zhe ci kaoshi Xiao Li cuo le san dao ti.

(48a) zhe ci kaoshi Xiao Li cuo de *shi* san dao ti

"In this test, it is three questions that Xiao Li got wrong."

(48b) zhe ci kaoshi Xiao Li *shi* cuo le san dao ti

"In this test, Xiao Li got WRONG with three questions."

(48c) zhe ci kaoshi *shi* Xiao Li cuo le san dao ti

"In this test, it is Xiao Li who got three questions wrong."

(48d) *shi* zhe ci kaoshi Xiao Li cuo le san dao ti

"It is in this test that Xiao Li got three questions wrong."

(49) shuiguo ta mai le xiangjiao

(49a) shuiguo ta mai de *shi* xiangjiao

"As for fruit, it is bananas that he bought."

(49b) ?shuiguo ta *shi* mai de xiangjiao

(49c) #shuiguo *shi* ta mai le xiangjiao

(49d) #*shi* shuiguo ta mai le xiangjiao

Once it is recognized that the main function of a range topic TC like (49) is to present a referent in the remaining part of the sentence as the top member within the range specified by the S-topic, the fixed focus structuring illustrated by (49a-d) is precisely what is to be expected (cf. N. McCawley 1976: 953). A frame topic TC, on the other hand, is not subject to such constraints on the placement of focus information, due to the fact that it is not confined to such a highly specialized function.

It is worthwhile to repeat that, as will be discussed in section 6, the differentiation drawn here between the three pragmatic interpretations of the S-topic plays an indispensable role in the account of the correlation between the TC and the RC in Chinese.

5.3. Relationship between types of S-topic and P-topic

The distinctions between the three pragmatic interpretations of the S-topic in Chinese TC are closely related to, but drawn independently of, the three types of S-topic that are distinguished on the basis of the syntactic features of the construction. While the TOP and LD TCs normally have an S-topic that is interpreted as an instance topic, the Chinese-style S-topic may be any of the three types of P-topic, as illustrated by the following examples:

(50) zhe ben shu ta xie de tai congmang le
this CL book he write CSC too hurry CRS
"This book, he wrote in too much of a hurry."

(51) zhexie shiqing nimen bu bi fang zai xin shang
these thing you not need put in heart up
"These things you don't have to take to heart."

(52) shang xinqisan, Lao Qian qu le Riben
last Wednesday Lao Qian go PFV Japan
"Last Wednesday, Lao Qian went to Japan."

(53) ta shenti hen hao
he body very good
"He is in good health."

(54) shenti Lao Zhao zui hao
body Lao Zhao most good
"As for health, Lao Zhao is the best."

(55) haixian, wo zui ai chi longxia
seafood I most love eat lobster

"As for seafood, I like lobster most."

The S-topics in (50) and (51) are interpreted as instance topics. As there is neither a gap nor a coreferential pronoun for the S-topic in the remaining part of the sentence, they are, by definition, TCs with a Chinese-style S-topic, in spite of the fact that the S-topic plays a participant role, rather than a circumstantial role, in the situation expressed by the TC. When the S-topic is related to the predicate verb in terms of case frame like this, it is normally interpreted as an instance topic. When the S-topic plays a circumstantial role in the situation, as in (52), or is not directly related to the predicate, as in (53)-(55), it is interpreted either as a frame topic or a range topic.

It is evident from the above that what have been subsumed under the heading of Chinese-style S-topic constitute a heterogeneous category in so far as their pragmatic interpretations, in terms of the distinction established above, are concerned. This, as we noted above, has important implications for the status of such S-topics within the grammatical organization of the language.

6. Correlation between three pragmatic interpretations of S-topic and the TC in Chinese

A close examination of the examples given earlier reveals that a neat and elegant account of whether a Chinese TC can be converted to an RC and a nominalization depends crucially upon the differentiation of the S-topic in terms of the three pragmatic interpretations.

A TC with an instance topic can be relativized and nominalized, independently of the syntactic distinctions drawn between the three types of S-topic. Examples (13)-(16), which share the feature that the S-topic is interpreted as an instance topic, belong to this category.

The TC with a range topic, on the other hand, categorically forbids either relativization or nominalization, as illustratedby (20) and (21).

The correlations are less clear-cut with TCs with a frame topic. While they are all amenable to relativization, some of them can be nominalized, under the condition that the referent of the deleted head NP is readily recoverable from the context, as in (17), and some cannot, no matter what the context, as in (19). What is it that underlies the differentiation?

Upon closer examination, it is found that the TCs with a frame topic can be nominalized only if the referent of S-topic stands in a possessor-possessed relationship with another referent in the remaining part of the sentence. Compare the following sentences with a frame S-topic:

(56a) zhe   zhong   xigua,   zir   da
      this   type   watermelon seed   big
      "This type of watermelons has big seeds."

(56b) shuodao   xigua,   wo bu   xihuan [zir da DE]
      speaking-of   watermelon I   not like
      "Speaking of watermelons, I don't like those that have big seeds."

(57a) nei   wei   xiansheng, wo   wang   le   mingzi le
      that   CL   gentleman   I   forget PFV   name   CRS
      "That gentleman, I forgot his name."

(57b) [wo wang le   mingzi DE], dangran mei fa   jiao le
      I   forget PFV name   of-course have-not method call CRS
      "Those whose name I forgot, I of course cannot call."

(58a) nei   ci   lüxing ta   daidui
      that   CL   tour   he   lead

"That tour, he led the team."

(58b) shuodao lüxing, *wo bu xihuan [ta daidui DE]

The S-topics *xigua* 'watermelon' and *nei wei xiansheng* 'that gentleman' stand in a possessor-possessed relationship to *zir* 'seeds' and *mingzi* 'name' respectively in (56)-(57), whereas there is no such relationship between the S-topic and any of the NPs in the remaining part of the sentence (58). The same distinction is found between all the frame topic TCs that can be nominalized and those that cannot. The correlation discussed above can be neatly summarized in Fig. 1.

	Relativization	Nominalization
instance topic	Yes	Yes
frame topic	Yes	(Yes)*
range topic	No	No

Fig. 1. Correlation between pragmatic interpretations of S-topic and relativization/nominalization of TC in Chinese

(* on the condition that the S-topic stands in a possessor-possessed relationship with an NP in the remaining part of the sentence)

It has thus been established that the distinction of S-topic in terms of the three pragmatic interpretations, namely instance topic, frame topic, and range topic, provides the crucial basis for an appropriate account of the interrelationship between the TCs and relativization and nominalization in Chinese.

7. Concluding remarks

In this paper, it has been established that, in Chinese, independent of the syntactic characterization of the TC in question, three pragmatic interpretations of S-topic can be identified, each characterized by its specific thematic structuring of the TC involved. What is more important, it has been demonstrated that whether the TC can be converted into an RC in Chinese, with or without an NP as its head, is best accounted for with reference to the pragmatic interpretation of the S-topic. An instance topic TC can be converted to a relative clause with a head NP, and to a nominalization, while a range topic TC cannot. Whereas a frame topic TC can be converted to a relative clause with a head NP, it can be nominalized only if the S-topic NP stands in a possessor-possessed relationship with another NP in the remaining part of the TC. The logical conclusion from these findings is that, at least as far as relativization and nominalization are concerned, what is defined as S-topic does not constitute a homogeneous grammatical function in Chinese. How the pragmatic differentiations of S-topic relate to other grammatical processes in Chinese, and whether and how such differentiations are established in other languages are topics that are worthy of further investigation.

References

Bresnan, Joan and Jane Grimshaw. 1978. The syntax of free relatives in English. *Linguistic Inquiry* 9:331-391.

Chafe, Wallace L. 1976. Givenness, contrastiveness, definiteness, subjects, topics, and point of view. In: Charles N. Li, ed., 1976, 25-55.

Chafe, Wallace L. 1994. *Discourse, Consciousness, and Time*. Chicago. IL: The University of Chicago Press.

Chen, Ping. 1986. Referent introducing and tracking in Chinese narratives. Ph.D. dissertation, The University of California, Los Angeles.

Chen, Ping. 1994. Shi lun Hanyu zhong san zhong juzi chengfen yu yuyi chengfen de peiwei yuanze [On principles of argument selection in Chinese]. *Zhongguo Yuwen* [*Chinese Language and Writing*] 3:161-168.

Chomsky, Noam. 1977. On wh-movement. In: Peter Culicover, Thomas Wasow and Adrian Akmajian, eds., *Formal Syntax*, 72-132, New York: Academic Press.

Chomsky, Noam. 1981. *Lectures on Government and Binding*. Dordrecht: Foris.

Davison, Alice. 1984. Syntactic markedness and the definition of sentence topic. *Language* 60: 797-846.

Dik, Simon. 1978. *Functional Grammar*. Amsterdam: North-Holland.

Dooley, Robert A. 1982. Options in the pragmatic structuring of Guarani sentences. *Language* 58:307-331.

Gundel, Jeanette. K. 1977. The role of topic and comment in linguistic theory. Bloomington, In: Indiana University Linguistics Club.

Gundel, Jeanette. K. 1985. "Shared knowledge" and topicality. *Journal of Pragmatics* 9: 83-107.

Gundel, Jeanette. K. 1988. Universals of topic-comment structure. In: Michael Hammond, Edith Moravcsik and Jessica Wirth, eds., *Studies in Syntactic Typology*, 209-239. Amsterdam: Benjamins.

Halliday, Michael A.K. 1967. Notes on transitivity and theme in English. Part I and Part 11. *Journal of Linguistics* 3: 37-81, 177-274.

Halliday, Michael A.K. 1985. *An Introduction to Functional Grammar*. London: Edward Arnold.

Huddleston, Rodney. 1988. Constituency, multi-functionality and grammaticalization in Halliday's Functional Grammar. *Journal of Linguistics* 24:137-174.

Jiang, Zixin. 1991. Some aspects of the syntax of topic and subject in Chinese. Ph.D. dissertation . The University of Chicago.

Justus, Carol. 1976. Relativization and topicalization in Hittite. In: Charles N. Li, ed, 1976, 215-245.

Keenan, Edward L. and Bernard Comrie. 1977. Noun phrase accessibility and universal grammar. *Linguistic Inquiry* 8: 63-99.

Kitakawa, Chisalo. 1982. Topic constructions in Japanese. *Lingua* 57 : 175-214.

Kuno, Susumu. 1972. Functional sentence perspective: A case study from Japanese and English. *Linguistic Inquiry* 3:269-230.

Kuno, Susumu. 1973. *The Structure of the Japanese Language*. Cambridge, MA: MIT Press.

Lehmann, Christian. 1986. On the typology of relative clauses. *Linguistics* 24: 663-680.

Lehmann, Christian. 1992. Relativization. In: William Bright, ed., *International Encyclopedia of Linguistics*, Vol. 3: 333-335. New York and Oxford: Oxford University Press.

Li, Charles N. ed. 1976. *Subject and Topic*. New York: Academic Press.

Li, Charles N. and Sandra A. Thompson. 1976. Subject and topic: A new typology of language. In: Charles N. Li, ed., 1976, 457-489.

Li, Charles N. and Sandra A. Thompson. 1981. *Mandarin Chinese: A Functional Reference Grammar*. Berkeley and Los Angeles, CA: University of California Press.

McCawley, James. 1976. Relativization. In: Masayoshi Shibatani, ed., *Syntax and Semantics*, Vol. 5, *Japanese Generative Grammar*. 209-306. New York: Academic Press.

McCawley, James. 1988. *The Syntactic Phenomena of English*, Vol. 1 and Vol. 2. Chicago. In: The Universityof Chicago Dress.

McCawley, Noriko A. 1976. Review of *The Structure of the Japanese Language* by Susumu Kuno. *Language* 52: 942-960.

Prince, Ellen. 1981. Topicalization, focus movement and Yiddish movement: A pragmatic differentiation. *Proceedings of Berkeley Linguistics Society* 7: 249-264.

Prince, Ellen. 1985. Fancy syntax and 'shared knowledge'. *Journal of Pragmatics* 9:65-81.

Prince, Ellen. 1992. Informational and rhetorical structure. In: William Bright, ed., *International Encyclopedia of Linguistics*, Vol. 3: 399-401. New York and Oxford: Oxford University Press.

Reinhart, Tanya. 1981. Pragmatics and linguistics: An analysis of sentence topics. *Philosophica* 27: 53-94.

Schachter, Paul. 1976. The subject in Philippine languages: Topic, actor, actor-topic, or none of the above. In: Charles N. Li, ed., 1976, 493-518.

Teng, Shou-Hsin. 1979. Remarks on cleft sentences in Chinese. *Journal of Chinese Linguistics* 7:101-114.

Tsao, Feng-Fu. 1990. *Sentence and Clause Structure in Chinese: A Functional Perspective*. Taipei: Student Book Co.

van Dijk, Teun. 1977. *Text and Context: Explorations in the Semantics and Pragmatics of Discourse*. London: Longman.

van Dijk, Teun. 1981. *Studies in the Pragmatics of Discourse*. The Hague: Mouton.

van Oosten Jeanne. 1986. *The Nature of Subjects, Topic and Agents*: A Cognitive Explanation. Bloomington, In: Indiana University Linguistics Club.

Xu, Liejiong and D. Terence Langendoen. 1985. Topic structures in Chinese. *Language* 61:1-27.

汉语结构话题的语用解释和关系从句化

提　要　话题结构和关系从句两者之间的关联早已引起学界注意。本文首先区分句法话题和语用话题，从语用角度将话题分为三种，即事例话题（instance topic）、框架话题（frame topic）和范围话题（range topic），三种话题所在的话题结构各有其独特的语用特点。本文证明，我们只能根据相关话题的语用特征而不是句法特征来解释话题结构和关系从句之间的关联，话题结构能否转换为关系从句、转换为什么样的关系从句都取决于话题的语用特点。本文提出的另一个观点是，就本文的研究对象来说，汉语句法话题成分复杂，不具备内部一致的语法功能。

关键词 话题结构 关系从句 句法话题 语用话题 事例话题 框架话题 范围话题 话题组织

（This article was first published in *Journal of Pragmatics* 26(3), 389-406, in 1996. Permission by Elsevier to reprint the article in the present volume is gratefully acknowledged.）

Aspects of referentiality*

Abstract Semantic referentiality, pertaining to the semantics of expressions of certain grammatical categories, is defined in terms of *pointing* to some existent entity in a model of discourse, whereas pragmatic referentiality pertains to language use, and is defined crucially in terms of context dependency and speaker's intention and cognitive status over and above semantics. A discourse thematic referential expression is regarded to be one high in thematic importance, which pertains to the purpose of performance of the referring function in discourse. While some expressions are generally taken, based on their semantics, as inherently referential or nonreferential semantically, there are no specific linguistic devices, other than preferred encoding types, in English or Chinese to mark the pragmatic referentiality of an expression. On the other hand, English and Chinese are found to be more sensitive to distinction in discourse thematic referentiality. Chinese strongly favors the same grammatical encoding for pragmatic and thematic nonreferentials and referents of low thematic referentiality, irrespective of

---

* Many people have helped me develop and clarify ideas formulated in this article when previous versions were presented at conferences and seminars, and circulated for critical comments. I am in particular indebted to Fang Mei, Thomas H.T. Lee, Shen Jiaxuan, Sandy Thompson, Benjamin K. T'sou and Xu Jiujiu for their help and valuable suggestions. I also wish to express my special gratitude to an anonymous reviewer of *Journal of Pragmatics* and Jacob Mey for their detailed insightful comments and expert editorial advice. Any remaining errors or shortcomings in this work are my own.

Following are the abbreviations used in this article. For a detailed explanation of the terms, cf. Li and Thompson (1981).

CL   Classifier
CRS Currently Relevant State
DUR Durative Aspect
EXP Experiential Aspect
PFV Perfective Aspect
TM   Topic Marker

their semantic referentiality, which provides further empirical evidence for the conceptual link between pragmatic referentiality and discourse thematic referentiality.

Keywords referential; nonreferential; semantic referentiality; pragmatic referentiality; thematic importance; Chinese

1. Introduction

Logicians and philosophers initiated research into referentiality in natural languages, which has had significant influence on linguists. Linguists, however, differ from logicians and philosophers in that they focus more on the cognitive status of referentiality in the discourse model established between interlocutors, and linguistic encoding of referentiality in languages. As one of the most basic concepts in linguistic studies, referentiality has been given a variety of definitions in the literature, and is also used in the characterization of a broad and diverse range of linguistic phenomena in grammar and discourse. The main aims of this paper are:

1) to explicate three aspects of the concept of referentiality- semantic, pragmatic, and discourse-thematic, with particular reference to their defining features, linguistic phenomena involved, and their encoding in English and Chinese;

2) to examine whether, and if so, how a broad range of linguistic phenomena characterized in the current literature as illustrative of NPs in nonreferential use relate to, and differ from, each other in a way that justifies the grouping of the broad and otherwise diverse range of linguistic phenomena into one category;

3) to discuss how the three aspects of referentiality are conceptually distinct from, and also related to, each other.

2. Semantic referentiality

2.1 Definition

Linguistics expressions in certain formal categories, as noted in Lyons (2002:297), "may be factorized, semantically if not syntactically and lexically, into two components. One of these is descriptive (e.g. the word 'man' in 'the man'); the other is purely referential (e.g. the definite article 'the' in English)". Semantic referentiality, which essentially serves the function of *pointing* to some existent entity in a model of discourse, defines the referential part of the expression. Whereas pragmatic referentiality to be discussed later relates mainly to the use of linguistic expressions in a given context, semantic referentiality is a property that is encoded in the semantics of linguistic expressions. Some linguistic expressions, most notably proper names, pronouns and demonstratives, are formally encoded in such a way that they are regarded as "inherently" semantically referential with little or no descriptive content. And there are also some linguistic expressions which are characterized by nonreferentiality of the referential component of their semantics. Let us have a closer examination of these expressions below.

2.2 Encoding of semantic referentiality in English and Chinese

As noted above, two semantic components can be identified in some types of linguistic expressions, a referential component and a descriptive component. Three grammatical categories which are generally taken as semantically referential, namely proper names, pronouns and demonstratives, are characterized by relative paucity of descriptive content, and prominence of the other referential component of their semantics. Their essential semantic value or function is taken to be that of directly referring, or pointing to an entity in the context of use, rather than describing any of its context-independent properties. In contrast, there are some inherently nonreferential expressions, like quantifiers 'none', 'no', and 'neither', which serve to negate the referential existence of the relevant denotations. On the other hand, what are known as partitive quantifiers, such as 'each', 'every', 'all', 'both' and 'most', while entailing the existence of a background set, are also inherently nonreferential in that they refer to a sub-set of the background set, rather than a specific individual entity in the set[1]. All of these quantifiers are taken to be semantically nonreferential. Table 1 presents a summary of the characterization of the semantic referentiality of expressions in major grammatical categories in English based on discussions by Fodor and Sag (1982):

Table 1 Semantic referentiality of grammatical categories of English NPs

	Semantic referential	Semantic nonreferential
Definite		
proper NP	+	−
personal pronoun	+	−
demonstrative	+	−
the	+	+

[1] The partitive quantifiers in Table 1 also differ in that some of them, for example 'most' and 'few', refer to a proper sub-set of the background set, and the others to a sub-set that is equal to the whole background set.

	Semantic referential	Semantic nonreferential
Indefinite		
a	+	+
two, three (cardinal numeral)	+	+
some	+	+
several	+	+
many	+	+
few	+	+
bare NP	+	+
Partitive Quantifiers		
every	−	+
all	−	+
each	−	+
most	−	+
few	−	+
no	−	+

What Fodor and Sag (1982), as well as many other linguists such as Partee (1970) and Lyons (1977), maintain here is that definite and indefinite NPs introduced by such determiners as 'the' and 'a' are semantically ambiguous in referentiality, susceptible to both a referential and a nonreferential reading. Not all linguists agree with Fodor and Sag (1982) on the characterization in Table 1. Kripke (1979), Ludlow & Neale (1991) and other neo-Russellians, basically holding on to Russell's position in (1905, 1911, 1919) that only proper names, pronouns and demonstratives are semantically referential, maintain that NPs in the other grammatical categories are semantically nonreferential. On the other hand, they do accept that semantic nonreferential expressions may have referential uses, through a pragmatic process captured in terms of Gricean conversational implicature.

Notwithstanding the differences in opinion, it has been generally acknowledged since Strawson (1950, 1964) that, in addition to the semantic features characterized by the lexical and grammatical encoding of expressions, no account of linguistic referentiality is complete without a pragmatic component, and both semantic and pragmatic factors need to be involved in the comprehensive characterization of linguistic referentiality. I will come back to this point later.

It is also worth noting at this point that expressions that are generally taken to be semantically referential, such as demonstratives and personal pronouns, may have nonreferential uses, as in the following examples:

(1) HE who has a thousand friends has not a friend to spare, and HE who has one enemy will meet him everywhere.

(2) THOSE who can, do. THOSE who can't, teach.

Studies on referentiality have so far been based mainly on data in major Indo-European languages, and findings similar to those in English have been reported for languages such as German and French with regard to the grammatical encoding of referential and nonreferential expressions. As Chinese is a language genetically and typologically quite different from English, an examination of the related phenomena in this language would enrich our knowledge of the linguistic encoding of referentiality in its cross-linguistic variety and complexity.

While English, like other major Germanic and Romance languages, has grammaticalized the distinction of NPs in identifiability in terms of definiteness, it does not provide systematically for the distinction in referentiality, as discussed above. Chinese differs from English with regard to the extent of grammaticalization of identifiability, as elaborated in Chen (2004). So far as formal marking of identifiability is concerned, NPs in Chinese fall into three major categories, definite, indefinite, and indeterminate. Indeterminate NPs differ from definite and indefinite NPs in that while the latter are interpreted as being of identifiable and nonidentifiable reference respectively regardless of what syntactic roles the NPs play in sentences, the former depend mainly on their positioning in sentence for their interpretation with regard to identifiability.

Referentiality is even less distinctively marked in Chinese than identifiability. Table 2 summarizes the semantic referential properties of NPs in major formal categories in Chinese, basically on the same theoretical assumptions as in Fodor and Sag (1982).

Table 2 Semantic referentiality of grammatical categories of Chinese NPs

	Semantic referential	Semantic nonreferential
Definite		
proper NP	+	−
personal pronoun	+	−
demonstrative *zhe/na* 'this/that'	+	−
zhe/na 'this/that' + (NP)	+	−
Indefinite		
yi 'one' + (CL) + NP	+	+
CL + NP		
Indeterminate		
numeral/*ji* 'several' ··· + CL + NP	+	+
bare NP	+	+
Partitive Quantifier		
mei 'each', 'every'	−	+
suoyou 'all'	−	+
yiqie 'all'	−	+
daduoshu 'majority', 'most'	−	+
duoshu 'most'	−	+
shaoshu 'few'	−	+

Similar to the case with English, other than some "inherently" referential or nonreferential categories, most Chinese NPs in other formal encodings can have both pragmatically referential and nonreferential uses, as will be exemplified in the next section.

3. Pragmatic referentiality

3.1 Definition

Linguistic referentiality is both a semantic concept, and more substantially, a pragmatic concept. Semantics, on the strict interpretation of the term, is mainly concerned with user-independent, decontextualized meanings of expressions. A pragmatically referential NP, in contrast, is one which is used by the speaker to refer to an entity, or a set of entities, in the universe of discourse that is of specific reference to the speaker. As linguistic referentiality relates mainly to the use of an expression by the speaker to perform an act of referring in a particular context, it pertains fundamentally to utterance meaning rather than sentence meaning. It is defined crucially in terms of context-dependency, speaker's intention and cognitive status over and above semantics of expressions, thus making it primarily a subject of pragmatic enquires in linguistic studies.

Pragmatic referentiality, instead of being a single unitary concept, comprises three components:

>(3)a. The existence of an individual entity is presupposed in the model of discourse that has been established or is being negotiated between the interlocutors of the speech act.

b. The entity in question is one of specific reference, characterized by unique individuation, and differentiation from other entities by the same linguistic description.
c. The speaker has the intention to use the expression to refer to the specific entity in question.

With regard to the existential presupposition in the first component, two points need to be emphasized. First, the existence of the entity is presupposed first and foremost in the discourse model, and only indirectly and through the mediation of the beliefs and assumptions of interlocutors, in the real world. Related to this is the second point that whether the existential presupposition holds does not hinge upon the truth and falsity of the descriptive content of the referent in the ontological sense. The description may not fit the entity in question as a matter of fact in the actual world, or may only be employed in a sarcastic or jokingly manner, as when an actual usurper is referred to as 'the king', or the term 'boss' is used by a husband to refer to his wife. So long as the speaker knows that, by means of the linguistic expression, the addressee is able to assign reference in the way he intends him to, that expression is used referentially and the existential presupposition of a referent is held by both the speaker and the addressee in the particular context of utterance.

Underlying the concept of specificity in this definition is speaker's familiarity with the referent in question, which is by nature a matter of degree. The speaker may know the exact identity of the referent so that he/she can use other linguistic expressions to refer to the same entity. Or it may be the case that all the speaker knows about the entity in question is that it is a particular individual that has been singled out from the set of all individuals that are denoted by the descriptive content of the linguistic expression in the context of use. He/she is unable to provide any additional information about it beyond the present description. As amply discussed in the literature, the specificity of an entity is often a function of accompanying modifiers, increasing in degree with the elaboration of the details of its identifying attributes (Fodor and Sag 1982; Givón 1982, 2001; inter alia).

Pragmatic referentiality, on this definition, is essentially a context-dependent and speaker-oriented concept. Whether the entity in question is one of specific reference to the speaker depends on the familiarity of the speaker about the referent in the context, with little regard for the cognitive status of the referent in the mind of addressees beyond the presupposed existence. More importantly, it depends crucially on the intention of the speaker to use the expression to refer in the particular context. Linguistic referentiality under discussion here is thus both a semantic and a pragmatic notion—semantic in that some aspects of the meaning are marked by the grammatical and lexical encoding of expressions, as presented in Tables 1 and 2, and pragmatic because of its user- and context-dependent features. For an expression to be pragmatically referential, it has to fulfill all the three conditions in (3), whereas a nonreferential expression is one that fails to fulfill one or more of them.

3.2 Pragmatic aspect of non-referentiality

Such a wide range of linguistic phenomena has been characterized, without much discussion by way of justification, as nonreferential in current linguistics literature that it is not always clear whether, and if so, what features they have in common to warrant the same characterization. There is furthermore a tendency in the literature, as noted by Lyons (1999: 171), to use different terminology for different types of nonreferential NPs, "but the distinction may well be the same and require the same explanation". In view of the controversy and lack of consensus among linguists as to the way in which terms such as 'nonreferential', 'nonspecific', 'attributive', 'quantificational', 'narrow-scope', 'generic' and so on are defined, and the relevant phenomena are explicated, the best approach, in my view, is to present, as much as possible, the original examples and their characterizing terms as they were put forward by their authors to illustrate the range and diversity of what are regarded as nonreferential uses of NPs in the literature. I will first list the major types of NPs in nonreferential use, as discussed by some of the most representative authors on this issue and, in many cases, referred to in various terms. I will then explore what these nonreferential uses of NPs have in common and how they differ in terms of the definition of linguistic referentiality as formulated in (3).

What are generally characterized in the current literature as nonreferential uses of NPs, I propose, fall into five major groups. They differ, among other features, with regard to which of the three components of the definition of referentiality in (3) they fail to satisfy. Expressions in the first three groups are nonreferential in that they do not presuppose the existence of an entity as described by the linguistic encoding of the expression, and those in the last two groups may also fail to satisfy the other one or two components of the definition.

Generic

(4) A/THE TIGER is a large, fierce animal.

(5) TIGERS are large, fierce animals.

Qualitative

(6) John is A MATH TEACHER.

(7) He was promoted CAPTAIN.

(8) Laura is THE CLASS REPRESENTATIVE this year.

Idiomatic

(9) John went to COLLEGE at the age of sixteen.

(10) She is ON THE PHONE right now.

Nonspecific

(11) (specific vs.) nonspecific in opaque contexts (Partee 1970: 359)

John would like to marry A GIRL HIS PARENTS DON'T APPROVE OF.

(12) (wide-scope specific vs.) wide-scope and narrow-scope nonspecific (Ioup 1977:243)

Everyone believes that A WITCH blighted their mares.

a. If they ever find out who she is, they'll try to catch her.

(wide-scope non-specific)

b. If they ever find out who they are, they'll try to catch them.

(narrow-scope non-specific)

The NPs in nonspecific use in (13) and (14), unlike the NPs in (11) and (12), presuppose the existence of an entity by the description of the NP, which, however, does not stand for an entity that is of specific reference to the speaker:

(13) (specific vs.) nonspecific (Lyons 1977:189)

A FRIEND has just sent me a lovely Valentine card.

(14) (referential vs.) quantificational (Fodor and Sag 1982:355)

A STUDENT IN THE SYNTAX CLASS cheated on the final exam.

Non-ostensive

(15) (referential vs.) attributive (Donnellan 1966:297)

The MURDERER OF SMITH is insane.

(16) (referential vs.) nonreferential or attributive (Partee 1970:364)

I heard that from A DOCTOR.

Even if a speaker is acquainted with the specific reference of an expression, he/she can still use it in a non-referential manner if he/she does not have the intention to draw the attention of the addressee to that particular referent. It is this feature of non-ostensivity that characterizes the second member of the dichotomies of Donnellan (1966)'s referential vs. attributive, and Partee (1970)'s referential vs. nonreferential or attributive, as exemplified in (15) and (16).

Other than some inherently referential and nonreferential grammatical categories, as presented in Table 1, there are no special grammatical markings in English that formally encode the distinction between pragmatically referential and nonreferential uses of NPs. Expressions in nonreferential uses may assume any grammatical form ranging from definite to indefinite as illustrated in the above examples and also amply discussed in the literature.

Similar to the case of English, there is no lexical or grammatical device in Chinese which marks NPs in nonreferential use in a specific and unambiguous way. NPs in nonreferential use in the five groups illustrated above may assume a form in any of the three grammatical categories—definite, indefinite, and indeterminate. Consider the following examples:

Generic

(17) a. ZHE REN   na,   dei   you   liangxin.
    this person TM   must   have   consciousness

"One has to have a clear consciousness."

b. YI   GE   REN   dei   you   liangxin.
    one   CL   person must   have   consciousness

"One has to have a clear consciousness."

c. REN   dei   you   liangxin.

person must have consciousness

"One has to have a clear consciousness."

Chinese NPs in generic use may assume the formal encoding of a definite NP as in (17a), an indefinite NP as in (17b), or an indeterminate bare NP as in (17c). Bare NP, it is to be pointed out here, is the most common encoding for all nonreferential uses in Chinese. Following are more illustrative examples:

Qualitative

(18) Ta   shi   (YI) (GE) REN,   bu   shi   jiqi.

he be one CL person not be machine

"He is a human being, not a machine."

Idiomatic

(19) Ta   kanshangqu   XIANG   WAIGUOREN.

he look like foreigner

"He looks like a foreigner."

Nonspecific and Non-ostensive

(20) You   (YI) (GE) XIAOTOU   lai   guo.

have one CL thief come EXP

"There has been a thief here."

The above examples illustrate the range and diversity of NPs in nonreferential use that have been discussed in current literature on referentiality. We can now explore what these nonreferential uses of NPs have in common and how they differ in terms of the definition of pragmatic referentiality in (3). Table 3 presents a summary of what features all of them have in common to justify them being characterized as nonreferential as defined in (3), and how the various nonreferential uses differ from each other:

Table 3 Features of major nonreferential uses of NPs

	Existential presupposition	Of specific reference	Speaker's intention to refer
Generic (Exx 4-5; 17)	−	−	−
Qualitative (Exx. 6-8; 18)	−	−	−
Idiomatic (Exx. 9-10; 19)	−	−	−
Nonspecific			
nonspecific in opaque context (Ex. 11)	−	−	−
wide-scope nonspecific (Ex. 12a)	+	−	−
narrow-scope nonspecific (Ex. 12b)	−	−	−
nonspecific (Exx. 13; 20)	+/−	−	−
quantificational (Exx. 14; 20)	+/−	−	−
Non-ostensive			
attributive (Exx. 15; 20)	+/−	+/−	−
attributive or nonreferential (Exx. 16; 20)	+	+/−	−

As Table 3 demonstrates, all the examples which have been proposed in the literature as illustrative of expressions in nonreferential use fail to fulfill one or more of the conditions of pragmatic referentiality as formulated in (3). Most NPs in nonreferential use discussed above do not carry a presupposition of the existence of a referent that meets the linguistic description of the expression, as is the case with (4-11; 12b) and (17-19). Some of the expressions that do or may carry such a presupposition, as exemplified in (12a), (13-14) and (20), denote an entity that is of no specific reference to the speaker. Some denote referents which may be of specific reference to the speaker, but are taken to be in nonreferential use as a result of lack of intention on the part of the speaker to use them to refer, as in (15-16) and (20).

It follows from the above discussion that the concept of pragmatic referentiality, as defined in (3) and illustrated by those examples, is a matter of degree. All the NPs in nonreferential use presented above share the feature that they do not fulfill all of the three conditions in the definition. Some meet none of the conditions; some meet one, but not the other two, and some meet the first two, but fail to meet the third. Those that fail to carry a presupposition of existence are most nonreferential of all. Those that do carry an existential presupposition, but fail to fulfill the second condition of specificity are more nonreferential than those that meet the first two, but not the last condition of referentiality. The difference in the degree of nonreferentiality is reflected, up to a point, in whether, and if so, how they are susceptible to anaphoric reference in ensuing discourse. The most nonreferential NPs do not allow any anaphoric reference. Consider the following example:

(21) He does not have ANY/A FRIEND/has no FRIEND.

No anaphoric reference can be made to 'a friend' in (21). The same is normally true of NPs in predicative or attributive use as in (6-8). Some nonreferential NPs which do not carry an existential presupposition, however, may be followed by a short-term anaphoric pronoun or NP, as observed by Karttunen (1976:383), provided the discourse continues "in the proper mode", as illustrated by the following example from (1976:377):

(22) Every time Bill comes here, he picks up A BOOK and wants to borrow it. I never let him take THE BOOK.

A generic NP can be followed by a pronoun, or a definite NP referring to the same genus rather than a specific member of the genus, in apparently the same way as in the case of a referential NP:

(23) THE DINOSAUR is now extinct. IT is no longer found live anywhere in the world.

An NP in generic reference, however, differs from an ordinary referential NP in that a following indefinite NP with the same denotation normally refers to the same genus as the initial generic NP, as illustrated by the following example:

(24) A TEACHING MACHINE is an automatic device for implementing a teaching method known as "programmed instruction." ... A TEACHING MACHINE is not intended to be a substitute for a teacher ... It is their claim that the speed of learning with the aid of A TEACHING MACHINE will revolutionize education (from Collier's *Encyclopedia*).

It is also to be noted that the generic 'a teaching machine' in the first clause of (24) may be followed by a plural 'they' referring to many tokens of the same type, as in:

(25) A TEACHING MACHINE is an automatic device for implementing a teaching method known as "programmed instruction." ... Today a variety of THEM are on sale, ranging in prize from $20 to $6,500.

Whereas it is justified to maintain that the first, the second, and the third indefinite NP 'a teaching machine' in (24) have the same reference, referring to one and the same genus, an NP in referential use as the first 'a young prisoner' in (26), as observed by Chastain (1975:206), must normally be in disjoint reference with following indefinite NPs in the same form:

(26) At eleven o'clock that morning, an ARVN officer stood A YOUNG PRISONER$_1$, bound and blindfolded, up against a wall. He asked A YOUNG PRISONER$_2$ several questions, and, when A YOUNG PRISONER$_3$ failed to answer, beat him repeatedly.

It is evident from the above discussion that nonreferential NPs which fail to fulfill the first condition of existential presupposition either do not allow anaphoric reference at all, or are subject to severe restrictions in this regard, or display different features from those of NPs in referential use. Nonreferential NPs that fulfill the existential presupposition, but fail to satisfy the specificity condition may behave in much the same way as referential NPs in that they are amenable to anaphoric reference like regular referential NPs, except that the speaker sometimes may need to make an arbitrary decision on the gender of the anaphoric pronoun. The NP 'a friend' in (13) 'A friend has just sent me a lovely Valentine card', as observed earlier, is open to a specific and a nonspecific interpretation. As pointed out by Lyons (1977:189), no matter whether the speaker has a particular person in mind or not when he utters the sentence, 'a friend' can be subsequently referred to by means of an expression like 'my friend' or 'your friend' (cf. Neale 1990; Rouchota 1994:447 for similar observations). The logical conclusion to be drawn from the differences between NPs in nonreferential use in behaviors with regard to anaphoric reference is that pragmatic (non)referentiality is a matter of degree, and 'a friend' in (13) under nonspecific interpretation is less nonreferential than 'a book' in (22), which in turn is less nonreferential than 'a friend' in (21).

3.3 Encoding of pragmatic referentiality in English and Chinese

How the distinction between referential vs. nonreferential uses of NPs is encoded in languages has become an important subject of empirical investigation starting from the 1960s, largely in the context of a debate on the demarcation of syntax, semantic and pragmatics in the construction of grammatical models for language. It is assumed by many researchers that if the referential vs. nonreferential readings of

NPs are distinctively and consistently marked in grammatical terms, the distinction is to be represented in the semantic or syntactic component of the model. In cases where no formal differentiation is attested, it may be assigned to pragmatics and considered to be outside the proper realm of the theory of grammar per se. Different readings of NPs, from the latter perspective, are treated as instances of pragmatic indeterminacy, which may be resolved in the use of the expressions in specific context of discourse.

It has been established that some languages, like Russian, Spanish, and Turkish, are sensitive to the distinction in terms of pragmatic referentiality of NPs (cf. Dahl 1970; Rivero 1975; Enç 1991). However, no language so far has been found that systematically and consistently encodes all the distinctions between the referential versus nonreferential uses of NPs as presented in Table 3. Furthermore, the grammatical distinction, when there is one, tends to apply to uses that differ in terms of existential presupposition rather than being of particular reference. What is marked grammatically is first and foremost the presence vs. absence of the existential presupposition, and derivatively the specificity vs. nonspecificity, of the entity in question. It accords well with the observation made above that linguistic referentiality, on the definition in (3), is a matter of degree, and expressions that do not carry an existential presupposition in the context of use are more nonreferential than those who do carry an existential presupposition but are of no particular reference to the speaker. It is only to be expected that when the distinction in referentiality is grammatically marked at all in a language, it is more likely to be made in exemplar situations than in other less prototypical cases.

Leaving aside what are generally regarded as inherently referential proper names, pronouns and demonstratives, as well as inherently nonreferential partitive quantifiers, the conclusion we draw from the discussions in the above sub-section is that there is no special linguistic device that systematically and consistently marks an expression as pragmatically referential or nonreferential in English or in Chinese. As is the situation with English, the interpretation of Chinese expressions in terms of referentiality depends mainly on the relevant features of the containing sentence and on the context of utterance. Of the Chinese expressions in various encodings illustrated in the examples in 3.2, it must be pointed out, the most common form used for nonreferential entities is bare NP. As elaborated in Lü (1944) and Chen (2003), the more nonreferential a NP is, the more likely is it to drop the indefinite marker *yi* 'one' and the classifier, and assume the form of bare NP. The preference for bare NP for nonreferential uses is not difficult to explain. Bare NP and non-bare NP in Chinese differ most prominently in that nouns in the latter group are typically preceded by a classifier. The major function of classifiers in languages characterized by this grammatical feature, as extensively discussed in the literature, is to individuate entities. As the most prototypical nonreferential expressions do not presuppose the existence of an entity denoted by the expression, they have no need for an encoding device that marks the individuation of an entity, or other markers that characterize features accompanying individuated entities such as numeration. The fit in form and function between bare NPs and nonreferentiality makes the former the encoding type par excellence for the latter in Chinese.

Fundamentally speaking, linguistic referentiality, and also identifiability, are context-dependent notions, involving intentions and assumptions of language users in the context of discourse. Identifiability, as detailed in Chen (2004), relates to the speaker's assumptions about the nature of the information on the part of addressee about the identity of the entity involved. Referentiality, as discussed in this paper, is mainly a speaker-oriented concept. It relates crucially to whether he/she has a specific referent in his/her own mind, with little regard for the cognitive status of the entity in the mind of the addressee, and to whether the speaker has the intention to draw the addressee's attention to the entity by means of the linguistic expression[①]. In some cases, as Lyons (1977:188) remarks with regard to (27):

(27) Every evening at six o'clock A HERON flies over the chalet. "We cannot tell whether an indefinite noun-phrase is being used with specific reference or not; the speaker himself might be hard put to decide." From the point of view of facilitating effective communication, whether an NP is used by the speaker to introduce a referent of importance in the development of discourse is of greater relevance to the addressee than whether or not the speaker has a specific referent in his or her mind. Grammar, as has been amply attested in languages of the world, tends to encode most distinctively those differences in meaning that are of high importance in communication. It is thus only to be expected that, in terms of linguistic encoding, Chinese is more sensitive to what many researchers regard as another aspect of referentiality, which is called discourse thematic referentiality in this paper, than to semantic and pragmatic referentiality. This leads us to the subject of the next section.

4. Discourse thematic referentiality

4.1 Definition

There is another important dimension to the speaker-dependency and

---

① This view is far from being shared by all researchers in the field. Some regard referentiality as a concept that involves both the speaker and addressee (cf. Enç 1991; Ludlow and Neale 1991; Kennedy 1999).

context-dependency of referentiality that has become an interesting subject of theoretical and empirical exploration since the 1980s. As emphasized above, whether or not the speaker has the intention to use a linguistic expression to refer is one of the defining factors in the pragmatic referentiality of the expression. Closely related to the intention (or lack thereof) to refer, and to some extent underlying this intention, is the function that each NP is meant to play in the development of discourse in the context of utterance. In this regard, NPs in referential use from the semantic and the pragmatic perspective as elaborated in the above section may differ significantly in terms of the importance of the referents they stand for to the thematic progression of the discourse in which they are used. The feature is commonly characterized in the current literature as thematicity of referents, and it is this feature that lies at the core of what is presented here as discourse thematic referentiality—referentiality in terms of thematic importance of objects in discourse.

Most linguists, particularly those inclined to discourse-functional approaches to studies of language, hold the view that the conceptual and functional bases underlying the grammatical categories of noun, adjective and verb serve as the key to a proper understanding of the nature of these categories. Prototypical nouns, adjectives and verbs denote objects, properties and actions, and perform the function of reference, modification and predication respectively. These and other grammatical categories, it is further maintained, have evolved primarily as grammaticalization of the prominent underlying conceptual and functional features. It is on the grounds of these theoretical assumptions that we regard thematicity as characterizing another essential aspect of the nominal function of reference which pertains to the purpose of performance of the referring function in discourse. In addition to the theoretical considerations, the assumed close connection between thematicity and the other aspects of referentiality, as will be discussed in more detail below, also finds support from empirical evidence reported in several languages that semantically and pragmatically nonreferential objects or objects of low pragmatic referentiality are typically encoded in the same way as objects of low thematicity, which would otherwise appear to be a mere coincidence.

Some referents play an important role in the development of the discourse, some only play a secondary role in the process, and some may be just mentioned in passing by the speaker, serving as the prop for the scene, or providing background information to the referents in the foreground. From the perspective of thematic progression in discourse, an NP in referential use is first and foremost one that indicates a clearly delineated, bound entity with continuous identity over time, which, due to this continuous identity over time, is available for further tracking after it is introduced into the universe of discourse (Thompson 1997:69; Du Bois 1980:208). Referentiality, from this perspective, "is not so much of a speaker having a referent in mind at the time of the utterance, as of a speaker assessing the relative discourse significance of an entity and presenting to hearers in such a way as to successfully foreground it" (Hopper and Thompson 1993:360).

Thematic referentiality, thus, relates to the importance of the entity in the thematic organization of the discourse. A thematically nonreferential NP, in this sense, stands for an entity which is taken by the speaker as of no or little importance in discourse, and a thematically referential NP is one that stands for an entity of relatively higher importance. It is, by nature, a matter of degree how thematically referential an entity is in the context of use.

Instead of activating or referring back to an independent mental file, a discourse nonreferential NP, according to Du Bois (1980) and Thompson (1997), typically plays a non-tracking role in discourse, serving one of the following three major functions: classifying, predicating, and orienting or backgrounding. They are exemplified respectively by 'a carpenter', 'ornaments' and 'Christmas Day' in (28-30):

(28) John is A CARPENTER.
(29) You put up ORNAMENTS.
(30) G: Well, ... two years ago, I was in bed.
K: You have nothing to complain about.
G: On CHRISTMAS DAY.

Semantic/pragmatic referentiality and discourse thematic referentiality, as defined here, are closely related, yet distinct and orthogonal concepts. As expected, many semantically and pragmatically nonreferential NPs are also discourse thematically nonreferential, as is the case with 'a carpenter' in (28) and 'ornaments' in (29). Semantically and pragmatically referential NPs, however, can be discourse nonreferential, as exemplified by expressions such as 'Christmas Day' in (30). On the other hand, pragmatically nonreferential NPs can be discourse thematically referential. Consider (31):

(31) The tiger is a carnivorous animal ...

Its subject 'the tiger' is a generic NP, which is by definition nonreferential. However, it may well be followed by a long paragraph that elaborates on various aspects of the species, as is customarily found in descriptions of entries in an encyclopedia. Similarly, as Lyons (1977:189) observes, regardless of whether 'a friend' in (10) is pragmatically referential or nonreferential, "the speaker can go on to say something more about the referent", with the possibility that the pragmatically nonreferential 'a friend' may turn out to be an NP high in discourse referentiality.

4.2 Encoding of discourse thematic referentiality in English and Chinese

Languages, it is extensively reported, may be sensitive to distinction in discourse thematicity, and both English and Chinese fall into this category. There are morpho-syntactic devices the primary function of which is to mark degrees of thematic importance registered by discourse entities in the context of use. A well-known example is *this* in English in its relatively recent use as an indefinite determiner. An entity of indefinite reference may be introduced for the first time into discourse by means of the indefinite article *a(n)*, or what is called indefinite *this*, as in the following examples:

(32) a. I walked out of the café, and bumped into A BOY ON BIKE.

b. I walked out of the café, and bumped into THIS BOY ON BIKE.

It is more likely for the speaker to elaborate on 'this boy' in the discourse following (32b) than on 'a boy' after (32a) (cf. Prince 1981; Wright and Givón 1987; inter alia). Similar linguistic devices have been attested in other languages, including Chinese. Sun (1988), for instance, reports that 80% of the major participants in Chinese are introduced by means of numeral-classified constructions in spoken narratives. Wright and Givón (1987:15) also find that the grammatical contrast between the *yi* 'one' +CL+NP construction and bare NP in introducing indefinite nouns for the first time into discourse in Chinese codes the pragmatics of importance, with the former marking entities of pragmatic importance, and the latter entities of minor or no importance in discourse. Similar findings have been reported in Li (2000) and Wang

(2001). Their conclusions, as will be discussed below, receive qualified support from findings in this study.

In addition to the contrast between encoding devices such as numeral-classified NPs and bare NPs in Chinese, other grammatical constructions have also been found to differ significantly in terms of the discourse thematicity of the NPs that occur in them. Hopper and Thompson (1993:363-4), for instance, report that in a study based on text counts, 97% of English subject NPs in their data are discourse-manipulable, whereas 65% of object NPs are discourse nonreferential, serving a predicating role as 'ornaments' in (29). Below, I will report on the results of my examination of the discourse thematic referentiality of two groups of NPs in Chinese, one in the form of an indefinite NP in the *yi*+CL+NP construction and the other in the form of bare NP, in connection with some other important grammatical constructions in order to establish whether, and if so how, discourse thematicity is systematically encoded in Chinese.

The corpus of data is composed of 80 narrative stories of similar length, with approximately 850 characters in each story, in the collection entitled *Zhongguo Yuyan Gushi* 'Chinese Fable Stories' edited by Jia Bu (Yuanfang Press, 1999). Intended to serve as readings for children and adolescents, the stories are of a vernacular style, but polished to some extent, as is normally the practice with printed materials.

Text frequency is generally regarded as one of the simplest and also the most reliable indicators of the thematic importance of discourse entities. Thematically important entities are usually those which maintain continuity of identity over an extended stretch of discourse, and consequently receive most anaphoric mentions in the following context. In other words, they display strong persistence in discourse. Entities of little or no thematic importance, on the other hand, most likely receive few or no subsequent mentions after they appear in the context for the first time. The correlation between thematic importance and text frequency is supported by other collaborative evidence based on speakers' judgement or other psychometric measures which independently assess the importance of the discourse participants (cf. Sun 1988; Wright and Givón 1987; Redeker 1987; Givón 1992; Downing 1993; Cumming 1995; inter alia). Entities high in frequency of mention in discourse are normally those which stand high in thematic importance as measured by other independent methods. Frequency of mention after being introduced for the first time into discourse is thus taken in this study as the indicator of the degree of discourse thematic referentiality of entities. At one extreme are entities with not a single anaphoric mention in the story, and at the other extreme are those with mention of 20 times and more, which are taken as indicators of discourse thematic nonreferentiality and very high thematicity respectively. Three ranks of thematic importance are set up in this paper—low, medium, and high, depending on whether the referent is followed by 0-3, 4-9, and 10 or more anaphoric mentions respectively in ensuing discourse.

My data shows that the two most common types of form assumed by entities on their first occurrence in discourse are *yi*+CL+NP and bare NP. Table 4 gives the text counts of NPs in each encoding type and their rankings in thematic importance, with numbers in parentheses under Low, Medium and High referring to numbers of ensuing mention in the stories.

Table 4 Thematicity and two types of encoding for initial-mention entities in Chinese

	yi+CL+NP %	Bare NP %	Total %
Thematicity			
Low (0)	74 (22%) 35	263 (78%) 204	337 (100%)

续表

	yi+CL+NP %	Bare NP %	Total %
(1-3)	39 (45%)	95 (91%)	
Medium (4-9)	24 (52%) (14%)	22 (48%) (8%)	46 (100%)
High (10-19) (20+)	68 (97%) 23 45 (41%)	2 (3%) 2 0 (1%)	70 (100%)
Total %	166 (37%) (100%)	287 (63%) (100%)	453 (100%) (100%)

Table 4 shows that bare NP, which is the typical encoding device for semantically and pragmatically nonreferential NPs, is clearly also a preferred marker of low thematicity, or more accurately, a preferred maker of thematic nonreferentiality, with 85% (204 out of 239) instances of nonreferential NP encoded in this form. Referents encoded as bare NP on first mention are seldom ones that stand high in thematicity. On the other hand, 97% of the referents high in thematicity assume the form of *yi*+CL+NP on their first mention, with those highest in thematicity (with 20 or more anaphoric mentions) categorically encoded as *yi*+CL+NP. The difference in preference for encoding form between the three groups of Low, Medium and High thematicity is highly significant ($\chi^2 = 146$, df=2, $p < 0.001$). It is also evident from Table 4 that the indefinite NP in the form of *yi*+CL+NP is not necessarily associated with high thematicity, as has been claimed in the literature (cf. Sun 1988; Li 2004; inter alia). NPs in this form are dispersed along the scale of thematicity measured in terms of the frequency of anaphoric mention.

The overwhelming majority of the 453 instances of *yi*+CL+NP and bare NP in Table 4 are found to be in one of four grammatical positions in sentences—as subject or object, and as the main argument in the Chinese *you* 'have' construction or the locative construction. As the distinction in encoding between numerically classified and bare NP alone does not always appear to be a reliable indicator of the thematic importance of the referent, let us examine whether the grammatical position of these NPs in sentence also plays a role in marking thematicity of the referents.

Table 5 examines thematicity of subject NPs in the two types of grammatical encoding.

Table 5　Thematicity and two types of encoding for initial-mention NPs in subject position

	yi+CL+NP %	Bare NP %	Total %
Thematicity			
Low	8（18%）	37（82%）	45（100%）
（0）	1	30	
（1-3）	7	7	
	（28%）	（82%）	（61%）
Medium	6（46%）	7（54%）	13（100%）
（4-9）			
	（20%）	（16%）	（17%）
High	15（94%）	1（3%）	16（100%）
（10-19）	6	1	
（20+）	9	0	
	（52%）	（2%）	（22%）
Total	29（39%）	45（61%）	74（100%）
%	（100%）	（100%）	（100%）

Here are two examples from my corpus:

(33) YI   PI   MA   zhengtuo le   shuan ma   shengzi,
one CL horse break   PFV   tie   horse reins
pao dao le   fujin de di   li.
run to   PFV   nearby   field in
"A horse got off its reins, and escaped to the nearby fields."

(34) PUREN song   shang yi   pan   lingjiao.
servant send   up   one   plate water:chestnut
"The/A servant presented a plateful of water chestnuts."

It has been much discussed in the literature that, all other things being equal, referents of relatively high thematic importance, are more likely to occur in the syntactic position of subject than elsewhere in the sentence (cf. Downing 1993; Shimojo 2004 for related findings in Japanese). Table 5, however, suggests that the grammatical encoding as bare NP is a better indicator of the thematicity of referents than positioning in the subject slot: of the 45 bare NPs in the subject position, 82% stand low in thematicity, and 30 instances out of 37 are thematically nonreferential. Meanwhile, Table 5 also shows that of the 21 instances of *yi*+CL+NP in subject position, 72% are in the groups of medium or high thematicity with at least four anaphoric mentions in the ensuing discourse, in comparison with the figure of 55% for all instances of NP in this encoding as given in Table 4. However, an examination of all the instances of *yi*+CL+NP in subject position in contrast with those in other sentential positions with regard to their thematic importance, as presented in Table 6, indicates that whether they are in subject position or not is not related to their thematicity in a statistically significant manner ($\chi^2 = 4.892$, df=2, p = 0.087).

Table 6 Thematicity and *yi*+CL+NP in subject versus non-subject positions

	Subject %	Non-subject %	Total %
Thematicity			
Low	8（11%） （27%）	66（89%） （50%）	74（100%） （46%）
Medium	6（27%） （21%）	16（73%） （12%）	22（100%） （13%）
High	15（23%） （52%）	51（77%） （38%）	66（100%） （41%）
Total %	29（18%） （100%）	133（82%） （100%）	162（100%） （100%）

Next, let us consider NPs in object position in Table 7.

Table 7 Thematicity and two types of encoding for initial-mention NPs in object position

	yi+CL+NP %	Bare NP %	Total %
Thematicity			
Low （0） （1–3）	41（22%） 22 19 （61%）	143（82%） 111 32 （91%）	184（100%） （81%）
Medium （4–9）	11（48%） （17%）	12（52%） （8%）	23（100%） （10%）
High （10–19） （20+）	15（88%） 8 7 （22%）	2（12%） 2 0 （1%）	17（100%） （11%）
Total %	67（31%） （100%）	157（69%） （199%）	227 （100%）

Following are two examples from my corpus:

(35) Lieren waichu dalie, budao YI ZHI XIAO LU.
     hunter go:out hunt, catch one CL small dear
     "The hunter went hunting, and caught a fawn."

(36) Ta lianhe le ji wei tiejiang, da qi HUOLU.
     he unite PFV some CL blacksmith, set up stove
     "He worked together with several blacksmiths, and built a stove."

Table 7 demonstrates that the object NPs in Chinese in both types of encoding are generally low in thematic importance, which concords with similar findings reported in Hopper and Thompson (1993) with regard to object NPs in English. 71% (111 instances out of 157) of bare NPs in the object position are thematically nonreferential, and 20% (32 out 157) are in the other sub-group of low thematicity. On the other hand, 61% of the *yi*+CL+NPs in the object position are entities of low thematicity.

Finally, let us examine two other grammatical constructions in Chinese which are regarded as characteristically marking the relevant NPs in the constructions as being very high or low in thematicity respectively. One is the canonical presentative construction in Chinese beginning with *you* 'have', and the other is the so-called *fangwei jiegou* 'locative construction' composed of a localizer such as *li* 'in', *wai* 'out', *shang* 'up', and *xia* 'down' after the NP and an optional preposition before the NP. Let us first examine the thematicity of NPs in the two types of grammatical encoding in the Chinese *you*-presentative construction presented in Table 8:

Table 8 Thematicity and two types of encoding for initial-mention NPs in *you* construction

	yi+CL+NP %	Bare NP %	Total %
Thematicity			
Low	14（50%）	14（50%）	28（100%）
（0）	5	11	
（1-3）	9	3	
	（25%）	（100%）	（41%）
Medium	5（100%）	0（0%）	5（100%）
（4-9）	（9%）	（0%）	（7%）
High	36（100%）	0（0%）	36（100%）
（10-19）	8	0	
（20+）	28	0	
	（66%）	（0%）	（52%）
Total	55（80%）	14（20%）	69（100%）
%	（100%）	（100%）	（100%）

Here are two illustrating examples from my corpus:

(37) YOU YI GE SHANGREN, zai waimian zuo shengyi
     have one CL business:man, in outside do business
     zhuan le   bushao   qian.
     earn   PFV   much   money
     "There was a business man who had made lots of money in his outside business."

(38) YOU REN   zhuanmen baifang ta, xiang ta qiujiao.
     have person special visit   he, toward he seek:advice
     "There was someone who paid him a special visit to seek his advice."

The *you*-presentative construction in Chinese is generally taken as a device that is commonly used to introduce noteworthy referents, or referents of high discourse referentiality into discourse. Table 8, however, shows that, similar to the situation with bare NPs in the subject position, the grammatical encoding of bare NP as a marker of low thematicity overrides the effect of the *you*-construction as a canonical construction to introduce entities of thematic importance. 79% (11 instances out of 14) of the referents in the form of bare NP introduced by the construction are thematically nonreferential. On the other hand, Table 8 demonstrates that, although either the *you*-presentative construction or the form of *yi*+CL+NP itself may not necessarily encode entities of high thematicity, their combination, namely *you*+*yi*+CL+NP, is clearly the most preferred form to introduce entities of thematic importance. In fact, of the 45 referents of the strongest persistence which are mentioned for 20 times or more in the ensuing discourse, 28 are introduced into discourse on their initial mention in the form of *yi*+CL+NP in the *you*-presentative construction. A comparison of the thematicity of *yi*+CL+NP in *you* construction and elsewhere also indicates that, so far as the form of *yi*+CL+NP is concerned, the correlation between thematicity and the *you* construction, as shown in Table 9, is significant ($\chi^2 = 20.43$, df=2, $p < 0.001$).

Table 9 Thematicity and *yi*+CL+NP in *you* construction versus elsewhere

	You Construction %	Elsewhere %	Total %
Thematicity			
Low	14 (19%) (25%)	60 (81%) (54%)	74 (100%) (46%)
Medium	5 (23%) (9%)	19 (77%) (17%)	22 (100%) (13%)

	You Construction %	Elsewhere %	Total %
High	36（55%）	32（45%）	66（100%）
	（66%）	（29%）	（41%）
Total	55（18%）	111（82%）	162（100%）
%	（100%）	（100%）	（100%）

The results in Tables 4-8 suggest that, whereas bare NP can be characterized as a marker of thematic nonreferentiality or low thematicity in Chinese, the indefinite NP in the form of *yi*+CL+NP, in and of itself, is a much less consistent marker of thematicity. It may encode an entity of low thematic importance just as likely as an entity of high thematic importance. In this respect, it displays some similarity to the English indefinite article *a*, which, although originally a marker of thematic importance, has gradually expanded its scope to entities of various degrees of discourse thematic referentiality (cf. Hopper and Martin 1987; Wright and Givón 1987; Heine 1997; Chen 2003).

Finally, let us examine the thematic importance of NPs in the Chinese locative construction:

Table 10　Thematicity and two types of encoding for initial-mention NPs in locative construction

	yi+CL+NP %	Bare NP %	Total %
Thematicity			
Low	11（15%）	63（85%）	74（100%）
（0）	7	47	
（1-3）	4	16	
	（100%）	（100%）	（100%）
Total	11（15%）	63（85%）	74（100%）
%	（100%）	（100%）	（100%）

It is evident from Table 10 that the locative construction is a most consistent and strongest marker of discourse thematic nonreferentiality or low thematicity in Chinese. Irrespective of whether they appear as a numerically classified NP or bare NP, NPs in the locative construction are either discourse thematically nonreferential or of low thematicity. Note that most of the NPs in the locative construction are of specific reference, referring to identifiable referents in the context of discourse. Some stand for existent, but nonidentifiable and nonspecific entities. Consider the following two examples from my corpus:

(39) Zhuren jiang keren yin dao YUANZI li sanbu.
host take guest lead to courtyard in stroll
"The host took the guest to the courtyard for a stroll."

(40) Xiangshu shang zhu zhe yi zhi chan,
oak:tree up live DUR one CL cicada
chan zhan zai SHUZHI shang, butingde jiao.
cicada stand on branch up, incessantly chirp
"There was a cicada on the oak tree, clinging onto a branch and chirping incessantly."

Yuanzi 'courtyard' in (39) is of specific and identifiable reference in the context of utterance, referring to the courtyard that is a part of the house of the host in the typical cognitive scheme or scenario of a house, as the head is to a person, and the wheel to a car. *Shuzhi* 'branch' in (40) is of unidentifiable reference in the sentence, as there are normally many branches to a tree, and the speaker cannot reasonably assume the addressee knows which uniquely identifiable branch is involved. As a matter of fact, we are in no position to know if the speaker him-/herself had a specific branch in his or her mind, which means that the pragmatic referentiality of the NP in this case is a matter of indeterminacy. The distinction in identifiability and pragmatic referentiality, however, is neutralized in the circumstances in question, where the entities are obviously discourse thematically nonreferential, or are of low thematicity, serving a mere circumstantial role in the development of the major theme of the discourse. Irrespective of whether or not they are of specific and identifiable reference, the NPs in the locative construction are predominantly encoded as bare NP, the form par excellence for both semantically/pragmatically nonreferential entities and thematically nonreferential entities. The fact that pragmatically specific NPs like *yuanzi* in a locative construction as in (39) are typically encoded in the same way as pragmatically nonreferential entities suggests that when semantic/pragmatic and discourse/thematic features conflict, as in the Chinese locative construction, more often than not the semantic/pragmatic distinction is neutralized, and the distinction in thematic importance prevails. Irrespective of their semantic and pragmatic features in referentiality, they usually assume the typical encoding for semantic/pragmatic nonreferentiality if they stand very low in discourse thematicity.

5. Conclusion

Three aspects of linguistic referentiality are discussed in this paper. A semantically referential expression, thus, is one whose semantics contains a component the essential function of which is to point to an existent entity in a model of discourse. A pragmatically referential expression is one that carries an existential presupposition, is of specific reference to the speaker, and is used by the speaker with the intention to refer the entity in the context of utterance. A nonreferential expression is one that fails to fulfill one or more of the conditions. An examination of a broad range of diverse linguistic phenomena that have been characterized in the literature in various terms including *nonreferential, nonspecific, attributive, quantificational, narrow-scope nonspecific and distributive, generic*, and *qualitative* has established that all of them fail to fulfill one or more of the conditions in the definition of pragmatic referentiality formulated in this paper. It is by virtue of this fact that it is justified to put this broad, and otherwise diverse range of linguistic phenomena into one category, and characterize them as pragmatically nonreferential. A discourse thematically referential expression is taken to be one high in thematic importance, as measured in terms of high frequency of anaphoric mention in ensuing discourse. Both pragmatic referentiality and discourse thematic referentiality are strongly speaker-oriented and context-dependent concepts, pertaining primarily to the cognitive status of the entity involved in speaker's mind and to the intention of the speaker in the utterance of the relevant expression.

Other than what are generally taken, in semantic terms, as inherently referential or nonreferential forms, there are no specific linguistic devices in English or Chinese which are used primarily or mainly to mark the pragmatic referentiality of an expression, although it is found in Chinese that encoding as bare NP strongly favors a nonreferential reading in situations where a nominal expression is susceptible to a referential and a nonreferential interpretation. On the other hand, both English and Chinese are found to be more sensitive to distinction in discourse thematic referentiality, with encoding devices which characteristically serve to indicate the thematic importance of referents in the discourse of utterance. Furthermore, the fact that Chinese strongly favors the same grammatical encoding of bare NP for pragmatic and thematic nonreferentials and referents of low thematic referentiality, irrespective of their semantic referentiality, provide further empirical evidence for the conceptual link between pragmatic referentiality and discourse thematic referentiality.

References

Chastain, Charles. 1975. Reference and context. In: Gunderson, Keith, ed., *Minnesota Studies in Philosophy of Science*, Vol. VII. *Language, Mind and Knowledge*. University of Minnesota Press, Minneapolis, Pp. 194-269.

Chen, Ping. 2003. Indefinite determiner introducing definite referent: A special use of *yi* 'one' + classifier in Chinese. *Lingua* 113, 1169-1184.

Chen, Ping. 2004. Identifiability and definiteness in Chinese. *Linguistics* 42(6), 1129-1184.

Cumming, Susanna. 1995. Agent position in the *Sejarah Melayu*, In: Downing, Pamela and Noonan, Michael, eds., *Word Order in Discourse*. John Benjamins, Amsterdam, Pp. 51-38.

Dahl, Östen. 1970. Some notes on indefinites. *Language* 46(1), 33-41.

Donnellan, Keith S. 1966. Reference and definite descriptions. *Philosophical Review* 75, 281-394.

Downing, Pamela. 1993. Pragmatic and semantic constraints on numeral quantifier position in Japanese. *Journal of Linguistics* 29 (1), 65-93.

Du Bois, John W. 1980. Beyond definiteness: The trace of identity in discourse, In: Chafe, Wallace, ed., *The Pear Stories: Cognitive, Cultural and Linguistic Aspects of Narrative Production*. Albex Publishing Corporation, Norwood, N.J., Pp. 203-274.

Enç, Mürvet. 1991. The semantics of specificity. *Linguistic Inquiry* 22, 1-25.

Fodor, Janet Dean and Sag, Ivan. 1982. Referential and quantificational indefinites. *Linguistics and Philosophy* 5, 355-398.

Givón, Talmy. 1982. Logic vs. pragmatics, with natural language as the referee: Toward an empirically viable epistemology. *Journal of Pragmatics* 6(1), 81-133.

Givón, Talmy. 1992. The grammar of referential coherence as mental processing instructions. *Linguistics* 30, 5-55.

Givón, Talmy. 2001. *Syntax*. Vols. I-II. John Benjamins Publishing Company, Amsterdam.

Heine, Bernd. 1997. *Cognitive Foundations of Grammar*. Oxford University Press, Oxford.

Hopper Paul and Martin, Janice. 1987. Structuralism and diachrony: The development of the indefinite article in English. In: Ramat, Anna Giacalone, et al., eds., *Papers from the Seventh International Conference on Historical Linguistics*. John Benjamins Publishing Company, Amsterdam, Pp. 295-304.

Hopper, Paul and Thompson, Sandra A. 1993. Language universals, discourse pragmatics, and semantics. *Language Sciences* 15 (4), 357-376.

Ioup, Georgette. 1977. Specificity and the interpretation of quantifiers. *Linguistics and Philosophy* 1, 233-245.

Karttunen, Lauri. 1976. Discourse referents. In: McCawley, James, ed., *Syntax and Semantics* Vol. 7: *Notes from the Linguistics Underground*. Academic Press, New York, Pp. 363-385.

Kennedy, Becky. 1999. Specific NP in scope. In: Kamio, Akio, Takami, Ken-Ichi, eds., *Function and Structure: In Honor of Susumu Kuno*. John Benjamins Publishing Company, Amsterdam, Pp. 251-287.

Kripke, Saul. 1979. Speaker's reference and semantic reference. In: French, P.A. et al., eds., *Contemporary Perspectives in the Philosophy of Language*. University of Minnesota Press, Minneapolis, Pp.6-27; Also in: Ostertag, Gary, ed., 1998, Pp. 225-256.

Li, Charles N. and Thompson, Sandra A. 1981. *Mandarin Chinese: A Functional Reference Grammar*. University of California Press, Berkeley and Los Angeles.

Li, Wendan. 2000. The pragmatic function of numeral-classifiers in Mandarin Chinese. *Journal of Pragmatics* 32(8), 1113-1133.

Ludlow, Peter, and Neale, Stephen. 1991. Indefinite descriptions: In defense of Russell. *Linguistics and Philosophy* 14, 171-202.

Lü, Shuxiang. 1944. *Ge* zi de yingyong fanwei, fu lun danweici qian *yi* zi de tuoluo [Scope of the uses of *ge* and omission of *yi* in front of classifiers]. In: *Lü Shuxiang Wenji* [*Collected Works of Lü Shuxiang*], Vol. 2, Shangwu Yinshuguan [The Commercial Press], Beijing, 1990, Pp. 144-175.

Lyons, John. 1977. *Semantics*. Vols. I-II. Cambridge University Press, Cambridge.

Lyons, John. 2002. *Linguistic Semantics*: *An Introduction*. Cambridge University Press, Cambridge.

Neale, Stephen. 1990. *Descriptions*. MIT Press, Cambridge, Massachusetts; Also in: Ostertag, G., ed., 1998, Pp. 309-368.

Ostertag, Gary. ed. 1998. *Definite Descriptions*: *A Reader*. MIT Press, Cambridge, Massachusetts.

Partee, Barbara H. 1970. Opacity, coreference, and pronouns. *Synthese* 21, 359-385.

Prince, Ellen. 1981. On the inferencing of indefinite-*This* NP. In: Joshi, Avavind, Webber, Bonnie and Sag, Ivan, eds., *Elements of Discourse Understanding*.

Cambridge University Press, Cambridge, Pp. 231-250.

Redeker, Gisela. 1987. Introductions of story characters in interactive and non-interactive narration. In: Verschueren, Jef, Bertuccelli-Papi, Marcella, eds., *The Pragmatic Perspective: Selected Papers from the 1985 International Pragmatics Conference*. John Benjamins Publishing Company, Amsterdam, Pp. 339-355.

Rivero, Maria-Luisa. 1975. Referential properties of Spanish noun phrases. *Language* 51 (1), 32-48.

Rouchota, Villy. 1994. On indefinite descriptions. *Journal of Linguistics* 30, 441-475.

Russell, Bertrand. 1905. On denoting. *Mind* 14; Reprinted in Zabeeh et al., eds., 1974, Pp. 141-158.

Russell, Bertrand. 1911. Knowledge by acquaintance and knowledge by description. *Proceedings of Aristotelian Society* 11, 108-28; Also in Russell, Bertrand, 1912, *The Problems of Philosophy*. Second edition, 1998, Oxford University Press, Oxford and New York, Pp. 25-32.

Russell, Bertrand. 1919. *Introduction to Mathematical Philosophy*. G. Allen & Unwin, London.

Shimojo, Mitsuaki. 2004. Quantifier float and information processing: A case study from Japanese. *Journal of Pragmatics* 36(3), 375-405.

Strawson, Peter F. 1950. On referring. *Mind* 59, 320-344; Reprinted in Zabeeh et al., eds., *Readings in Semantics*, University of Illinois Press, Urbana, Pp. 159-192.

Strawson, Peter F. 1964. Identifying reference and truth value. *Theoria*, Vol. XXX, 96-108; Reprinted in: Zabeeh et al., eds., *Readings in Semantics*, University of Illinois Press, Urbana, Pp. 193-216.

Sun, Chaofen. 1988. The discourse function of numeral classifiers in Mandarin Chinese. *Journal of Chinese Linguistics* 16(2), 298-323.

Thompson, Sandra A. 1997. Discourse motivations for the core-oblique distinction as a language universal. In: Kamio, Akio, ed., *Directions in Functional Linguistics*. John Benjamins Publishing Company, Amsterdam, Pp. 59-82.

Wang, Hongqi. 2001. Zhicheng Lun [On Reference]. Unpublished PhD. Dissertation, Nankai University, Tianjin.

Wright, S. and Givón, Talmy. 1987. The pragmatics of indefinite reference: Quantified text-based studies. *Studies in Language* 11(1), 1-33.

Zabeeh, Farhang, Klemke, E. D., and Jacobson, Arthur, eds. 1974. *Readings in Semantics*. University of Illinois Press, Urbana.

指称现象研究

提　要　本文详细分析指称现象的三个主要方面——语义、语用和话语。指称的语义属性同相关词语形式本身表现的涉及指称的意义相关，指称的语用属性除了词语形式表现的指称意义之外，还同具体语境和发话人的意图有关，指称的话语属性除了上述的语义和语用因素以外，还涉及发话人在话语环境中使用有关词语的目的。本文侧重研究指称三个主要方面的交互关系，揭示指称三种属性在汉语中的表现形式。

关键词　有指　无指　语义有指　语用有指　话题重要程度　汉语

（This article was first published in *Journal of Pragmatics* 41(8), 1657-1674, in 2009. Permission by Elsevier to reprint the article in the present volume is gratefully acknowledged.）

Referentiality and definiteness in Chinese[*]

Abstract Four aspects of referentiality are discussed in this chapter, logico-philosophical, semantic, pragmatic and discourse thematic. While some expressions are generally taken as inherently referential or nonreferential semantically based on their semantics, there are no specific linguistic devices, other than preferred encoding types, in Chinese to mark the pragmatic referentiality of an expression. Chinese is found to be sensitive to distinction in discourse thematic referentiality. It strongly favors the same grammatical encoding, bare NP, for pragmatic and thematic nonreferentials and referents of low thematic referentiality. The term "definiteness" denotes a grammatical category featuring formal distinction whose core function is to mark a nominal expression as identifiable or nonidentifiable. Whereas pragmatic and discourse thematic referentiality is a speaker-oriented notion, identifiability is taken as an addressee-oriented, pragmatic notion relating to the assumptions made by the speaker on the cognitive status of a referent in the mind of the addressee in the context of utterance. The pragmatic distinction between identifiability and nonidentifiability is expressed in Chinese in terms of distinctive lexical and morphological encodings and in terms of the positioning of nominal expressions in sentences. Unlike many other languages, distinctive features of definiteness and indefiniteness cannot be obligatorily and uniquely specified for nominal expressions in Chinese, which leads to the conclusion

---

* (1) I would like to acknowledge that portions of this chapter were originally published in Chen (2004, 2009). Readers are referred to the two articles for more detailed discussion.

(2) Following are the abbreviations used in this article. For a detailed explanation of the terms, cf. Li and Thompson (1981).

    CL   Classifier
    CRS Currently Relevant State
    EXP Experiential Aspect
    PFV Perfective Aspect

that definiteness as a grammatical category has not been fully developed in Chinese.

Keywords   referential; definite; indefinite; discourse thematicity

1. Referentiality

The concept of referentiality has attracted attention from logicians, philosophers and linguists since Greco-Roman times as being essential to capturing many intriguing features concerning the relationship between language, human cognition and the external world, and most importantly for linguists, the structure, use and evolution of languages. More recent research focuses on four major aspects of the concept—logico-philosophical, semantic, pragmatic, and discourse thematic.

1.1 Logic-philosophical referentiality

Logicians and philosophers, Frege (1892), Russell (1905, 1919), Strawson (1950, 1964), and Donnellan (1966) among the most influential, took a keen interest in the referentiality of linguistic expressions since the turn of the twentieth century, as they aimed to determine how to ascertain what people say or believe is true or false as part of their research agenda to establish a general theory of meaning. Their works have had strong impact and ramifications on linguists both in the delineation of the range of linguistic phenomena coming under investigation, and in the definition and use of important terms and concepts related to referentiality. To Bertrand Russell, and most logicians, philosophers and linguists working in the broadly neo-Russellian framework, the term "referential" is confined to logically proper names, demonstratives like *this* and *that*, and indexicals like *I*. Logically proper names, demonstratives and indexicals, in the Russellian tradition, are inherently referring expressions, whereas other linguistic words and phrases, such as definite and indefinite descriptions, are not.

1.2 Semantic referentiality

Semantic referentiality is a property encoded in the semantics of linguistic expressions that essentially serves the function of directly "referring" or pointing to some existent entity in a model of discourse. Semantics of expressions in some grammatical categories may be factorized into two components, one descriptive, like "city" in "in the city", the other purely referential, as "the" in the same phrase. Some linguistic expressions, most notably proper names, pronouns, demonstratives, and definite articles like the English *the*, because of the semantics encoded in their form, are regarded as "inherently" semantically referential with little or no descriptive content. In contrast, there are some inherently nonreferential expressions, like English quantifiers *none*, *no*, and *neither*, which serve to negate the referential existence of the relevant denotations. What are known as partitive quantifiers, such as *each*, *every*, *all*, *both* and *most*, while entailing the existence of a background set, are also inherently nonreferential in that they refer to a subset of the background set, rather than a specific individual entity in the set. All of these quantifiers are taken to be semantically nonreferential.

As will be discussed in more detail later, noun phrases (NPs) in Chinese fall into three major formal categories in terms of how the pragmatic property of identifiability is encoded: definite, indefinite, and indeterminate (cf. Chen 2004). The property of semantic referentiality of some major types of Chinese NPs in the three categories, as well as Chinese partitive quantifiers, is summarized by Chen (2009: 1160) in Table 1, basically on the same theoretical assumptions as in Fodor and Sag (1982).

Table 1 Semantic referentiality of grammatical categories of Chinese NPs

	Semantic referential	Semantic nonreferential
Definite		
Proper NP	+	−
Personal pronoun	+	−
Demonstrative *zhe/na* 'this/that'	+	−
zhe/na 'this/that' + NP	+	−
Indefinite		
yi 'one' + (CL) + NP	+	+
CL + NP		
Indeterminate		
Numeral/*ji* 'several' ... + CL + NP	+	+
Bare NP	+	+
Partitive Quantifier		
mei 'each', 'every'	−	+
suoyou 'all'	−	+
yiqie 'all'	−	+
daduoshu 'majority', 'most'	−	+
duoshu 'most'	−	+
shaoshu 'few'	−	+

As in English, semantic referentiality is not distinctively marked in Chinese. Other than some "inherently" referential or nonreferential encodings, such as proper names and pronouns, Chinese NPs in other formal categories may be semantically referential or nonreferential, as shown in Table 1.

1.3 Pragmatic referentiality

While semantic referentiality is mainly concerned with user-independent, decontextualized meaning of expressions that is marked by the grammatical and lexical encoding of expressions, pragmatic referentiality relates mainly to the use of linguistic expressions in a given context.

Pragmatic referentiality comprises three components: (1) presupposed existence of an individual entity in the universe of discourse established between the speaker and the addressee; (2) of specific reference to the speaker; (3) with speaker's intention to use the expression to refer to the specific entity in question. It is essentially a context-dependent and speaker-oriented concept. Whether the entity in question is one of specific reference to the speaker depends on the familiarity of the speaker about the referent in the context, with little regard for the cognitive status of the referent in the mind of addressees beyond the presupposed existence. More important, it depends crucially on the intention of the speaker to use the expression to refer in the particular context. For an expression to be pragmatically referential, it has to fulfill all the three conditions, whereas a nonreferential expression is one that fails to fulfill one or more of them.

There is no special linguistic device that systematically and consistently marks an expression as pragmatically referential or nonreferential in Chinese, or in English for that matter, as discussed in Chen (2009). Of the Chinese expressions in various encodings presented in Table 1, the most common form used for nonreferential entities is bare

NP. As observed in Lü (1944) and Chen (2003), the more nonreferential an NP is, the more likely is it to drop the indefinite marker *yi* and the classifier (CL), and assume the form of bare NP. The preference for bare NP for nonreferential uses is not difficult to explain. Bare NP and non-bare NP in Chinese differ most prominently in that nouns in the latter group are typically preceded by a classifier. The major function of classifiers in languages characterized by this grammatical feature, as extensively discussed in the literature, is to individuate entities. As the most prototypical nonreferential expressions do not presuppose the existence of an entity denoted by the expression, they have no need for an encoding device that marks the individuation of an entity or other markers that characterize features accompanying individuated entities such as numeration. The fit in form and function between bare NP and nonreferentiality makes the former the encoding type par excellence for the latter in Chinese.

1.4 Discourse thematic referentiality

Discourse thematic referentiality relates to the importance of the entity in the thematic organization of the discourse. A thematically nonreferential NP stands for an entity which is taken by the speaker as of no or little importance in discourse, and a thematically referential NP is one that stands for an entity of relatively higher importance.

Some referents play an important role in the development of the discourse, some only play a secondary role in the process, and some may be just mentioned in passing by the speaker, serving as the prop for the scene, or providing background information to the referents in the foreground. From the perspective of thematic progression in discourse, an NP in referential use is first and foremost one that indicates a clearly delineated, bound entity with continuous identity over time, which, due to this continuous identity over time, is available for further tracking after it is introduced into the universe of discourse. Referentiality, from this perspective, "is not so much of a speaker having a referent in mind at the time of the utterance, as of a speaker assessing the relative discourse significance of an entity and presenting to hearers in such a way as to successfully foreground it" (Hopper and Thompson 1993:360). Instead of activating or referring back to an independent mental file, a discourse thematic nonreferential NP, according to Du Bois (1980) and Thompson (1997), typically plays a non-tracking role in discourse, serving one of three major functions of classifying, predicating, and orienting or backgrounding.

Languages may be sensitive to distinction in discourse thematicity. There are morphosyntactic devices whose primary function is to mark degrees of thematic importance registered by discourse entities in the context of use. A well-known example is *this* in English in its relatively recent use as an indefinite determiner to introduce into discourse referents of thematic importance. Grammatical constructions have also been found to differ significantly in terms of the discourse thematicity of the NPs that occur in them. Hopper and Thompson (1993:363-4), for instance, report that in a study based on text counts, 97% of English subject NPs in their data are discourse-manipulable, whereas 65% of object NPs are discourse nonreferential.

Similar linguistic devices have been attested in Chinese. Sun (1988), for instance, reports that 80% of the major participants in Chinese are introduced by means of numeral-classified constructions in spoken narratives. Wright and Givón (1987:15) also find that the grammatical contrast between the *yi*+CL+NP construction and bare NP in introducing indefinite nouns for the first time into discourse in Chinese codes the pragmatics of importance, with the former marking entities of pragmatic importance, and the latter entities of minor or no importance in discourse.

Chen (2009) examines the discourse thematic referentiality of two groups of NPs in Chinese, one in the form of an indefinite NP in the *yi*+CL+NP construction and the other in the form of bare NP, in connection with some other major grammatical constructions in order to establish whether, and if so how, discourse thematicity is systematically encoded in Chinese. It is found that whereas bare NP can be characterized as a marker of thematic nonreferentiality or low thematicity in Chinese, the indefinite NP in the form of *yi*+CL+NP, in and of itself, is a much less consistent marker of thematicity. It may encode an entity of low thematic importance just as likely as an entity of high thematic importance. In addition to the contrast between encoding devices such as numeral-classified NP and bare NP in Chinese, other grammatical constructions have also been found to differ significantly in terms of the discourse thematicity of the NPs that occur in them. Irrespective of whether or not they are of specific and identifiable reference, the NPs in the locative construction are predominantly encoded as bare NP, the form par excellence for both semantically/ pragmatically nonreferential entities and thematically nonreferential entities. In contrast, the effect of the subject position and the *you* presentative construction which are traditionally taken as canonical devices to introduce entities of thematic importance is overridden by the grammatical encoding of bare NP as a marker of low thematicity, with 67% and 79% of the referents in the form of bare NP introduced in the subject position and in the *you* construction respectively being thematically nonreferential.

2. Definiteness

The term "definiteness" denotes a grammatical category featuring formal distinction whose core function is to mark a nominal expression as identifiable or nonidentifiable. Identifiability is taken as an addressee-oriented, pragmatic notion relating to the assumptions made by the speaker on the cognitive status of a referent in the mind of the addressee in the context of utterance. A referent is considered to be identifiable if the speaker assumes that the addressee, by means of the linguistic encoding of the NP and in the particular universe of discourse, is able to identify the particular entity in question among other entities of the same or different class in the context. Otherwise it is considered to be nonidentifiable.

The formal distinction in terms of definiteness may be expressed by a variety of grammatical means in languages, including phonological, lexical, morphological, and word order. Most typically, the grammatical category is encoded in terms of a contrast between a definite article like *the*, and an indefinite article like *a* in English. A definite expression with *the* differs essentially from an indefinite expression with *a* in that the former is marked as being identifiable and the latter as nonidentifiable. Whether or not a language is considered to have a grammatical category of definiteness is decided, to a large extent, on the basis of whether there are specialized grammatical means primarily for this particular function on a par with definite and indefinite articles in languages like English. As observed by Chesterman (1991: 4), "it is via the articles that definiteness is quintessentially realized, and it is in analyses of the articles that the descriptive problems are most clearly manifested.

Moreover, it is largely on the basis of the evidence of articles in article-languages that definiteness has been proposed at all as a category in other languages."

Three major types of linguistic devices—lexical, morphological, and positional—are employed in Chinese to indicate or suggest to the addressee whether the nominal expressions should be interpreted as being of identifiable or nonidentifiable reference.

2.1 Lexical and morphological

In terms of lexical encoding, aside from proper names and personal pronouns, three major groups of definite determiners serve the function of marking a referent as identifiable in Chinese: demonstratives, possessives, and universal quantifiers. Monosyllabic classifiers in Chinese, and occasionally monosyllabic nouns as well, may undergo the morphological process of reduplication to gain the same meaning as that of distributive universal quantifiers. There is no *the*-like definite article in Chinese. Of the major definite determiners in Chinese, demonstratives are developing functions, more advanced in spoken Chinese than in written Chinese, which are served by the definite article in English in marking referents whose identifiability is established through shared general knowledge, and in anaphoric and associative uses, although they have still preserved their deictic force to a considerable extent in these situations. All definite articles in languages evolved from demonstratives through the process of grammaticalization. To the extent that the Chinese demonstratives have retained their deictic force, they don't always behave in the same way as fully grammaticalized markers of definiteness like the English *the*, and thus cannot be treated on a par with a fully developed definite article.

The most important indefinite determiner in Chinese is *yi*+classifier. *Yi* on its own is a numeral, and can still be used in the same way as all the other numerals in Chinese. Unlike the other numerals, however, *yi*+classifier has undergone the process of grammaticalization toward a marker of indefiniteness in much the same way as the English indefinite article was derived from the numeral 'one.' Other than the fact that *yi*+classifier can be used both as a pronominal and as a determiner, it serves all the major functions of a regular indefinite article as the English *a*, and moreover extends to other uses that have not been reported for indefinite determiners in English or other languages (cf. Chen 2003, 2004).

NPs which are lexically or morphologically encoded as definite or indefinite, on the assumption that they are used referentially, are always interpreted as of either identifiable or nonidentifiable reference in utterance, no matter what position they occupy in sentences. The encodings are determinate in relation to the interpretation of identifiability.

There are other types of NPs that, so far as their lexical or morphological encodings are concerned, are neutral with respect to the interpretation of identifiability: the bare NP, and the cardinality expression, which is an NP modified by a cardinal numeral or a quantifier like *ji* 'several'. They constitute what I call the indeterminate encodings of NP with respect to the interpretation of identifiability. In most, but not all, instances, whether the indeterminate expressions are to be interpreted as identifiable or nonidentifiable is indicated, or suggested, by the position of the NP in sentences.

2.2 Positional

Syntactic positions in sentences may display strong inclination in terms of interpretation of the NP in the slot as referentially identifiable or nonidentifiable. It has been a well-known fact in studies of Chinese grammar that a bare noun in subject position, like *keren* 'guest' in the subject position in *keren lai le* 'the guest(s) has/have come' is normally interpreted as identifiable, and the same word in the postverbal position, as in *lai keren le* 'here come(s) guests/a guest', nonidentifiable. Relevant positions in Chinese sentences fall into two categories, definiteness inclined and indefiniteness inclined, as presented in Table 2:

Table 2 Definiteness-and indefiniteness-inclined positions in Chinese

Definiteness-inclined	Indefiniteness-inclined
Subject	Object of the presentative verb *you*
Ba object	Postverbal NP in presentative sentence
Preverbal object	Postverbal NP in existential sentence
First object of ditransitive sentence	Second object of ditransitive sentence

Nominal expressions which are lexically or morphologically encoded as definite or indefinite may be subject to restrictions in their eligibility to occur in some of the positions shown in Table 2. It is ungrammatical, for example, to have a reduplicated classifier or noun in any of the indefiniteness-inclined positions, as exemplified by (1):

(1) *You   ren   ren   lai   guo   zher
     have   person   person   come   EXP   here

"Everybody has been here."

Indefinite expressions can hardly occur as subject with stative predicate, as illustrated by (2):

(2) *Yi   ge   ren   hen   congming
     one   CL   person   very   smart

"One person is very smart."

In the great majority of cases, the inclination is manifested, not in terms of grammatical restriction, but in terms of higher frequency of expressions of one category in contrast with the other in texts. As amply demonstrated in statistical studies of Chinese sentences and discourse, NPs in subject, *ba* object, and the other definiteness-inclined positions are overwhelmingly definite, and those in indefiniteness-inclined positions are overwhelmingly indefinite. Similar findings are reported in other languages as well (cf. Givón 1984/1990).

Expressions which are lexically and morphologically indeterminate with regard to identifiability are not subject to the same kind of restrictions as expressions of determinate encodings. Generally speaking, they occur freely in positions of either inclination, as well as in other positions. At the same time, they display a strong inclination to be interpreted as identifiable in definiteness-inclined positions, and as nonidentifiable in indefiniteness-inclined positions. The strength of the inclination varies with the types of indeterminate encoding and the sentential positions that are occupied by the expressions. There is, however, no absolute correlation between the interpretation in respect of identifiability of reference and the inclination of the position occupied by indeterminate expressions in sentences. Sometimes the same NP in indeterminate encoding may have different interpretations in the same sentential position. Consider (3) and (4):

(3) Liang ge qiangdao cong zheli zou guo, kandao zhouwei
    two CL bandit   from here walk by   see   around
    meiyou ren,   zhiyou Ou Ji zheme yi ge xiaohaizi,
    have:not person only   Ou Ji this one CL kid
    jiu qi   le   huaixin ... Liang ge qiangdao
    then arise PFV evil:idea   two   CL bandit
    ba Ou Ji de shuangshou fan bang zhu.
    BA Ou Ji DE two:hand   back tie   up
    "Two bandits passed by, saw nobody around except the

kid Ou Ji, and then had an evil idea ... The two bandits tied Ou Ji's hands behind his back."

The cardinality expression *liang ge qiangdao* 'two bandits' in the two clauses has exactly the same lexical encoding, and occupies the same syntactic position; it is nonidentifiable on the first occurrence, and identifiable on the second.

(4) Zuowan lianyouchang da huo, tie men dou shao hua le.
last:night refinery big fire iron gate even burn melt CRS
"There was a big fire at the refinery last night. The/an iron gate/gates melted in the fire."

The bare noun *tie men* 'iron gate' in (4) can refer to an identifiable referent, in the situation where there is only one iron gate at the refinery that is supposed to be known to the addressee as part of their shared background knowledge or as a frame triggered entity. The sentence is also appropriate in the context in which the addressee is not assumed to know, and probably the speaker himself does not know either, how many iron gates there were to the refinery and which one or ones were melted in the fire. All that the speaker intends to tell the addressee is that the fire was so destructive that it melted one or more iron gates. In the latter case, the expression obviously refers to a nonidentifiable referent.

In conclusion, there is no simple, fully grammaticalized marker of definiteness in Chinese, like the definite article in English. In spite of the fact that demonstratives in Chinese have developed some uses that are normally served by definite articles in other languages, their basic or primary functions are still far from being those of deictically neutral determiners of definiteness like English *the*. While the Chinese numeral *yi* has arguably reached the endpoint of grammaticalization into an indefinite article, there is no paradigmatic contrast between it and a highly grammaticalized marker of definiteness. Furthermore, it is not obligatory to mark a nominal expression as either definite or indefinite in Chinese, as is the case in English. To the extent that situations are abundant in Chinese in which the interpretation of bare NPs and cardinality expressions with respect to identifiability cannot be determined solely in terms of their position in sentences, and may even be ambiguous or indeterminate with regard to identifiability, the features of definiteness and indefiniteness cannot be uniquely and unambiguously specified for nominal expressions in Chinese. This leads to the conclusion that definiteness as a grammatical category has not been fully developed in Chinese.

References

Chen, Ping. 2003. Indefinite determiner introducing definite referent: A special use of "*yi* 'one' + classifier" in Chinese. *Lingua* 113: 1169-1184.

Chen, Ping. 2004. Identifiability and definiteness in Chinese. *Linguistics* 42.6: 1129-1184.

Chen, Ping. 2009. Aspects of referentiality. *Journal of Pragmatics* 41: 1657-1674.

Chesterman, Andrew. 1991. *On Definiteness*. Cambridge: Cambridge University Press.

Donnellan, Keith S. 1966. Reference and definite descriptions. *Philosophical Review* 75: 281-394.

Du Bois, John W. 1980. Beyond definiteness: The trace of identity in discourse. In: *The Pear Stories: Cognitive, Cultural and Linguistic Aspects of Narrative Production*, ed. by Chafe, Wallace, 203-274. Norwood, N.J.: Albex Publishing Corporation.

Fodor, Janet Dean and Ivan Sag. 1982. Referential and quantificational indefinites. *Linguistics and Philosophy* 5: 355-398.

Givón, Talmy. 1984/1990. *Syntax: A Functional-Typological Introduction*. Vols. I and II. Amsterdam and Philadelphia: John Benjamins.

Hopper, Paul and Sandra A. Thompson. 1993. Language universals, discourse pragmatics, and semantics. *Language Sciences* 15.4: 357-376.

Li, Charles N. and Sandra A. Thompson. 1981. *Mandarin Chinese: A Functional Reference Grammar*. Berkeley and Los Angeles: University of California Press.

Lü, Shuxiang. 1944. *Ge* zi de yingyong fanwei, fu lun danweici qian *yi* zi de tuoluo

("个"字的应用范围，附论单位词前"一"字的脱落) [Scope of the uses of *ge* and omission of *yi* in front of classifiers]. In: *Lü Shuxiang Wenji* [*Collected Works of Lü Shuxiang*], Vol. 2, 144-175. Beijing: The Commercial Press, 1990.

Russell, Bertrand. 1905. On denoting. *Mind* 14. Reprinted in *Readings in Semantics*, ed. by Zabeeh, et al., 141-158. Urbana: University of Illinois Press, 1974.

Russell, Bertrand. 1919. *Introduction to Mathematical Philosophy*. London: G. Allen & Unwin.

Strawson, Peter F. 1950. On referring. *Mind* 59: 320-344.

Strawson, Peter F. 1964. Identifying reference and truth value. *Theoria* Vol. XXX: 96-108.

Sun, Chaofen. 1988. The discourse function of numeral classifiers in Mandarin Chinese. *Journal of Chinese Linguistics* 16.2: 298-323.

Thompson, Sandra A. 1997. Discourse motivations for the core-oblique distinction as a language universal. In: *Directions in Functional Linguistics*, ed. by Kamio, Akio, 59-82. Amsterdam: John Benjamins Publishing Company.

汉语中的有指与定指

提 要 本文阐释有指/无指和有定/无定的语用、话语和认知特点，并且系统分析这两对概念在汉语中的语法形式特点。有指/无指和有定/无定这两组概念都同事物的指称属性有关。发话人如果用名词性成分指称自己认知领域里某个具体事物，该事物就是有指成分，否则是无指成分。发话人如果认为受话人能将某个事物从同类事物之中辨认出来，该事物就是可辨识事物，否则就是不可辨识事物。可辨识事物语法上一般表现为有定成分，不可辨识事物一般表现为无定成分。有指/无指是从发话人的角度出发（speaker-oriented）的概念，而有定/无定是基于受众（addressee-oriented）的概念。汉语无指成分最典型的表现形式是光杆名词，而有指/无指的区别则可以通过词法、语法成分和语序表达。

关键词 有指　定指　无定　话语主题性

(This article was first published in *The Oxford Handbook of Chinese Linguistics* edited by William S-Y Wang and Chaofen Sun, Oxford University Press, pp.404-413, in 2015. Permission by Oxford University Press to reprint the article in the present volume is gratefully acknowledged.)

Identifiability and definiteness in Chinese*

Abstract This article explores how the pragmatic notion of identifiability is encoded in Chinese. It presents a detailed analysis of the distinctive linguistic devices, including lexical, morphological, and position in sentence, which are employed in Chinese to indicate the interpretation of referents in respect of identifiability. Of the major determiners in Chinese, demonstratives are developing uses of a definite article, and *yi* 'one' + classifier has developed uses of an indefinite article, although morphologically and in some cases also functionally they have not yet been fully grammaticalized. What makes Chinese further different from languages like English is the interpretation in this regard of what are called indeterminate lexical encodings, which include bare NPs and cardinality expressions. They by themselves are neutral in respect of the interpretation of identifiability. For indeterminate expressions, there is a strong but seldom absolute correlation between the interpretation of identifiability or nonidentifiability and their occurrence in different positions in a sentence. Unlike the cases with several other languages without articles like Czech, Hindi, and Indonesian, the features of definiteness and

---

* I am grateful to Sandra A. Thompson and two anonymous reviewers of *Linguistics* for their valuable comments, criticisms, and suggestions on an earlier draft of this paper.

Following are the abbreviations used in this paper. For a detailed explanation of the terms, cf. C. Li & Thompson (1981).

    BA   preverbal object marker (*ba*)
    CL   classifier
    CRS Current Relevant State (*le*)
    CSC complex stative construction (*de*)
    DE   nominalizer (*de*)
    DUR durative aspect marker (*zhe*)
    PFV perfective aspect marker (*le*)
    SFP sentence-final particle

indefiniteness cannot be obligatorily and uniquely specified for nominal expressions in Chinese. The findings in this article lead to the conclusion that definiteness as a grammatical category defined in the narrow sense has not been fully developed in Chinese.

Keywords identifiability; definiteness; definite article; indefinite article; demonstrative; numeral 'one' ; grammaticalization

1. Introduction

The term "identifiability" in this paper denotes a pragmatic concept, and the term "definiteness" denotes a grammatical category featuring formal distinctions whose core function is to mark a nominal expression as identifiable or nonidentifiable. The formal distinctions may be expressed by a variety of grammatical means in languages, including phonological, lexical, morphological, and word order. Most typically, and also most extensively in languages, the grammatical category is encoded in terms of a contrast between a definite article like *the*, and an indefinite article like *a* in English. A definite expression with *the* differs essentially from an indefinite expression with *a* in that the former is marked as being identifiable and the latter as nonidentifiable. Whether or not a language is considered to have a grammatical category of definiteness is decided, to a large extent, on whether there are specialized grammatical means primarily for this particular function on a par with definite and indefinite articles in languages like English. As observed by Chesterman (1991:4), "it is via the articles that definiteness is quintessentially realized, and it is in analyses of the articles that the descriptive problems are most clearly manifested. Moreover, it is largely on the basis of the evidence of articles in article-languages that definiteness has been proposed at all as a category in other languages."

As is the case with other grammatical categories in language like tense, number, gender, proximity, animacy, etc., the form and function do not always match. Definite expressions typically, but need not always, mark identifiability, just as a verb in past tense may be found in uses which have nothing to do with past time.

There is no fully grammaticalized definite article in Chinese. I aim to address the following issues in this paper:

i. How is the pragmatic notion of identifiability encoded in Chinese?

ii. How is Chinese in this respect similar to, or different from, languages with articles like English, and languages without articles like Czech, Hindi and Indonesian?

iii. Is it justified—and if so, to what extent and in what sense— to assert that definiteness as a grammatical category exists in Chinese?

Given the relevance of identifiability and definiteness to a wide range of linguistic phenomena, findings in this paper, I would hope, would have implications for other studies involving these concepts, in particular relating to Chinese and those languages lacking *the*-and *a*-like articles, and also to other languages in general.

1.1 Definition of identifiability and definiteness

Identifiability in this paper is taken as a pragmatic notion relating to the assumptions made by the speaker on the cognitive status of a referent in the mind of the addressee in the context of utterance. A referent is considered to be identifiable if the speaker assumes that the addressee, by means of the linguistic encoding of the noun phrase and in the particular universe of discourse, is able to identify the particular entity in question among other entities of the same or different class in the context. Otherwise, it is considered to be nonidentifiable. For instance,

(1) a. George finally bought *a house*.

b. George finally bought *the house*.

By using 'a house' in (1a), the speaker assumes that the addressee is not in a position to identify which particular house George bought; in uttering (1b), on the other hand, he assumes that the addressee knows which house he is talking about. The entity of house is presented as nonidentifiable in (1a), and identifiable in (1b).

The terms "entity" and "referent" used in the paper, it is to be noted, are shorthand for mental presentations, or mental files, of entities denoted by linguistic expressions in the universe of discourse constructed by the speaker and the addressee. I follow Lambrecht (1994:36-7) in taking the universe of discourse as composed of two parts, the text-external world, and the text-internal world. The former comprises the participants and the spatio-temporal setting of a speech event, and the latter comprises the linguistic expressions and their meanings. Whether or not the entities exist in the "real world", and whether they have been established in physical or linguistic terms seldom affect how the linguistics expressions are actually used to draw attention to what we are talking about, which is what linguists are really interested in, as different from philosophers and logicians, who are equally, if not more, interested in the ontological and epistemological aspects of the issue.[①]

[①] To illustrate this point, let us consider the following sentences ([i] and [ii] are from Givón 1984:120):
 (i) There was once *a unicorn*. The unicorn loved lettuce.
 (ii) There was once *a rabbit*. The rabbit loved lettuce.
 (iii) There was once *a rabbit* under this tree. The rabbit loved lettuce.
 Unicorns do not exist in the real world; the existence of 'rabbit' in (ii) is established in linguistic

The pragmatic notion of identifiability, or notions of a very similar nature, comes under different names in the literature, such as old vs. new (Halliday 1967), given vs. new (Clark & Clark 1977), definite vs. indefinite (Chafe 1976; J. Lyons 1977; Givón 1984-1990), and uniquely identifiable vs. nonidentifiable (Gundel et al. 1993). The terminological, and in some cases substantive differences between writers need not concern us here. This paper follows Chafe (1994:93) and Lambrecht (1994:77-79) in the usage of the terms of identifiable and nonidentifiable as defined above.

Definiteness, on the other hand, is used in this paper as a grammatical concept, relating to the formal grammatical means in which identifiable and nonidentifiable referents are encoded distinctively in language. The formal grammatical means include phonological, lexical, morphological, positional and other linguistic devices whose function it is to indicate whether a nominal expression is to be interpreted as identifiable or nonidentifiable. Whether definiteness is a grammatical category in a particular language depends on how the notion is defined. Generally speaking, there are two senses, a broad one and a narrow one, in which definiteness is claimed to be a grammatical category. In the broad sense, it is understood as characterizing the major types of identifiable referring expressions, mainly personal pronouns, proper names, and definite noun phrases featuring one of the definite determiners in that language. Assuming that almost all languages in one way or another provide for these types of identifiable expressions, we would come to the natural conclusion that definiteness, in the broad sense of the term, is language universal. In the current literature, however, the notion of definiteness as a grammatical category is usually

---

terms, and in (c), in both physical and linguistic terms. Yet, *the unicorn* in (i) and *the rabbit* in (ii) and (iii) display exactly the same set of features in terms of both form and function.

understood in a narrow sense: the defining criteria are whether there is a linguistic form, or forms, whose core, or primary function it is to indicate identifiability, and whether the features of definiteness and indefiniteness are obligatorily and uniquely specified for nominal expressions in the language.

It is not always straightforward to decide on the basis of the above criteria whether a particular language has definiteness or not. When definiteness is marked by typically grammatical or functional morphemes in the form of affixes, clitics or morphophonologically weak free forms (most importantly articles like the definite article *the* in English), which are called simple definites in C. Lyons (1999:279), it is normally a clear case for the presence of definiteness as a grammatical category. Languages in this category include English, French, and other Germanic and Romance languages. In other languages which are genetically and geographically as diversely scattered as Chinese, Japanese, Czech, Russian, Warlpiri, Lango, Ik, Hindi and Indonesian, identifiability is indicated primarily by forms such as proper names, demonstratives, personal pronouns and possessives, which are called complex definites in C. Lyons (1999), or other grammatical means like word order. The major difference between simple definites and complex definites, apart from morphological autonomy and phonological weight, is that the encoding devices in the former group, whatever they may be diachronically derived from, have undergone the full process of grammaticalization and developed highly specialized uses to indicate identifiability or nonidentifiability of entities, while those in the latter group simultaneously, or even primarily, encode other grammatical features like deixis, person, saliency, topicality and so on, in addition to identifiability. Linguists may look further into the languages that only have complex definites to determine whether definiteness is obligatorily and unambiguously encoded for nominal expressions in that language. If it is, it may be treated as a language with definiteness as a grammatical category; if it is not, it is taken as a language lacking definiteness as a grammatical category. While identifiability, as a pragmatic concept, plays an important role in the form and function of human languages, definiteness, as a grammatical category defined in the narrow sense, may not be fully developed in some languages. It is, in the words of C. Lyons (1999:278), the grammaticalization of identifiability.[1] Like almost all other grammatical categories such as number, tense, or voice, it is present in some languages, and absent in others.

The notion of definiteness in this article is used in its narrow sense. Applying the above criteria to Chinese, as will be elaborated in this paper, I will conclude that definiteness as a grammatical category has not been fully developed in Chinese. On the other hand, the terms of definite and indefinite are also extensively used in the current literature, sometimes rather loosely, to refer to two distinctive groups of formal expressions which are normally, but not necessarily interpreted as identifiable versus nonidentifiable in addition to other accompanying grammatical and pragmatic attributes. It is in the latter use that proper nouns, personal pronouns, demonstratives, some types of quantified NPs, etc. are referred to as definite expressions by many writers, with

---

[1] It has been argued that there are semantic and pragmatic components other than identifiability to the grammatical notion of definiteness, the most prominent of which is inclusiveness (cf. Hawkins 1977). C. Lyons (1999:278) notes that in languages like Chinese and Korean which do not have an explicit definiteness marker such as the English definite article, what is customarily referred to as definiteness is usually an element of discourse organization, relating to whether the referents are familiar or already established in the discourse. It is obviously identifiability rather than inclusiveness that is involved here. Furthermore, C. Lyons argues that demonstratives when used as markers of definiteness indicate identifiability, not inclusiveness. It is also suggested by Epstein (1993) on the basis of data from Old French, that some definite articles may also serve the function of marking referents that are nonidentifiable but prominent. I leave the issue open whether and how the notion of inclusiveness, or other relevant notions, also plays a role here.

no commitment to any claim on whether there is definiteness as a grammatical category in the language in question. For convenience of exposition, and to ensure comparability, I also follow this practice in this paper.

1.2 Definition of other related notions

It is appropriate in this connection to discuss briefly another two pairs of related notions, which are referential vs. nonreferential, and specific vs. nonspecific.

There is a striking lack of general consensus on the definition and denotation of these terms in the current literature. Seldom do we find two writers who adopt same definitions for these terms, or use the same term to cover the same range of linguistic phenomena. The differences are both terminological and substantive—in a way that one might ask whether or not these terms have passed their use-by date.[1] What is presented below is a very sketchy account of my views on the relevant issues (cf. Chen 2004 for details). It is, I hope, sufficient for the purpose of this article.

I follow Payne & Huddleston (2002:399) in defining a referential NP as one which refers to "some independently distinguishable entity, or set of entities" in the universe of discourse, where "independently distinguishable" means "distinguishable by properties other than those inherent in the meaning of the expression itself". Nonreferential uses of nominal

---

[1] To give an example illustrating the diversity of the usage of the terms in question, let us consider the following sentence:
(i) *A friend* has just sent me a lovely Valentine card.
J. Lyons (1977:189) maintains that the subject NP is subject to both specific and nonspecific interpretation. However, it is argued in Krifka et al. (1995:16) that this NP, as the subject of a particular predication, can only make specific reference.

expressions, I propose, fall into three major groups.

First, and the "most non-referential" are instances of what I call "nonindividuated", as the nominal expressions in this group are used primarily for the quality denoted by the expressions, rather than as individuals. They are considered to be "nonreferential in the semantic sense" by Hopper & Thompson (1984:711) and Du Bois (1980), who have identified five types of this nonreferential use of nominals, as exemplified in the following sentences:

(2) a. incorporation of patient:

I only wear one in my left when I'm wearing *my lenses*.

b. incorporation of oblique:

We went to *school* yesterday.

c. noun compounding:

pear tree, *letter* box

d. predicative nominal:

He is *the Prime Minister of Australia*.[①]

e. nominal in the scope of negation:

Please don't say *a word*.

In terms of formal encoding, the nominals in the nonreferential use can be indefinite (2e), definite (2a and 2d), or bare nouns (2b and 2c). Nonreferential expressions in this group are all characterized by the fact that they do not have continuous identity in the following discourse, and do not allow anaphoric reference .

The second group of nominals in the nonreferential use are nonspecific expressions. An expression is specific if the speaker uses it to refers to a particular entity in the universe of discourse, which may be identifiable or nonidentifiable; otherwise it is nonspecific. One of

---

① The nominal expression in question is in predicative use. It can also be interpreted as being in equative use in this sentence, in which case it is referential and identifiable.

the most important defining features is that with a specific referent, the speaker may be able to provide more identifying information about it, or to use another referring expression of different linguistic encoding to refer to it. While with a nonspecific referent, all the speaker knows is that it fits the description of the nominal expression. Consider the following examples.

(3) a. Everyday *the chef* comes to cook the dinner for us.

b. Everyday *a chef* comes to cook the dinner for us.

'the chef' in (3a) is specific, and identifiable. There are two readings for 'a chef' in (3b), one specific, and the other nonspecific. On the specific reading, the speaker may, though not necessarily, tell us more about his/her personal attributes such as age, appearance, etc. With 'a chef' on nonspecific reading, on the other hand, the speaker is unlikely to know anything beyond his/her type membership.

There are three major types of context in which a nominal expression may be subject to a specific and a nonspecific interpretation. First is represented by the so-called narrow-scope NP, which is in the scope of another term that is quantified, as exemplified by (3b).

The second is marked by the irrealis, or non-fact modality of the proposition where the nominal is embedded, which, according to Givón (1984-1990:393ff.), characterizes all of the following situations:

(4) a. sentences in future or habitual tense;

b. within the scope of world-creating verbs like 'want', 'look for', 'imagine', etc.;

c. within the scope of complements of non-implicative verbs and nonfactive verbs such as 'believe', 'think', 'say', 'claim', etc.;

d. within the scope of probabilistic modal operators like 'can', 'may', and 'must';

e. within the scope of irrealis adverbial clauses, imperative or interrogative sentences.

Consider (5), a classic example illustrating the distinction between a specific and a nonspecific interpretation of the nominal in a sentence of irrealis modality:

(5) John intends to marry *a Norwegian girl*.

John may already have a Norwegian girl in mind, whom he intends to marry. She may be known or unknown to the speaker. Or John simply intends to marry a Norwegian girl, whomever it may be. The noun phrase 'a Norwegian girl' is specific in the first case, and nonspecific in the second.

Finally, following an approach initiated in Partee (1970), the distinction traditionally drawn between the referential and the attributive use of definite expressions since Donnellan (1966) is captured in this paper in terms of the contrast between specific and nonspecific. Consider the nominal 'Smith's murderer' in (6):

(6) *Smith's murderer* is insane.

It can have a referential or specific interpretation, or an attributive or nonspecific interpretation. The expression in the specific use can be replaced with other descriptions of the same person, which is not possible with the expression in the nonspecific or attributive use.

While all of them are nonreferential, nonspecific expressions differ from the non-individuated expressions in that they may allow anaphoric reference in subsequent discourse, although usually subject to some restrictions. As observed by Karttunen (1976), for instance, it is possible for a nominal in the nonspecific use to be followed by a short-term anaphoric pronoun or definite noun phrase, "provided the discourse continues in the same mode". Under either interpretation, the nominal expression in (5) can be followed by an anaphoric pronoun (also cf.

Heim 1988:249ff.).

(7) a. John intends to marry *a Norwegian girl*. She is a linguist. (specific)

b. John intends to marry *a Norwegian girl*. She must be a linguist. (nonspecific)

The third major use of nonreferential expressions is for generic reference. It refers to a kind or a genus, instead of a particular object. Since it has no direct relevance to the subject of this article, we will not discuss it here (cf. Krifka et al. 1995).

2. Cognitive basis of identifiability

As a cognitive concept, identifiability denotes a status of the referent in the mental representations of the participants of a speech event. Its social and expressive functions aside, a speech event may be taken as a process by which the speaker instructs the addressee to reconstruct a particular mental representation of events and ideas that the speaker himself has in his mind. When he chooses among a range of possible alternatives what he believes to be the most felicitous way to encode and send the message to the addressee, the speaker depends crucially on his assumptions regarding the various statuses of the entities, attributes and their links which comprise the mental discourse model in the minds of the speech participants, particularly in the mind of the addressee—such statuses as relating to their location in memory, predictability, attention state, and so on. These assumptions, furthermore, are continuously adjusted and updated in the on-going, dynamic process of communication.

What are the factors on the basis of which the speaker comes to assumptions one way or another on the identifiability of entities for the addressee? The status of being identifiable can be assumed by the speaker to have been established for an entity between him and the addressee by virtue of a variety of identificatory resources. Roughly speaking, they fall into two major categories. In the first category, the identifiability is directly evoked from its presence in the context of discourse, which is composed of the physical situation of utterance, and the linguistic text; in the second category, the identifiability of the entity in question is established on the basis of shared background knowledge between speaker and addressee, or inferable from other entities in discourse by virtue of the knowledge shared by participants of the speech event about the associations between the former and the latter.

2.1 Direct physical or linguistic co-presence

The identity of an entity is considered to be contextually evoked when the entity in question is located in the spatio-temporal universe of discourse where the speaker and the addressee are co-present and can be uniquely identified by means of the linguistic expression used with or without accompanying paralinguistic expressions. For instance, catching sight of someone who has just entered the room, the speaker, most likely with accompanying bodily gesture or sight in the direction of the person, may ask the following question to the addressee without having provided any other information about the person prior to the utterance:

(8) Do you know who *he/that man/the man* is?

In addition to the physical situation of utterance, a more common type of the context of discourse is constructed through the use of language by the participants of the speech event. In so far as identifiability is concerned, entities that have been introduced into the text by the speaker are comparable to those that make their first appearance in the physical environment. After a referent has been introduced into the context, it can be treated as identifiable on subsequent mentions, given that enough identificatory linguistic encoding is provided. The identifiability of such a referent is taken as textually evoked, as illustrated by the following example:

(9) There is a dog and a cat in my backyard. *The dog* loves to chase *the cat*.

'the dog' and 'the cat' refer backward to the correlated entities introduced into the text by 'a dog' and 'a cat'. They represent the typical use of definite expressions in anaphoric reference.

2.2 Shared background knowledge

The identity of a referent is also established on the basis of the shared knowledge between the participants of the speech event about their physical and linguistic environments, which may vary considerably in terms of scope and nature. It may involve only the speaker and the addressee, or it may be so broad as to cover all those who live in the same social and cultural environments. In the situation of a family that has a pet dog, the husband may ask his wife the following question when he returns from work in the evening, with the assumption that the addressee is able to establish the identity of the noun phrase 'the dog':

(10) Where is *the dog*?

In this particular context, it is normally impossible for the speaker to accompany the utterance with any deictic gestures as the dog in question is physically absent; it is not necessary for the dog to be verbally introduced into the discourse before being treated as identifiable. The identifiability of the dog derives from the background knowledge shared between the husband and the wife that they have a dog, and a dog only. It is by the same token that the identity of the referents of such noun phrases like 'the house', 'the river', 'the City Council', 'the Prime Minister', 'the President' and 'the sun', as well as proper nouns, is established in contexts of varying scope and nature. The knowledge involved can be very specific, as is the case with the dog in (10), or very general, as with the sun.

The identity of a referent can also be inferred from other entities or activities in the discourse through logical reasoning on the basis of the general knowledge of the interrelationship among the entities or activities involved. They are often interrelated in such a way that the mention of one will automatically bring the mental representation of others that are customarily associated with it into the consciousness of the participants of the speech event. The knowledge of such interrelationships among entities is generally shared by all the members of the group, constituting an important feature defining the membership of a certain community. Such organization of knowledge in memory is captured in terms of theoretical constructs such as frame, schema, script, scenarios etc. in cognitive sciences. Consider the following example:

(11) David bought an old car yesterday. *The horn* didn't work.

That cars have horns can be assumed, in the context of the modern society, to be part of general knowledge in the possession of ordinary language users. This enables the speaker to assume that, once the referent of a car has been introduced into discourse, the addressee is able to establish the identity of the horn as being the part of the car. In this case, the antecedent of the horn is not directly mentioned in the previous discourse; instead, it is identified as the horn of the car through what Clark (1977) calls "indirect reference by association", which is a type of bridging cross-reference. Consider another example:

(12) Joe bought a used car yesterday, but *the seller* later claimed that he didn't get *the money* from Joe.

Among the major stereotypical information slots that a selling frame, as presented in the first clause, characteristically has are a buyer, a seller, an object and money that change hands. Although the seller and the money in the second clause are mentioned for the first time in the discourse, their identity has been established through the evocation of the frame as the seller and the money, which are the fillers of the slots of the transaction.

Indirect reference by association involves anaphora and shared general knowledge simultaneously. It looks backward to an entity or situation that has already been present in the universe of discourse, in a way similar to the normal anaphoric reference. Rather than in a direct reference to the correlated referent in previous discourse, it refers to one whose identifiability is inferred through association with another referent or situation in the general knowledge of the participants.

Referents which derive their identifiability through association may display varying degrees of identifiability, depending on the types of frames and referents, as well as on the extent of familiarity with the frames on the part of addressees. A distinction is drawn in the literature between two kinds of bridging cross-reference: one represented by (13) quoted from Haviland & Clark (1974:515), and the other by (14) from Sanford & Garrod (1981:104):

(13) a. We got some beer out of the trunk. *The beer* was warm.

b. We checked the picnic supplies. *The beer* was warm.

(14) a. Mary put the baby's clothes on. *The clothes* was

made of pink wool.

b. Mary dressed the baby. *The clothes* were made of pink wool.

In contrast to the direct anaphoric reference to the antecedent in the previous sentence in (13a) and (14a), the identity of the definite nominals in (13b) and (14b) is indirectly established through association in terms of the frames of 'picnic supplies' and 'dressing'. It is reported in Haviland & Clark (1974) that in psycholinguistic experiments, it takes more processing time for most subjects to establish the connection between the anaphoric definite expression in the second sentence and its "trigger" indirect antecedent in (13b) than is the case with the direct antecedent in (13a). However, no significant difference in processing time is found between (14a) and (14b) in the comprehension experimentation by Sanford & Garrod (1981). The results of the two experiments suggest that some associations are easier to establish than others. The association between 'the clothes' and the 'dressing' frame is part of the general knowledge of ordinary people so that the frame will easily or automatically activate 'clothes' in our mental representation. On the other hand, as noted by Brown & Yule (1983:263), the connection between picnic supplies and the beer is not as readily made by readers other than "a group of real ale enthusiasts who often indulge their enthusiasm on picnics at the local park." In other words, the 'clothes' in (14b) is more identifiable than the 'beer' in (13b) with most addressees. In spite of the difference, all the referents in question are encoded in the same way as a definite NP marked by the definite article.

The identifiability of a referent may also derive from its association with information that is contained in the nominal expression itself. Consider the following example:

(15) Do you know *the man that she went to dinner with last night*?

It may well be that the referent of 'the man' appears for the first time in the universe of discourse. It is treated as an identifiable referent through the identifying function of the restrictive relative clause that follows it: she went to dinner with a man last night, and 'the man' refers to that particular man (cf. C. Lyons 1999:5 for a detailed discussion of the relevant issues). A similar case called "containing inferrable" is discussed by Prince (1981:236-7), who gives the following illustrative example:

(16) Have you heard *the incredible claim that the devil speaks English backwards*?

in which the identifiability of the definite referent 'claim' is inferenced off from the following clause that is properly contained within the inferrable NP itself.

2.3 Degrees of identifiability

It is evident from the above discussion that identifiability, as a pragmatic concept, is a matter of degree. From full identifiability to complete nonidentifiability is a continuum with no clear line of demarcation anywhere along it.① In languages in which identifiability

---

① The relativity of the identifiability of referents often manifests itself in the grammatical structure of language. It is illustrated by Prince (1981:476) in the following sentences:
(i) *A friend of yours* bought a Toyota.
(ii) *A friend of Steve's* bought a Toyota.
(iii) *A friend of my neighbors* bought a Toyota.
(iv) *A friend of a guy I know* bought a Toyota.
(v) ?*A friend of a guy's* bought a Toyota.

There is a scale of identifiability for the referent 'a friend', which correlates with the identifiability of the anchor in the postnominal phrase. The referent becomes less and less identifiable as the identifiability of the anchor decreases. As shown in the above sentences, the subject position of the English

is grammaticalized in terms of definiteness, speakers are usually forced to make a decision on whether to encode entities of varying degrees of identifiability in definite or indefinite terms. The cut-off line between definite vs. indefinite encoding along the continuum of identifiability is not always readily obvious in any language. It is a common phenomenon that a referent of partial identification is treated as identifiable, receiving a definite encoding in the same way as a referent of full identification. Consider the following example from Du Bois (1980:232):

(17) The boy scribbled on *the living-room wall*.

As argued by Du Bois (1980:232), it is not a necessary condition for the definite encoding of the referent of 'the living-room wall' for the addressee to be able to identify precisely which of the four walls of the living room is involved. Du Bois (1980:232) maintains that the definite encoding here is justified so long as the speaker assumes that "the addressee is able to identify the particular living room in question, and to narrow down the range of possible referents to one of the four walls." He also notes that the speaker could be "violating the Gricean maxim of relevance by giving more information than people care to know", if he specifies exactly which wall, as in (18):

(18) He scribbled on *the north living-room wall*.

Du Bois (1980) also points out that to present the wall as nonidentifiable as (19)

(19) He scribbled on *a living room wall*.

would be violating the maxim from the other direction, because it presupposes an excessive curiosity about the walls on the part of the addressee. To explain the phenomenon, Du Bois (1980:233) has

---

sentence, while admitting indefinite expressions, displays a clear inclination to have an NP at the higher end of the scale of identifiability. For similar observations, cf. Givón (1984-1990:431) and Lambrecht (1994:85-86).

proposed what he calls the curiosity principle:

> "A reference is counted as identifiable if it identifies an object close enough to satisfy the curiosity of the hearer. The identification need not to be one to satisfy a philosopher or a Sherlock Holmes, who may of course be led to demand 'Which wall?' In special circumstances even an ordinary speaker might desire more precise identification. But in everyday speech such partial identification is quite common."

The lack of full identification for referents which are encoded as definite is mostly confined to those which derive their identifiability from semantic frames discussed above. It is noted in Löbner (1985:302) that frame-triggered referents may stand in a one-to-one relationship to the anchor, like driver to a car and president to a state, or in a one-to-many relationship, like daughter to a parent and friend to a person. Löbner argues that the identifiability of a definite expression need not be determined in an absolute sense, and a definite article can be used to mark a noun so long as the referent is one that stands in a one-to-one relationship to the anchor in spite of the fact that the overall NP may be nonidentifiable. Thus the grammaticality of (20):

(20) *The mayor* of a small village in Wales.

A case is presented in Lambrecht (1994:91) and C. Lyons (1999:26) in which a referent is treated as identifiable where the conditions for identifiability defined in Löbner's terms do not strictly hold. In (21), for instance, there is no implication that the speaker has only one brother.

(21) I'm going to stay with *my brother* for a few days.

And (22) would be appropriate, as Lambrecht (1994) remarks, even if the unidentified king in question has more than one daughter.

(22) I met *the daughter* of a king.

As long as the information provided by the noun phrase is sufficient for the communicative purpose of the utterance, there is no need to specify it any further. Obviously, the same curiosity principle as formulated by Du Bois (1980) is at work here.

The above issue arises, I maintain, to a large extent as a result of the fact that the speaker is obliged, as a result of the grammatical constraints of definiteness as a grammatical category in English, to make a selection between definite vs. indefinite encoding for the referent in question. It may no longer be an issue in a language without definiteness as a obligatory grammatical category for nominal expressions, such as Chinese, where the referent may be encoded in a way that is neutral with respect to the interpretation of identifiability. The difference between English and Chinese in this respect is readily seen when (17) is translated into Chinese: the referent in question will most likely assume the form of an indeterminate expression (to be explained in Section 4) in a sentence position that does not make any clear indication or suggestion to the addressee regarding whether the expression is to be interpreted as identifiable or nonidentifiable.[1] I will return to this point later.

3. Linguistic encodings of identifiability

Irrespective of whether there is definiteness as a grammatical category, the distinction between identifiability vs. nonidentifiability can be encoded in one way or another in all the languages of the world (cf.

---

[1] Note in this connection the following quote from J. Lyons (1977:188): "It is a characteristic feature of the grammar of English that common nouns in the singular (except when they are used as mass nouns) must be introduced with an article (whether definite or indefinite), a demonstrative adjective, or some other determiner. Not all languages that have what might be described a definite or indefinite article are like English in this respect." It would be interesting to investigate how referents like 'the living-room wall' in (13) are encoded in those languages with respect to definiteness.

Haspelmath 1997; C. Lyons 1999 inter alia). While it is typically encoded in terms of respective formal markings which can be phonological, lexical, morphological, and syntactic, languages vary considerably in the types of encodings most commonly used for the purpose and in how they are used. To bring a cross-linguistic perspective to definiteness in Chinese, let us start with a brief account, based on recent findings reported in the literature, of the linguistic encodings of identifiability in two types of languages, one with and the other without definite or indefinite articles. The former is represented by English, and the latter by Czech, Hindi, and Indonesian.

3.1 English

Definite expressions in English fall into three major categories, namely, definite NPs, proper nouns, and personal pronouns. Definite NPs feature one of the following definite determiners:

1) definite article *the*;

2) demonstratives *this/these, that/those*;

3) possessives like *my, our, his*, and so on;

4) universal quantifiers like *all, every*, random *any*, and so on.

3.1.1 Definite article

As the most important definite determiner, the definite article represents an exemplar par excellence of the grammaticalization of identifiability. Its core function is to indicate that the referent, or more precisely the mental representation of the referent in the universe of discourse, that it is used with is to be interpreted as an entity that the addressee can identify from among the other members of the class in the context. Unlike other definite expressions such as demonstratives, proper nouns or personal pronouns, the article itself does not have any descriptive content other than the ostensive function. As is the case with the overwhelming majority of the languages in the world, and certainly with all the Germanic and Romance languages, the English definite article derives diachronically from a demonstrative pronoun. As a fully grammaticalized marker of definiteness to indicate the identifiability of the noun phrase it modifies, it is neutral with regard to deixis, person, number, gender or any other grammatical features.

Given the highly specialized role of the definite article, it is only to be expected that it stands to serve as a marker of definiteness in all the situations in which identifiability of reference is derived. The uses of the English definite article fall into four major categories, namely situational, anaphoric, shared specific or general knowledge, and associative, covering all the sources of identifiability of referents as discussed in the last section. Following are examples illustrating each of them (cf. Christopherson 1939; Hawkins 1978; C. Lyons 1999; inter alia):

(23) situational:
Get a knife for me from *the table*.

(24) anaphoric:
I saw a man pass by with a dog. *The dog* was very small and skinny, but *the man* was very large.

(25) shared specific knowledge:
Be quiet. Do not wake up *the baby* (who is sleeping in the next room).

(26) shared general knowledge:
The sun is brighter than *the moon*.

(27) frame-based association:
They bought a used car. *The tires* were all worn out.

(28) self-containing association:

Do you know *the man who lived in this room last year*?

(29) self-containing association:

He broke the window glass with *the handle of a bike*.

(23) is an example of the situational use of the definite article. By using the definite article, the speaker indicates to the addressee that the reference is to the table that is most easily accessible in the context of utterance. The use of the definite article here is different from the deictic use of demonstratives to be discussed shortly in that it is ostentive, but does not provide any information in deictic terms. The definite article in (24) is used anaphorically in both nominal expressions, referring back to the referents that have been introduced into the discourse in the first clause. The identifiability of the referents of the nominal expressions in (25) and (26) derives from the shared background knowledge of the speech participants that there is a baby in the house in the case of (25), and a sun and a moon in the case of (26). As noted earlier, the scope of the context covered by the shared background knowledge is a continuum that begins with the immediate situation and extends gradually to the very broad physical, cultural and societal environments we find ourselves in. (27), (28) and (29) exemplify the associative uses of the definite article. (27) illustrates the frame-based association, in which the mention of 'car' triggers the identifiability of all the things that are typically associated with it. On the basis of the general knowledge that cars have tires, 'the tires' in the second clause is most naturally interpreted as referring to those of the car in the first clause. In (28) and (29), the identifiability of the nominal expressions is established on the basis of the information that is contained in the nominal itself.

The uses of *the* as discussed above will serve as a template in the examination of the uses of other definite determiners in English and

Chinese.

3.1.2 Demonstratives

Demonstratives differ from definite articles in two major aspects. First, while definite articles have adjectival uses only, demonstratives typically have adjectival, pronominal and adverbial uses as well[①]. Second, the primary function of demonstratives in English is that of deixis, which has been extended to other uses as well (cf. Fillmore 1982, 1997; Himmelmann 1996; Diessel 1999). They serve to locate and identify entities with reference to their distance in relation to the speech participants in the spatio-temporal space of discourse. As determiners of definiteness, they are mainly found in deictic uses, signaling to the addressee in one way or another that the referent in question is accessible to him in relation of the position of the participants in the context of utterance. Definite articles, in contrast, are deictically neutral.

The uses of demonstratives, following Himmelmann (1996), fall into four major types, which are situational, discourse deictic, anaphoric and recognitional.

(30) situational:

Could you please give me a hand with *this big box*?

(31) discourse deictic:

He did not answer our phone call as promised. *This* is not good.

(32) anaphoric:

---

① Diessel (1999:5) has identified a fourth use, called identificational, as exemplified in the following sentence:

(i) C'est Pascal.
　This/It is Pascal.
　"It/This is Pascal."

There is a zoo a couple of miles down the road. You won't see many animals in *that zoo*.

(33) recognitional:

It was filmed in California, *those dusky kind of hills that they have out here by Stockton and all*.

Demonstratives in situational use differ from definite articles in that the former are subject to the restriction that the referent in question must be visible to the addressee. Compare the following examples:

(34) a. Beware of *the dog*.

b. Beware of *that dog*.

(34a), but not (34b), is be felicitous if the dog is invisible, but its existence can be inferred from the context. As Hawkins (1978:112) notes, "demonstratives are only possible in these cases if the interlocutors can actually see a dog at the time of the utterance." The explanation lies in the deictic component in the semantics of the demonstratives, which distinguishes them from the definite article. The use of the deictics assumes that the addressee is able to locate the referent in terms of its location relative to the participants of the speech event. The assumption would be invalidated if the referent is physically absent from the immediate situation of the utterance.

Anaphora, as enunciated by J. Lyons (1977:670), involves the transference of what are basically spatial notions to the temporal dimensions of the context of utterance and the reinterpretation of deictic location in terms of what may be called location in the universe of discourse. With deixis underlying anaphora, the English demonstratives are found in anaphoric use as well. The anaphoric uses of the demonstratives are much less common in comparison with their deictic uses, and also in comparison with the anaphoric uses of other definite determiners like the definite article and personal pronouns. When they are used anaphorically, it is usually with a contrastive sense.[①]

(33) is quoted from Himmelmann (1996:230), who characterizes it as "recognitional", a term borrowed from Sacks & Schegloff (1979). It is first observed in Sacks & Schegloff (1979), and later developed in Schegloff (1996) that when the speaker does not know with certainty whether a referent is identifiable enough for the addressee, as happens very often in informal talks, he usually prefers a definite expression, either in the form of a proper name, or "recognitional" descriptions, which presumes some familiarity on the part of the addressee with the referent, rather than using an indefinite expression which treats the referent as nonidentifiable. The speaker will often try different wordings, called "try-marked" recognitionals by Sacks and Schegloff, for this definite expression until he perceives recognition on the part of the addressee (cf. Ford & Fox 1996; also cf. Grice 1989 and Levinson 2000 for an explanation). Demonstratives in such recognitional uses are mainly found in situations where the speaker is not very sure whether the relevant knowledge that is crucial to the identifiability of the entity is shared by the addressee or not. As is the case when recognition on the part of the addressee is in doubt, demonstratives in such uses are typically accompanied by expressions like *you know?* and *remember?*, seeking confirmation of the information being shared by the addressee. For a detailed discussion, cf. Sacks & Schegloff (1979), Himmelmann (1996), and Schegloff (1996).

Demonstratives in recognitional use are used to refer to referents that have been previously introduced into discourse, or to introduce referents into discourse for the first time. It is, in my view, a combination of the

---

[①] Note the observation by Clark & Marshall (1981:44) that the use of *that* in the sentence *I met a woman yesterday; that woman was a doctor* "attracts contrastive stress and implies that there is a contrasting set of women."

shared knowledge and self-containing uses of definite determiners. On the one hand, the speaker appeals to the knowledge that he assumes, albeit without much certainty, to be shared by the addressee; on the other hand, he phrases the expression in a way that he hopes will provide sufficient identifying information for the addressee to identify the referent in question.

Apart from the recognitional use which is accompanied by some restrictions, the English demonstratives are normally unacceptable for referents which derive their identifiability through shared specific or general information, as in (35) and (36), or through association, as in (37) and (38):

(35) Be quiet. *Don't wake up *that baby* (who is sleeping in the next room).

(36) *That sun* was covered by dark clouds.

(37) They bought a used car. *These/those tires* are all worn out.

(38) *He broke the window glass with *this/that handle of a bike*.

3.1.3 Grammaticalization of demonstratives into definite articles

It is well-attested in the languages of the world that demonstratives are the most common sources from which definite articles are derived through the process of grammaticalization. In the discussion of the cycle of the definite article, Greenberg (1978:61) describes how a demonstrative, which he calls Stage 0, develops into a definite article, which he calls Stage 1. In a number of instances that have been studied in detail, Greenberg finds that the process of grammaticalization starts when a purely deictic element has come to identify an element as previously mentioned in discourse. Furthermore,

"The point at which a discourse deictic becomes a definite article is where it becomes compulsory and has spread to the point at which it means 'identified' in general, thus including typically things known from context, general knowledge, or as with 'the sun' in non-scientific discourse, identified because it is the only member of its class." (Greenberg 1978:61-62)

His view can be summarized in the diagram of (39):

(39) Stage 0   transitional   Stage 1
     situational deictic   > anaphoric >   shared knowledge
                                              association

The view is shared by Diessel (1999:128-129), who maintains that "the use of anaphoric demonstratives is usually confined to non-topical antecedents that tend to be somewhat unexpected, contrastive or emphatic. When anaphoric demonstratives develop into definite articles their use is gradually extended from non-topical antecedents to all kinds of referents in the preceding discourse. In the course of this development, demonstratives lose their deictic function and turn into formal markers of definiteness".

The above will serve as our guiding criteria when we examine the emerging uses of Chinese demonstratives as definite articles. As markers of definiteness, demonstratives and definite articles differ crucially in that the former are deictic and the latter are not. The process of grammaticalization of demonstratives into definite articles is one in which the deictic force of the demonstratives is gradually bleached out, which is often accompanied by phonological reduction, loss of morphological and grammatical autonomy, etc. As a result of which the demonstratives gradually extend their uses to situations that call for a deictically neutral determiner of definiteness. It has been attested in all the languages that did not, or do not have definite articles. As grammaticalization is by its nature a gradual process, we are more likely to be concerned with transitional stages and borderline cases rather than distinct categories in the studies of the development of demonstratives into definite articles in particular languages. Demonstratives in Chinese, as we will show shortly, display some features characteristic of a transitional stage in the process.

3.1.4 Possessives

English noun phrases with possessives such as *my, his, John's*, as pre-modifiers are definite expressions. It is ungrammatical to insert an indefinite determiner between the possessive and the head noun. However, as C. Lyons (1999:24) points out, it would be wrong to assume that possessives are definite determiners cross-linguistically. In languages like Italian and Greek, possessives do not impose an interpretation of identifiability on the head noun: if the head noun is to be interpreted as identifiable, a definite article is used; and if it is nonidentifiable, an indefinite article is used, as shown by the Italian examples: *il mio libro* 'lit. the my book' ("my book") and *un mio libro* 'lit. a my book' ("a book of mine").

The difference between English and Italian in this regard is captured by C. Lyons (1999: 24) in terms of a typological distinction between a determiner-genitive (DG) language and an adjectival-genitive (AG) language. In DG languages possessives appear in positions reserved for definite determiners, while in AG languages they are in adjectival or some other position. It is also observed by C. Lyons that while a nonidentifiability reading is impossible with the basic possessive structure in DG languages, a prepositional construction is most commonly used when the head noun is nonidentifiable, with or without the co-occurrence of an indefinite marker. Examples from C. Lyons are English *a friend of mine,* French *un ami a moi* 'a friend to me', German *ein Freund von mir* 'a friend of mine' and Irish *cara liom* 'friend with me' ("a friend of mine").

3.1.5 Indefinite markers

The most important indefinite marker in English is the indefinite article *a*. Unstressed *some* and *any* are also used as indefinite markers to indicate that the entity they modify is to be interpreted as nonidentifiable. The weakly stressed *this* also serves as indefiniteness marker, mainly in colloquial speech and typically for referents of high thematic importance with continuing presence in the ensuring discourse.

As is the case in the great majority of languages that have indefinite articles, the indefinite article in English derives from the numeral *one*. It is proposed in Givón (1981, 1984-1990) that there are a few major steps along the functional continuum along which the numeral develops gradually into an indefinite article through the process of grammaticalization:

(40) quantification > referentiality/denotation > genericity/connotation

The English article *a* serves all the three major functions, as exemplified in the following examples:

(41) quantification:

It needs *an hour* and *a quarter*.

(42) referentiality/denotation:

He bought *a book*.

(43) genericity/connotation:

He is *a teacher*.

It is further proposed in Heine (1997) that the second stage of referentiality/denotation consists of three uses, namely as a presentative marker, a specific marker, and a nonspecific marker. The article at the final stage of development is called a 'generalized' article by Heine.

It is important to note that, as argued in C. Lyons (1999:33-4), a noun phrase in English is indefinite if it has no definite determiner, whether or not it has an indefinite determiner. Thus, count nouns in the plural and mass nouns, as in (44) and (45), are indefinite where they are not interpreted generically:

(44) John has gone out to buy *milk*.

(45) I have already put *spoons* on the table.

Cardinality terms like *two*, *three*, and *many* are neutral with respect to definiteness. They can be preceded by a definite determiner, as in:

(46) Pass me those *three books*.

(47) I've only read *a few of the many books she's written*.

When they occur without any determiner, they are indefinite, in a way similar to count nouns in the plural and mass nouns.

3.2 Languages without definite articles

Two recent studies, Cummins (1998) and Porterfield & Srivastav (1988), have explored the correlation between identifiability and definiteness in Czech, Hindi and Indonesian, which, like Chinese, are languages that lack simple definiteness markers such as the English definite article. For want of space, what is presented here is a very brief summary of their main points. Readers are referred to the two papers for a detailed account of their findings.

Identifiability in Czech, according to Cummins (1998), is marked in terms of various linguistic devices including word order and intonation. Bare NPs and cardinality NPs in sentence-initial positions are definite expressions. Their default reading in sentence final positions is indefinite. Bare NPs in final positions are definite only when the entity in questions is "at hand in context or in memory". A demonstrative *ten* is often used as a definiteness marker in the language, serving as the most close approximate to an definite article like the English *the*. Both bare NPs and *ten*-modified NPs are found in anaphoric uses.

Bare singular NPs in Hindi, as concluded by Porterfield & Srivastav (1988), are always to be interpreted as definite expressions. In situations where they are apparently indefinite, they are in kind-level generic use. In Indonesia, bare NPs are always in generic use (cf. Porterfield & Srivastav 1988).

What the three languages have in common is that the bare NPs, cardinality NPs, and demonstrative modified NPs have only one reading in the sentence, which is assigned to them according to their lexical and morphological encodings and word order. Generic uses aside, they are to be interpreted as identifiable in certain positions or uses, and as nonidentifiable in other positions or uses. It is claimed in Cummins (1998:567) that the underlying notions of definite and indefinite appear to be as unitary and as central to the semantics and pragmatics of NPs in Czech as they are in language with articles like English and German. Based on his studies of Czech as an article-less language, Cummins (1998) proposes that as a grammaticalized subcategory of nominal determination, definiteness is a linguistic universal. It is further claimed in Porterfield & Srivastav (1988) that the feature of definiteness vs. indefiniteness should be obligatorily and uniquely specified in all languages.

While apparently belonging to the same group of languages without articles, Chinese, as I will demonstrate below, represents a case that is different from what has been established for the three languages.

4. Definiteness in Chinese

The identifiable vs. nonidentifiable contrast is encoded in a more complex manner in Chinese. Three major types of linguistic devices, namely, lexical, morphological, and positional, are employed to indicate or suggest to the addressee whether the nominal expressions should be interpreted as of identifiable or nonidentifiable reference.

4.1 Lexical

There is no *the*-like definite article in Chinese. In terms of lexical encoding, other than proper names and personal pronouns, three major groups of definite determiners serve the function of marking a referent as identifiable in Chinese. They are demonstratives, possessives, and universal quantifiers.

4.1.1 Demonstratives

The most important definite determiners in Chinese are demonstratives *zhe* 'this' and *na* 'that' and their plural forms *zhexie* 'these' and *naxie* 'those'. In contemporary Chinese, particularly in the Beijing dialect, *zhe* and *na* can also take the form of *zhei* and *nei* respectively, when the deictic distinction is highlighted as in situational uses (cf. Lü 1990[1985]; Zhang & Fang 1996; Fang 2002).① They are used both as pronouns and adjectives. It is to be noted that the singular vs. plural distinction is not strictly observed in the use of Chinese demonstratives, or for that matter, Chinese personal pronouns and nouns. More often than not, a singular form is used where semantics would dictate a plural form. As discussed earlier, demonstratives are the most common source from which definite articles or similar determiners of definiteness derive. Chinese is no exception in this regard. With phonological

---

① For the relationship between contemporary Chinese and the Beijing dialect, cf. Chen (1999).

reduction and the deictic component in their meanings weakened in varying degrees, *zhe* and *na* in Chinese are the closest to definite articles in other languages, as has often be noted in the literature (cf. Lü 1990[1956], 1990[1985], 1990; S. Huang 1999; Tao 1999; Fang 2002).

As demonstratives, *zhe* and *na* serve all the major functions of demonstratives as discussed in the last section. Consider the following examples:

(48) situational:
Qing ba zhe/na zhang yizi ban dao na jian fangjian qu.
Please BA this/that CL chair move to that CL room go
"Please remove this/that chair to that room."

(49) discourse deictic:
Ta xiang huiqu? Zhe ni ke buneng daying.
He want return this you surely cannot agree
"He wants to go back? You surely cannot give your permission to that."

(50) anaphoric (contrastive):
Yi ge xiaohaizi... lu zhong de shihou ne,
one CL kid road middle DE time SFP
pengdao le yi ge nühaizi,... zhe ge shihou, *zhe*
run:into PFV one CL girl this CL time this
ge xiaohaizi you kan le *na ge nühaizi*, kan
CL kid again look PFV that CL girl look
le yi yan.
PFV one eye
"A kid in the middle of the road ran into a girl, ... this time the kid had another look at the girl."

When used anaphorically, *zhe* is preferred for a referent that has just been introduced into discourse. When the referent is referred to later in the discourse, particularly after several other intervening referents, *na* is more often used than *zhe*. Consider the following example from a story in *Zhongguo Yuyan Gushi*:①

(51) Zai tong xiang cheng li de yi tiao da lu   pang,
     on lead to town in DE one CL big road side
     zhang zhe yi ke da shu. *Zhe ke shu* de shugan
     grow DUR one CL big tree this CL tree DE trunk
     shang you yi ge hen da de dong. Yi tian,
     up   have one CL very big DE cavity one day
     yi ge dayude ren   xiang jin   cheng mai yu...
     one CL fisherman person intend enter town sell fish
     zhe wei yufu   jimang   pao dao *na ke you da*
     this CL fisherman   hurriedly run to that CL have big
     shudong de   shu xia duo   yu... Yi tian, *na*
     cavity DE   tree down dodge rain   one day that
     wei wang shudong li fang yu de yufu   you
     CL to   cavity in put fish DE fisherman again
     jingguo zheli.
     pass   here

"On the side of a main road leading to the town, there was a big tree. On the trunk of the tree there was a very big cavity. One day, a fishermen wanted to go to the town to sell fish... The fisherman rushed to the tree with a big cavity to take shelter from the rain... One day, the fisherman who had put a fish in the cavity passed by

---

① My corpus is composed of twenty-four narrative stories in *Zhongguo Yuyan Gushi* [*Chinese Fables*], edited by Jia Bu, published by Yuangfang Press in Beijing in 1999, and the transcriptions of forty-seven pear stories narrated by twenty Chinese students in Taiwan and twenty-seven Chinese students in Singapore. I am grateful to Hongyin Tao for sharing with me his transcripts of the pear stories by twenty-seven Chinese students in Singapore. For a detailed account of the pear story, cf. Chafe (1980).

again."

The proximal *zhe* is used for the tree and the fisherman right after they have just been introduced into the discourse. When the referents appear again later in the story, both of them are introduced by the distal *na*. This is the normal pattern for the selection of demonstratives in such anaphoric uses.

(52) recognitional:

Ta jiu gei *na* ... xiaohaizi ..., gei *na ge huan ta*
he then give that   kid   giv that CL return he
maozi de xiaohaizi san ge bale.
cap   DE kid   three CL pear

"He then gave the ... boy, ... the boy who returned the cap to him three pears."

Na is the determiner that is used to introduce such try-marked recognitionals in Chinese, as illustrated in (52). The speaker of (52) is uncertain from the beginning whether the addresses is able to identify which boy he is referring to, as evidenced by his pauses of hesitation; after the first try with *na* ... *xiaohaizi*, he offers another more detailed description with a relative restrictive clause. *Na* is used with both try-marked recognitionals in the utterance.

Compared with the English demonstratives, the Chinese demonstratives are subject to less restriction when used as markers of definiteness. In fact, they are found in some of the contexts where in English the definite article is regularly used as a marker of definiteness and the demonstratives are not generally allowed. Such uses of the Chinese demonstratives are illustrated in the following examples:

(53) anaphoric (non-contrastive):

You yi ge lieren ... yang zhe yi zhi gou. *Zhe*
have one CL hunter   keep DUR one CL dog this

zhi gou hen dongshi.
CL dog very intelligent
"There was a hunter who had a dog. The dog was very intelligent."

(54) shared general knowledge:
Zhe tianqi zhen guai, shi-er yue le, ke
This weather really strange twelve month CRS but
yidian bu leng.
bit not cold
"The weather is really strange. It is December now, but it is not cold at all."

(55) frame-based association:
Ta mai le yi liang jiu che, *na luntai* dou
he buy PFV one CL old car that tire even
mo ping le.
wear flat CRS
"He bought an old car. All the tires are worn out."

(56) self-containing association with accompanying restrictive relative clause:
Shang ge yue lai kan ni de na ge ren,
last CL month come see you DE that CL person
wo jintian you jian dao ta le.
I today again see to he CRS
"The person who came to see you last month, I saw him again today."

Unlike the situation in English, the use of the Chinese demonstratives in non-contrastive anaphoric reference as in (53), and with restrictive relative clauses as in (56) is very common in Chinese of all styles. On the other hand, uses of the Chinese demonstratives with referents whose identifiability stems from shared general knowledge or frame-based association as exemplified in (54) and (55), are only found in texts of the vernacular style.

Demonstratives in Chinese, as is obvious from the above discussion, have extended their use to definite articles, serving some of the functions that are characteristic of the definite article like *the* in English. It is by virtue of the functions beyond those of pure deictics that Lü (1990), S. Huang (1999), Tao (1999), and Fang (2002) rightly claim that *zhe* and *na* are used, in some situations, as definite articles.

While it is clear that *zhe* and *na* have started on the path of grammaticalization into definite articles, there is evidence which suggests that they are still far from reaching the endpoint yet.

First, most of the instances of *zhe* and *na* which apparently have much weakened or no deictic force are found in anaphoric and recognitional uses, as reported in studies based on text counts in S. Huang (1999) and Tao (1999). These uses, as argued in Greenberg (1978) and Himmelmann (1996), are characteristic of the beginning or transitional stage of the grammaticalization of demonstratives toward definite articles, rather than representing typical uses of fully grammaticalized definite articles.

There is evidence that *zhe* and *na* have preserved their deictic force, to a certain extent, in these uses which are considered to be transitional. When *zhe* and *na* are found in contrastive anaphoric use, as discussed above, *zhe* is preferred over *na* as the anaphoric device for an antecedent that is recently introduced into discourse. In non-contrastive anaphoric use, *zhe* outnumbers *na* by approximately three to one in my corpus. In textual deictic uses, where no contrast between referents is normally involved, *zhe* outnumbers na by approximately six to one (Tao 1999:82). This makes best sense if we assume that the proximity of *zhe* makes it a better anaphoric device than the distal *na* in referring to an antecedent recently introduced into discourse.

The deictic distinction may also play a role in a more delicate manner in those circumstances which are apparently neutral with regard to proximity. No deictic element appears to be involved when referents depend on accompanying relative clauses for their identifiability: the referents become identifiable through the qualitative information provided by the relative clause and the noun itself, and no locative information is at play in the process. Table 1 presents the distribution of *zhe* and *na* as the definite determiner of an NP modified by a relative clause.

Table 1 Distribution of *zhe* and *na* as determiner for nouns with a relative clause

	zhe number of instances	PCT	*na* number of instances	PCT
NP+restrictive relative clause	3	8%	33	92%
NP+nonrestrictive relative clause	4	50%	4	50%

Table 1 shows that while both *zhe* and *na* are found in such uses, *na* is by far the preferred determiner with a head noun modified by a restrictive clause. A total of thirty-six such instances are found in my corpus of data. *Na* is used in thirty-three instances and *zhe* only in three. When the referent is used with a non-restrictive relative clause, no preference is evident. A total of eight such instances are found in the corpus, with *zhe* used in four instances, and *na* in the other four. One explanation for the differential is that of the two demonstratives, *na* is the more grammaticalized, or unmarked, determiner of definiteness for referents which are neutral with respect to the deictically based distinctions, and is thus more appropriate for uses with nouns modified by restrictive relative clauses. It may also be explained, I propose, in terms of the inherent deictic distinctions between the two demonstratives. When a referent depends crucially on the accompanying restrictive relative clause for identifying information, it is very likely that it is further away from the speaker, both physically and cognitively, than a referent that has established its identifiability through other means. Given the circumstances, the distal demonstrative is more appropriate for that referent than the proximal demonstrative.

Second, *zhe* and *na* are either not allowed, or very rarely found for the uses which are considered to be prototypical of definite articles, namely for uses with referents which derive their identification through shared specific and general knowledge or frame-based association. Consider (57):

(57) Anjing dianr, bie ba *na* haizi chaoxing le.
quiet bit don't BA that baby wake:up CRS
"Be quiet. Don't wake up that baby."

In a way similar to the behaviors of the English demonstratives in (34) and (35), the Chinese demonstrative would be infelicitous if the baby is not visible to the addressee, and the addressee has no previous knowledge that there is a baby in the house,

Sentences like (54) and (55), while acceptable in colloquial speech, are statistically very rare. Only three instances in my corpus are found in which a demonstrative is used as a marker of definiteness for referents which derive their identification from shared general knowledge as in (54), and two instances for uses of frame-based association as in (55). All of the five instances occur in the vernacular pear stories, and not a single instance is attested in the written Chines fables. Even these five instances are open to another interpretation, not as adnominal determiner, but as markers of hesitations and false starts, which abound with some speakers.

Granted that *zhe* and *na* are sometimes used in deictically neutral contexts, neither of the Chinese demonstratives has developed in the direction of a definite article to such an extent that their primary function is to serve as a deictically neutral marker of definiteness like the English *the*. In his studies of the historical development of definite articles in languages, Greenberg (1978: 61) observes that a definite article "develops from a purely deictic element which has come to identify an element as previously mentioned in discourse. Such a use is often an additional function of an element which is also a pure deictic, but sometimes there is a particular demonstrative which has assumed this as its basic function." From the above discussion, it is clear that the anaphoric use, as well as the recognitional use, are better taken as additional functions, rather than basic functions, of *zhe* and *na*. More importantly, uses characteristic of fully grammaticalized definite articles, like those marking shared specific and general knowledge, and frame-based association, are exceptional rather than the norm with either *zhe* or *na*. It is even unclear, based on the text frequency studies of the uses of *zhe* and *na* as definite determiners, which of the two has developed more deictically neutral uses characteristic of a definite article. Lü (1990:592) and S. Huang (1999) maintain that *na* has developed further than *zhe* toward a definite article, while Tao (1999) and Fang (2002) suggest *zhe* as the most likely candidate for definite article in Chinese. It is an issue open to further investigation.

Finally, the Chinese demonstratives, at the current stage of development, fail to fulfill what Greenberg (1978:61) takes to be a crucial criterion for deciding when a discourse deictic has become a definite article: the criterion of being "compulsory" when definiteness is marked for a referent in discourse. It is argued in Xu (1987), for instance, that a zero NP is the unmarked form for non-contrastive anaphoric uses that is functionally equivalent to the English definite article, and *zhe* and *na* are marked forms for such uses.

In sum, while demonstratives in Chinese have developed some functions which are typically served by definite articles in languages like English, they are, generally speaking, still much closer to demonstratives than definite articles on the path of grammaticalization.

4.1.2 Possessives

Chinese possessives, which are formed by suffixing the possessive marker *de* to personal pronouns or nouns, do not have the same distribution and interpretation as those in English. In English, as we know, an indefinite article cannot come between a possessive and the head noun, and the possessive imposes a reading of definiteness on the nominal expression. A Chinese possessive, on the other hand, can be separated from the head noun by an indefinite marker, with an interpretation of nonidentifiability for the nominal expression, as illustrated in (58):

(58) Zhe shi *wo-de yi* ge *pengyou* gaosu wo de.
This be my one CL friend tell I DE
"A friend of mine told me this."

In terms of the typological distinction between DG languages and AG languages drawn by C. Lyons (1999), as discussed earlier in this paper, it appears that while English is a DG language, Chinese is an AG language.

Chinese possessives, however, cannot be counted as those of a typical AG language like Italian. In Italian, as discussed earlier, whether the NP with a possessive is definite or indefinite depends on the presence of a definite or an indefinite article. In Chinese, the possessive does impose a definiteness interpretation on the nominal expression when the head of the expression is a bare NP, which in itself is unmarked for identifiability or nonidentifiability. Consider the following example:

(59) *Wo-de qianbi* zenme zhao bu dao le?
    my pencil how find not arrive CRS
    "How come I cannot find my pencil/ *a pencil of mine?"

In other words, whether the nominal expression with a possessive and a bare noun is to be interpreted as identifiable or nonidentifiable in Chinese depends on the presence or absence of an indefinite determiner between the possessive and the bare noun. Since an indefinite determiner is perfectly grammatical in that position in Chinese, its absence strongly implicates an interpretation of identifiability on the nominal expression in a way that is theoretically captured in terms of Gricean conversational implicature (cf. Grice 1989; Levinson 2000).

4.1.3 Universal quantifiers

Also used as markers of definiteness in Chinese are universal quantifiers, which include collective universal quantifiers *suoyou* 'all', *yiqie* 'all', and distributive universal quantifiers *mei* 'each, every', and *ge* 'each, every'. Consider the following examples:

(60) *Yiqie yinsu* dou dei kaolü jinqu.
    all factor all must consider in
    "All factors have to be taken into consideration."

(61) *Mei ge xuesheng* dou you ziji de fangjian.
    every CL student all have self DE room
    "Every student has his own room."

Interrogative words in Chinese like *shenme* 'what', *shei* 'who' and *nei* 'which', in their stressed form, are used as what are called free-choice quantifiers, referring to any arbitrary member of a whole class. They are treated by some linguists as indefinite determiners (cf. Lü 1990[1956]; Chao 1968:324). There are close semantic connections, as noted by (Haspelmath 1997: 12, 154), between the distributive universal quantifiers and the free-choice quantifiers, and free-choice quantifiers may diachronically evolve into universal quantifiers. The free-choice quantifiers in Chinese have the same semantics as the universal quantifiers in terms of scope behaviors. Consider the following sentences:

(62) *Mei   ge   xuesheng dou   dei   xue   liang   men*
     Every   CL   student   all   must   learn two   CL
     waiyu.
     foreign:language

(63) *Nei   ge   xuesheng dou   dei   xue   liang   men*
     Every   CL   student   all   must   learn two   CL
     waiyu.
     foreign:language

"Every student has to learn two foreign languages."

the NP *liang men waiyu* 'two foreign languages' in the two sentences is subject to the same scope ambiguity in terms of specificity.

Furthermore, *yiqie* in (60) and *mei* in (61) can be replaced by free-choice quantifiers, with no change in the meaning of the sentence:

(64) *Shenme yinsu* dou dei kaolü jinqu.
     "All factors have to be taken into consideration."

(65) *Nei ge xuesheng* dou you ziji de fangjian.
     "Every student has his own room."

Finally, the free-choice quantifiers in Chinese behave much more like universal quantifiers than indefinite determiners in that they usually occupy a pre-verbal position in sentence, and are not allowed in some indefiniteness-inclined sentential positions (more detail on this term later). Consider the following sentence:

(66) a. Ta *suoyou de cai* dou chang le yidianr.
he all DE dish all taste PFV bit
"He had a taste of all the dishes."

b. Ta *ge yang cai* dou chang le yidianr.
he every CL dish all taste PFV bit
"He had a taste of every dish."

c. Ta *shenme cai* dou chang le yidianr.
he any dish all taste PFV bit
"He had a taste of all the dishes/every dish."

(67) a. */? Ta chang le yidianr *suoyou de cai*.
d. */?? Ta chang le yidianr *ge yang cai*.
c. * Ta chang le yidianr *shenme cai*.

No such restriction is applicable to words like *shenme* in stressed form as an interrogative, as in (68), or in unstressed form as an indefinite determiner as in (69).

(68) interrogative *shenme* in stressed form:
Ta chang le yidianr *shenme cai*?
he taste PFV bit what dish
"What dish/dishes did he have a taste of ?"

(69) indefinite *shenme* in unstressed form:
Rang ta chang yidianr *shenme cai* ba.
let he taste bit sm dish SFP
"Let him have a taste of some dish/dishes."

It is thus justified both on the grounds of semantics and syntactical behaviors to treat the freedom-choice quantifiers in Chinese as definite determiners on a par with collective and distributive universal quantifiers.

4.1.4 Indefinite determiners

The most important indefinite determiner in Chinese is *yi* 'one' + classifier. *yi* on its own is a numeral, and can still be used in the same way as all the other numerals in Chinese. Unlike the other numerals, however, *yi* + classifier has undergone the process of grammaticalization toward a marker of indefiniteness in much the same way as the English indefinite article was derived from the numeral 'one'. Other than the fact that *yi* + classifier can be used both as a pronominal and as a determiner, it serves all the major functions of a regular indefinite article as the English *a*, and moreover extends to other uses that have not been reported for indefinite determiners in English or other languages. It is found in uses characteristic of each of the five stages of development from a numeral to a grammatical indefiniteness marker as proposed by Givón (1981) and Heine (1997), namely, as a numeral, a presentative marker, a marker of nonidentifiable specific reference, a marker of nonidentifiable nonspecific reference, and what Heine (1997) calls a generalized article. They are illustrated respectively in the following examples:

(70) numeral:
Wo zhi yao *yi* zhi pingguo jiu gou le.
I only want one CL apple then enough CRS
"I only want one apple."

(71) presentative marker:
Yi zhi xiao qi'e yaoyaobaibai zou le shanglai.
one CL little penguin swaying walk PFV up
"A little penguin was waddling up."

(72) nonidentifiable specific reference:
Zhe jian shi wo zuotian qing le (*yi*) ge
this CL issue I yesterday invite PFV one CL

    ren   lai.
    person come

"For this issue I invited a person here yesterday."

(73) nonidentifiable nonspecific reference:

    Gankuai qu zhao (*yi*) ge *ren*   lai,   shenme ren
    Hurriedly go find one CL person come any   person
    dou xing.
    all   fine

"Hurry up and get somebody; anybody will be just fine."

(74) generalized article:

    Ta   kan   shangqu xiang (*yi*) ge *faguoren*.
    he   look   up   like   one CL Frenchman

"He looks like a Frenchman."

It is proposed in Heine (1997:76) that the more stages an item has passed through on its way from numeral to indefinite article, the more it is affected by grammaticalization processes such as bleaching, cliticization, and phonetic erosion. The behaviors of *yi* + classifier in Chinese have provided another piece of evidence in support of the claim. While *yi* in (70) must be stressed, it is unstressed in other uses, and is in fact commonly omitted, leaving as it were the function of indefiniteness marking served by the classifier alone. In his seminal analysis of the uses of *yi* + classifier, Lü (1990[1944)]) has discussed in detail the conditions under which *yi* can be omitted. It is observed in his paper that, apart from prosodic constraints, *yi* is more likely to be omitted when used as a marker of nonidentifiable nonspecific reference, as in (73), than as a marker of nonidentifiable specific reference, as in (72) (cf. Lü 1990[1944]:167). A more inclusive, and theoretically more revealing account, I would propose, is that, other prosodic conditions as elaborated in Lü (1990[1944]) being equal, the further down the grammaticalization continuum of the uses of the indefiniteness marker, the more weakened is the morphological and phonological weight of *yi* in *yi* + classifier. *Yi* in (70) always appears in stressed form; *yi* in (71) cannot be omitted, but is usually unstressed; naturalness of the sentences with *yi* omitted increases from (72) through (73) to (74): while it is more natural to have *yi* in (72), (74) sounds much better without *yi*. The extent of the phonological reduction of the Chinese numeral *yi* correlates perfectly with the order of its development through the five stages along the continuum of grammaticalization.

What is more interesting is the fact that the Chinese indefinite determiner has developed uses that are not reported for indefinite articles in other languages. Heine (1997:73) observes that at the final stage of development, the generalized article is no longer restricted to singular nouns, but is extended to plural and mass nouns as is the case in Spanish. At the same time, he asserts that it still may not be used with a noun marked for definiteness or a proper noun. This restriction is relaxed in Chinese.

In addition to the uses in (70-74), *yi* + classifier can also be used with identifiable referents such as proper names.[①] Consider the following examples ((75) and (76) are quoted from Lü (1990 [1944])):

(75) An   na   meizi.... taiju   de   *ge zhangfu*   jun
     I   that sister   praise CSC   CL   husband   smart
     shang tian   jun.
     up   plus   smart
     "My sister praised her husband in such a way that he looked even smarter."

---

① The uses to be discussed here have little to do with the use of *a* in *A Mr. Smith came to see you this morning*, where *a* means 'a certain', indicating that the referent is nonidentifiable for the addressee. *yi* + classifier can be used in a similar way in Chinese, which need not concern us here.

(76) Dangxia   ba   *ge*   Zhang   San   Li   Si   xia   de
instantly   BA   CL   Zhang   San   Li   Si   scare   CSC
mudengkoudai.
dumbstruck
"Zhang San and Li Si were instantly struck dumb with fear."

(77) Lao   Zhang   bei   pengyou   ba   *ge*   *taitai*   gei   pian
Old   Zhang   BEI   friend   BA   CL   wife   by   cheat
zou   le.
go   CRS
"Lao Zhang was cheated by his friend and lost his wife."
"Lao Zhang was cheated by his friend out of his wife."

(78) Ta   ba   *ge*   *pibao*   gei   diu   le.
he   BA   CL   hat   lose   CRS
"He lost his bag."

Unlike the cases of (70-74), the nominal expressions modified by the indefinite determiner in (75-78) are all of identifiable reference.

The function of (*yi*)+ classifier in (75-78), as I have argued in detail in Chen (2003), is to de-individuate the referent it is used with to make it less likely to serve as a topic of continuing reference in ensuing discourse. It serves as a backgrounding device in a way that is opposite to the indefinite use of *this* in English. Originally and still primarily a definite demonstrative, *this* in the new usage as an indefinite determiner to introduce new referents into discourse serves to mark a nonidentifiable referent as of high thematic importance. *Yi* + classifier in Chinese, on the other hand, operates in the opposite direction. As an indefiniteness determiner, it has developed uses with an identifiable referent, otherwise of high inherent saliency as is the case with the proper names in (76) and with "wife" in (77), to mark it as of low thematic importance.

In the final stage of the development, as discussed earlier, the indefinite determiner *yi* + classifier is used with nominal expressions whose referentiality is completely bleached out, leaving us with only genericity and connotation, as is the case with the predicative nominal in (74). Other nominal expressions used with this generalized indefinite determiner, through the process of analogy, may acquire some of the features that characterize the nonreferential nominal expressions that are commonly used with the determiner at this stage of development, with their referentiality in effect bleached out to a certain extent. In other words, the use of the indefinite determiner at its final stage of development is further extended to definite expressions to induce sense of nonreferentiality to identifiable entities, which is in turn suggestive of lower thematic importance (cf. Chen 2003 for a more detailed discussion).

In terms of the typical functions representing the five major stages of grammaticalization of the numeral 'one' into an indefinite article, we conclude that the numeral *yi* in Chinese has undergone the full process of grammaticalization, and has developed into an *a*-like indefinite article. The conclusion, however, has to be qualified. Unlike the indefinite article in English, as noted earlier, *yi* has both an attributive and a pronominal use, which means it has retained a higher degree of morphological autonomy than a fully grammaticalized indefinite article. If we follow the assumption in Heine (1997:71) that an indefinite article cannot be used as a pronoun (e.g. *I want *a* vs. I want *one*), we cannot accept without any reservations the claim that there is an *a*-like indefinite article in Chinese. As will be discussed later in the paper, moreover, *yi* differs from *a* in another more important respect: while it is compulsory for an nonidentifiable referent in English to be marked by *a* or another device of indefiniteness, it is not the case in Chinese.

Other markers of indefiniteness in Chinese include interrogative-turned indefinite determiners like *shenme* 'some/any', and *shei* 'soneone/anyone', which are always in weakened phonological form (cf. Chao 1968:651-657). Consider the following examples:

(79) Ta   meiyou   shuo   *shenme*   yaojin   de   shir.
     He   not:have say   any   important DE   thing
     "He did not say anything important."

(80) Na   zhi   beizi   bei   *shei*   da   po   le.
     that CL   cup   BEI   somebody   hit   break   PFV
     "That cup was broken by somebody."

What are sometimes called mid-scalar quantifiers like *few*, *several* and *many* are often grouped with indefinite pronouns in many languages (cf. Haspelmath 1997:11-12). They do not constitute a single category in Chinese. While *yixie* 'several' is an indefinite determiner, *ji* 'several', as will be discussed shortly, should be treated as a modifier of cardinality expression on a par with numerals like *liang* 'two' and *san* 'three', which may have a identifiability reading in certain sentential positions when not accompanied by other definite or indefinite determiners.

4.2 Morphological

Monosyllabic classifiers in Chinese, and occasionally monosyllabic nouns as well, may undergo the morphological process of reduplication to gain the same meaning as that of distributive universal quantifiers, as illustrated in the following examples:

(81) *Zhong-zhong*   yinsu   dou   dei   kaolü   jinqu.
     CL   factors   all   must   consider   in
     "Every factor has to be taken into consideration."

(82) *Ren-ren* dou shuo ta shi ge hao ren.
person all say he be CL nice person
"Everybody says he is a nice person."

The reduplicated classifier or noun gives rise to the same scope ambiguity with regard to quantified NPs in sentences as universal quantifiers, which is illustrated in (62) and (63); it also displays the same syntactic behaviors as universal quantifiers in that they are not allowed in the indefiniteness inclined positions like that in (67).

(83) *Ta chang le yidianr *yang-yang cai*.
he taste PFV bit CL dish
"He had a taste of every dish."

4.3 Indeterminate expressions

The lexical and morphological markings of NPs in Chinese we have discussed so far fall into two groups, definite and indefinite. NPs which are lexically or morphologically encoded as definite or indefinite, on the assumption that they are used referentially, are always interpreted as of either identifiable or nonidentifiable reference in utterance, no matter what position they occupy in sentences. The encodings are determinate in relation to the interpretation of identifiability.

There are other types of NPs which, so far as their lexical or morphological encodings are concerned, are neutral with respect to the interpretation of identifiability. One is the bare NP, by which I mean an NP that is not marked by any of the definite or indefinite determiners we have discussed above, and has not undergone the morphological process of reduplication either. The other is the cardinality expression, a term borrowed from C. Lyons (1999), which is an NP modified by a cardinal numeral or a quantifier like *ji*. They constitute what I call the indeterminate encodings of NP with respect to the interpretation of identifiability.

In most, but not all, instances, whether the indeterminate expressions are to be interpreted as identifiable or nonidentifiable is indicated, or suggested, by the position of the noun phrase in sentences. It has been a well-known statement in studies of Chinese grammar that a bare noun in subject position, like *keren* 'guest' in the classic example (84a), is identifiable, and one in post-verbal position, in *keren* in (84b), is nonidentifiable.

(84) a. *Keren* lai le.
guest come PFV
"The guest has arrived."

b. Lai *keren* le.
"A guest/guests has/have arrived."

The statement, as I will show shortly, needs qualification and modification to account for the full range of relevant phenomena in Chinese.

It has been elaborated in this paper that definite expressions derive their identifiability from a variety of sources, and there is some correlation, and overlapping, between the particular types of definite determiners and the ways in which the identification of the referents is established. For instance, while both the definite article and the demonstratives in English are used for simple anaphoric reference, the former, but not the latter, is used for referents of frame-based association. When interpreted as of identifiable reference, indeterminate expressions in Chinese are used for referents which derive identifiability from the whole range of sources that is covered by the English definite article and demonstratives, as illustrated in the following sentences:

(85) bare noun: situational
Xiaoxin, bie ba *haizi* chaoxing le.
careful don't BA baby wake CRS

"Be careful. Don't wake up the baby."

(86) cardinality expression: situational
Xiaoxin, bie ba *liang ge haizi* chaoxing le.
careful don't BA two CL baby wake CRS
"Be careful. Don't wake up the two babies."

(87) bare noun and cardinality expressions: anaphoric
Ta yang le yi zhi maor he ji tiao gou,
He raise PFV one CL cat and several CL dog
maor you fei you da, *ji tiao gou* que shou de
cat both fat and big several CL dog but thin CSC
pi bao gu.
skin cover bone
"He has a cat and several dogs. The cat is big and fat, but the dogs are very skinny."

(88) bare noun: shared specific knowledge
Ganggang jie dao tongzhi, *laoban* xiawu
just receive arrive notice boss afternoon
lai jiancha gongzuo.
come inspect work
"The notice has just come: The boss is coming for an inspection in the afternoon."

(89) cardinality expression: shared specific knowledge
Ba *wu shan chuangzi* dou guan shang.
BA five CL window all shut up
"Shut all the five windows."

(90) bare noun: shared general knowledge
Yueliang sheng shang lai le.
moon rise up come CRS
"The moon has risen."

(91) cardinality expression: shared general knowledge
Zai nar, si ge jijie dou you gezi
in there four CL season all have self
de tezheng.
DE characteristics
"Each of the four seasons there has its own charateristics."

(92) bare noun and cardinality expression: frame-based association
Ta mai le yi liang jiu che, (si zhi) luntai
he buy PFV one CL old car four CL tire
dou mo ping le.
all wear flat CRS
"He bought a used car. (The four tires) The tires are all worn out."

(93) bare noun and cardinality expression: self-containing association
Ni renshi zuotian lai de (san ge) ren ma?
you know yesterday come DE three CL person Q
"Do you know the (three) people who came yesterday?"

Indeterminate expressions on nonidentifiable reading also serve the major functions that are served by indefinite determiners like (*yi*)+classifier exemplified in (72) through (74). Following are some examples:

(94) bare noun and cardinality expression: nonidentifiable specific
Wo jia li lai le (ji wei) keren.
I home in come PFV several CL guest
"I have had (several visitors) a visitor/visitors at home."

(95) bare noun: nonidentifiable nonspecific
Women dei zhao ren bangmang, shenme ren
we must find person help any person

dou xing.

all   fine

"We must get somebody to help us; anybody will be just fine."

(96) cardinality expression: nonidentifiable nonspecific

Women dei   zhao *san ge ren*   bangmang, shenme

we   must find three CL person help   any

ren   dou   xing.

person all   fine

"We must get three people to help us; anybody will be just fine."

(97) bare noun and cardinality expression: generic/connotation

Li Ming he   Zhang Hong kan   shangqu xiang

Li Ming and Zhang Hong look up   like

(*liang   ge*)   *faguoren.*

two   CL   Frenchman

"Li Ming and Zhang Hong look like Frenchmen."

Factors which govern the choice between the determinate and the indeterminate encoding for identifiable or nonidentifiable referents will be addressed in a separate paper.

4.4 Positional

In addition to the lexical and morphological encodings, position in sentences also serves as an important device to indicate identifiability or nonidentifiability of nominal expressions in Chinese. It is extensively attested in both languages with definite articles, like English, or languages without articles, like Czech and Russian, that most sentential positions, or semantic roles which typically occupy particular syntactic positions in sentence, differ in their preference for nominal expressions characterized by various degrees of identifiability. Subject as well as other pre-verbal positions in an SVO language usually display a strong inclination for definite expressions; some post-verbal positions display a inclination for indefinite expressions (cf. Keenan & Comrie 1977; Chafe 1980; Givón 1979, 1983, 1984-1990; Du Bois 1987; Hopper & Thompson 1994; Thompson 1997 inter alia). I call the former definiteness-inclined positions, and the latter indefiniteness-inclined positions. There are also positions which show relatively weak inclination one way or the other. The inclination may be grammaticalized in a way that expressions of the opposite encodings in terms of the definite versus indefinite dichotomy are simply ungrammatical in the syntactic slot. In the overwhelming majority of cases, however, instead of in the form of grammatical restrictions, the inclination is manifested in terms of higher text frequencies of the nominal expressions of definite versus indefinite encodings occupying the particular position in sentences.

The major types of definite or indefinite expressions discussed earlier also differ with regard to the degree of identifiability of reference, which may relate to their grammaticality or naturalness in some positions of sentences. Of proper names, personal pronouns and NPs modified by definite determiners, for example, the referent of a personal pronoun normally registers a higher degree of identifiability than that of the other two types (cf. Ariel 1990). The strength of inclination of sentential position for definite or indefinite expressions correlates positively with the degree of identifiability of the referent. I will come to this point shortly.

The discourse pragmatic notion of topic, as demonstrated in the studies by Hopper & Thompson (1980, 1984), Givón (1983, 1984-1990), Tomlin (1983), van Oosten (1986), Du Bois (1987), and Thompson

(1997), stands as a most important factor underlying the correlation between the definiteness inclination of syntactic positions (and semantic roles that typically assume the respective positions) and the identifiability, as well as referentiality and activation status, of nominal expressions that occupy those positions. I am adopting the notion of topic as defined by Lambrecht (1994:131):

> (98) "A referent is interpreted as the topic of a proposition if in a given situation the proposition is construed as being about this referent, i.e. as expressing information which is relevant to and which increases the addressee's knowledge of this referent."

The topic expression of a sentence, furthermore, typically contains information that bears close relevance to the preceding discourse. It is more likely, although by no means an absolute certainty, for the subject expression of the sentence than other sentential components to serve at the same time as the topic of the utterance. A highly identifiable referent, which is by definition referential, is more likely to serve as the topic of the utterance than a referent with a lower degree of identifiability. Hence the high correlation between subject and identifiability of reference.

It has been established in the literature that the following sentential positions display an inclination for definiteness or indefiniteness in Chinese (cf. Lü 1990[1956]; Chao 1968; C. Li & Thompson 1975, 1981; Sun & Givón 1985; Chen 1986; L. Li 1986; J. Huang 1987; LaPolla 1995; Shen 1999 inter alia):[①]

---

① Chinese linguists often disagree over the definition and application of the terms for sentential components as listed in (99) and (100). In this article I am using these terms in a way that is, to the extent possible, fairly uncontroversial and compatible with different theoretical frameworks. For want of space to do full justice to the issues involved, I have left aside in this article the notion of 'topic' as a syntactic component (cf. Chen 1994, 1996).

(99) **Definiteness-inclined positions in Chinese:**
   Subject
   ba object
   preverbal object
   first object of ditransitive sentence

(100) **Indefiniteness-inclined positions in Chinese:**
   object of the presentative verb *you*
   postverbal NP in presentative sentences
   postverbal NP in existential sentences
   second object of di-transitive sentences

After subject, *ba* object is the next most likely topic expression in a Chinese sentence, which is characterized as "secondary topic" by some writers. Nominal expressions in the other two positions in (99) also display features of high topicality (cf. Tsao 1990; Zhang & Fang 1996 inter alia). The primary function of the four positions in (100), on the other hand, is to introduce new and nonidentifiable referents into discourse, which are highly unlikely to serve as the topic of utterance.

Now let us consider how the sentential positions correlate with definite expressions, indefinite expressions, and expressions of indeterminate encodings in Chinese with regard to the interpretation of identifiability of reference.

4.4.1 Positions and determinate expressions

Nominal expressions which are lexically or morphologically encoded as definite or indefinite may be subject to severe restrictions in their eligibility to occur in some of the positions listed in (99-100). It is ungrammatical to have a reduplicated classifier or noun in any of the indefiniteness-inclined positions:

(101) a. *You   ren-ren   lai   le.
          have   person   come   CRS
     b. *Qianmian   lai   le   ren-ren.
          front   come   PFV   person
     c. *Qianmian   zuo   ge-ge   daibiao.
          front   sit   CL   representative
     d. *Women   gei   le   ta   yang-yang   liwu.
          we   give   PFV   he   CL   present

Indefinite expressions can hardly occur as subject with stative predicate, as illustrated by (102a). Explanation for this phenomenon in Chinese and other languages is captured in terms of the thetic vs. categorical distinction in Sasse (1987).

(102) a. *Yi   ge   ren   hen   shanchang   dalie.
          one   CL   person very   good:at   hunt
     b. You   yi   ge   ren   hen   shanchang   dalie.
          have   one   CL   person very   good:at   hunt
     "There was someone who was a very good hunter."

In the great majority of cases, as said earlier, the inclination is manifested, not in terms of grammatical restriction, but in terms of higher frequency of expressions of one category in contrast with the other in texts. As amply demonstrated in statistical studies of Chinese sentences and discourse, subject, *ba* object, and the other definiteness-inclined positions are overwhelmingly definite, and the indefiniteness-inclined positions are overwhelmingly indefinite. Similar findings are reported in other languages as well (cf. Givón 1983, 1984-1990).

The text frequency findings of my studies, which will be presented below, demonstrate that nominal expressions of definite or indefinite encodings may also occur in some sentential positions of the opposite inclination, with frequency in texts varying from relatively low to extremely low. It is reported by L. Li (1986) that definite expressions as the postverbal NP in presentative and existential sentences are attested in his corpus of data, although such occurrences are very rare in text counts. (103), (105) and (106) are quoted from L. Li (1986):

(103) You   zuo   men   zou   jin   le   *Hu Si   he*
      from   left   door   walk   in   PFV   Hu Si   and
      Gu Ba   Nainai.
      Gu   Ba   Nainai
      "From the left foor walk in Hu Si and Gu Ba Nainai."

(104) Pingmu   shang   jianjian   chuxian   le   *Wang   Gang*
      screen   on   gradually appear   PFV   Wang   Gang
      de   miankong.
      DE   face
      "Wang Gang's face gradually took shape on the screen."

(105) Ta...   shen   pang   jiu   tang   zhe   *Chen   Changjie.*
      he   body   side   then   lie   DUR   Chen   Changjie
      "Besides him lies Chen Changjie."

(106) Ta   huiguo   shen   qu,   yan   qian   jiu   zhan
      she   turn   body   go   eye   front   then   stand
      zhe   ta.[①]
      DUR   he
      "She turned around, and he stood right in front of her."

Furthermore, indefinite expressions are found in use as *ba* object, as in (107), although much less frequently than definite expressions (cf. Lü (1990[1948]; Zhang 2000).

[①] While the postverbal NP in this existential sentence is a personal pronoun, no case has been reported in L. Li (1986) where a personal pronoun occurs in the postverbal slot in a presentative sentence.

(107) Ta zhongyu ba *yi kuai shitou yiyang de dongxi*
he finally BA one CL stone same DE thing
wale   chulai.
dig PFV   out
"He finally dug out something like a stone."

On the other hand, while statistically many more definite and indeterminate expressions occupy subject position, indefinite expressions serving as subject with dynamic predicate as in (71), repeated below as (108), are actually quite common in Chinese, so long as certain conditions are met (cf. Fan 1985; Sasse 1987).①

(108) *Yi zhi xiao qi'e*   yaoyaobaibai zou le   shanglai.
one CL little penguin swaying   walk PFV up
"A little penguin was waddling up."

The subject in (108) presents a nonidentifiable referent that is introduced for the first time into discourse. The grammaticality, and fairly common occurrence of sentences like (108) clearly demonstrate that, as expected, there is no one-to-one correlation between the discourse pragmatic role of topic and the syntactic position of subject, just as there is no one-to-one correlation between semantic roles and syntactic roles. There are many competing pragmatic, semantic, and syntactic factors at work which may result in the separation of subject and topic in utterances.

Other positions in sentences, like post-verbal object in transitive sentences and oblique object, normally admit determinate expressions of

---

① A distinction is drawn in the studies of Aktionsart between stative and dynamic sentences. While it occurs frequently in a dynamic sentence, as illustrated by (108), an indefinite expression is normally unacceptable as subject of a stative sentence in Chinese, as in other languages, as shown in the following example:

(i) **Yi zhi xiao qi'e hen e.*
one CL little penguin very hungry
"A little penguin was very hungry."

either category, as well as indeterminate expressions. Text counts may reveal a reference for one category of expressions rather than another, but not as strong and obvious as is the case with the positions in (99) and (100).

4.4.2 Positions and indeterminate expressions

Expressions which are lexically and morphologically indeterminate with regard to identifiability are not subject to the same kind of restrictions as expressions of determinate encodings. Generally speaking, they occur freely in positions of either inclination, as well as in other positions. At the same time, they display a strong inclination to be interpreted as identifiable in definiteness-inclined positions, and as nonidentifiable in indefiniteness-inclined positions. The strength of the inclination varies with the types of indeterminate encoding and the sentential positions that are occupied by the expressions.

I have examined twenty-four narrative stories in *Chinese Fables* in my corpus to ascertain how the indeterminate encodings and the interpretation in respect of identifiability correlate. I have chosen for the purpose two most prominent definiteness-inclined positions, subject and *ba* object, and two most prominent indefiniteness-inclined positions, which are object of the presentative verb *you* and the postverbal NP in presentative sentences. Postverbal object in transitive sentences is also included as representing positions not belonging to either category. The outcomes are presented in Table 2 and Table 3.

Table 2 Interpretation of bare NPs in five syntactic positions

	subject	*ba* object	postverbal object in transitive sentences	object of presentative verb *you*	postverbal NP in presentative sentences
Identifiable	81	34	62	0	0
Nonidentifiable	3	2	57	9	7

Table 3 Interpretation of cardinality expressions in five syntactic positions

	subject	*ba* object	postverbal object in transitive sentences	object of presentative verb *you*	postverbal NP in presentative sentences
Identifiable	23	3	4	0	0
Nonidentifiable	7	1	11	5	6

It is evident from Table 2 and Table 3 that the great majority of the expressions of indeterminate encodings in the position of subject and as *ba* object are interpreted as identifiable. The percentage of identifiability reading is even higher for those in the subject position than as *ba* object. In this limited corpus of data, all the indeterminate expressions in the two indefiniteness-inclined positions, namely, object of presentative verb *you* and post-verbal NP in presentative sentences, are of nonidentifiable reference, although it is attested in L. Li (1986), as discussed above, that they can be of identifiable reference. Identifiable and nonidentifiable referents encoded as bare NP are fairly equally divided in the position of postverbal object in transitive sentences, while the ratio is about one to three for cardinality expressions in the same position. The typical uses and interpretations of indeterminate expressions in the relevant positions are illustrated by the following examples:

(109) Qianyuan da   shu   xia   ji   tian qian pa
      front:yard big   tree down several day   ago creep
      man   le   *mayi*, dao   zuotian, *mayi* dou   pa
      full PFV   ant   to   yesterday ant   all   creep
      zou   le,   di   shang zhi   jian yi   gen
      away CRS   ground   on   only   see   several CL
      niao mao.
      bird feather

"Several days ago there were ants all over the bottom of the big tree in the front yard. Yesterday, the ants all disappeared, and there were only a few bird feathers on the ground."

(110) Zhangfu zhao lai le *ji* wei niwagong.
husband find come PFV several CL tiler
Ji wei niwangong yong le ji tian
several CL tiler use PFV several day
shijian ba fangding xiu hao le.
time BA roof fix fine CRS

"The husband hired several tilers. The tilers spent a few days and fixed the roof."

The referent *mayi* 'ant' in (109) assumes the same lexical form, as a bare NP, on its two occurrences in the sentence; and so does the referent *niwangong* 'tiler' in (110), as a cardinality expression. In each case, the nominal expression on the two occurrences differ in its position in the sentence. The bare NP *mayi* in (109) appears as postverbal NP in the presentative sentence on the first occurrence, interpreted as a nonidentifiable referent; and, as subject on the second occurrence, the expression is in anaphoric use, referring to an identifiable referent. The cardinality expression *ji wei niwagong* on the first occurrence as the object of the transitive verb refers to a new referent that is introduced into the discourse for the first time, and on the second occurrence, in subject position it is interpreted as a fully identifiable referent co-referential with the previously introduced referent.

While the identifiability or nonidentifiability of reference of determinate expressions is unambiguously indicated by the lexical and morphological encodings of expressions irrespective of their positioning in sentences, the interpretation of indeterminate expressions in respect of identifiability is inferred by the addressee, or is expected by the speaker to be inferred by the addressee, based on his assessment of how likely the expression in question is meant to serve as the topic of the utterance as well as on his whole range of knowledge of the utterance and its context of use. When he hears an utterance like *keren lai le* 'The guest/guests has/have arrived', he will start searching in the universe of discourse for a referent that meets the description of the NP *keren*, and which is supposed to be already identifiable for him: he knows that it is highly likely that the expression, because of its position as subject, is meant to be the topic of the utterance, and as such, normally has to be assumed by the speaker to be identifiable for him. In the overwhelming cases, he will easily locate that referent, in spite of the fact that the encoding itself is less informative in comparison with encodings marked by definite determiners like demonstratives. On the other hand, with a utterance like *lai keren le* 'A guest/guests has/have arrived; here arrives/arrive a guest/some guests', instead of searching for an identifiable referent fitting the description, most likely he will simply establish a new file in his mental representation of the event for a referent that is not supposed to have been known to him: he knows that position in sentence is normally used for introducing new referents into discourse.

  Since identifiability or nonidentifiability is encoded unequivocally and irrevocably in the case of determinate encoding, communication breaks down when the addressee cannot find an identifiable referent in the universe of discourse that meets the description of the definite expression. There is more flexibility with indeterminate expressions in definiteness-inclined positions which are normally expected to be interpreted as identifiable. As we have discussed earlier, the possibility is great that the subject expression is also the topic of the utterance, but it is not an absolute certainty. Subject can also serve as the position in which new referents, encoded in indefinite terms, are introduced into discourse, as illustrated by (108). Given that possibility, when the addressee cannot find a suitable identifiable referent satisfying the description of the indeterminate expression in the subject position, he will most likely read it in the same way as he interprets the indefinite subject in (108), treating it as a new referent making its first appearance in discourse, particularly when some other conditions are met (cf. Sasse 1987; Lambrecht 1994).[1]

In comparison, cardinality expressions in definiteness-inclined positions are even more likely to receive a nonidentifiability reading than bare NPs, presumably due to the fact that the descriptive content of numerals and quantifiers makes the expression more compatible than bare NP with a presentative use. Consider the following sentences:

(111) *Wuyun   piao le   guolai, jianjian ba   yueliang*
      dark:cloud float PFV come   gradually BA moon
      zhezhu   le.
      blot:out   CRS
      "Dark clouds float over, and gradually blot out the moon."

(112) *Da qun de lu   tingdao tonglei   de zhaohuan,*
      big group DE deer   hear   same:kind DE call

---

[1] I myself recently heard the following utterance from the manager to a waiter in a Chinese restaurant:
  (i) *Keren   lai le, ling libian qu.*
      customer come CRS lead inside go
      "There are some customers coming. Lead them to the inside."
When it was obvious from the body language of the restaurant staff and the customers that the customers had not patronized the restaurant before.

```
            beng  zhe  tiao  zhe  lai  dao  lieren  shenbian.
            leap  DUR  lump  DUR  come to   hunter  side
```
"Deer in large numbers ran vivaciously to the hunter when they heard the calls from other deer."

(113) *Liang ge qiangdao* cong zheli zou guo, kandao
      two CL bandit   from here walk by   see
      zhouwei meiyou   ren,   zhiyou Ou Ji zhenme
      around have:not person only   Ou Ji this
      yi ge xiaohaizi, jiu   qi   le   huaixin... *Liang*
      one CL kid   then arise PFV evil:idea two
      ge qiangdao ba Ou Ji de shuangshou fan bang zhu.
      CL bandit   BA Ou Ji DE two:hand   back tie up

"Two bandits passed by, saw nobody around except the kid Ou Ji, and then had an evil idea... The two bandits tied Ou Ji's hands behind his back."

Both (111) and (112) are felicitous when the referents of *wuyun* 'dark clouds' and *da qun de lu* 'deer in large numbers' appear for the first time in discourse. (113), which is quoted from a Chinese fable in my corpus of data, offers another illustrative example. The cardinality expression *liang ge qiangdao* 'two bandits' in the two clauses has exactly the same lexical encoding, and occupies the same syntactic position; it is nonidentifiable on the first occurrence, and identifiable on the second.

Finally, there are situations where the same indeterminate expression in an utterance can be interpreted either as an identifiable referent or a nonidentifiable referent. Consider the following as the opening sentence for a conversation:

(114) Zuowan   lianyouchang da   huo, *tie* *men* dou
      last:night refinary   big fire iron   gate   even

>
> shao hua le.
> burn melt CRS
>
> "There was a big fire at the refinery last night. The/An iron gate/gates melted in the fire."

(115) Xiao Li de bing   hen   zhong, yiyuan   de *san*
      Xiao Li DE illness very serious hospital DE three
      wei xinzhangbing zhuanjia shuo dei   like
      CL heard:ailment expert   say must immediately
      dong   shoushu.
      move   operation

"Xiao Li is seriously ill. (The) three cardiologists at the hospital said that he needed to undergo an operation immediately."

The bare noun *tie men* 'iron gate' in (114) can refer to an identifiable referent, in the situation where there is only one iron gate at the refinery that is supposed to be known to the addressee as part of their shared background knowledge or as a frame triggered entity. The sentence is also appropriate in the context in which the addressee is not assumed to know, and probably the speaker himself does not know either, how many iron gates there were to the refinery and which one or ones were melted in the fire. All the speaker intends to tell the addressee is that the fire was so destructive that it melted one or more iron gates. In the latter case, the expression obviously refers to a nonidentifiable referent. The same applies to (115). The referent of *san wei xinzhangbing zhuanjia* 'three cardiologists' can be three out of many cardiologists at the hospital, or it can be the three cardiologists that the hospital has, or the three doctors that the speaker and the addressee have mentioned earlier in discourse. It is out of the question to interpret the indeterminate expressions in (114) and (115) as in generic use.

By putting indeterminate expressions in sentence positions of two distinctive categories in respect of inclination for definite or indefinite expressions, the speaker indicates, or suggests, to the addressee whether the expressions are meant to be interpreted as identifiable or nonidentifiable. While it works in the majority of cases, it is to be stressed that, unlike the lexical and morphological encodings, position in sentences does not function as an unambiguous, watertight encoding device for marking identifiability or nonidentifiability of reference for nominal expressions in Chinese, except in one or two syntactic slots such as the postverbal NP in presentative sentences. So far as determinate expressions are concerned, most sentential positions in Chinese, as in many other languages, favor definite or indefinite expressions, as the case may be, but seldom reject categorically expressions of the other category. With regard to indeterminate expressions, most sentential positions invite, some more strongly than others, but seldom impose categorically, a reading of identifiability or nonidentifiability. There is simply no sentential position, or specific word order in Chinese whose core or primary function is to mark the distinction of the constituent in terms of identifiability.

It is appropriate in this connection to make a comparison between Chinese and the other four languages discussed earlier with respect to the use of zero NP as a coding device for identifiability. Count nouns in the plural and mass nouns with zero determiner in English, as observed earlier in this article, are always interpreted as nonidentifiable, standing in a paradigmatic contrast with the same nouns preceded by the definite article. Bare NPs in Czech are interpreted as definite or indefinite, depending on their position in sentences. Those in Hindi and Indonesian are either definite or for generic use. The four languages all share the feature that the interpretation of zero NPs with regard to identifiability of the referents is unambiguously determined. In contrast, the interpretation of zero NPs in Chinese with respect to identifiability correlates closely, but imperfectly, with their grammatical position in sentences; it is sometimes ambiguous or indeterminate.

5. Concluding remarks

In conclusion, we now summarize our answer to the first two questions raised at the beginning of this article: (i) how is identifiability encoded in Chinese? and (ii) how is Chinese in this respect similar with, or different from, the other languages that are briefly discussed in this article?

The pragmatic distinction between identifiability and nonidentifiability is expressed in Chinese in terms of distinctive lexical and morphological encodings and in terms of the positioning of nominal expressions in sentences. Of the major definite determiners in Chinese, demonstratives are developing functions, more advanced in spoken Chinese than in written Chinese, which are served by the definite article in English in marking referents whose identifiability is established through shared general knowledge, and in anaphoric and associative uses, although they have still preserved their deictic force to a considerable extent in these situations. The most important marker of indefiniteness in Chinese is *yi*+classifier, which has developed all the major functions, and more, that are served by indefinite articles in languages like English. In terms of morphology, and also in terms of function in the case of demonstratives, the definite and indefinite determiners in Chinese have not yet acquired the full status of specialized grammatical marker of definiteness and indefiniteness like the articles in English. Possessives in Chinese display features characteristic of AG languages like Italian, rather than DG language like English, although they at the same time have their own features not shared by those of typical AG languages. Monosyllabic classifiers and nouns in Chinese undergo reduplication to gain the additional meaning as that of universal quantifiers, which in Chinese are taken as definiteness markers on the grounds of their semantics and syntactic behaviors.

What makes Chinese further different from languages like English is the existence of what I call indeterminate expressions, which consist of bare NPs and cardinality expressions, and the correlation between the interpretation of the expressions in respect of identifiability and their positioning in sentences. As far as their lexical and morphological encodings are concerned, the indeterminate expressions are neutral with respect to the interpretation of identifiability. Whether the speaker intends them to be interpreted by the addressee as identifiable or nonidentifiable is indicated, or suggested, by their positioning in sentences. Some sentential positions in Chinese display a strong inclination for definite expressions, and some for indefinite expressions. They are called definiteness-inclined and indefiniteness-inclined positions respectively. With regard to indeterminate expressions, there is a strong, but not absolute, correlation between the interpretation in respect of identifiability of reference and the inclination of the position occupied by the expressions in sentences. While the pragmatic status of identifiability is unequivocally and irrevocably expressed for nominal expressions in referential use when they are encoded in determinate lexical and morphological terms, the interpretation of indeterminate expressions in respect of identifiability is expected by the speaker to be inferred by the addressee, on the basis of the topicality of the position occupied by the expression, the availability of an identifiable referent in the context that meets the descriptive content of the expression, as well as other relevant information of the utterance in the universe of discourse.

Finally, we turn to the last question: is it justified to assert that definiteness as a grammatical category, in the narrow sense of the term, exists in Chinese? English presents an exemplar case for the existence of definiteness as a grammatical category, as the language displays a paradigmatic contrast between two simple, fully grammaticalized articles, one definite and the other indefinite. A language which only has complex definite markers or other grammatical devices to encode the distinction between identifiability and nonidentifiability may also be treated, as discussed earlier, as having definiteness as a grammatical category if definiteness is obligatorily and unambiguously marked in that language. Czech, Hindi and Indonesian, based on the findings by Porterfield & Srivastav (1988) and Cummins (1998), meet this criterion, since the features of identifiability and nonidentifiability are obligatorily and unambiguously encoded in those languages in terms of a variety of linguistic devices including word order.

Chinese, however, represents a case that does not accord very well with what has been established for these languages in the current literature. To begin with, there is no simple, fully grammaticalized marker of definiteness in Chinese, like the definite article in English. In spite of the fact that demonstratives in Chinese have developed some uses that are normally served by definite articles in other languages, their basic or primary functions are still far from being those of deictically neutral determiners of definiteness like the English *the*. While the Chinese numeral *yi* 'one' has arguably reached the endpoint of grammaticalization into an indefinite article, there is no paradigmatic contrast between it and a highly grammaticalized marker of definiteness.

Furthermore, it is not obligatory to mark a nominal expression as either definite or indefinite in Chinese, as is the case in English. To the extent that situations are abundant in Chinese where the interpretation of bare NPs and cardinality expressions in respect of identifiability cannot be determined solely in terms of their position in sentences, and may even be ambiguous or indeterminate with regard to identifiability, the features of definiteness and indefiniteness cannot be uniquely and unambiguously specified for nominal expressions in Chinese. This leads to the conclusion that definiteness as a grammatical category, as defined in the narrow sense of the term, has not been fully developed in Chinese.

References

Ariel, Mira. 1990. *Accessing Noun-phrase Antecedents*. London: Routledge.

Brown, Gillian and George Yule. 1983. *Discourse Analysis*. Cambridge: Cambridge University Press.

Chafe, Wallace L. 1976. Givenness, contrastiveness, definiteness, subjects, topics, and point of view. In: *Subject and Topic*, Charles N. Li, ed., 25-55. New York: Academic Press.

Chafe, Wallace L. ed., 1980. *The Pear Stories: Cognitive, Cultural and Linguistic Aspects of Narrative Production*. Norwood, N.J.: Albex Publishing Corporation.

Chafe, Wallace L. 1994. *Discourse, Consciousness, and Time: The Flow and Displacement of Conscious Experience in Speaking and Writing*. Chicago: Chicago University Press.

Chao, Yuen Ren. 1968. *A Grammar of Spoken Chinese*. Berkeley and Los Angeles: University of California Press.

Chen, Ping. 1986. Referent introducing and tracking in Chinese narrative. PhD. dissertation, University of California, Los Angeles.

Chen, Ping. 1994. Shi lun Hanyu zhong san zhong juzi chengfen yu yuyi chengfen de peiwei yuanze [On principles of argument selection in Chinese]. *Zhongguo Yuwen* [*Chinese Language and Writing*] 1994 (3), 161-168.

Chen, Ping. 1996. Pragmatic interpretations of structural topics and relativization in Chinese. *Journal of Pragmatics* 26, 389-406.

Chen, Ping. 1999. *Modern Chinese: History and Sociolinguistics*. Cambridge: Cambridge University Press.

Chen, Ping. 2003. Indefinite determiner introducing definite referent: A special use of "*yi* 'one' + classifier" in Chinese. *Lingua* 113(2), 1169-1184.

Chen, Ping. 2004. Referentiality in grammar and discourse: With special reference to Chinese.

Chesterman, Andrew. 1991. *On Definiteness*. Cambridge: Cambridge University Press.

Christopherson, Paul. 1939. *The Articles: A Study of Their Theory and Use in English*. Copenhagen: Munksgaard.

Clark, Herbert H. 1977. Bridging. In: *Thinking: Readings in Cognitive Science*, Philip Nicholas Johnson-Laird and Peter Cathcart Wason, eds., 411-420. Cambridge: Cambridge University Press.

Clark, Herbert H. and Eve V. Clark. 1977. *Psychology and Language*. New York: Harcourt, Brace, Jovanovich.

Clark, Herbert H. and Catherine R. Marshall. 1981. Definite reference and mutual knowledge. In: *Elements of Discourse Understanding*, Avavind Joshi, Bonnie Webber and Ivan Sag, eds., 10-63. Cambridge: Cambridge University Press.

Cummins, George M. III. 1998. Definiteness in Czech. *Studies in Language* 22(3): 567-596.

Diessel, Holger. 1999. *Demonstratives: Form, Function and Grammaticalization*. Amsterdam: John Benjamins Publishing Company.

Donnellan, Keith S. 1966. Reference and definite descriptions. *Philosophical Review* 75, 281-394.

Du Bois, John W. 1980. Beyond definiteness: The trace of identity in discourse. In: *The Pear Stories: Cognitive, Cultural and Linguistic Aspects of Narrative Production*, Wallace Chafe, ed., 203-274. Norwood, N.J.: Albex Publishing Corporation.

Du Bois, John W. 1987. The discourse basis of ergativity. *Language* 63(4), 805-855.

Epstein, Richard. 1993. The definite article: Early stages of development. In: *Historical Linguistics 1991: Papers from the Tenth International Conference on Historical Linguistics*, Jaap van Marle, ed., 111-134. Amsterdam: John Benjamins Publishing Company.

Fan, Jiyan. 1985. Wuding NP zhuyu ju [Sentences with indefinite NP subject] *Zhongguo Yuwen* [*Chinese Language and Writing*] 1985 (5), 321-328.

Fang, Mei. 2002. Zhishici 'zhe' he 'na' zai Beijinghua zhong de yufahua [On the grammaticalization of the demonstratives *zhe* and *na* in Beijing Mandarin].

Zhongguo Yuwen [*Chinese Language and Writing*] 2002(4), 343-356.

Fillmore, Charles J. 1982. Towards a descriptive framework for spacial deixis. In: *Speech, Place, and Action: Studies in Deixis and Related Topics*, Jarvella Robert J. and Wolfgang Klein, eds., 31-59. John Wiley & Sons Ltd.

Fillmore, Charles J. 1997. *Lectures on Deixis*. CSLI Publications, Center for the Study of Language and Information, Stanford, California.

Ford, Cecilia E. and Barbara A. Fox. 1996. Interactional motivations for reference formulation: *He* had. *This* guy had, a beautiful, thirty-two O:lds. In: *Studies in Anaphora*, Barbara Fox, ed., 145-168. Amsterdam: John Benjamins Publishing Company.

Givón, Talmy. 1979. *On Understanding Grammar*. New York: Academic Press.

Givón, Talmy. 1981. On the development of the numeral 'one' as an indefinite marker. *Folia Linguistica Historica* 2(1), 35-53.

Givón, Talmy. ed. 1983. *Topic Continuity in Discourse: Quantitative Cross-language Studies*. Amsterdam: John Benjamins Publishing Company.

Givón, Talmy. 1985. The pragmatics of referentiality. In: *Meaning, Form and Use in Contact*, Deborah Schiffrin, ed., 120-138. Washington, D.C.: Georgetown University Press.

Givón, Talmy. 1984-1990. *Syntax: A Functional-Typological Introduction*. Vols. I & II, Amsterdam/Philadelphia: John Benjamins Publishing Company.

Greenberg, Joseph H. 1978. How does a language acquire gender markers? In: *Universals of Human Language*. Vol. III *Word Structure*, Joseph H. Greenberg, ed., 47-82. Stanford: Stanford University Press.

Grice, Paul. 1989. *Studies in the Way of Words* (*The William Jones Lectures*). Cambridge, Mass.: Harvard University Press.

Gundel, Jeanette K., Nancy Hedberg and Ron Zacharski. 1993. Cognitive status and the form of referring expressions in discourse. *Language* 69(2), 274-307.

Halliday, Michael A. K. 1967. Notes on transitivity and theme in English. Part I & Part II. *Journal of Linguistics* 3, 37-81, 177-274.

Haspelmath, Martin. 1997. *Indefinite Pronouns*. Oxford: Clarendon Press.

Haviland, Susan E. and Herbert H. Clark. 1974. What's new? Acquiring new information as a process in comprehension. *Journal of Verbal Learning and Verbal Behaviors* 13, 512-521.

Hawkins, John A. 1978. *Definiteness and Indefiniteness*. Atlantic Highlands, N. J.: Humanities Press.

Heim, Irene. 1988. *The Semantics of Definite and Indefinite Noun Phrases*. New York & London: Garland Publishing, Inc.

Heine, Bernd. 1997. *Cognitive Foundations of Grammar*. Oxford University Press.

Himmelmann, Nikolaus P. 1996. Demonstratives in narrative discourse: A taxonomy of universal uses. In: *Studies in Anaphora*, Barbara Fox, ed., 205-254. Amsterdam: John Benjamins Publishing Company.

Hopper, Paul and Sandra A. Thompson. 1980. Transitivity of grammar and discourse. *Language* 56(2), 251-299.

Hopper, Paul and Sandra A. Thompson. 1984. The discourse basis for lexical categories in universal grammar. *Language* 60(4), 703-752.

Hopper, Paul and Sandra A. Thompson. 1994. Language universals, discourse pragmatics, and semantics. *Language Sciences* 15 (4), 357-376.

Huang, James C.-T. 1987. Existential sentences in Chinese and (in)definiteness. In: *The Representation of (in) definiteness*, Eric J. Reuland and Alice G. B. ter Meulen, eds., 226-253. Cambridge, Mass.: MIT Press.

Huang, Shuanfan. 1999. The emergence of a grammatical category definite article in spoken Chinese. *Journal of Pragmatics* 31, 77-94.

Karttunen, Lauri. 1976. Discourse referents. In: *Syntax and Semantics,* Vol. 7: *Notes from the Linguistics Underground*, James McCawley, ed., 363-385. New York: Academic Press.

Keenan, Edward L. and Bernard Comrie. 1977. Noun phrase accessibility and Universal Grammar. *Linguistic Inquiry* 8(1), 63-99.

Krifka, Manfred, Francis Jeffry Pelletier, Gregory N. Carlson, Alice ter Meulen, Godehard Link, and Gennaro Chierchia. 1995. Genericity: An introduction.In: *The Generic Book*, Gregory N. Carlson and Francis Jeffry Pelletier, eds., 1-124. Chicago & London: The University of Chicago Press.

Lambrecht, Knud. 1994. *Information Structure and Sentence Form: A Theory of Topic, Focus, and the Mental Representation of Discourse Referents*. Cambridge: Cambridge University Press.

LaPolla, Randy J. 1995. Pragmatic relations and word order in Chinese. In: *Word Order in Discourse*, Pamela Downing and Michael Noonan, eds., 297-329. Amsterdam: John Benjamins Publishing Company.

Levinson, Stephen C. 2000. *Presumptive Meaning: The Theory of Generalized Conversational Implicature*. Cambridge, Mass.: MIT Press.

Li, Charles N. and Sandra A. Thompson. 1975. The semantic function of word order: A case study in Mandarin. In: *Word Order and Word Order Change*, Charles N. Li, ed., 163-195. Austin: University of Texas Press.

Li, Charles N. and Sandra A. Thompson. 1981. *Mandarin Chinese: A Functional Reference Grammar*. Berkeley and Los Angeles: University of California Press.

Li, Linding. 1986. *Xiandai Hanyu Juxing* [*Sentence Patterns in Modern Chinese*]. Beijing: Shangwu Yinshuguan [The Commercial Press].

Löbner, Sebastian. 1985. Definites. *Journal of Semantics* 4, 279-326.

Lü, Shuxiang. 1990 [1944]. Ge zi de yingyong fanwei, fu lun danweici qian *yi* zi de tuoluo [Scope of the uses of *ge* and omission of *yi* in front of classifiers]. In: *Lü Shuxiang Wenji* [*Collected Works of Lü Shuxiang*], Vol. 2, 144-175. Beijing: Shangwu Yinshuguan [The Commercial Press].

Lü, Shuxiang. 1990[1948]. Ba zi yongfa de yanjiu [Studies in the uses of *ba*]. In: *Lü Shuxiang Wenji* [*Collected Works of Lü Shuxiang*], Vol. 2, 176-199. Beijing: Shangwu Yinshuguan [The Commercial Press].

Lü, Shuxiang. 1990 [1956]. *Zhongguo Wenfa Yaolue* [*Essentials of Chinese Grammar*]. In: *Lü Shuxiang Wenji* [*Collected Works of Lü Shuxiang*], Vol. 1, 1-463. Beijing: Shangwu Yinshuguan [The Commercial Press].

Lü, Shuxiang. 1990[1985]. *Jindai Hanyu Zhidaici* [*Demonstratives and Pronouns in Early Modern Chinese*]. In: *Lü Shuxiang Wenji* [*Collected Works of Lü Shuxiang*], Vol. 3, 1-406. Beijing: Shangwu Yinshuguan [The Commercial Press].

Lü, Shuxiang. 1990. Zhishi daici de erfenfa he sanfenfa [Binary and ternary distinctions of demonstrative pronouns]. In: *Lü Shuxiang Wenji* [*Collected Works of Lü Shuxiang*], Vol. 3, 591-601. Beijing: Shangwu Yinshuguan [The Commercial Press].

Lyons, Christopher. 1999. *Definiteness*. Cambridge: Cambridge University Press.

Lyons, John. 1977. *Semantics*, Vols. I-II. Cambridge: Cambridge University Press.

Partee, Barbara Hall. 1970. Opacity, coreference, and pronouns. *Synthese* 21, 359-385.

Payne, John and Rodney Huddleston. 2002. Nouns and noun phrases. In: *The Cambridge Grammar of the English Language*, Rodney Huddleston and Geoffrey K. Pullum, Chapter 5, 323-524. Cambridge: Cambridge University Press.

Porterfield, Leslie and Veneeta Srivastav. 1988. (In)definiteness in the absence of articles: Evidence from Hindi and Indonesian. In: *Proceedings of the Seventh West Coast Conference on Formal Linguistics*, Hagit Borer, ed., 265-276. Stanford University: The Center for the Study of Language and Information.

Prince, Ellen. 1981. Towards a taxonomy of given-new information. In: *Radical Pragmatics*, Peter Cole, ed., 223-255. New York: Academic Press.

Sacks, Harvey and Emanuel A. Schegloff. 1979. Two preferences in the organization reference to persons in conversation and their interaction. In: *Everyday Language: Studies in Ethnomethodology*, George Psathas, ed., 15-21. New York: Irvington Publishers.

Sanford, Anthony and Simon C. Garrod. 1981. *Understanding Written Language.* Chichester: Wiley.

Sasse, Hans-Jurgen. 1987. The thetic/categorial distinction revisited. *Linguistics* 25, 511-580.

Schegloff, Emanuel A. 1996. Some practices for referring to persons in talk-in-interaction: A partial sketch of a systematics. In: *Studies in Anaphora*, Barbara Fox, ed., 437-485. Amsterdam: John Benjamins Publishing Company.

Shen, Jiaxuan. 1999. *Buduicheng he Biaojilun [Asymmetry and A Theory of Markedness]*. Nanchang: Jiangxi Jiaoyu Chubanshe [Jiangxi Education Publishing House].

Sun, Chaofen and Talmy Givón. 1985. On the so-called SOV word order in Mandarin Chinese: A quantified text study and its implications. *Language* 61(2), 329-351.

Tao, Hongyin. 1999. The grammar of demonstratives in Mandarin. *Journal of Chinese Linguistics* 27 (1): 69-103.

Thompson, Sandra A. 1997. Discourse motivations for the core-oblique distinction as a language universal. In: *Directions in Functional Linguistics*, Akio Kamio, ed., 59-82. Amsterdam: John Benjamins Publishing Company.

Tomlin, Russell S. 1983. On the interaction of syntactic subject, thematic information, and agent in English. *Journal of Pragmatics* 7, 411-432.

Tsao, Feng-fu. 1990. *Sentence and Clause Structure in Chinese: A Functional Perspective*. Taipei: Student Book Company.

van Oosten, Jeanne. 1986. *The Nature of Subjects, Topic and Agents: A Cognitive Explanation*. Bloomington: Indiana University Linguistics Club.

Xu, Yulong. 1987. A study of referential functions of demonstratives in Chinese discourse. *Journal of Chinese Linguistics* 15(1), 132-151.

Zhang, Bojiang. 2000. *Ba zi ju de jushi yuyi* [A construction grammar approach to the meaning of *ba* construction], *Yuyan Yanjiu* [*Studies in Language*] 1/2000 (38), 28-40.

Zhang, Bojiang and Mei Fang. 1996. *Hanyu Gongneng Yufa Yanjiu* [*Studies in Chinese grammar: A Functional Perspective*]. Nanchang: Jiangxi Jiaoyu Chubanshe [Jiangxi Education Publishing House].

汉语中的可辨识性与定指范畴

提　要　"可辨识性"指的是个体事物是否能由受话人将它从同类事物中辨识出来，是有定/无定语法范畴的认知基础，也是语法和话语分析研究领域里的重要概念。

本文研究"可辨识性"在汉语语法中的形式表现手段，涉及词义、词法和句法。可辨识性最典型的语法表现手段是定冠词，不可辨识性最典型的语法表现手段是不定冠词，本文侧重比较汉语指代词"这/那"以及数词"一"同西方语文的定冠词和不定冠词在语法化程度方面的异同，同时揭示汉语在表现可辨识/不可辨识性事物方面展示出来的有关特点。

关键词　可辨识性　有定　定冠词　不定冠词　指示词　数词"一"　语法化

（This article was first published in *Linguistics* 42(6), 1129-1184, in 2004. Permission by Walter de Gruyter GmbH to reprint the copyright material in the present volume is gratefully acknowledged.）

Indefinite determiner introducing definite referent: A special use of "*yi* 'one' + classifier" in Chinese[*]

Abstract The indefinite determiner "*yi* 'one' + classifier" is the most approximate to an indefinite article, like the English *a*, in Chinese. It serves all the functions characteristic of representative stages of grammaticalization from a numeral to a generalized indefinite determiner as elaborated in the literature. It is established in this paper that the Chinese indefinite determiner has developed a special use with definite expressions, serving as a backgrounding device marking entities as of low thematic importance and unlikely to receive subsequent mentions in ensuing discourse. '*yi* + classifier' in the special use with definite expressions displays striking similarities in terms of semantic bleaching and phonological reduction with the same determiner at the advanced stage of grammaticalization characterized by uses with generics, nonspecifics and nonreferentials. An explanation is offered in terms of an implicational

---

[*] I am grateful to an anonymous reviewer of *Lingua* for helpful comments and suggestions on the draft of this paper.

Following are the abbreviations used in this paper. For a detailed explanation of the terms, cf. Li & Thompson (1981).

BA   preverbal object marker (*ba*)
CL   classifier
CRS Current Relevant State (*le*)
CSC complex stative construction (*de*)
DE   nominalizer (*de*)
DUR durative aspect marker (*zhe*)
PFV perfective aspect marker (*le*)
PM   passive marker (*gei*)
SFP sentence-final particle

relation between nonreferentiality and low thematic importance which characterize the two uses of the indefinite determiner. While providing another piece of evidence in support of the claim that semantically nonreferentials and entities of low thematic importance tend to be encoded in terms of same linguistic devices in language, findings in this paper have shown how an indefinite determiner can undergo a higher degree of grammaticalization than has been reported in the literature – it expands its scope to mark not only indefinite but also definite expressions as semantically nonreferential and/or thematically unimportant.

Keywords   numeral 'one'; indefinite determiner; grammaticalization; thematic importance; nonreferentiality

1. Introduction

Yi is the numeral for 'one' in Chinese. When it is used with a common noun, it is mandatory to have a sortal classifier inserted between the numeral and the noun, as is normally the case with all numerals and determiners, like demonstratives, in Chinese when they are used with common nouns. Characteristic of what are known as classifier languages, like Chinese, Vietnamese and many other Southeastern Asian languages, a sortal classifier, in the words of Lyons (1977:463), "is one which individuates whatever it refers to in terms of the kind of entity that it is". For a detailed discussion of the use of classifiers in Chinese and other languages, see Erbaugh (1986), Hopper (1986), Sun (1988), inter alia. Following are two examples:

(1) Qianmian turan   tiao chulai *yi*   zhi   laohu.
    front   suddenly jump out   one   CL   tiger
    "Suddenly a tiger jumped out in front of us."

(2) Ta mai   le   *yi*   zhuang   fangzi.
    he buy   PFV   one   CL   house
    "He bought a house."

The numeral 'one' is the most common source from which indefinite articles in languages are derived, as is extensively attested in the literature (cf. Givón 1981; Wright & Givón 1987; Heine 1997). It is proposed in Heine (1997) that there are five stages in the process of grammaticalization through which the numeral 'one' has developed into a fully grammaticalized marker of indefiniteness. The five stages are characterized respectively by the use of 'one' as a numeral, by its presentative use, and by its use to introduce expressions of nonidentifiable specific reference, expressions of nonidentifiable nonspecific reference, and nonreferential expressions like a nominal predicative in ascriptive use. They are illustrated by the English indefinite article *a* in the following sentences respectively:

(3) a. NUMERAL

   I need *an hour and a half*.

   b. PRESENTATIVE USE

   A man came up the front stairway.

   c. NONIDENTIFIABLE SPECIFIC REFERENCE

   He bought *a house* last year.

   d. NONIDENTIFIABLE NONSPECIFIC REFERENCE

   He wants to buy *a house* in this area; any house will do.

   e. NONREFERENTIAL USE

   He is *a good chef*.

It is not always easy to establish for a particular language whether the numeral has undergone the full process of grammaticalization on its way to a bona fide indefinite article. Criteria used for the purpose include the semantic bleaching of its original meaning, phonological reduction, and morphological autonomy, which converge to indicate how far the numeral has gone along the path of grammaticalization marked by the five stages. Although there is a lack of consensus as to whether there is a bona fide indefinite article in Chinese, linguists of various theoretical backgrounds seem to agree that '*yi* + classifier' is the most approximate to an indefinite article in Chinese. As an indefinite marker, '*yi* + classifier' is employed for all the five uses of the indefinite article in English as illustrated in (3). They are illustrated in the following examples respectively:

(4) a. NUMERAL

Zhe jian shi bu nan ban, wo zhi yao *yi*
this CL thing not hard do I only need one
ge zhongtou jiu gou le.
CL hour then enough CRS
"This is not hard. I only need one hour for it."

b. PRESENTATIVE USE

Yi jia feiji cong women tou shang fei
one CL airplane from we head above fly
le guoqu.
PFV go
"An airplane flew over us."

c. NONIDENTIFIABLE SPECIFIC REFERENCE

Ta qunian mai le (*yi*) zhuang fangzi.
he last:year buy PFV one CL house
"He bought a house last year."

d. NONIDENTIFIABLE NONSPECIFIC REFERENCE

Ta xiang mai (*yi*) zhuang fangzi, shenme fangzi
he want buy one CL house any house
dou xing.
all do
"He wants to buy a house; any house will do."

e. NONREFERENTIAL USE

>   Ta   shi   (*yi*) ge   maimairen.
>   he   be   one   CL   businessman
>
>   "He is a businessman."

The further '*yi* + classifier' goes down the continuum of grammaticalization, the greater is its phonological reduction. *Yi* is often omitted when '*yi* + classifier' is used with nonidentifiable or nonreferential expressions, as shown in the above examples, leaving as it were the classifier alone to play the role of indefinite marker. With nonreferential expressions, it is much more natural to leave out *yi* in the expression. Regardless of whether *yi* is present or not, a countable noun introduced by the indefinite marker, as illustrated in (4a-d), is always understood as of singular reference. I will return to this point later in the paper.

The Chinese indefinite determiner displays a higher degree of morphological autonomy than the English indefinite article in that it has both pronominal and adjectival uses, as in the following example:

>   (5) Lao Li   xiang mai   (*yi*) zhuang fangzi, Lao Zhang
>   Lao Li   want   buy   one   CL   house   Lao Zhang
>   ye   xiang mai *yi* zhuang.
>   also want   buy one CL
>
>   "Lao Li wants to buy a house, and Lao Zhang wants to buy one too."

In other words, '*yi* + classifier' in the sentence serves the functions of both 'one' and 'a' in English.

2. '*yi* + classifier' used with definite referents

The indefinite determiner in Chinese has a special use that has not been reported for indefinite articles or the numeral 'one' in other languages.

It was first observed in Lü (1990[1944], 1990 [1948]) that '*yi* + classifier' can be used, normally with *yi* omitted, with expressions of definite reference. Let us consider the following example taken from Lü (1990[1944]:164):

(6) Zhi zhe yi ju, ba (*yi*) ge Jiang Ping hu
Only this one utterance BA one CL Jiang Ping scare
le yitiao.
PFV jump
"Just this one utterance gave Jiang Ping a fright."

where '*yi* + classifier' introduces a definite referent by the name of Jiang Ping.

It is to be noted that the use of '*yi* + classifier' with definite expressions in the above sentence is not to be confused with its use in the following sentence:

(7) You (*yi*) ge Jiang Ping xiang yao jian ni.
have one CL Jiang Ping think want see you
"There is a certain Jiang Ping who wants to see you."

In (7) '*yi* + classifier' introduces a referent that the speaker takes to be nonidentifiable to the addressee. It is used in exactly the same way as the English indefinite article in front of a proper name, meaning 'a certain', as illustrated by the English translation of the sentence. On the other hand, the proper name 'Jiang Ping' after the indefinite determiner '*yi* + ge' in (6) must refer to a person that is uniquely identifiable by that name to the addressee in the context of utterance. The sentence would be infelicitous if the addressee is not supposed to know who Jiang Ping is. In other words, the indefinite determiner '*yi* + classifier' in (6) is used to introduce a definite expression of uniquely identifiable reference to the addressee.

Definite referents introduced by the indefinite determiner '*yi* +

classifier' as illustrated in (6) fall into two major categories. They are either proper names, or kinship terms that are very similar in use to proper names in Chinese, or common nouns in the specific position of preverbal object introduced by the object marker *ba*. Below are more examples of the first category ((8) is adapted from Lü 1990 [1994]:159-164):

    (8) Dangxia xia de (*yi*) ge *Zhang San* mudengkoudai.
        instantly scare CSC one CL Zhang San dumbstruck
        "Zhang San was instantly struck dumb with fear."

    (9) Ta bei pengyou ba (*yi*) ge *taitai* gei pian
        he BEI friend BA one CL wife PP cheat
        zou le.
        away CRS
        "He was cheated by his friend out of his wife." or
        "He suffered from his friend cheating his wife away from him."

    (10) Ta qiannian si le *ge die*, qunian you
        he year:before:last die PFV CL father last:year again
        si le *ge niang*.
        die PFV CL mother
        "His father died the year before last, and his mother died last year."

'Zhang San' in (8) is a proper name with unique reference known to the addressee. The identifiable unique reference of the nominals of 'taitai' "wife" in (9) and 'die' "father" and 'niang' "mother" in (10) is inferable from the meaning of the kinship terms in the context of utterance. 'taitai', 'die' and 'niang' share an important feature with proper names in Chinese in that they all commonly serve both the vocative function as well as the referential function, which are taken as features characteristic of proper names (Lyons, 1977:216).

All of the nominals introduced by '*yi* + classifier' in the above sentences are definite expressions, and retain their interpretation of uniquely identifiable reference in spite of the presence of the indefinite determiner in front of them. When translated into a language like English, the indefinite determiner needs to be dropped.

'*yi* + classifier' is also used with nominal expressions which are interpreted as of definite reference due to their position after *ba* in sentences. As discussed in detail in Chen (2004), lexical encodings of NPs with regard to the interpretation of identifiability fall into three groups in Chinese, definite, indefinite, and indeterminate. While definite and indefinite NPs are interpreted as of identifiable and nonidentifiable reference respectively no matter what grammatical role they assume in the sentence, the interpretation of indeterminate NPs, such as a bare NP, usually depend on their position in sentences. There is a very strong tendency for a bare NP as the preverbal *ba* object to be interpreted as of uniquely identifiable reference. Consider (11):

(11) Ta   ba   *pibao*   diu   le.
     he   BA   bag   lose CRS
     "He lost his/the bag."

where the bare NP '*pibao*' is typically interpreted as of definite reference. The sentence would normally be infelicitous if the referent is nonidentifiable to the addressee in the context of utterance.

Now, consider the following sentence where '*pibao*' serves as the *ba* object, and is at the same time preceded by the indefinite determiner '*yi* + classifier':

(12) Ta   ba   (*yi*)   ge   *pibao*   diu   le.
     he   BA   one   CL   bag   lose CRS
     "He lost his/the bag."

There is a potential conflict in (12) between the function of '*yi*+

classifier' and the interpretation of 'pibao' with regard to identifiability. The lexical encoding of the referent in the form of bare noun, in itself, is neutral with regard to the interpretation of identifiability. On the one hand, '*yi* + classifier', as an indefinite determiner, presumably marks the common noun introduced by it as of nonidentifiable reference, as is customarily the situation elsewhere as illustrated in (4). On the other hand, the position of the nominal expression as the preverbal *ba* object in the sentence shows a strong tendency to assign to the expression an interpretation of definite reference, as illustrated in (11). With reference to (12), Chao (1968:344) remarks that "the advanced position of the object, brought about by the pretransitive (*ba*), has a stronger effect than the presence of *g* (= *ge*) or *ig* (= *yi* + *ge*) in deciding the definiteness of reference". In other words, in spite of the presence of the indefinite determiner, the bare NP 'pibao' in (12) is to be interpreted as of definite reference.

In his seminal discussion of the uses of '*yi* + classifier', Lü (1990[1944]) observes that the Chinese indefinite determiner indicates quantification and indefiniteness in a way similar to the indefinite article in English. At the same time, he points out that '*yi* + classifier' is used for a wider range of functions in comparison with the indefinite article in English. The special use of '*yi* + classifier' with definite expressions, as illustrated in the above sentences, is one that is not displayed by the indefinite article in English or other languages. The view is echoed by Chao (1968:344), who follows Lü in the characterization of '*yi* + classifier' as an indefinite marker, and adds that "there is no reason why forms like *g* or *ig* in Chinese should be delimited to indefinite reference because *a* or its equivalent in other Indo-European languages is the indefinite article."

The description of the uses of '*yi* + classifier' in Lü (1990[1944]) is comprehensive and highly insightful; and the interpretation by Lü, and also by Chao (1968), of the nominal expressions introduced by the indefinite determiner with respect to definite and indefinite reference as illustrated in the above examples is accurate and perceptive. There are two questions, however, that remain unanswered:

1) what is the function of the indefinite determiner 'yi + classifier' when it is used to introduce an expression of definite reference?
2) how is this special use of 'yi + classifier' related to the other uses of the indefinite determiner?

I will attempt an answer to the two questions in the remainder of this paper.

3. Function of 'yi + classifier' with definite referents

Let us start with the first question. As discussed above, on the one hand, we have the same indefinite determiner 'yi + classifier' used with indefinite referents or nonreferentials in (4) but with definite expressions in (6), (8), (9), (10) and (12); on the other hand, the definite expressions in question, namely the proper names, proper name-like kinship terms, and bare NPs in the position of the *ba* object, all retain their interpretation of definite reference in the context of utterance despite being apparently introduced by an indefinite determiner. What, then, is the function of 'yi + classifier' in these instances where it is used with definite referents? To put the question another way, what is the difference between these sentences and the corresponding ones without 'yi + classifier' in front of the definite expressions?

'*yi* + classifier' in the special use in these sentences, I would argue, serves as a backgrounding device which indicates that the nominal expression it modifies, which is otherwise marked as of high thematic importance, is to be taken as low in thematic importance in the context of utterance.

The concept of thematic importance used in this paper, which is borrowed from Givón (1984-1990), refers to the importance of a referent in discourse. Referents often differ in respect of their role in the development of discourse. Some play a central role, some play a relatively less important or peripheral role, and still some may only serve as props in an action or event. Referents of high thematic importance characteristically receive more mentions in the following discourse than referents of lower importance. The information status of referents in this respect is also captured in the literature in terms of concepts such as plot centrality (Clancy 1980), salience (Du Bois 1980), thematic subjecthood (Garrod & Sanford 1988), newsworthiness (Chafe 1994), foregrounding (Hopper & Thompson 1993), protagonism (Cumming 1995), referential importance (Givón 1984-1990; Chafe 1994:88-91), main characterhood (Downing 1996:114), and overlaps with what is covered by notions like topicality (Givón 1983) and thematicity (Nichols 1985).

The pragmatic concept of thematic importance, as noted in Cummings (1995:78) in reference to protagonism, "relates primarily to speakers' representations" of referents in discourse. There are a variety of linguistic devices, some language specific and some language universal, that speakers may utilize to indicate to the addressee whether a referent is characteristic of such information status. A case in point is the contrast between 'a' and 'this' as an indefinite marker in spoken English. If the noun refers to an entity that is thematically important, and will probably receive more mentions later in the discourse, 'this' is more likely to be chosen, whereas the use of 'a' does not indicate such an intention on the part of the speaker, as exemplified in the following sentences:

(13) a. He was walking in the forest and saw *this big bear*...

b. He was walking in the forest and saw something that looked like *a big bear* ...

It is more likely for *this big bear* in (13a) to receive more subsequent mentions in discourse than *a big bear* in (13b).

As discussed above, the referents of definite reference that are introduced by '*yi* + classifier' fall into two major categories in terms of morphosyntactic encoding, which are proper names or kinship terms, and objects of the preverbal *ba*. It is important to note that high thematic importance in discourse of utterance has been shown to be characteristic of both types of morphosyntactic encoding.

It has been established in the literature that, among the wide range of referential choices for a particular referent in discourse, proper name is characteristically used for referents which the speaker treats as high in thematic importance. In the experimental studies on reading and writing, Sanford, Moar & Garrod (1988: 48) report that an individual denoted by a proper name is "more likely to be a character of importance in a full narrative than is one denoted by a role description", and the encoding serves as "a discourse-triggered instruction to register the individual so denoted as of special importance". As a result, "introducing a character by means of a proper name enhances the character's availability for continuation production, and enhances accessibility for pronominal anaphora". A similar claim is made in Givón (1984-1990:937) that "typically, only globally important referents are given a proper name". Based on a preliminary examination of her collected data,

Downing (1995:115) also proposes that "it does seem likely ... that main character status will turn out to be one of the factors promoting the use of proper names in conversational contexts."

Similar characterization has been made of nominal expressions that serve as the *ba* object in Chinese. Expressions as the *ba* object, as those in the subject position, are typically of high thematic importance in the context of utterance, which are likely to be more frequent in the ensuing development of discourse. While the subject expression often assumes the pragmatic role of topic, the *ba* object is the next most likely expression in the sentence to be interpreted as a pragmatic topic in discourse. It is for this reason that the *ba* object is characterized as a secondary topic by some Chinese grammarians (cf. Tsao 1990; also Tomlin 1983, 1995; van Oosten 1986; inter alia).

When expressions in the two types of morphosyntactic encoding are preceded by the indefinite determiner '*yi* + classifier' in Chinese, they retain the interpretation of identifiability but lose the high thematic importance normally associated with the encoding. The indefinite determiner in the special use with definite referents serves to indicate that the entity in question is of low thematic importance, thus canceling the otherwise high expectation for the expression to recur frequently in the following discourse. Consider the following examples:

(14) a. Ta na   yi   fan hua   shuo de   *Zhang Zhicheng*
     He that one CL   words say CSC Zhang Zhicheng
     mudengkoudai. Guo   le   hao   yihuir, Zhang
     dumbstruck   Pass PFV   very while   Zhang
     Zhicheng cai   manman mingbai   guolai.
     Zhicheng then slowly understand over

   b. Ta na yi fan hua shuo de *ge Zhang Zhicheng* mudengkoudai.
      Guo le hao yihuir, ?? Zhang Zhicheng cai manman

mingbai guo lai.

"His words dumbfounded Zhang Zhicheng. After quite a while, Zhang Zhicheng slowly started to make sense of what he had said."

(15) a. Ta ba *pibao* diu le,   houlai you   zhao dao le.
        he BA bag   lose CRS later again find to CRS
    b. Ta ba *ge pibao* diu le, ?? houlai you zhao dao le.

"He lost his bag, but found it later."

The two sentences in each pair differ only in whether or not the definite expression in question is preceded by '*yi* + classifier' in the first part of the sentence. The nominal expressions in question, no matter whether introduced by '*yi* + classifier' or not, are interpreted as of definite reference, referring to entities whose identity has been established in the context of utterance. When ensuing mentions are made of the expressions in question, (a) is much more natural than (b) in both sentences. The contrast between (a) and (b) in the minimal pairs reveals the role of '*yi* + classifier' in the sentence, which is to mark the referent in question as less likely to recur in the following discourse than is otherwise the case.

It is to be noted that '*yi* + classifier' in the special use illustrated here displays three distinctive features. They are all related to the bleaching out of the individuation and referentiality of the entity introduced by the indefinite determiner.

First, while it is still possible to have '*yi*' in front of the classifier, it is much more common to omit it when the indefinite determiner is in its special use with definite expressions, leaving only the classifier in front of the noun. Second, the semantic component of quantification in '*yi* + classifier' is greatly bleached, particularly when *yi* is omitted, to such an extent that, in spite of the inherent meaning of oneness in the indefinite determiner, '*yi* + classifier' may be used to introduce plural referents, as illustrated by the following example from Lü (1990 [1944]:159):

(16) Dangxia ba *ge Zhang San he Li Si* xia de
instantly BA CL Zhang San and Li Si scare CSC
mudengkoudai.
dumbstruck
"Zhang San and Li Si were instantly struck dumb with fear."

Third, unlike the cases involving the other uses of the indefinite determiner, the classifier is almost always *ge* when '(*yi*) + classifier' is in the special use with definite referents.

As noted at the beginning of this paper, nouns in Chinese have their own special sortal classifiers, which serve the purpose of individuation and enumeration of the object denoted by the noun. The classifiers indicate, in an explicit or suggestive manner, the shape, texture, function and so on of the entities they are used with. For instance, the special sortal classifier for 'pen' in Chinese is *zhi*, literally "branch", which suggests the long slender shape of a pen; that for 'hat' is *ding*, literally "top", which denotes an essential part of the object; and that for 'table' is *zhang* "stretched, spread", which suggests the function of the entity. When '*yi* + classifier' is in the special use with definite expressions, the classifier *ge* is normally used, instead of the special sortal classifiers that are customarily used with the nominal expressions elsewhere. Consider the following examples:

(17) a. Ta diu le *yi fu yanjing*.
he lose PFV one CL glasses
b. *Ta diu le *yi ge yanjing*.
"He lost a pair of glasses."

(18) a. ?Ta ba (*yi*) *fu yanjing* gei diu le.
   he BA one CL glasses PM lose CRS
b. Ta ba (*yi*) *ge yanjing* gei diu le.
   he BA one CL glasses PM lose CRS
"He lost his glasses."

The special sortal classifier for glasses is *fu* 'pair' in Chinese, as in (17a), and *ge* is normally not allowed, as in (17b), except with children, who, generally speaking, overwhelmingly prefer *ge*, as established in Erbaugh (1986:413). In the special use of '*yi* + classifier' with a definite referent as in (18), however, *ge* is much preferred over *fu*. While (18a) may be acceptable to some speakers, (18b) is much more natural and idiomatic. In comparison with the other special sortal classifiers like *zhi*, *ding*, *zhang* and *fu*, *ge* is the most generalized classifier in Chinese without any special semantic characteristics.

A sortal classifier, as discussed earlier, serves to individuate the entity for which it is used. While the omission of *yi* weakens the force of quantification of the indefinite marker, the substitution of *ge* for the special sortal classifier for the particular noun further weakens the individuation of the entity introduced by the indefinite determiner. The combined effect of these features of '*yi* + classifier' in the special use is underscored by Chao (1968:344) when he translates (19)

(19) Ta ba *ge zhangfu* si le.
   she BA CL husband die CRS

as "she suffered her husband to die on her". What underlies this rendition is that instead of being taken as an individuated entity of high thematic importance, her husband is treated as a prop in an event that has happened to her. What is being talked about in this utterance is 'she', not 'her husband'. In the particular context of utterance, it is far more likely to expect more subsequent mentions of her than of her husband.

4. Connection between the special use of '*yi* + classifier' and the other uses of the indefinite marker

The three features characteristic of '*yi* + classifier' in its special use with definite referents, it is revealing to note, are all displayed by '*yi* + classifier' at the advanced stage of development as an indefinite determiner.

In the first section of this paper, I have discussed the five uses of '*yi* + classifier' as an indefinite determiner in Chinese. The five uses, as proposed in Givón (1981) and Heine (1997), represent the stages of grammaticalization through which the numeral 'one' has evolved into a grammatical marker of indefiniteness. In the final stage of the process, as argued in Givón (1981:51), each of the two more remarked semantic features of the numeral 'one', namely quantification and referentiality, are bleached out, leaving only the connotation/genericity of the nominal expression introduced by the indefinite marker. The most typical use of the indefinite article at the final stage of development is with a nonreferential predicative nominal as in the following sentence:

(20) John is *a teacher*.

The indefinite marker at the final stage is called the "generalized article" by Heine (1997:73), which "can be expected to occur on all types of nouns, ... no longer restricted to singular nouns but is extended to plural and mass nouns". Based on cross-linguistic evidence, Heine (1997) observes that the bleach-out of the number-specific features of the numeral 'one' at the advanced stage of grammaticalization is also likely to correlate with loss of morphological autonomy and reduction of phonological form.

Heine's remarks accurately characterize the Chinese indefinite determiner '*yi* + classifier' in its development as an indefinite marker. As discussed at the beginning of this paper, (4) represents the typical uses of the numeral-indefinite marker in Chinese at five representative stages of development. The likelihood of omission of *yi* increases as we go from (4a) through to (4d), correlating with the weakening of quantification and referentiality of '*yi* + classifier + NP'. It is observed in Lü (1990[1994]:167) that *yi* in '*yi* + classifier' is more likely to be omitted when used as a marker of nonidentifiable nonspecific reference, as in (4d), than as a marker of nonidentifiable specific reference, as in (4c). Chen (2004) further observes that it is much more natural to omit *yi* when '*yi* + classifier' is used with nonreferentials as in (4e). While speakers may vary in their judgement on whether it is more natural to omit *yi* in particular instances representing intermediate stages of development such as (4b), (4c), and (4d) (also cf. Huang 1987), there is general agreement that the extent of the phonological reduction of the Chinese indefinite determiner correlates perfectly with the order of its development through the five stages of grammaticalization: the less referential a nominal is, the more likely it is for *yi* to be omitted.

Furthermore, '*yi* + classifier' in the numeral and the presentative use, as well as in its uses with nonidentifiable specific or nonspecific reference, is always to be interpreted as referring to a singular noun regardless of whether or not *yi* is omitted. When used with nonreferential nominals in sentences like (4e), however, '*yi* + classifier' may be used to be ascriptive of plural nouns. Consider the following sentence:

(21) Tamen fuzi kanshangqu xiang (*yi*) ge faguoren.
They father:son look like one CL Frenchman
"The father and the son look like Frenchmen."

Finally, the special sortal classifiers of particular nouns are more likely to be replaced by the general classifier *ge* when '*yi* + classifier' is used with nonreferentials, further weakening the individuation and referentiality of the noun. Consider the following sentences:

(22) *Yi   wei/ge   faguoren   zou   le   guolai.*
     One   CL/CL   French   walk PFV   over
     "There is a Frenchman coming over."

(23) *Wo zuotian   jiandao   (yi)   wei/ge   faguoren.*
     I   yesterday see   one   CL CL   French
     "I met a Frenchman yesterday."

(24) *Ta kanshangqu xiang ge/*?wei faguoren.*
     he   look   like   CL CL   French
     "He looks like a Frenchman."

(25) *Tamen fuzi   kanshangqu xiang ge/*?? wei faguoren.*
     they   father:son look   like   CL   CL   French
     "The father and the son look like Frenchmen."

In the presentative and the nonidentifiable specific use of '*yi* + classifier' as in (22) and (23) respectively, both the specific sortal classifier *wei* for the noun, and the general classifier *ge* can be used. In the nonreferential use as in (24), *ge* is much more common than *wei*. The preference is even stronger when the subject is in the plural as in (25).

It is suggested in Lü (1990[1944]:165-166) that the use of '*yi* + classifier' with definite expressions may have derived by analogy from the use of the indefinite determiner introducing a nonidentifiable noun. While we do not have large-scale data to prove that '*yi* + classifier' in the special use with definite expressions has diachronically followed the use of '*yi* + classifier' as an indefinite article for nouns with nonidentifiable reference and as what Heine (1997) calls a "generalized article" introducing a nonreferential nominal, it would be theoretically unproductive to brush aside as mere coincidence the fact that '*yi* + classifier' in the two uses displays the same important features.

Heine (1997:75) notes that at the advanced stage of development "the article can be expected to occur on all types of nouns, even if there may remain a number of exceptions—for instance, if the noun is marked for definiteness, or is a proper noun". What has been established for '*yi* + classifier' in this paper suggests that the generalized article in Chinese has extended beyond the use of nonreferentiality into another function to mark a definite expression as of low thematic importance. The plausibility of this view is based on the fact that '*yi* + classifier' as a generalized article introducing nonreferentials and '*yi* + classifier' introducing definite referents share important behavioral features which otherwise could not be explained. More importantly, it is also supported by the well attested connection between nonreferentiality and low thematic importance that respectively characterize the two uses of '*yi* + classifier' under discussion.

A distinction is drawn in the literature between semantic or objective referentiality and pragmatic or discourse referentiality. A semantically or objectively referential entity is defined in Payne (1997: 264) as one that "exists as a bounded, individuated entity in the message world", whereas generics, nonspecifics, and nonreferentials are semantically nonreferential. Pragmatic referentiality, on the other hand, relates to the importance of the entity in the discourse of utterance. Pragmatically referential entities are normally semantically referential, but semantically referential entities may be pragmatically important or unimportant. When semantics and pragmatics conflict, grammar follows one or the other. Some grammatical features hinge upon the distinction between semantic referentiality and nonreferentiality. For example, whether human direct objects take the preposition *a* or no preposition in Spanish, as described in Payne (1997:264), depends on whether they are semantically referential or nonreferential. More grammatical features, however, are sensitive to the distinction of entities with regard to their pragmatic referentiality or importance.

In their empirical studies of the grammatical markings of indefinite referents in Hebrew, Krio and Chinese, Wright & Givón (1987) have demonstrated that semantically referential indefinites which are pragmatically unimportant tend to receive the same encoding as semantically nonreferential indefinites, which is distinct from that for pragmatically important entities. In the words of Wright & Givón (1987:9), "the grammar marked nominals as 'referential' not merely because the speaker intends them to exist in the universe of discourse, but rather because their specific, referential identity was important— it mattered—in the discourse." With regard to those pragmatically unimportant indefinite entities, they are treated in the same way regardless of whether or not they are semantically referential. In other words, the semantic referentiality and nonreferentiality in the case with entities of low thematic importance is neutralized in terms of the formal encoding of the nominals involved.

It follows from the above reasoning that there is an implicational relation between nonreferentiality and low thematic importance which characterize the two uses of the Chinese indefinite determiner '*yi* + classifier' under discussion in this paper:

(26) A nominal marked as semantically nonreferential is necessarily pragmatically unimportant.

The three features displayed by '*yi* + classifier' in its use with nonreferentials reflect the semantic bleaching and phonological reduction characteristic of the indefinite determiner at the advanced stage of grammaticalization, where the individuation and numeration of indefinite nominals introduced by it have been almost completely bleached out. The indefinite determiner at the advanced stage of development, when used with a definite expression, strongly implicates that the entity is to be interpreted as pragmatically unimportant, by virtue of the fact that it is encoded in much the same way as a semantically nonreferential nominal. From the use of '*yi* + classifier' as a numeral 'one' to its special use with definite referents to mark low thematic importance, its use with semantic nonreferentials as represented in (4e) is a pivotal development. At this stage, and to some extent in the previous one or two stages represented by (4d) and (4c), with the phonological reduction of *yi*, the general classifier *ge* itself apparently serves as an article, as suggested in Lü (1990[1944]:174), or as what is called a "quasi-article" in Hopper (1986) and Hopper & Thompson (1993:371). It paves the way for its further use with definite referents as a marker of low thematic importance in two important respects.

First, with *yi* almost always omitted, there is less potential semantic conflict between '*yi* + classifier' and definite reference. Second, semantic nonreferentiality bears a close affinity to thematic low importance, which, as demonstrated in Wright & Givón (1987), is often manifested in language in terms of same grammatical encoding. It explains why the indefinite determiner '*yi* + classifier' at the advanced stage of grammaticalization characterized by its use with nonreferentials shares important features with the determiner in the special use with definite expressions as a marker of low thematic importance.

In the cases discussed by Wright & Givón (1987), semantic referentiality or nonreferentiality of entities is neutralized in terms of grammatical encoding when they are thematically unimportant.

In the case of the Chinese '*yi* + classifier' used as a generalized indefinite article and as an indefinite determiner introducing definite expressions, both semantic referentiality and pragmatic identifiability of nominals are neutralized: the speaker treats them as entities that do not matter in the subsequent discourse, no matter whether they are semantically referential or nonreferential, or pragmatically identifiable or nonidentifiable.

5. Concluding remarks

The Chinese indefinite determiner '*yi* + classifier', in a way fairly similar to the indefinite article *a* in English, has developed functions characterizing each of the representative stages of grammaticalization from a numeral to a generalized indefinite determiner as elaborated in Heine (1997). More interestingly, it has been established in this paper that the Chinese indefinite determiner has developed a special use with definite expressions, serving as a backgrounding device marking the entities as of low thematic importance and unlikely to receive subsequent mentions in ensuing discourse. The indefinite determiner in the special use displays striking similarities in terms of semantic bleaching and phonological reduction with the determiner at its advanced stage of grammaticalization characterized by uses with generics, nonspecifics and nonreferentials.

Based on the findings in this paper, I would like to make two further points of more general interest.

First, referential encoding as proper names, and syntactic encoding as the *ba* object in Chinese have been characterized in the literature as being associated with a specific function in discourse, which is to mark entities as of high thematic importance. It is evident from the discussion in this paper that the characterized function is a 'default' one, which can be overridden. It indicates that there are other functions coded by these linguistic devices. What these functions are and how they relate to each other are interesting topics for further investigation.

Second, the five stages of grammaticalization of the indefinite determiner in various languages all relate to the quantification and referentiality of the nominal introduced by the determiner. The special use of '*yi* + classifier' with definite expressions has demonstrated how the indefinite determiner in Chinese has extended beyond the referential properties of the nominal, and acquired a new discourse function that is implicated by nonreferentiality featured at the advanced stage of grammaticalization of the determiner. While providing another piece of evidence in support of the claim that semantically nonreferentials and entities of low thematic importance tend to be encoded in terms of same linguistic devices in language, the findings in this paper have shown how an indefinite determiner can undergo a higher degree of grammaticalization than has been reported in the literature—it expands its scope to mark not only indefinite but also definite expressions as semantically nonreferential and/or thematically unimportant.

References

Chafe, Wallace L. 1994. *Discourse, Consciousness, and Time: The Flow and Displacement of Conscious Experience in Speaking and Writing.* Chicago University Press.

Chao, Yuen Ren. 1968. *A Grammar of Spoken Chinese.* University of California Press, Berkeley and Los Angeles.

Chen, Ping. 2004. Identifiability and definiteness in Chinese. *Linguistics* 42(6), 1129-1184.

Clancy, Patricia. 1980. Referential choices in English and Japanese narrative discourse. In: Chafe, Wallace, ed., *The Pear Stories: Cognitive, Cultural and Linguistic Aspects of Narrative Production*. Albex Publishing Corporation, Norwood, N.J., Pp.127-202.

Cumming, Susanna. 1995. Agent position in the Sejarah Melayu. In: Downing, Pamela A. and Noonan, Michael, eds., *Word Order in Discourse*. John Benjamins Publishing Company, Amsterdam, Pp. 51-38.

Downing, Pamela A. 1996. Proper names as a referential option in English conversation. In: Fox, Barbara, ed., *Studies in Anaphora*. John Benjamins Publishing Company, Amsterdam, Pp. 95-143.

Du Bois, John W. 1980. Beyond definiteness: The trace of identity in discourse, In: Chafe, Wallace, ed., *The Pear Stories: Cognitive, Cultural and Linguistic Aspects of Narrative Production*. Albex Publishing Corporation, Norwood, N. J., Pp. 203-274.

Erbaugh, Mary S. 1986. Taking stocks: The development of Chinese noun classifiers historically and in young children. In: Craig, Colette, ed., *Noun Classes and Categorization*. John Benjamins Publishing Company, Amsterdam, Pp. 399-436.

Garrod, Simon and Sanford, Anthony. 1988. Thematic subjecthood and cognitive constraints on discourse structure. *Journal of Pragmatics* 12, 519-534.

Givón, Talmy. 1981. On the development of the numeral 'one' as an indefinite marker. *Folia Linguistica Historica* 2(1), 35-53.

Givón, Talmy. ed. 1983. *Topic Continuity in Discourse: Quantitative Cross-Language Studies*. John Benjamins Publishing Company, Amsterdam.

Givón, Talmy. 1984-1990. *Syntax: A Functional-Typological Introduction*, Vols. I & II, John Benjamins Publishing Company, Amsterdam.

Heine, Bernd. 1997. *Cognitive Foundations of Grammar*. Oxford University Press.

Hopper, Paul. 1986. Some discourse functions of classifiers in Malay. In: Craig, Colette, ed., *Noun Classes and Categorization*. John Benjamins Publishing Company, Amsterdam, Pp. 309-325.

Hopper, Paul. and Thompson, Sandra. A. 1993. Language universals, discourse pragmatics, and semantics. *Language Sciences* 15 (4), 357-376.

Huang, James. C.-T. 1987. Existential sentences in Chinese and (in)definiteness. In: Reuland, Eric J., ter Meulen, Alice G. B., eds., *The Representation of (In) definiteness*. MIT Press, Cambridge, MA, Pp. 226-253.

Li, Charles N. and Thompson, Sandra A. 1981. *Mandarin Chinese: A Functional Reference Grammar*. Berkeley and Los Angeles: University of California Press.

Lü, Shuxiang. 1990 [1944]. *Ge zi de yingyong fanwei, fu lun danweici qian yi zi de tuoluo* [Scope of the uses of *ge* and omission of *yi* in front of classifiers]. In: *Lü Shuxiang Wenji [Collected Works of Lü Shuxiang]*. Vol. 2. Shangwu Yinshuguan [The Commercial Press], Beijing, Pp. 144-175.

Lü, Shuxiang. 1990[1948]. *Ba zi yongfa de yanjiu* [Studies in the uses of *ba*]. In: *Lü Shuxiang Wenji*, Vol. 2. Shangwu Yinshuguan [The Commercial Press], Beijing, Pp. 176-199.

Lyons, John. 1977. *Semantics*, Vols. I-II. Cambridge University Press.

Nichols, Johanna. 1985. The grammatical marking of theme in literary Russian. In: Flier, Michael S. and Brecht, Richard D., eds., *Issues in Russian Morphosyntax*. Slavica Publishers, Columbus, Ohio, Pp. 170-186.

Payne, Thomas. 1997. *Describing Morphosyntax: A Guide for Field Linguists*. Cambridge University Press.

Sanford, Anthony, Moar, J. K. and Garrod, Simon C. 1988. Proper names as controllers of discourse focus. *Language and Speech* 31, 43-56.

Sun, Chaofen. 1988. The discourse function of numeral classifiers. *Journal of Chinese Linguistics* 16 (2), 298-323.

Tomlin, Russell S. 1983. On the interaction of syntactic subject, thematic information, and agent in English. *Journal of Pragmatics* 7, 411-432.

Tomlin, Russell S. 1995. Focal attention, voice, and word order. In: Downing, Pamela A. and Noonan, Michael, eds., *Word Order in Discourse*. John Benjamins Publishing Company, Amsterdam, Pp. 517-554.

Tsao, Feng-fu. 1990. *Sentence and Clause Structure in Chinese: A Functional Perspective*. Student Book Company, Taipei.

van Oosten, Jeanne. 1986. *The Nature of Subjects, Topic and Agents: A Cognitive Explanation*. Indiana University Linguistics Club, Bloomington.

Wright, S. and Givón, Talmy. 1987. The pragmatics of indefinite reference: Quantified text-based studies. *Studies in Language* 11(1), 1-33.

引进定指成分的无定限定词：汉语"一＋量词"的一个特殊用法

提　要　"一＋量词"是汉语中最接近西语不定冠词的成分。普通语言学研究证实，不定冠词由数词"一"通过语法化过程演化而来，语言学文献中广泛报道，数词"一"语法化过程一般经历五个阶段，这五个阶段的有关特征，都可以从汉语数词"一"的用法中看到。不仅如此，汉语数词"一"还可以同语义定指成分连用，起着削弱其话语角色、将其退居边缘的作用，与语义无指成分的典型用法相同。这种现象从另一个角度说明语义无指事物同话语边缘成分的内在联系。
关键词　数词"一"　无定限定词　语法化　主题重要程度　无指

(This article was first published in *Lingua* 113, 1169-1184, in 2003. Permission by Elsevier to reprint the article in the present volume is gratefully acknowledged.)

人名索引

A

Aikhenvald, Alexandre Y. 23, 36
Ariel, Mira 311, 328
Aristotle 见"亚里士多德"
Austin, John L. 99

B

柏拉图（Plato） 97, 98, 100, 101
Bache, Carl 43, 73
Berwick, Robert C. 165, 166
Birner, Betty 23, 36
Bresnan, Joan 172, 192
Brown, Gillian 270, 328

C

曹逢甫（Tsao, Feng-Fu） 176, 178, 181, 194, 313, 333, 347, 360
陈平（Chen, Ping） 16, 21, 23—25, 27, 36, 37, 49, 62, 73, 77, 92, 95, 102, 107, 109, 110, 112, 114, 119, 120, 135, 137, 140, 142, 145, 155, 159, 165, 178, 192, 201, 215, 230, 234, 238, 241—243, 245, 248, 252, 261, 287, 303, 304, 312, 328, 329, 342, 352, 358
Carlson, Gregory N. 331
Carlson, Lauri 43, 73
Chafe, Wallace L. 18, 36, 95, 171, 180, 184, 192, 234, 252, 258, 289, 311, 328, 329, 345, 358, 359
Chao, Yuen Ren 见"赵元任"
Chastain, Charles 212, 234
Chen, Ping 见"陈平"
Chesterman, Andrew 125, 142, 246, 252, 255, 329
Chierchia, Gennaro 30, 37, 331
Chomsky, Noam 见"乔姆斯基"
Christopherson, Paul 276, 329
Clark, Herbert H. 258, 269, 270, 280, 329, 330
Comrie, Bernard 43, 45, 48, 56, 74, 178, 193, 311, 331
Cumming, Susanna 222, 234, 345, 359
Cummins, George M. III. 285, 286, 327, 329

D

邓守信（Teng, Shou-Hsin） 2, 13, 44—46, 73, 186, 187, 194
丁声树 21, 36
Dahl, Östen 214, 234
Daneš, František 152, 165, 166
Davison, Alice 181, 182, 193
Diessel, Holger 132, 142, 278, 282, 329

Dik, Simon 180, 193
Dixon, R. M. W. 36
Donnellan, Keith S. 120, 207, 208, 234, 252, 264, 329
Dooley, Robert A. 181, 184, 193
Downing, Pamela 222, 225, 234, 331, 345, 347, 359, 360
Dowty, David 1, 3, 12, 43, 74
Du Bois, John W. 92, 95, 218, 219, 234, 244, 252, 262, 272, 274, 311, 329, 345, 359

E

Enç, Mürvet 214, 234
Epstein, Richard 260, 329
Ernst, Thomas 37
Euclides 100

F

范继淹（Fan, Jiyan） 2, 5, 10, 12, 16, 27, 28, 36, 60, 73, 91, 95, 316, 329
范晓 57, 73
方梅（Fang, Mei） 14, 24, 27, 36, 196, 287, 288, 292, 295, 313, 329, 333
弗雷格（Gottlob Frege） 99, 101, 103, 104, 108, 120, 239
傅承德 57, 60, 73
Fan, Jiyan 见"范继淹"
Fang, Mei 见"方梅"
Fillmore, Charles J. 1, 12, 278, 330
Fodor, Janet Dean 30, 37, 109, 120, 199, 200, 202, 205, 207, 234, 241, 252
Foley, William A. 1, 6, 12
Ford, Cecilia E. 330
Fox, Barbara A. 280, 330, 331, 333, 359
Frege, Gottlob 见"弗雷格"
Fretheim, Thorstein 17, 21, 25, 28, 34, 37

G

Gabelentz, Georg von der 见"甲柏连孜"
Givón, Talmy 21, 38, 92, 95, 133, 138, 142, 156, 166, 205, 220, 222, 230, 234, 236, 244, 250, 252, 257, 258, 263, 272, 284, 300, 311, 312, 314, 330, 333, 337, 345, 351, 355, 356, 359, 360
Greenberg, Joseph H. 131, 142, 281, 282, 292, 295, 330
Grice, Paul 99, 100, 280, 330
Grimes, Joseph E. 159, 166
Grimshaw, Jane 172, 192
Gundel, Jeanette K. 15, 17, 18, 21, 25, 28, 34, 37, 169, 171, 180—182, 193, 258, 330

H

韩礼德（Michael A. K. Halliday） 15, 37, 181, 193, 258, 330
胡裕树 21, 36
黄正德（Huang, James C.-T.） 295, 312, 331, 352, 359
Halliday, Michael A. K. 见"韩礼德"
Haspelmath, Martin 275, 298, 305, 330
Haviland, Susan E. 269, 270, 330
Hawkins, John A. 126, 142, 260, 276, 279, 330
Heim, Irene 265, 330
Heine, Bernd 133, 138, 142, 230, 234, 284, 300—302, 304, 331, 337, 351—

354, 357, 359
Heraclitus 97
Himmelmann, Nikolaus P. 278, 280, 292, 331
Hockett, Charles F. 15, 18, 37
Hopper, Paul 1, 3, 6, 12, 16, 37, 74, 92, 95, 166, 218, 221, 227, 230, 235, 244, 252, 262, 311, 331, 336, 345, 356, 359
Huang, James C.-T. 见"黄正德"
Huang, Shuanfan 288, 292, 295, 331
Huddleston, Rodney 181, 193, 261, 332
Huth, Alexander G. 129, 142

I

Ioup, Georgette 207, 235

J

甲柏连孜（Georg von der Gabelentz） 15, 37
Jackendoff, Ray S. 1, 13
Jacob, Joachim 37
Jacobson, Arthur 120, 143, 236
Jespersen, Otto 见"叶斯帕森"
Jiang, Zixin 176, 178, 184, 185, 193
Justus, Carol 176, 193

K

奎因（William Van Orman Quine） 103
Karttunen, Lauri 211, 235, 264, 331
Keenan, Edward L. 178, 193, 311, 331
Kennedy, Becky 216, 235
Kitakawa, Chisalo 176, 193
Klemke, E. D. 120, 143, 236
Krifka, Manfred 261, 265, 331
Kripke, Saul 200, 235

Kuno, Susumu 176, 180, 181, 193, 194, 235

L

黎锦熙 21
李临定（Li, Linding） 2, 12, 48, 73, 91, 95, 312, 332
李行德（Lee, Thomas H. T.） 196
廖秋忠 155, 165
刘丹青 25, 36
刘月华 70, 73
陆俭明 29, 36
吕叔湘（Lü, Shuxiang） 1, 3, 6, 11, 12, 19, 21, 23, 25, 27, 36, 42, 73, 86, 90, 91, 93, 95, 146, 163, 165, 235, 252, 253, 287, 288, 298, 301, 312, 332, 341, 360
罗素（Bertrand Russell） 15, 38, 99, 102—106, 108, 120, 126, 143, 200, 235, 236, 239, 253
Lakoff, George 1, 13
Lambrecht, Knud 23, 25, 37, 126, 142, 257, 258, 272, 273, 312, 321, 331
Langacker, Ronald 41, 74
Langendoen, Terence D. 171, 194
LaPolla, Randy J. 312, 331
Lee, Thomas H. T. 见"李行德"
Leech, Geoffrey 72, 74
Lehmann, Christian 172, 193
Levinson, Stephen C. 280, 297, 331
Li, Charles N. 15, 18, 36, 37, 60, 74, 91, 95, 156, 166, 167, 172, 173, 178, 181, 187, 192—194, 196, 235, 238, 252, 254, 328, 331, 335, 359
Li, Linding 见"李临定"
Li, Wendan 220, 235
Longacre, Robert E. 159, 166

Löbner, Sebastian　273, 332
Ludlow, Peter　200, 216, 235
Lü, Shuxiang　见"吕叔湘"
Lyons, Christopher　259, 260, 271, 273, 275, 276, 283, 284, 296, 306, 332
Lyons, John　19, 38, 45, 74, 83, 95, 112, 120, 124, 142, 198, 200, 205, 207, 213, 216, 219, 235, 258, 261, 274, 279, 332, 336, 341, 360

M

马庆株　44, 46, 73
马希文　60, 73
孟琮　60, 73
Mann, William　159, 166
Martin, Janice　16, 37
McCawley, James　176, 179, 184, 185, 194, 235, 331
McCawley, Noriko A.　176, 179, 184, 187, 194
McConnell-Ginet, Sally　30, 37
McKeown, Kathleen R.　166
Meulen, Alice ter　331
Milsark, Gary L.　30, 38
Mourelatos, Alexander　43

N

Neale, Stephen　200, 213, 216, 235

O

Onishi, Masayuki　36
Ostertag, Gary　235

P

潘文娱　60, 73
Partee, Barbara H.　200, 207, 208, 235, 264, 332

Payne, John　261, 332
Payne, Thomas　354, 355, 360
Pelletier, Francis Jeffry　331
Plato　见"柏拉图"
Porterfield, Leslie　285, 286, 327, 332
Prince, Ellen F.　28, 38, 131, 143, 181, 194, 220, 235, 271, 332

Q

乔姆斯基（Noam Chomsky）　97, 98, 110, 170, 176, 192
Quine, William Van Orman　见"奎因"
Quirk, Randolph　72, 74

R

Redeker, Gisela　222, 236
Reichenbach, Hans　68, 74
Reinhart, Tanya　25, 28, 38, 180—182, 194
Rile, Gilbert　99
Rivero, Maria-Luisa　214, 236
Rouchota, Villy　213, 236
Rozwadowska, Bozena　1, 3, 13
Russell, Bertrand　见"罗素"

S

沈家煊（Shen, Jiaxuan）　22, 23, 36, 196, 312, 333
苏格拉底（Socrates）　97, 98
孙朝奋（Sun, Chaofen）　21, 38, 120, 220, 222, 223, 236, 244, 253, 312, 333, 336, 360
Sacks, Harvey　280, 332
Sag, Ivan　30, 37, 109, 120, 199, 200, 202, 205, 207, 234, 235, 241, 252, 329
Sanford, Anthony　269, 270, 333, 345,

346, 359, 360
Sasse, Hans-Jurgen　314, 316, 321, 333
Schachter, Paul　176, 194
Schegloff, Emanuel A.　280, 332, 333
Schlobinski, Peter　25, 38
Schütze-Coburn, Stephan　25, 38
Seuren, Peter　102, 120
Sgall, Petr　152, 166
Shen, Jiaxuan　见"沈家煊"
Shimojo, Mitsuaki　225, 236
Sidner, Candace L.　165, 166
Smith, Carlota　43, 44, 50, 74
Socrates　见"苏格拉底"
Srivastav, Veneeta　285, 286, 327, 332
Strawson, Peter F.　15, 25, 38, 99, 105, 106, 120, 126, 143, 201, 236, 253
Sun, Chaofen　见"孙朝奋"

T

陶红印（Tao, Hongyin）　288, 289, 292, 295, 333
Tao, Hongyin　见"陶红印"
Tedeschi, Philip J.　73, 74
Teng, Shou-Hsin　见"邓守信"
Thompson, R. McMillan　60, 74
Thompson, Sandra A.　1, 3, 6, 12, 15, 18, 37, 60, 74, 91, 92, 95, 156, 159, 166, 167, 172, 173, 178, 181, 186, 187, 193, 194, 196, 218, 219, 221, 227, 235, 236, 238, 244, 252—254, 262, 311, 312, 331, 333, 335, 345, 356, 359
Tomlin, Russell S.　311, 347, 360
Tsao, Feng-Fu　见"曹逢甫"

V

van Dijk, Teun A.　156, 166, 181, 194

van Oosten, Jeanne　1, 3, 13, 181, 194, 311, 333, 347, 360
van Valin, Robert D.　1, 6, 12
Vendler, Zeno　43, 45, 58, 74, 103
Verkuyl, Henk　43, 74

W

王还　70, 73
王红旗（Wang, Hongqi）　25, 36, 220, 236
维特根斯坦（Ludwig Wittgenstein）99, 106
Wang, Chengchi　21, 37
Wang, Hongqi　见"王红旗"
Ward, Gregory　23, 36, 37
Weil, Henri　152
Wittgenstein, Ludwig　见"维特根斯坦"
Wright, S.　220, 222, 230, 236, 244, 337, 355, 356, 360

X

徐烈炯（Xu, Liejiong）　25, 36, 171, 194
Xu, Liejiong　见"徐烈炯"
Xu, Yulong　295, 333

Y

亚里士多德（Aristotle）　43, 97, 100—102
叶斯帕森（Otto Jespersen）　126, 142
于根元　60, 73
Yule, George　270, 328

Z

张伯江（Zhang, Bojiang）　287, 313, 315, 333
赵元任（Chao, Yuen Ren）　15, 16, 18, 21, 36, 43, 73, 298, 305, 312, 328, 343,

344, 350, 358
郑怀德　57, 73
朱德熙　21, 36
Zabeeh, Farhang　38, 120, 143, 236, 253

Zacharski, Ron　330
Zaenen, Annie E.　73, 74
Zhang, Bojiang　见"张伯江"
Zhang, Ning　22, 38

主题索引

B

被动句　15
悖论 paradox　100
必要条件　11, 144, 164
变化性　4
标示词 indexical　104, 105, 240
标准理论　97
表层句法结构特征　17
表现 coding　58
宾语　1—3, 5—10, 12, 16, 22, 25, 32, 36, 40, 47, 49, 53, 61—63, 87, 88, 90, 92, 113, 114, 117, 118, 139, 141, 147, 152, 155, 156, 164
宾语前置句　21
宾语倒装句　21, 22
补语　40, 47, 59, 63—65, 90, 92
不定（indeterminate）形式　135, 139, 140, 201, 202, 208, 209, 241, 248, 250, 252, 254, 274, 306, 307, 309, 310, 313, 316—318, 320, 321, 323—326, 328, 342
不定冠词 indefinite article　16, 37, 104, 105, 110, 113, 121, 125, 130, 133, 134, 138, 139, 142, 220, 230, 235, 246, 248, 251, 254, 255, 274, 275, 283, 284, 296, 300—302, 304, 325, 327, 334, 335, 337—340, 343, 351, 357, 360
不定名词短语　109, 110
不定性用法　121, 142
不定指 indefinite　28, 75, 77—80, 82—84, 86—93, 95, 107, 121, 123, 124, 135, 142, 200—202, 208, 209, 211, 212, 215, 216, 220, 221, 223, 230, 234—236, 239—241, 243—246, 248—250, 252, 255, 258, 260, 262, 272, 274, 280, 283—286, 296, 299, 303, 306, 311, 313—316, 321, 324, 326—328, 330, 336, 338, 339, 342—345, 350—352, 355, 356, 358, 359
不定指性 indefiniteness　87—89, 92, 142, 238, 248—250, 252, 255, 259, 284, 286, 299—306, 312—314, 317, 318, 325, 326, 328, 330, 337, 343, 351
不可辨识 nonidentifiable　126, 127, 130, 133—135, 139—141, 202, 231, 238, 246—251, 253, 255, 257, 258, 260, 262, 272—274, 280, 283, 284, 286, 287, 297, 300—304, 306, 307, 309, 310, 313, 316—319, 322—324, 326, 337—340, 342, 343, 352, 353, 357
不可辨识性 nonidentifiability　130, 238, 254, 259, 271, 274, 283, 296, 297, 310, 319—321, 324, 325, 327,

334
不可数 62, 63, 122
不完全态 imperfective 71
布拉格学派 15
Bedeutung 所指对象 103, 120
Begriffswort 概念词，抽象名词 62, 63, 104
Broca 区 129

C

参项 15
参与成分 participant role 146, 155, 189
参照时间 40, 67
插入句 157, 162, 163
常态句式 canonical construction 17, 23, 24, 229
陈述 14—18, 25, 29, 34
成就 achievement 43, 45
承前性 150, 155, 156, 164
持续 durative 40, 44, 45, 48—52, 54—60, 62, 66, 71
初级时制 primary tense 68
处所 19, 51—53, 55, 61, 73, 90, 92
传信/传疑 evidentiality 121, 122
词法 112, 253, 334
词法自主性 134
词类 41, 64, 121
词序 15, 21, 27, 30
词语的形式 107, 110, 113, 114
次级时制 secondary tense 68
从发话人的角度出发 speaker-oriented 107, 127, 205, 215, 238, 242, 253
存现句 28, 87, 88, 90, 133, 139
存现句的典型标记"有" 28, 29

D

达成 45, 46
大小主语 21
大主语 21, 153, 154
代词 15, 17, 20, 21, 29, 75, 81, 83, 85, 87, 97, 109, 112, 131, 134, 135, 144, 145, 154
代词复指 21
代词性回指 pronominal anaphora 144, 145
单变 simple change 39, 50, 56, 58, 59, 61, 63—65
单复数 122
单指 individual 75, 83, 94, 95, 184, 199, 203, 204, 240, 242, 262, 346
独一无二 uniqueness 126
当前指示 deictic reference 80
当事 1
"的"字结构 75, 84
等立 42, 159, 161, 163
低次谓词 159
地点 5, 7, 8, 11, 19, 24, 31, 78, 114, 131, 146, 147
地点理论 localism 19
递归 recursive 159, 163
典型动词 39, 60, 61, 63, 65, 66, 72
定冠词 definite article 37, 104, 105, 108, 121, 123, 125, 126, 128, 131, 132, 134—139, 141, 198, 240, 246, 247, 251, 254—256, 259, 260, 270, 273, 275—279, 281—283, 285—288, 290, 292, 294—296, 307, 310, 324, 325, 327, 329, 331, 334
定语中心词 130
定指 definite 16, 18, 25, 28, 33, 35, 37, 75, 77—84, 86—93, 95, 107, 120, 121, 123—128, 130, 132, 133, 135, 137, 138, 142, 151, 166, 184, 199—202, 208, 234, 235, 239—241,

246, 248—252, 255, 256, 258—260, 262, 264, 267, 270—275, 280, 283, 285, 286, 296, 303—307, 311, 313—316, 320, 324, 325, 327, 330, 332, 335, 336, 339, 340, 342—350, 353, 354, 356—358

定指范畴　121, 123, 125, 126, 132, 333

定指名词 definite NPs　80, 131, 200, 202, 209, 211, 212, 221, 223, 230, 245, 270, 275, 306, 329, 342

定指倾向性位置　121, 139, 140

定指性 definiteness　81, 87—92, 95, 119, 120, 125, 142, 192, 201, 234, 238, 239, 246, 247, 249—252, 253—256, 258—261, 272, 274—276, 278, 282, 285—287, 290, 293, 295—297, 299, 302, 312, 325—332, 343, 354, 359

动宾结构　39, 53, 62, 63, 72

动补结构　39, 57, 59, 64, 65, 72

动词　1—3, 5, 6, 8, 12, 18—22, 25, 27, 39—41, 43—55, 57—66, 70, 72, 73, 75, 86, 92, 139, 146—148, 152, 155—159, 164, 165

动词重叠　70, 73

动词性成分　75

动态　42, 48, 51—56, 58, 61, 73

对比　11, 26, 27, 36, 159, 162

《对话录》Cratylus 篇　97

definite　见"定指""有定"

definite article　见"定冠词"

definite determiner　247, 258, 275, 277, 279, 281, 283, 285, 287, 293, 295, 299, 307, 311, 325

definite NPs　见"定指名词"

definiteness　见"定指性"

designatum　103

discourse thematicity　见"话语主题性"

demonstrative　见"指示词"

E

Electra 悖论　101
extension 外延　103

F

发话人　14, 15, 71, 76—79, 81, 82, 94, 107, 109, 110, 112, 113, 124, 126—130, 133—135, 137, 148, 150, 152, 154, 162, 237, 253

反身代词　97

反指 cataphoric reference　161

范围话题 range topic　167, 168, 179, 180, 184—187, 189—192, 195

非常态句式 non-canonical construction　17, 20, 23

非持续性情状　48, 49

非动词谓语句　146, 147

非基本句式　23

非零形回指　145

非特指 non-specific　111, 112, 207

非完成　49, 52, 58

非谓语焦点句　34

非语言环境 nonlinguistic context　80, 148

非指向性 non-ostensive　112, 113, 207, 209, 210

分量词 partitive quantifier　109, 199, 200, 202, 214, 240, 241

分裂句式　23

分析哲学　99, 105

复变 complex change　39, 50, 56—58, 61, 63—65

复合趋向补语　90, 92

复指　17, 18, 21

附带成分 circumstantial role　146, 189,

主题索引 371

232
附庸性 4
frame topic 框架话题 167, 168, 180, 184, 185, 187, 189—192, 195

G

概念词 Begriffswort 104
感事 4, 5, 7, 9, 24, 30
感知性 4
高次谓词 159
格 121, 122, 125
个体量词 123, 137
工具 1, 5, 7—9, 11, 19, 24, 31, 33
功能结构 6, 11
功能/话语/认知学派 100
构式语法 98
关系从句 relative construction 167—169, 172, 194, 195
管约理论 97
冠词 121, 125, 126
惯用语 (idiomatic) 用法 111, 112
光杆名词 bare noun 83—85, 104, 105, 109, 113—119, 121, 125, 135, 139—142, 249, 251, 253, 262, 297, 307—310, 323, 343
过去时 past tense 68—70, 131, 256
grammaticalization 见"语法化"

H

汉语式话题 18
核磁共振（MRI）技术 129
核心成分 41
宏观连续性 macro continuity 144, 150, 156, 157, 161, 162, 164
后事时 posterior 68, 69
话题 14—18, 25—29, 33—36, 114, 116, 150, 195

话题-陈述结构 14—18, 24—26, 33, 36
话题化结构 topicalization（简称 TOP） 17, 18, 20—22, 25, 38, 170—173, 177, 188, 193, 194
话题结构 topic construction 25, 167—169, 193—195
话题突出 15, 18, 35,
话题重要程度 thematic importance 196, 197, 217, 220—222, 224, 225, 227, 229, 230, 232, 233, 237, 244, 245, 284, 303, 304, 335, 336, 345—347, 350, 354—358
话题组织 thematic structuring 167, 168, 185, 192, 195
话语 14—16, 20, 25, 34, 35, 75—79, 81, 91, 98, 100, 107, 110, 115, 119, 136, 144, 145, 148—165, 237, 253, 333, 360, 361
话语分析 95—97, 102, 113, 114, 119, 139, 144, 145, 165, 333
话语结构 144, 148, 149, 156, 157, 161, 163, 164
话语主题性 discourse thematicity 220, 221, 232, 239, 244, 245, 253
回指 anaphoric reference 20, 76, 77, 79, 80, 111, 112, 127, 132, 136, 141, 144—150, 152, 154—157, 160, 164, 211, 213, 262, 264, 267, 269, 270, 291, 307
回指代词 20
回指对象 anaphor 144—150, 152, 154—157, 160—166
回指形式 anaphora 144—146, 148, 154, 156, 165, 166, 269, 279, 330, 331, 333, 359
混合结构 28

活动 activity　39, 43, 45, 49, 52—55, 61—63, 65

I

identifiable　见"可辨识"
identifiability　见"可辨识性"
instance topic　见"事例话题"
indefinite　见"不定指""无定"
indefinite article　见"不定冠词"
indefinite determiner　见"无定限定词"
indefinite NPs　200, 202, 209, 211, 212, 221, 223, 230, 245, 306, 329, 342
indefiniteness　见"不定指性"

J

基本句式　11, 22, 23
基于受众 addressee-oriented　126, 238, 253
激活 activated　129
激活状态 activation state　25, 124
及物动词　152
集群激活　129
集群聚合　129
计量功能　121, 138, 142
计算机自然语言处理　148
价 valence　146, 159
简单时 simple tense　68
间接宾语　146
剑桥分析学派、剑桥学派　99, 100, 102, 103
渐变成分 grade term　57
渐成性　4, 5
将来时 future tense　68—70, 131
交替　159
焦点　14, 15, 36, 124, 152
焦点-预设结构　25
焦点结构　6, 11, 15, 35

焦点信息　11
结构关系　73, 75
结构主义　21, 23, 24, 96
结构主义理论　96
结束 accomplishment　39, 40, 43, 45—46, 50, 54—56, 58, 61—63, 71
近宾语　90, 92, 139
静态 static　48—52, 54
句法　2, 6, 14, 17, 18, 21—23, 25, 27—30, 32—36, 54, 55, 59, 64, 86—89, 91—93, 95—97, 114, 118, 119, 140, 145, 148, 153, 155, 157, 159, 165, 195, 334
句法话题 syntactic topic　17, 18, 21—23, 25, 27—30, 32—35, 167—169, 194, 195
句法话题结构 syntactic-topic construction　17, 18, 21, 22, 25
句法结构　14, 17, 21, 64, 153, 157, 159
句式　10, 11, 15—18, 20, 22—24, 27, 28, 35
句子成分　1, 2, 5, 7—11, 15, 16, 23, 25, 29, 36, 39, 40, 42, 47, 61, 66, 72, 89, 90, 92, 121, 131, 139
聚合关系上的对立 paradigmatic contrast　23, 251, 324, 327
均质 homogeneous　48

K

可辨识 identifiable　126, 128, 130, 132—137, 139—141, 202, 231, 232, 238, 245—251, 253, 255—258, 260, 262, 263, 266—268, 270—274, 280, 283, 286, 287, 293, 297, 302—304, 306, 307, 310, 312, 317—324, 326, 340—342, 357
可辨识性 identifiability　37, 119, 121,

126—133, 136, 137, 142, 201, 202, 215, 231, 234, 238, 240, 246—248, 250, 252, 254—256, 258—260, 265—277, 280, 281, 283, 285, 292—294, 297, 305—307, 310—313, 317—320, 324—328, 333—334, 342, 343, 347, 357, 358

可数　62, 63, 122
肯定/否定　121, 122
空间位置　41
框架话题 frame topic　167, 168, 180, 184, 185, 187, 189—192, 195
扩充标准理论　97
Knowledge of Meaning—An Introduction to Semantic Theory　96

L

类指　111, 138
连续体 continuum　57, 271, 272, 277, 284, 302
连续性 continuity　38, 144, 149, 150, 156, 164, 166, 221, 330, 359
量化（quantificational）成分　105
零标记　43
零形回指 zero anaphora　144, 145, 147—149, 154—157, 160—162, 164, 165
零形式　15, 125, 144, 149, 150, 156, 157, 161, 162, 164
领属性定语　88, 90
论元 argument　12, 18, 159, 160, 163, 192, 224, 328
论元焦点 argument focus　34
逻辑主语、逻辑谓语　105

M

《马氏文通》　40, 73

矛盾律　100
名词重叠　94
名词短语　15, 16, 94, 104, 105, 108—110, 113, 138, 144
名词谓语句　146
名词性成分　2—6, 14, 18, 19, 22, 24, 25, 28—30, 32—35, 73, 75—84, 86—92, 94, 95, 97, 104, 105, 110—112, 115, 119, 121—123, 126, 127, 130, 131, 133, 134, 137—142, 146, 147, 149, 152—155, 253
名词性短语　105, 109
名词性回指 nominal anaphora　144, 145, 165
模糊语境 opaque context　111, 207, 210
摹状词　104—106
Megarian School 哲学学派　100
MIT 形式学派　99

N

牛津日常语言学派 Oxford school of ordinary language　99—100
牛津学派　100, 102, 103, 105
Nature《自然》　129, 142
nonidentifiable　见"不可辨识"
nonidentifiability　见"不可辨识性"
nonreferential　见"无指"
nonreferentiality　见"无指性"
numeral 'one'　见"数词'一'"

P

排列顺序　2, 33, 35
排中律　100
配位　1, 2, 5—12, 23
配位原则　1, 2, 5, 6, 8, 12, 23, 36
篇章　107, 110, 129, 136, 150, 159, 161, 162, 165

评述 comment 150—152, 155
普通语言学 99, 360
pragmatic referentiality 见"语用有指"
pragmatic topic 见"语用话题"

Q

启后性 150—156, 164
倾向性 6, 8, 90—93, 113, 116, 117, 121, 139, 140
情状类型 situation type 39, 42, 43, 47, 60, 61, 66, 72
屈折 41, 122
全句焦点 sentence focus 28

R

人称代词 75, 81, 83, 85, 87, 109, 131, 135
人工智能研究领域 129
认知概念 126
日语中的 wa 17
弱化 some 125
range topic 见"范围话题"
referential 见"有指"
referentiality 见"指称"
relative construction 见"关系从句"

S

沙堆悖论 the sorites paradox 101
生成语法理论 97, 98
省略 23, 84, 89, 137, 138, 144, 165
施事 1, 3—12, 14, 16, 19, 24, 27, 28, 30—32, 35, 122, 146, 155
时间性 39—41, 46, 63—65, 69
时间系统 39, 40, 47, 60, 66, 67, 71—73
时量宾语 44, 45, 73
时态（aspect）结构 39, 40, 42, 71, 72

时态助词"了、着、过" 42
时相（phase）结构 39—47, 50, 52, 54, 56—61, 63, 65, 66, 71—73
时制（tense）结构 39—41, 43, 44, 46, 47, 67—74, 256, 260, 263
时轴 40, 42, 48—50, 54, 58, 60, 63—65, 67, 68, 71
实体 entity 42, 76, 77, 82
实指 specific 75, 81—83, 87, 93—95
使动性 4, 5
事例话题 instance topic 167, 168, 179, 180, 184, 188—192, 194, 195
受动性 4, 5
受话人 14, 76—80, 82, 107, 109, 123, 124, 126—130, 133—135, 137, 148, 150—152, 156, 162, 163, 253, 333
受事 1, 3—12, 16, 19, 24, 27, 30—31, 90, 92, 122, 146, 155
书面语 18, 65, 137, 145
熟悉 familiarity 126
属性（attributive）用法 106, 112, 113
数 number 41
数词 84, 109, 121, 123, 133, 135, 138, 142, 334, 360, 361
数词"一" numeral 'one' 29, 121, 133, 138, 142, 248, 255, 284, 300, 304, 330, 334, 336, 337, 339, 351, 356, 359—361
双宾语结构 90, 92, 139
双项名词句 14, 18—22, 24, 25, 27—30, 32—36
双主语结构 double-subject construction 18
顺连 159
瞬间动作 42, 61
所指 44, 62, 77—82, 103, 104, 108, 110, 114, 129, 130, 135, 154

所指对象（referent） 41, 75—83, 87, 89, 92, 101, 103, 104, 114, 131, 144—146, 148—153, 155—157, 160—164
所指对象是独一无二的事物 signular reference 104, 339
Sapir-Whorf 假说 122
semantic referentiality 见"语义有指"
Sinn 意义 103, 120
SOV 句式 22—24, 38, 333
SVO 句式 16, 17, 20, 22—25, 28, 32, 33, 35, 311
syntactic topic 见"句法话题"

T

提顿词 16
体 121, 122
通指 generic 18, 25, 28, 33, 34, 62, 75, 83, 90, 94, 95, 111, 206, 208—212, 219, 233, 286, 310, 323, 324, 331, 335, 357
同形异义结构 18
同一律 100
同一性 8, 98, 101, 145
同一性关系 coreference 145, 235, 332
同指 97, 98, 145, 161
头角悖论 the horns paradox 102
突显性 saliency 25, 259, 303
thematic importance 见"话题重要程度""主题重要程度"
thematic structuring 见"话题组织"
TOP 见"话题化结构"
topic construction 见"话题结构"

W

完成 telic 44, 45, 48—50, 52, 54, 56, 58, 62

完结 45
完全态 perfective 71, 167, 196, 238, 254, 335
微观连续性 micro continuity 144—150, 155, 156, 164
位移性 4, 5
无标记 6, 11, 23
无定 indefinite 14, 16, 18, 28, 30, 35, 36, 87, 95, 107, 110, 111, 114, 121, 124—127, 130, 131, 134—137, 140, 142, 152, 200—202, 208, 209, 211, 212, 215, 216, 220, 221, 223, 230, 234—236, 239—241, 243—246, 248—250, 252, 253, 255, 258, 260, 262, 272, 274, 280, 283—286, 296, 299, 300, 306, 311, 313—316, 321, 324, 326—328, 330, 333, 336, 338, 339, 342—345, 350—352, 355, 356, 358, 359
无定名词短语 104—110
无定倾向性位置 121, 139, 140
无定限定词 indefinite determiner 37, 119, 220, 234, 244, 248, 252, 283, 285, 297—300, 302—306, 309, 325, 329, 335, 336, 339, 340, 342—344, 347—353, 355—358, 360, 361
无指 nonreferential 14, 16, 18, 28—30, 33—35, 62, 75—78, 83—86, 95, 105—114, 127, 134, 138, 196, 197, 199—203, 205, 206, 208—215, 218, 219, 221—223, 225, 227, 229, 231—233, 237, 238, 240—245, 253, 261, 262, 264, 304, 335—339, 344, 351—358, 360, 361
无指性 nonreferentiality 62, 112, 113, 211—215, 222, 223, 230—232, 243, 245, 304, 336, 354—356, 358

物理共现　130
物主代词　131
Wernicke 区　129

X

系事　5, 6, 9, 20, 24, 28, 31
先事时 anterior　68, 69
先行词 antecedent　144—150, 152, 154—157, 160—164, 268, 270, 282, 292, 293, 328
现在时 present tense　68—70, 131
限定摹状词理论 Theory of Descriptions　104
小句　88, 144, 145, 147—149, 151, 157—159, 161—164
小句谓语　19, 23, 27, 33
心理焦点 psychological focus　25
新罗素学派 neo-Russellians　105, 200
信息焦点　17, 26, 27, 34
信息结构 information structure　6, 14—18, 21, 23, 24, 26—28, 34—37, 123, 124, 142, 153, 331
形容词谓语句　146
形式逻辑理论　100, 102
形式语义学研究　99, 105
形态变化　23, 41, 42
性 gender　41
虚化　42, 84, 121, 133, 134, 138
虚指 nonspecific　75, 77, 81—83, 93—95, 206, 207, 209, 210, 213, 231, 233, 261—265, 284, 300, 301, 309, 310, 335, 337, 338, 352
悬置话题 hanging topic　18, 21, 22

Y

压进 push down　163, 164,
演变　87, 121, 131, 133, 135—137, 141, 142
阳性　123
疑问词　16, 17, 29
疑问代词　29
已给信息 given information　150
异指 disjoint reference　97, 98, 212
异质的 heterogeneous　48
阴性　123
隐含　11, 27, 28
有标记　6, 23
有定 definite　16, 35, 107, 110, 111, 120, 121, 124, 125, 127, 130, 131, 134—136, 138—140, 152, 166, 184, 199—202, 208, 234, 235, 240, 241, 246—250, 252, 253, 255, 256, 258—260, 262, 264, 267, 270—275, 280, 283, 285, 286, 296, 304, 306, 307, 311, 313—316, 320, 324—330, 332—336, 339, 340, 342—344, 346—350, 353, 354, 356—358
有界的 bounded　63
有指 referential　14, 37, 63, 75—78, 84—86, 95, 96, 104—113, 120, 127, 134, 138, 184, 196—203, 205, 207, 208, 212—215, 217—219, 232—234, 237, 239, 240, 242, 243, 252, 253, 261, 262, 264, 312, 326, 333, 341, 345, 346, 352, 354, 355, 357—359
语段　145
语法标记　42—44, 46, 47, 122, 134
语法成分　23, 42, 59, 69, 121, 122, 125, 131, 134, 135, 138, 139, 253
语法范畴　39, 58, 121—125, 130, 131, 134, 139, 142, 333
语法关系　18, 20, 41, 146
语法化 grammaticalization　121, 131—138, 141, 142, 193, 201, 217, 247,

248, 251, 255, 259, 260, 275, 281, 282, 284, 292, 296, 300—302, 304, 327, 329, 334—337, 339, 351, 352, 356—358, 360, 361

语法化程度　121, 134, 136—138, 141, 142, 334

语法现象　2, 32, 39, 55, 60, 73, 157

语法位置　114, 117, 121, 139, 140, 142

语法形式　14, 35, 43, 66, 68, 72, 109, 112, 123, 135, 155

语法虚词　122

语法助词　17, 42, 69, 70

语境　14, 16, 25, 27, 29, 34, 35, 47, 76—83, 86, 87, 93, 108, 110, 112, 114, 115, 126, 131, 148, 237

语料　18, 107, 114, 145

语篇同现　127, 128, 130, 132, 136, 140

语式 schema　158—164

语序　21—23, 122, 253

语言成分　17, 101, 104, 105, 107—112, 121, 122

语言单位　43, 44, 46, 157

语言类型学　15

语言哲学 philosophy of language　96, 103—108, 111, 145

语言转向 linguistic turn　99

语义层次结构　159

语义成分　1—3, 5—12, 23, 36, 39, 146

语义格　1

语义关系　6, 39, 75, 158

语义结构　14, 56, 66, 157—159, 161—164

语义角色　1, 3, 5, 6, 8, 19, 23, 24, 27, 32, 33, 35

语义角色优先序列　1, 5, 6, 12, 19, 23, 28, 32, 33

语义类别　2, 3

语义属性　21, 30, 109, 110, 122, 237

语义网络　39

语义学　96, 99, 102, 105—110

语义有指 semantic referentiality　107, 109, 237, 196—199, 202, 233, 240—242, 354, 355, 357

语音弱化　134

语用话题 pragmatic topic　17, 18, 25—29, 33—35, 168, 180, 181, 194, 195, 347

语用学　96, 99, 100, 102, 106, 110—112, 114, 126

语用有指 pragmatic referentiality　112, 113, 196—198, 203, 205, 209, 210, 213, 214, 216—218, 231, 233, 234, 237, 238, 242, 354, 355

语缀　122

预设 presupposition　14, 102, 204, 210, 214, 232

原型 prototype　4—6, 155

原型施事、原型受事　3—5

原则与参数框架　97

远宾语　90, 92, 139

韵律　14, 15, 17

Z

"这/那"　83, 109, 121, 135—139, 141, 334

真值条件　15

直接宾语　146, 155

直接成分　2, 3

直指 deixis　121, 131—133, 136, 137, 141, 259, 276, 278, 279, 330

指称 referentiality　15, 24, 25, 30, 36, 83, 96—114, 126—128, 134, 135, 137, 145, 146, 196, 197, 201—203, 205, 206, 209, 211, 214, 219, 229,

230, 232—234, 237, 238, 239, 244, 252, 253, 284, 304, 312, 329, 330, 348, 351—354, 358

指称形式　14, 114

指代词　20, 84, 95, 104, 105, 108, 109, 334

指示词 demonstrative　109, 112, 121, 126, 131—137, 141, 142, 198—202, 214, 240, 241, 247, 251, 254, 255, 259, 260, 274—283, 285—288, 290—296, 303, 307, 325, 327, 329, 331—334, 336

指谓成分 denoting expressions　104, 105

中性　122, 123

周遍成分　14, 29

主从关系　159—161

主动句　15

主题　1—3, 5, 6, 9—12, 103, 124, 150—153, 155, 161—164

主题句　1, 3, 9, 11, 14

主题链 topic chain　165

主题性 thematicity　96, 114—119, 217, 218, 220—232, 345

主题重要程度 thematic importance　196, 197, 217, 220—222, 224, 225, 227, 229, 230, 232, 233, 244, 245, 284, 303, 304, 335, 336, 345—347, 350, 354—358, 361

主谓结构　15

主谓谓语句　3, 12, 21, 24, 36, 146, 153

主语　1—3, 5—12, 15, 16, 18, 21, 23, 25, 28, 29, 35, 36, 47, 65, 66, 81, 86—90, 92, 95, 104, 105, 114—117, 130, 131, 138, 139, 141, 144, 146, 147, 152—155, 162, 164

助词　17, 42, 51, 69—73

注意焦点 focus of attention　25

专有名词　63, 83, 104, 105, 108, 109, 131, 135

转换生成语法模式　22

状态 state　39—41, 43—46, 48—51, 53, 54—60, 61, 71, 72, 94

自含式定指　130, 132, 133

自立性　4, 5

自然语言　43, 99, 100, 102—104, 141, 148, 158

自然语义　121—123, 125

自主性　4

字类　40

最简方案　97

左向移位句 left dislocation（简称LD）17, 18, 20, 21, 25, 38, 170, 171—173, 177, 180, 188

后　记

　　文选收录的三十篇论文围绕现代汉语研究的各个方面展开，涉及现代汉语的语法和语义、汉语研究的理论与方法，以及同说汉语、学汉语的人相关的其他语言问题。文选共分三卷，标题分别为《汉语的形式、意义与功能》《引进·结合·创新——现代语言学理论与中国语言学研究》和《语言与中国的现代化进程》。

　　《汉语的形式、意义与功能》收录十二篇论文，研究对象是汉语句法、语义、语用和话语分析中具有较大理论意义的课题，从形式、意义和功能的角度对相关汉语现象作详尽的实证分析和深入的理论探讨，旨在揭示汉语句法、语义、语用和话语篇章的主要特点，并阐发有关汉语现象在普通语言学层面上的理论意义。

　　中国传统语言研究领域是文字、音韵和训诂。现代语言学着重关注的音系、句法、语义、语用等研究领域，所用的主要理论、概念和方法大都起源于西方语言研究。20世纪初以来中国语言学家所做的主要工作，是利用外来的理论、概念和方法分析本土材料，并以此为基础对前者进行补充、修正，进而提出描写和解释能力更为周延的新理论、新概念和新方法。要做好本土语言研究，两个前提条件必不可少：一是对语料全面、准确地掌握，二是对语言学理论和方法的深刻理解。《引进·结合·创新——现代语言学理论与中国语言学研究》收录十篇论文，主要内容是笔者就普通语言学和汉语研究两者关系所做的思考，以及对普通语言学主要理论、概念及方法的研究体会。

　　1898年出版的《马氏文通》开创了中国现代语言学研究的历史。《马氏文通》研究的是古代汉语。中国现代汉语研究的初创之年，可以定于

1917年。那一年白话文运动与《国语研究会》的代表人物双潮合一，整合19世纪下半叶中国开始步入现代化进程以来，社会有识之士提出的"我手写我口""汉语拼音化""文字改革""言文一致""国语统一"等语言文字改革思想，首次为现代汉语口语和书面语标准形式的属性拟定具体要求，为其发展提出可行路径。现代汉语语音、词汇、语法以及文字改革从此成为汉语研究的重点领域。《语言与中国的现代化进程》收录八篇论文，着重探讨汉语语言文字在中国现代化进程中所起的作用以及自身所经历的变化，并从社会发展的角度观察颇具中国特色的语言规划问题。

三十篇论文均曾刊于海内外学术期刊和文集。2016 年夏，徐赳赳教授和尚新教授分别向我建议，从历年发表的论文中选取较具代表性的编为文集出版，免去读者翻检搜寻之劳。该建议得到商务印书馆总编辑周洪波博士的大力支持，并委任何瑛博士担任文选的责任编辑。何瑛博士在时间紧、工作量大的情况下加班加点，高质量地完成了文选的编辑工作。徐赳赳教授也参与了文选英文论文的部分编辑工作。我在此向徐赳赳教授、尚新教授、周洪波博士和何瑛博士表示诚挚的谢意。

多年学术生涯中有幸得到很多师友的指教，文章中的许多思想都是在同他们的切磋辩难之中生发和成熟的，在此一并致谢。这些论文的完成还得益于我所工作的中国、美国和澳大利亚大学和研究机构提供的良好研究条件，得益于安宁的家庭氛围。妻子朱静、爱女 Fay 和 Laura 是我人生中最为珍惜的部分，她们对我的支持和关爱，我永远感激不尽。

整理文稿的过程中，时时浮现恩师吕叔湘先生的面容。写作也是对话，吕先生指引我走上汉语语言学研究的道路，也是我自中国社科院语言所学生年代起撰写论文时心目中的主要对话人。文选收录的文章，有好几篇初稿写成后，第一位读者便是先生，并且总能得到先生的悉心指教。先生离去后，我动笔开篇时，往往心目中的第一读者还是先生，只是初稿完成后寄送无由，再也无从聆听老人家的教诲了。

陈 平

2017 年 5 月

澳大利亚昆士兰大学

Epilogue

The thirty papers in the present three-volume anthology center around Modern Chinese, covering themes such as its grammar and semantics, theories and methodologies of Chinese language studies, and other language-related subjects concerning speakers and learners of Chinese. The respective titles of the three volumes are *The Chinese Language: Form, Meaning and Function, Introduction, Integration and Innovation: The Relationship between General Linguistics and Chinese Language Studies*, and *Language in a Modernizing China*.

The twelve papers in *The Chinese Language: Form, Meaning and Function* focus on subjects with theoretical impact in the areas of Chinese syntax, semantics, pragmatics and discourse analysis. They present findings from empirical and theoretical investigations into the form, meaning and function of the Chinese language, which aim to identify characteristic features of the Chinese language, and explore implications of the findings for issues of more general interest in modern linguistics.

Traditional Chinese language studies focus on script, historical phonology, and critical interpretation of ancient texts (*xungu*). Major theories, concepts and methodologies in the studies of phonology, syntax, semantics, pragmatics and other areas of modern linguistics have emerged and developed mainly on the basis of studies of Western languages. Since the beginning of the twentieth century Chinese linguists have undertaken to apply theories, concepts and methodologies originating in the West to the analysis of the Chinese language, and at the same time have endeavoured to revise and innovate based on findings from Chinese. Two pre-conditions must be met if one expects to conduct proper and meaningful studies of Chinese and other indigenous languages. One is a comprehensive collection of relevant language data, and the other is in-depth understanding of theoretical and methodological apparatuses related to the analysis of the data in question. The ten papers in *Introduction, Integration and Innovation: The Relationship between General Linguistics and Chinese Language Studies* present my reflections on the relationship between general linguistics and Chinese language studies, and investigations into some of the most influential theories, concepts and methodologies of modern linguistics.

The start of research on the Chinese language from a modern linguistic perspective is marked by the publication of *Grammar* by Ma Jianzhong in 1898. However, the subject of study in *Grammar* is Classical Chinese. 1917 was the year when studies on Modern Chinese began to take shape. Major proponents of the Vernacular Written Chinese Movement and members of the National Language Studies Association joined forces in that year to delineate the features of Standard Modern Spoken and Written Chinese, and propose how Modern Chinese should be developed in a way that incorporated major thought and initiatives in language and script reform since the second half of the nineteenth century such as "I write what I speak", phonetization of Chinese, script reform, consistency of speech and writing, and unification of the National Language. Starting from that year, the phonetics and phonology, vocabulary, grammar and script of Modern Chinese fast became major areas of linguistic study in China. The eight papers in

Language in a Modernizing China examine the role of language in a modernizing China, and explore how the Chinese language and script developed in the process partially as an outcome of language planning efforts.

All of the thirty papers have previously been published in scholarly outlets in China and overseas. Professor Xu Jiujiu and Professor Shang Xin proposed in 2016 that I select from my writings in Chinese linguistics for the publication of an anthology to provide easier assess to my work. The proposal received firm support from Dr Zhou Hongbo, Editor-in-Chief of the Commercial Press in Beijing, arguably the most prestigious academic publisher in the Chinese language world, who entrusted the editing of the anthology to Dr He Ying, an experienced editor at the Commercial Press. Putting in a large amount of time and effort, Dr He completed the editing work against a tight time frame with admirable efficiency and exactitude. Professor Xu Jiujiu also helped with the editing of the papers in English in the anthology. I am grateful to all four for their support and kind help, which have resulted in the present three-volume anthology.

I thank all of my friends who have inspired and helped me in the development of many of the ideas in the thirty papers. I have benefited from the stimulating academic environments where I have been working in China, the USA and Australia over the past decades, and also from the tranquility of family life. What I treasure most in my life are my wife Jean, and two daughters, Fay and Laura. I am always grateful to them for their love and support.

Professor Lü Shuxiang, my mentor since I embarked on my career as a Chinese linguist, often appeared in my mind as I was editing the thirty papers for publication in the anthology. Writing is also dialogue. It is Professor Lü who first guided me to the work that I love, and who was also a primary addressee I have kept in mind when writing research papers since my student years at the Institute of Linguistics of the Chinese Academy of Social Sciences. As a matter of fact, Professor Lü was the first reader of several papers in the present collection, and was always kind enough to promptly offer his feedback and advice. Long after his passing away, he is still often the first reader I visualize when writing, and I regret that I can no longer send drafts for his feedback.

Chen Ping

May 2017

The University of Queensland, Australia